The
Players Guide

THE COMPLETE SOURCEBOOK FOR PLAYERS OF VAMPIRE™

Credits

Concepts: Mark Rein•Hagen, Andrew Greenberg, Josh Timbrook

Authors: Andrew Greenberg, Mark Rein•Hagen, Graeme Davis, Bill Bridges, Daniel Greenberg, Ryk Strong, Frank Fry, Aaron Voss, Travis Williams.

Development: Mark Rein•Hagen, Andrew Greenberg, Stewart Wieck

Editing: Stewart Wieck, Andrew Greenberg, Ken Cliffe

Cover Art: Dan Frazier

Art: Tim Bradstreet, Gail Van Voorhis, Josh Timbrook, John Bridges, Larry McDougal, Seri Mohm

Layout: Sam Chupp

Layout Peons: Mark Rein•Hagen, Andrew Greenberg, Kelly Norwood

Production: Sam Chupp and Josh Timbook

Design Contributors: Ian Borchardt, Hank Driskill, Chet Allen Erez, Mary K. Kuhner, Dave P. Martin, Ron Jarrell, John Daly, James Dunson, Carl Rigney, Bernard Cana, James R. Dunson, Jim Summers (Many thanks to all of you on the Internet Vampire mailing list!)

Vampire: The Masquerade™ was created by Mark Rein•Hagen

Special thanks to:

Mark "John Holmes" **Rein•Hagen**. Very, very, very.

Stewart "Odds fixin'" **Wieck**, for seeming to win all his football games. Hmmm. . .

Josh "My quote!" **Timbrook**, for embracing the Brujah state of mind.

Wes "Hey, let's use this new power" **Harris**, for summoning unwanted Gremlins.

Travis "Bumbaras Clot" **Williams**, for being a wanted Gremlin.

Ken "Mythic Places is on schedule" **Cliffe**, for his overly optimistic attitude.

Chris "Coyotes are good people" **McDonough**, for really getting us in trouble.

Sam "How did you guess I stayed up all night" **Chupp**, for showing us the essence of a sugar rush.

Leigh Ann "Fertility Goddess" **Hildebrand-Chupp**, for somehow managing to be patient and pregnant at the same time.

Kelly "Road Warrior" **Norwood**, for designing some really rad wheels.

Dedication: To Anne Rice, whose boundless imagination so inspired us, and who understands so well what it all means. Thanks for the nightmares...

"Horror and mortal terror can never be exonerated. They have no real value. Pure evil has no real place....

Except, perhaps, the art that repudiates evil — the vampire comics, the horror novels, the old gothic tales — or in the roaring chants of the rock stars who dramatize the battles against evil that each mortal fights within himself."

Anne Rice, *The Vampire Lestat*

TABLE OF CONTENTS:

The time has come.
You know it in your soul.
For I am your soul . . .
Frank Miller, *Batman.*
The Dark Night Returns

Preface

The essence of **Vampire** lies in the undead characters, those doomed symbols of both good and evil. Powerful beyond human comparisons, yet damned with tragic defects of epic proportions, each Vampire is a unique reflection of its creator, and as such bears only limited resemblance to other Kindred. The soul of a Vampire is its individuality.

This means we should not pass up any opportunity to make each character even more special, even more unique. **The Players Guide** is a compilation of new information, rules and ideas aimed at making your creation the most interesting character it can possibly be. This book includes copious amounts of rules and background material relevant to the role of the player. It also contains advice for all types of players, including suggestions ranging from how to survive as a Vampire to spicing up your roleplaying experience.

A large amount of emphasis has been placed on demonstrating some of the different ways in which you can play **Vampire**. Each section of this book suggests a different style of play, only some of which will be appropriate for your Chronicle. Merits and Flaws enhance the roleplaying possibilities inherent in the game; new clans, traits and disciplines help bring your character concepts to life; and expanded equipment lists allow for everything from mortar fire to ghoul Chihuahuas.

This sourcebook is quite a change for us. Normally we like to focus monomanically on storytelling, roleplaying and setting — directing our efforts towards helping you tell good stories. However, because of the nature of this book as a sourcebook for *players*, we had to try something else.

We have designed this sourcebook to be of the greatest possible use to as many different brands of **Vampire** players as possible. For those who want to hunt Methuselah we have included the weapons and equipment best suited for such exacting work. For those who wish to advance in potence and power we have included new levels of Disciplines and thaumaturgical rituals. For those who want to create a more fully realized character we have included new Abilities and Archetypes. For those who want to gain status and influence in Kindred society we have an entire chapter devoted to Prestige and Prestation. For those who want to roleplay **Vampire** all the more intensely we have included personal advice on how we play. For those of you who want it all, it's all here.

Somewhere in this book you will find what you were looking for, and the rest of the prattle may be of interest to you as well. Don't hesitate to throw out what doesn't suit you or the Chronicle in which you play; not everything will be equally appropriate.

We had a lot of fun with this book. It's not as serious as most of our Vampire supplements are, but then this one is for you. And after all, it is just a game. We hope you have as much fun with it as we did.

PAX!

The World of the Kindred

Four copies of the following letter were recovered, and the holders of the documents, along with their families, were dispensed with. But by the intervention of unnatural providence we would not have been able to recover so many. I trust that no more such documents exist, and that if they do, they have not reached the wrong hands.

Vladmicov — Archon, Clan Ventrue

ear Friend,

Forgive me that I cannot give you personal salutations. You are one of several people to whom copies of this document are addressed. Perhaps you know me, and perhaps you do not. I am sending many copies, in the hope that not all may be intercepted and destroyed. You must make copies of it, and then send it on to others whom you can trust — you do not have much time.

I pray that you will take what I say seriously. I trust that you will then take action using the lore I have passed on to you. My time is short, and I must set down a lifetime's experience. My own life is of little importance, for others will always come after me — but for the sake of all of God's Children on earth, my knowledge must not die with me. Or with you.

When you receive this, as I pray you shall, I shall be dead… or perhaps worse. Trust nothing further that you hear from me; read on and you will understand why.

To begin at the beginning, as one always must, my name is Alfonso, and I am, or rather was, a priest for the Holy Father in Rome. For almost thirty years I was attached to The Society of Saint Leopold, an organiza-

tion whose existence is unknown to the laity and most of the clergy of my church. The Order confronts the Devil and his works directly, leaving parishes and souls to others more suited to such work. In a former age, we might have been called inquisitors or even by the name that they have for us, witchhunters.

Please, read carefully what follows, and keep your mind open to it. This the only thing of lasting value my life has ever produced. The truth is simple and the truth is plain — but there are not many who believe or understand it. It is the truth however, and of that I pledge to you my most solemn word.

THE EVIL

here exist in this world all manner of abominations. The human race is capable of almost every degradation and vice in the name of material profit, political advantage or physical gratification. We are sinful creatures, and we have created more than enough evil for ourselves.

But there is evil beyond our own sins, there are things which are diabolic beyond any mortal register, beside which the lowest and most shameful of humanity's dregs may be considered paragons of virtue, for to be mortal is to be always within reach of Salvation. For these creatures, Divine grace is forever denied, and even scorned.

In latter days they were known by us, and so they concealed themselves and would have little to do with us. There were many hunters, and they feared us and fled from our sight. They grew so practiced at concealing themselves that they even convinced us they did not exist. Over time, given the erosion of Faith by the advancement of material science, their existence has been discounted as mere superstition, quaint folk-tales to be collected for entertainment's sake. Now, it saddens me to admit, few within the Holy Church seriously believe that many of these creatures are real, much less that they constitute a grave and ever-present threat to the lives and souls of all mankind.

I find that I am reluctant to use the word *monsters* when I speak of them — though that is surely what they are, by any definition — for it has become degraded and diminished through popular entertainment. Now, the word smacks of make-up, of special effects, of plastic toys, and conveys nothing of their true evil. But I shall use that term, for it still has power for me. Would that it never be the same for you.

The Dark power seeks to cover the existence of his monstrous minions by fostering skepticism in the name of education, and by turning the holy lore of former years into works of fiction — novels, picture books, moving pictures. But there are a few still breathing who know the truth. I trust that it has pleased the Almighty that I should be one of those few, and that in my day I have come to know even more it. I have learned their habits and their needs and I have learned how to destroy them, and for that reason they now hunt me.

What I am about to write may seem incredible and irrational. I may seem to you depraved, though I am in fact but weary and soul-worn. I make no apology for that. I can merely recount what I have learned through my experiences, completely and truthfully.

My Calling has led me many times into battle with the creatures of Evil. I have faced many of these monsters, and seen many things which would have driven me mad had my faith not sustained me. Of all the abominations upon this earth, the most foul and insidious are those who drink our blood and call themselves the kindred.

THE KINDRED

These monsters call themselves *kindred* but I am not sure why, I presume because they believe themselves to be related. They are the blood suckers, the haunters of the night, the ones who fear the stake and the cross. Their blasphemous tradition has it that the first of their kind was Cain — when the Lord cast him out for the murder of his brother, he became a drinker of blood and his descendants have repeated his crime ever since. They consider themselves predators rather than murderers, and think of all of humanity as either thralls or prey.

I shall compile as best I can what little information I have. Some I have found in the writings of those who went before me, and the rest comes from having put several of them to the question over the years. I deem it reliable, at least in as much as those I questioned believed that they were telling me the truth. They were not lying to me, of that you can be sure. My techniques are ancient, and were perfected by many before me.

The kindred may be found anywhere humanity gathers in sufficient numbers to satisfy their bestial appetites. No city of any size is free of their evil. Their society reflects their attitudes — and, it may be argued, the age of the more powerful monsters.

These creatures have their own society, which stands apart from and yet mirrors the society of mortals. Indeed, they control much of our society, and that is only the least of their foul powers. If you begin to hunt them you cannot put your trust into any of our institutions, they control them all. Sometimes I think they even have influence with the church...

The society of kindred in a city is a diabolical parody of a medieval or Renaissance court. They are ruled by the most powerful of the creatures, who is styled the prince, and who is advised by the Elders of the city. The role of privy council is played by an assembly of the oldest and most powerful of their kind. The only constant of this council is that they forever battle among themselves. Their distrust of one another is a weakness that can be exploited.

These elders are the true power within a city, and are the most subtle, cunning and dangerous of monsters. At the first sign of any trouble they can crush an opponent like an insect, all without revealing their true identity or whereabouts. I have met an elder face-to-face but once, a few years ago in New Orleans. I only survived that meeting by claiming to be the servant of another elder, whose name I had gained (through my questioning) only a short time before .

They are therefore the ones I have searched for the most astutely, for they are the leaders behind it all. They are the monarchs of the evil. The others are mere window dressing, ploys and traps to keep us away from those who not only direct the evil, but create it.

CLANS

ccording to their own traditions, they are divided into a number of Clans. Each represents a bloodline which has somehow departed from the original foul spawner and established its own identity. Each of these groups calls itself a clan, and as diabolists of the worst nature, each worships a different demon lord. This demon actually controls the clan, and directs it in its evil ways. So clever are these brimstone-tainted devils that many of their followers do not realize who they are following and how they are used. They are in fact the lowly soldiers who wage war for their masters, playing out the games that are played by the demented demons who lord over them. It is much the same with the Kindred as it is with the misguided and contemptuous mortal spirits who engage in the black mass.

Though I do not know all of the clans, I shall describe them to you as best I can. I have also learned the names of the demons, through means I dare not describe to you, and I shall relate them to you as well.

First among the clans are the Ventrue, who are the absolute leaders of this evil congregation. Almost all of the Princes are Ventrue, and they exert a strange sort of control over the other Clans. They feign respectability, and control the souls of many well-known politicians and business executives. They are completely in the grip of the great Nebiros, Field Marshal of the great Satan himself, and none of them act without his direction and consent. Nebiros command three other demons, who go by the names of Ayperos, Nuberus and Glasyabolas — in this way he indirectly controls other clans.

The great allies of the Ventrue are the Toreador, who revel in decadence and denigration. They have perverted all of the human sensory pleasures to such a degree, that they must commit great evil in order to obtain it. They, in fact, must feed upon pleasure, and will

die if they do not obtain it. They are directed by Ayperos, the demon of sensory delight, who is given the souls of all those sinners who died because of excess.

One of the most mysterious of the clans are the Assamites, but despite their efforts I was able to pierce their veil of secrecy. They are the paid assassins of the Ventrue, vile warriors who enforce the word of their masters. Some of them also go by the name of Heliots. I believe them to be under the sway of the contemptible Glasyabolas, who is hated even among his own kind for his fratricidal tendencies.

Though the Brujah clan pretends to be the enemies of the Ventrue, they are in fact their secret allies — though none of its rank and file would ever believe it. They are so caught up in their eternal rebellion, that they do not understand, just as no insurrectionists understand, they are as much a part of the establishment as anyone else. These pathetic self-declared anarchists are under the influence of Nuberus, the most cynical of all demons.

The Ravnos seem to be independent from the other clans, perhaps due to their half-breed ancestry and ties with the vagrant Romany people. Theft and trickery are their favorite activities, and they actually gain honor for successful accomplishments of criminal activities. Social gatherings are important to these creatures; they seem to enjoy pretending that they are still mortal. They are controlled by no one save their dark lord, Sargatanas, the brigadier of invisibility, trickery and wiles.

The associates of the Ravnos clan are the Gangrel, who are the more individualistic cousins of the Ravnos. The Gangrel are arrogant enough think themselves apart from the others of their kind, and more free from their inner bestiality. They too are controlled by Sargantanas, but his lieutenant, Valefar, watches over them for his master.

The Malkavians and the Giovanni also worship the same Demon, though neither realizes it. The great Agaliarept, the grand general of Lucifer, is their guide and patriarch. He is the demon of ritual and rites, and uses the death-worshiping Giovanni to summon to our realm many of his lesser demon minions. He uses the feigned insanity of the Malkavians to cast a vastly complicated spell which will some day bring him to our realm — an eventuality which we must fight desperately against.

Among the most bizarre of all the Clans are those who call themselves the Followers of Set. These twisted creatures engage in practices I do not care to describe, but which are based on ancient heathen Egyptian practices. They are more sensitive to sunlight than any other clan, and are even sensitive to bright artificial lights (a weakness which can be easily used against them). They openly worship the demon who controls them, though they know him by a different names. The one they call Set, we know of as Sargatannas.

There are many other clans, but I have not been able to learn much about them, never having the opportunity or the leisure to question them. It is vital that you discover more about them however, the names of their dark lords must be learned.

Secret wars are being fought in many cities between the various clans. Nearly every of them I have questioned sought to give an organization called the Sabbat the full blame for every evil visited upon Humanity.

The more we can encourage friction between these Clans, the more we can weaken them. I have on two occasions manufactured incidents and evidence that caused two clans to come into open conflict. There is nothing more pleasing than to witness them exterminating one another, doing our work for us. If we are to defeat them, we must continue to use such devices of deception, just as they use them against us.

THE MASQUERADE

he Masquerade is the name which they give to the most sacred of their laws. It boils down to the continuing pretense that there are no monsters — for if there are no monsters, then they do not exist either, and in not believing in them, humanity can not harm them. They are appallingly successful in this, and if we are to ultimately succeed in our anointed task, we must somehow cause it to miscarry.

This so-called Masquerade operates on a number of levels. At the most basic level, each of them is obliged to take care not to be exposed, nor to allow others to be detected and revealed for what they are. This is the extent of most of their participation in the Masquerade, but it is taken with great seriousness, and enforced ruthlessly. As with our own criminals, any crime — including killing — may be forgiven, but threatening the security of the group is unforgivable. Treason is punishable with execution.

Most of them go to great lengths to fit into our society. Some of them retain the jobs or positions they held when they were mortal. I knew of one who still controlled the corporation he headed when he was human, I was able to put away another who still held his job as a nightwatchman. Yet another, I believe, controlled the entire police department of a major city.

In order to preserve their own secrecy, they have taken over, or even created, some of our most well-known institutions. You will be shocked by the following list, but through my questioning I have deemed it to be horrifyingly accurate.

They certainly control the media, which is so openly contemptuous of what they call "superstition." Secular humanism is their construct, as is the theory of evolution and those who support it. The so-called New Agers and other occultists are equally as much their pawns. They direct much of the counter-culture which has so racked our society, including rock music in all its incarnations, and they have become leading distributors of drugs. Even some influential churches are controlled by them, such as the Unification Church, the Mormons and even the divisionist Anglicans. Communism is one of their failed experiments, but no length of time is too short for them to control vast populations. They are the dark power behind the rise in interracial marriages, the introduction of sex education classes, and the conspiracy to add fluoride to our drinking water.

The Masquerade is a global, subtle and highly insidious conspiracy, and its efficacy should never be doubted. It is their primary advantage against us, and it is what I work most adamantly to end. Ending it is the key to our victory and somehow we must force them to commit to error. Besides working to maintain human disbelief in monsters, the Masquerade also covers the suppression of discoveries and the punishment of the inquisitive. I have long had to duel with kindred who sought to kill me for my work in exposing their kind.

Even now, my life is in constant danger, and only the strictest precautions have kept me alive this long. This, in part, is why I am writing now. I have been declared the subject of a blood hunt — an award of dubious honor which is seldom accorded to a mortal. They will find me soon.

HOW TO DESTROY THEM

One of their greatest advantages over other monsters is their human appearance. One of them which has recently fed can pass for human, even though it may have existed as a fiend for several centuries. However, there are various signs by which their true condition may be told.

This creature is a corpse to all intents and purposes — a cadaver maintained at the point of death and kept from decomposing by the diabolical forces of its nature. So long as it feeds on blood, this physical stasis is maintained — that is how the foul magic of their being is sustained. Once they are completely killed, the body decomposes in a matter of hours, leaving only dust. The older they are, it appears, the faster their bodies will decompose.

The internal organs of the creature apparently wither, since digestion does not follow its natural course. Upon dissection of three I found the liver, kidneys as well as the entire digestive tract to be shrivelled and atrophied. A slimming of the body also appears to occur after their "embrace" although the slimming may be concealed by any body fat which was present at the time of death.

As I have said, there are many ways to detect them, even though they may pass as human on a casual inspection. There as many ways to slay them as well. I shall summarize the conclusions of three decades of experimentation and dissection.

The first and surest sign is an aversion to sunlight. Exposure to sunlight causes second degree burns, as if the flesh were exposed to a blow-torch. Consequently, not surprisingly, they will not willingly venture into the sun. It is indeed appropriate, and somewhat ironic, that these creature of death cannot face the very source of life. Some of them can bear to be outside in the shade on dull, overcast days for short periods of time, but these are few.

I have conducted some experiments of my own using artificial ultraviolet light, and had mixed results. In weaker individuals it causes some pain, in others mere discomfort. It can serve to blind most of them. At any rate, it is not as deadly to them as the direct rays of the sun. However, it can sometimes be useful in questioning, especially against a weak and inexperienced stripling who believes that the full effect of the sun's rays can be artificially replicated.

They have a faint musky odor, the stench of death no doubt, which is very distinct after you have smelled it one or two times. The most bestial among them carry this smell the most strongly. Most of them don't seem to notice this smell themselves, though some do douse themselves with perfumes in order to conceal it.

One of the more interesting phenomena I have observed is their ability to control the blood they consume. They will not bleed, at least not in copious quantities, unless they so wish, but they can cry (with tears of blood) and if they cut themselves open they can will the blood to issue forth. However, the very touch of their blood is danger to us, for it gives them some small control over our baser selves. Never allow yourself to come in contact with it.

As a side note, using this blood they are able to regenerate their various body organs. When I would remove a portion of their body, such as a lung or even a arm, it would be but a matter of days before it was completely regrown (blood is indeed the only way in which they can heal, as our methods of healing are of no use to them). I have never seen such a thing, except in lizards and worms.

Fire is as deadly to them as it is to humans, and is one of the surest ways of killing them after exposure to sunlight. Experimentation has shown that the flame of a blowtorch is almost the equal of sunlight. The burns created are most severe when the blue flames are prominent. Though tricky to use, a welding torch is even more harmful, and the bright arcs of light is casts creates much terror.

When they burn, the blood will start to boil and leak out from their pores, and you can hear the bones crackle. If the process continues long enough they will be so starved of blood that they cannot heal themselves and will be exterminated. A most effective technique is to burn down the buildings in which they reside. I once ended the existence of one of them by burning down a museum around her. The loss of a few paintings cannot be compared with the importance of ending death of one of these creatures.

Traditional measures — garlic, the Cross, and the stake — are mixed in their effects, and cannot altogether be relied upon. The herbs seem to have no harmful effect at all, though the Cross cannot in itself harm these devils, it has always served me well to repel them. Be very sure in your Faith before trusting to this measure, but if you are strong it will serve you well.

As to the stake, it cannot kill a them, but it is still a most useful weapon. Driven through the heart, it causes a kind of paralysis, and thus renders the monster helpless without actually destroying it. This can be most valuable technique for preserving one of them for transportation and questioning. Furthermore, in many cases it is aware of what is happening around it while it is in this paralyzed state. This helplessness is intolerable to them, and may be combined with some physical coercion — typically fire or sunlight — to break down a subject for questioning very quickly. I use the mirrors of Sanfrucious, one of the first of my avocation, to direct the light most precisely. The stake must be placed with great care, however, for I have discovered that impalement through any part of the body but the heart has no paralyzing effect.

There are other weaknesses, which vary from creature to creature. Many are passed down the bloodlines of the so-called clans. Some of them may be forced to reveal their true bestial nature by goading and threats, until they lose their self-control and enter the state which they call frenzy. One clan, which calls itself Nosferatu, wears its beastliness openly, in its appearance, while another exhibits more and more of the beast in its appearance as time goes by.

The more we know of these frailties, the more deadly will be our tools to annihilate them with.

GENERATIONS

 have come to believe that the monsters exist in generations as much as humans, even though the nature of procreation is different. As I have said, most of them trace their kind from Cain of the Bible — they believe he is the first generation, and those whom he created were the second. And so it goes on, until today most of them are thirteen or more generations removed from him.

You should realize that their generation need not have any connection with age. This is something which confused me greatly, early on. While it is certainly true that those of early generations generally have spent a longer time in their cursed existence than those of the later generations, this is by no means invariable. If a third generation were to create progeny today, that creature would be of the fourth generation. Even though a kindred of the genetically inferior thirteenth generation might have several decades more experience, the new-made fourth generation would have far greater status and perhaps far greater intrinsic powers and potential — or would be believed to have by others — owing to its early generation. It is perhaps helpful to treat generation and experience as the two axes on a graph; the actual power of the monsters is a function of both.

Those of the earliest generations are rare indeed, most having died over the millennium through a combination of human action, encroaching madness and inter-fraternal wars. Indeed I have not, much to my regret, even encountered one. These Methuselahs, as they are called, are feared more than anything. Seldom seen, the few remaining Methuselahs are engaged in secret wars against one another, for reasons that no one seems to know. They never show their hands clearly, and always work through pawns and dupes, both those of their own kind and human. According to rumors current among them, some of the seemingly most significant events in human history were actually the result of plots concocted by one Methuselah or another. If this is true, we are in even more danger that I believed earlier.

Some attempt to feed only on animals, at least in the first few centuries of existence, but eventually the hunger grows too strong, as does the need to cause misery and pain, and they feed on humans. Clearly the devil works in them, and that it is impossible to resist his commands once he has taken you. Later still — so much later that few of sufficient age are known to exist, and this whole point is no more than rumor — human blood likewise ceases to nourish them. Such a monster is therefore obliged for them to feed henceforth upon its own kind. It does appear, though, that no additional potencies are gained by an elder kindred feeding on a stripling; only the blood of the eldest among them has this capacity.

This is an ironic development indeed, and if it be true, I should be most pleased. Would that all these monsters fed only upon one another, and soon we would be rid of them all.

Procreation and The Blood Oath

 his discussion of the blood and its reputed properties leads me, somewhat belatedly, to consider its role in the creation of one of them, and in the social contracts created among them by much the same method.

All the reliable reports I have seen, and all the informants I have questioned, agree that there is one way a human enters that accursed state. The subject is drained of blood — normally by the procreator's crazed feeding — until the point of death. Then, just as life ebbs away, the stripling is given a drop of blood to drink. This is sufficient to bring about the change, but the stripling must feed immediately or die. Only the very strongest will can resist the all-consuming need for blood, and many of the procreators delight in cruel jokes like parading their victim's family before them and inviting the poor mortal to drink.

In the end they shall be punished for such vile deeds. If not by us, in the near future, then later, in the afterlife.

Those who they serve now shall be their slave drivers in the Everafter.

The Hunger, as they call it, apparently replaces every other lust and drive known to the living. None of them can withstand it for long, but few even try, and the very appearance of blood can lead them to reveal their true bestial nature. Denying the opportunity to feed, and promising blood in exchange for confession, have proved to be most potent questioning techniques. These are fully the equal of fire and sunlight. If you can provoke it in them in public, then you have mastered a most valuable technique of subjugation.

This lack of self control is something which many of them wrestle with, for though they admire the bestial side of their nature, they loath the danger it exposes them to. Some of my informants have also asserted that they have greater physical strength when they have recently fed.

Finally, in regards to the blood of these creatures, there is a matter which may be superstition, but which is firmly believed by every one of them I have questioned. This is the matter of the blood oath. If it be true, it can explain much to us of the influence of the eldest ones among them.

As I have said, those of late generation may gain the powers of an early-generation by drinking that individual's blood. However, this power is only conferred if the donor is completely drained, and therefore destroyed. One who drinks but a little of the blood of an earlier generation becomes bound to the donor in some mystical way, unable to harm the donor and often bound to obey. Many Sires force this bond upon their new-made Progeny — the better to control them. Some believe that the blood must be taken on three successive days to complete the blood oath, but I believe this to be a myth, propagated by the ancients among them.

I have examined but one pair who claimed to be so bound in Dusseldorf many years ago. The younger was extremely protective of the elder, and apparently willing to face destruction rather than allow harm to befall its regnant, as such individuals are called. Although doused in kerosene and shown a blow-torch, this creature seemed incapable of harming its partner, even to save itself. The elder, it may be reported, showed no such compunction.

DEMONIC ABILITIES

he abilities I have so far described are inherent, and will be discovered by them at some time or another in its existence. Those which I am about to recount are learned, and are not restricted to these creatures; indeed, many seem to have their origins in the Black Arts, such as might be learned by any mortal willing to sacrifice his soul. It might be argued that lacking souls, they have these powers gratis; I am a theologian, but I still do not know enough to pursue this matter. All I know is that some of them have learned the arts of the devil-dealing sorcerer, and many others beside.

In my experience many kindred have the capacity to read and dominate the human mind — for some, it is an essential part of their hunting technique. One instance, in Vancouver, left me baffled for weeks before I realized that the creature had erased the memories of its victims, so that they had no conscious recollection of its assaults. Attacks of this kind may be resisted by Faith and willpower alone; there is no talisman or tool which can shield the mind from them. You must have complete trust in yourself and the Almighty Father. However, if you avoid any sort of eye contract, you will find the danger of it vastly mitigated.

Superior strength, stamina and speed are part of their diabolical gift, but many which I questioned confessed to augmenting their physical abilities further through the use of what they called "the Disciplines." Apparently, such powers are most useful in an emergency, but they cause great fatigue and an increased need to feed, so they are used with care by all but the most rash.

Some few of them, it is said, have the ability to change shape, just as reported by the Papal commissions to Hungary and elsewhere. These are apparently few; I myself have never seen this ability in use though I have attempted to provoke it many times. However, some of my informants have assured me, even under the most extreme questioning, that they have indeed witnessed it. This is certainly a line of questioning that needs pursuing. I worry what other forms they might be capable of taking. . .

There are many other powers which I have seen reported or heard hints of. As I have said, some of them are privy to the black arts of alchemy and thaumaturgy, some having practised them since before the Church so rightfully outlawed them. One entire bloodline claims descent from the medieval alchemists rather than the Biblical Cain. If this be true, then perhaps we have enemies even more powerful than these creatures whose extinction I have devoted my life to.

SERVANTS

hese monsters, when they are alone, are a fairly easy prey for a determined and devout hunter. I have captured many of them, always when they were out of contact with their "kindred," and only rarely have I experienced any difficulty. Even in the protection of their infernal society it is no arduous matter to hunt them all down by day when they are made immobile. But the creatures are aware of this fact, and many of them are sufficiently intelligent to protect themselves. All the elders have one or more servants who can protect them and transact their business during the hours of daylight.

Most of these servants are ordinary mortals who have been persuaded or coerced to serve the creatures. The mental powers I have described provide one means of doing this; other servants may be kept faithful by appealing to their greed, or by the hollow promise that one day they will share in eternal life. Whatever their moral state may be, these individuals are physically no less human than you or I. They are, however, weak in soul and spirit, and most certainly have forsaken their chances for salvation.

The most monstrous of there servants is the creature which they call a ghoul. This is a human who is allowed, from time to time, to drink the blood of its master. Since the ghoul is not first drained of blood, it does not become one of them, but it can no longer be said to be human. Aging ceases as in its master so long as the supply of blood is maintained, but the ghoul can derive no sustenance from human blood. However, it is able to go about by day, and the blood oath I have described seems to keep it faithful to its master.

It is nearly impossible to tell a ghoul from a human, since it lacks all of the kindred's characteristic weaknesses. However, if it is denied the opportunity to feed on the blood of its master, the ghoul will rapidly deteriorate to its true age, and may die. Some ghouls believe themselves to be kindred, and try to live on the blood of humans — no doubt they have been deceived by their masters, who promised them eternal life in exchange for faithful service.

Although the truth may never be known, the murderers Haarman and Haigh may have been creatures of this kind. Perhaps they were abandoned by their masters and forced to rely on an incomplete and fallacious understanding of their condition in order to survive. Many ghouls travel close to the edge insanity, many more have fallen over.

GOLCONDA

Among the most persistent of their legends is the myth that it is possible to reach a state of inner balance where a they can exist without becoming a monster. When they achieve this state, they believe they will have complete self-control and will no longer go into a blood-starved frenzy. They speak of the Man and the Beast, by which they mean their light and dark sides, according to a perverse moral standard, of course, for these are monsters and nothing but evil — and each fears the day when the "beast" shall defeat the "man" and they shall become monstrous even to their own eyes.

Perhaps this is the lie which allows them to live with themselves, to imagine a level of denigration beneath oneself is to imagine one as moral — at least to some extent. It is yet another one of the Dark Lord's tricks, and one to which many of our own kind fall prey.

Obviously, this concept of Golconda is a myth — a pathetic and blasphemous attempt to offer some hope of Salvation in the absence of Divine Grace. Lacking souls, the creatures offer themselves a Heaven on Earth for they deny themselves an afterlife. The end comes as oblivion, they believe, and the flames of Hell can never touch them. None of my informants have ever confessed to meeting one who had attained this blissful state. I believe this Golconda to be yet another myth which the Ancients have created in order to hold the lesser ones in line.

VALEDICTION

There is so very little time. I have attempted to set down what generalities I may as best I can. If truly great need arises, you will find some more detailed reports of individual cases in the library of the Society of St. Leopold, if the monsters have not reached it first. But I must warn you, Brethren of the Society will not let willingly allow you to inspect the documents, fearing you might be a servant of the dark one. This is what they fear me to be, and such is the danger in carrying the chase so closely as have I.

Now I must make as many copies of this letter as I can, and send them out to yourself and others. I pray that at least one may escape interception.

Beware of the monsters, for they will surely seek to destroy you now that you have a portion of my knowledge. Remember that although they appear to be human, they are not. They can scream in pain and weep and plead and offer such inducements as might vanquish all but a St. Anthony, but do not forget that they are monsters. Harden your heart against pity, for they are creatures of the Devil, without souls or salvation. Do not let them tempt you or move your feelings. Allow righteousness to guide you.

Carry on our crusade with courage and piety. My blessings go with you.

Alfonso Rialto

Father Alfonso Rialto

Chapter Two: Character Creation

*Poor Skeleton steps out, dressed up in bad
blood, bad brains, bad thoughts, and others'
deeds. Poor Skeleton no doubt, one of these days
you can cast aside your human, be free.*
XTC, *Poor Skeleton Steps Out*

This chapter describes two new ways to create a character — hyper-fast character creation using character templates in the use of Merits and Flaws to personalize your character in the most detailed degree imaginable.

This chapter assumes that all of the normal rules for character creation still apply; but these new rules are extras that can make the process easier or more complete. Both the templates and the Merits and Flaws are optional — do not feel any pressure to use either set of rules if they do not suit you.

Ensure that your Storyteller has okayed the use of these optional rules. Each Chronicle is individual and unique, so there is no telling what restrictions or changes your Storyteller has in mind.

Character Templates

The process of character creation in **Vampire** is quite detailed and can be time-consuming if you put a great deal of thought into it. Though it is possible to create a character in less than five minutes, the end result will not be as complete and real as it should be. The more you put into a character's creation, the more attached you will become to that character and the more rewarding your experience of playing her personality will be. However, there can be some times when you need a short-cut , or when you do not have the time or inclination to create a character from scratch, or perhaps when you simply do not have a concept for what kind of character you want.

The following Templates give you something to work from, and by using them you can mix around scores to your heart's desire to create the character of your dreams. These templates can also be quite useful to the Storyteller for creating minor characters without a lot of effort. Simply use a clan Template to get a basic idea of where to start from, and you cannot go very far wrong.

The character templates presented here give you a head-start. They are partly generated characters, like the half-baked bread you can buy in the supermarket and finish at home. In a way they are the archetypical example of what a character from a particular clan is like; they express the motives, strengths and weakness of that clan. You could even think of them as clan "heroes," for they reflect what those of that clan admire and the way in which they see themselves.

The templates list the scores all of your Traits, and reflect the basic concept of the character. All you need to do to draw your own character from the Template is to copy the example down, and then spend your fifteen 'freebie' points to flesh it out even more. If you want to make your character even more unique, then just switch around a point here and there — just make sure you do not break any rules in doing so. If you are using Virtues and Flaws, you can deal with these at the same time, gaining Merits or extra freebie points by purchasing points of Flaws.

If you hate the idea of character Templates, and many do, then do not use them. They are certainly not for everyone (but keep them in mind when you need a character *fast*).

BRUJAH REBEL

Quote: *"Everyone round here hits the streets like they the Mac. Here, that kind of Bullshit gets you smoked, quick, fast and in a hurry. Just cause you Kin, don't mean you don't fall, G. Just means you put up a good fight"*

Prelude: A life at the bottom breeds two types of people — those who give in and those who fight back. You've fought back since day one and have the scars to prove it. From the time you could walk you were a part of the gang, and you took it over when you were 15, killing a man eight years older than you. Being leader brought with it even more pain, as you saw life-long friends gunned down by enemy gangs and arrested by the police. The urge to fight back, already strong within you, rose with the passing of every day. Nothing could be more attractive to a Brujah, and one dark night you were finally given a power to fight back with which you never believed possible.

Concept: Since the Clan Brujah normally selects their Neonates from the youth of society who are the most contemptuous of authority, the concept for this character is a street-gang leader — a punk or gangsta. The character has adopted a flamboyant, rebellious exterior, but deep down is as much interested in having things go his way as he is in changing things. Attributes and Abilities of this character reflect the many years of life spent on the street and in a gang.

Contacts can be any street lowlife, while the character's Allies and Herd are likely to be drawn from the streetgang itself. Area knowledge focuses on the gang's turf, spreading out into surrounding areas (and eventually the whole city) with decreasing precision.

The character's main weakness is a Willpower of 4. Virtues — particularly Conscience — could do with boosting if you want to keep your Humanity, especially since the Brujah clan weakness makes it harder for the character to resist Frenzy. A few more points to Talents like Intimidation and Leadership would help the character maintain the street-tough image, and enhanced weapon skills are always handy. The character's Sire may still be around as a Mentor, using the character and the gang for odd jobs from time to time. It can help having someone speak for you to the Elders, as at some point you will be getting into trouble you will need to be getting out of.

Roleplaying Tips: You owned the street when you were human, and now you've just got a whole lot tougher. Project confidence and aggression with every word, every gesture. You're the hippest of the hip and the cruelest of the cruel and you'll take no grief from anyone. Well, no mortal, certainly. You're still learning about being a Vampire, but you'd die rather than let anyone know that you're unsure of yourself, even though you really are sometimes.

Equipment: Colt Anaconda, shoulder holster, switchblade, leather jacket, assorted Jewelry, combat boots.

VAMPIRE ™

Name: _____ Nature: **Bravo** Generation: **13th**
Player: _____ Demeanor: **Cavalier** Haven: _____
Chronicle: _____ Clan: **Brujah** Concept: **Street Gang Leader**

Attributes

Physical
Strength _____ ●●●●○
Dexterity _____ ●●●○○
Stamina _____ ●●●○○

Social
Charisma _____ ●●○○○,
Manipulation _____ ●●○○○
Appearance _____ ●●○○○

Mental
Perception _____ ●●●●○
Intelligence _____ ●●○○○
Wits _____ ●●●○○

Abilities

Talents
Acting _____ ○○○○○
Alertness _____ ●●○○○
Athletics _____ ○○○○○
Brawl _____ ●●●○○
Dodge _____ ●○○○○
Empathy _____ ○○○○○
Intimidation _____ ●○○○○
Leadership _____ ●○○○○
Streetwise _____ ●○○○○
Subterfuge _____ ○○○○○

Skills
Animal Ken _____ ○○○○○
Drive _____ ●●○○○
Etiquette _____ ○○○○○
Firearms _____ ●●●○○
Melee _____ ●●○○○
Music _____ ○○○○○
Repair _____ ○○○○○
Security _____ ○○○○○
Stealth _____ ●●○○○
Survival _____ ●○○○○

Knowledge
Bureaucracy _____ ○○○○○
Computer _____ ○○○○○
Finance _____ ○○○○○
Investigation _____ ○○○○○
Law _____ ●○○○○
Linguistics _____ ○○○○○
Medicine _____ ○○○○○
Occult _____ ○○○○○
Politics _____ ●○○○○
Science _____ ○○○○○

Advantages

Disciplines
Celerity _____ ●○○○○
Potence _____ ●○○○○
Presence _____ ●○○○○
_____ ○○○○○
_____ ○○○○○

Backgrounds
Contacts _____ ●○○○○
Allies _____ ●●○○○
Herd _____ ●●○○○
_____ ○○○○○
_____ ○○○○○

Virtues
Conscience _____ ●●○○○
Self-Control _____ ●●●●○
Courage _____ ●●●●○

Other Traits
Fast Talk _____ ●○○○○
Gambling _____ ●○○○○
Lock Picking _____ ●○○○○
Area Knowledge ●●●○○
_____ ○○○○○

Combat

Weapon	Difficulty	Damage

Humanity
●●●●●●●○○○○

Willpower
●●●●●○○○○○
□□□□□□□□□□

Blood Pool
○○○○○○○○○○○

Health
Bruised _____ □
Hurt -1 □
Injured -2 □
Wounded -3 □
Mauled -4 □
Crippled -5 □
Incapacitated □

Experience
[ ]

Attributes: 7/5/3 Abilities: 13/9/5 Disciplines: 3 Backgrounds: 5 Virtues: 7 Freebie Points: 15 (7/5/2/1)

GANGREL LONER

Quote: *"The woods are quiet tonight. That's the best time to run, when it's cold and the grass is crisp beneath your toes. You understand the mortals well at such times; when their breath crystalizes in the air it speaks of what they are. There is a feeling of raw nature on your face as you run, and you can hear their hearts beat so frantically and smell the anguish in their warm blood."*

Prelude: The woods were your home since you were a girl, and you came to know them as you knew your own bedroom. It seemed only natural that when you grew up you would become a park ranger fighting fires, tagging animals, and protecting the forests you loved.

A week of strange animal deaths in your park attracted your attention, and after another week of tracking, you managed to discover the killer's lair. The only trouble was that the killer was expecting you. The deaths were but a ruse to test you for your worth as one of the Undead. You fought back, but nothing could prevail against this unholy force of nature. Then it abandoned you to the earth.

Concept: The Gangrel Clan has a particular affinity with wild animals, so the concept for this character was a park ranger. Outdoors and survival skills are paramount, with little in the way of social graces.

Gangrels are not gregarious by nature, but band together loosely against the problems caused by others. The character's Sire is still on the scene as a Mentor (though you still know little about him), and Allies are probably drawn from friends and acquaintances in the National Park Service.

The character's Willpower needs building up, and enhanced combat skills (especially Firearms) would be useful. More outdoors skills would be entirely appropriate to the stereotype. To personalize the character, you might add a craft Skill or two for

a hobby, or a couple of Knowledges as outside areas of interest.

Roleplaying Tips: You are ill at ease around people and in developed areas. Speak little, and never raise your voice — always keep it soft, as though you are afraid of startling nearby game. Move slowly most of the time, and with blinding speed when it's necessary. When you speak to someone, look them directly in the eye and never let your gaze waver. Keep your eyes slightly narrowed at all times, and focused somewhere in the middle distance without appearing to dream: you are alert at all times.

Equipment: Remington M-700, sleeping bag, backpack, flashlight, maps.

VAMPIRE ™

Name: _____ Nature: **Survivor** Generation: **13th**
Player: _____ Demeanor: **Loner** Haven: _____
Chronicle: _____ Clan: **Gangrel** Concept: **Forest Ranger**

Attributes

Physical
Strength _____ ●●●○○
Dexterity _____ ●●●○○
Stamina _____ ●●●●○

Social
Charisma _____ ●●●●○
Manipulation _____ ●○○○○
Appearance _____ ●●○○○

Mental
Perception _____ ●●●●○
Intelligence _____ ●●○○○
Wits _____ ●●●○○

Abilities

Talents
Acting _____ ○○○○○
Alertness _____ ●●●○○
Athletics _____ ●●○○○
Brawl _____ ●●○○○
Dodge _____ ●●●○○
Empathy _____ ●○○○○
Intimidation _____ ○○○○○
Leadership _____ ○○○○○
Streetwise _____ ○○○○○
Subterfuge _____ ○○○○○

Skills
Animal Ken _____ ●●●○○
Drive _____ ●○○○○
Etiquette _____ ○○○○○
Firearms _____ ○○○○○
Melee _____ ○○○○○
Music _____ ○○○○○
Repair _____ ○○○○○
Security _____ ○○○○○
Stealth _____ ●○○○○
Survival _____ ●●○○○

Knowledge
Bureaucracy _____ ○○○○○
Computer _____ ○○○○○
Finance _____ ○○○○○
Investigation _____ ○○○○○
Law _____ ○○○○○
Linguistics _____ ○○○○○
Medicine _____ ●○○○○
Occult _____ ○○○○○
Politics _____ ○○○○○
Science _____ ○○○○○

Advantages

Disciplines
Protean ●○○○○
Animalism ●○○○○
Fortitude ●○○○○
_____ ○○○○○
_____ ○○○○○

Backgrounds
Allies ●●●○○
Mentor ●●○○○
_____ ○○○○○
_____ ○○○○○
_____ ○○○○○

Virtues
Conscience _____ ●●●○○
Self-Control _____ ●●●●○
Courage _____ ●●●○○

Other Traits:
Scrounging ●●○○○
Sense Deception ●○○○○
Tracking ●●○○○
Meteorology ●○○○○
Naturalist ●●●○○

Combat

Weapon	Difficulty	Damage

Humanity
●●●●●●●○○○

Willpower
●●●●●○○○○○
□□□□□□□□□□

Blood Pool
○○○○○○○○○○

Health
Bruised _____ □
Hurt -1 □
Injured -2 □
Wounded -3 □
Mauled -4 □
Crippled -5 □
Incapacitated □

Experience
_____

Attributes: 7/5/3 Abilities: 13/9/5 Disciplines: 3 Backgrounds: 5 Virtues: 7 Freebie Points: 15 (7/5/2/1)

MALKAVIAN MEDDLER

Quote: *"You're very pretty . . . hee, hee. Yes, of course I mean it; you're a lovely little creature. It doesn't matter what the others think, they can't touch you now. No, don't worry, you can go slow. I'll be back soon my little darling, so don't get all arroused and run about putting things in disaray. That would make me upset. Calm down child, why would you want to leave now? Your pumpkin is still a coach. Well, if you are so ungodly eager to leave, there is one thing you can do for me before you go..."*

Prelude: Your parents began to worry years ago, when you first started to hurt other children and small animals for fun. A succession of analysts and doctors led finally to a small but comfortable room in an exclusive sanitarium where you drew the attention of a strange presence. Your skill at creating confusion and misery amounted to an art, and was the main reason for the Embrace. You fought against it the whole time, but secretly loved every instant of it.

Concept: The Malkavians are the least predictable and least trusted of all the Clans, and this character is no exception. Delighting in chaos, you have made a lifetime's hobby of throwing a wrench in the works and making the plans of anyone within reach come crashing down in ruins. Attributes and Abilities are geared towards deception and sabotage.

Your Herd and Retainers are almost certainly inmates of an asylum which houses one of your Havens. It is probably a very high-class and discreet establishment, since the your Resources indicate that your family was well-off. Certainly your hands have never been soiled with work (not that you're even capable of it).

Again the character's weakest point is Willpower, and the low Conscience rating. While very much in keeping with the character concept, the latter could become a problem. Almost any Trait could be acquired or added to, since the character is a lifelong dilettante and has been able to indulge almost any interest.

Roleplaying Tips: You consider yourself to be a master manipulator, and the world in general to be an ant farm provided for your amusement. You love to drop in a rock from time to time and see them all scurrying around. On the surface you are polished and charming — perhaps you even work a little too hard at that — but every so often, you can't suppress a giggle or a flash of psychotic temper.

Equipment: Strait jacket, anti-psychotic drugs, hypodermic needle, crayons and coloring book.

VAMPIRE ™

Name: _____ Nature: **Jester** Generation: **13th**
Player: _____ Demeanor: **Gallant** Haven: _____
Chronicle: _____ Clan: **Malkavian** Concept: **Troublemaker**

Attributes

Physical
Strength _____ ●●○○○
Dexterity _____ ●●○○○
Stamina _____ ●●○○○

Social
Charisma _____ ●●○○○
Manipulation _____ ●●●●○
Appearance _____ ●●○○○

Mental
Perception _____ ●●●○○
Intelligence _____ ●●●○○
Wits _____ ●●●○○

Abilities

Talents
Acting _____ ●●●○○
Alertness _____ ●●○○○
Athletics _____ ○○○○○
Brawl _____ ○○○○○
Dodge _____ ○○○○○
Empathy _____ ●○○○○
Intimidation _____ ●●○○○
Leadership _____ ●●○○○
Streetwise _____ ○○○○○
Subterfuge _____ ●●●○○

Skills
Animal Ken _____ ○○○○○
Drive _____ ○○○○○
Etiquette _____ ●●○○○
Firearms _____ ●○○○○
Melee _____ ●○○○○
Music _____ ○○○○○
Repair _____ ○○○○○
Security _____ ○○○○○
Stealth _____ ●○○○○
Survival _____ ○○○○○

Knowledge
Bureaucracy _____ ●●○○○
Computer _____ ○○○○○
Finance _____ ●○○○○
Investigation _____ ○○○○○
Law _____ ●○○○○
Linguistics _____ ●●○○○
Medicine _____ ○○○○○
Occult _____ ●○○○○
Politics _____ ●○○○○
Science _____ ○○○○○

Advantages

Disciplines
Auspex _____ ●○○○○
Obfuscate _____ ●○○○○
Dominate _____ ●○○○○
_____ ○○○○○
_____ ○○○○○

Backgrounds
Herd _____ ●●○○○
Influence _____ ●○○○○
Resources _____ ●○○○○
Retainers _____ ●○○○○
_____ ○○○○○

Virtues
Conscience _____ ●●○○○
Self-Control _____ ●●●●●
Courage _____ ●●●○○

Other Traits
Mimicry _____ ●●○○○
Toxicology _____ ●●○○○
_____ ○○○○○
_____ ○○○○○
_____ ○○○○○

Combat

Weapon	Difficulty	Damage

Humanity
●●●●●○○○○○

Willpower
●●●●●○○○○○
□□□□□□□□□□

Blood Pool
○○○○○○○○○○

Health
Bruised _____ □
Hurt -1 □
Injured -2 □
Wounded -3 □
Mauled -4 □
Crippled -5 □
Incapacitated □

Experience

[ ]

Attributes: 7/5/3 Abilities: 13/9/5 Disciplines: 3 Backgrounds: 5 Virtues: **7** Freebie Points: 15 (7/5/2/1)

SKULKING NOSFERATU

Quote: *"What are you looking at, pretty boy? Never seen anything as beautiful as me before, have you? That's right, just keep staring and you won't have anything to stare with much longer!"*

Prelude: Nosferatu traditionally favor the twisted and forlorn, and those with nothing to lose, and you more than fit the bill. Literally born on the street, you bounced in and out of orphanages and foster homes your entire life. You escaped this life for a short while by joining the army, but soon found nothing in your life had prepared you for a jungle firefight. When you left the army you were but a shell of your old self, broken and scared. Unable to hold a job for more than a month, the streets seemed destined to be your grave as well as your crib. Alcohol became your only solace.

Indeed, you were killed on the street, only to be reborn as something more. Your quirky personality betrayed some spirit, a fire another outcast did not want to see lost. Now you are truly one of the homeless, for all of humanity has rejected you. Your home is now below the streets. There are weird things in the city sewers, things no sane person would believe, and Vampires are the least of them.

Concept: You move among the lowest levels of humanity, and are used to living on the street. Traits are geared towards urban survival, with the accent on Stamina, Alertness, Streetwise, Stealth and Survival.

The character's Herd and Retainers are almost certainly drawn from the city's homeless. The Mentor Background indicates that the character's Sire is still in touch, probably having re-

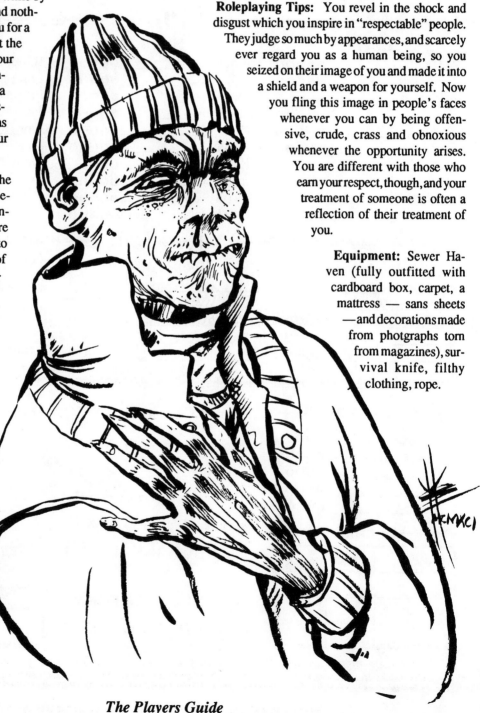

cruited the character as part of an intelligence-gathering network.

The character's Willpower of 4 is an obvious weakness, although low Courage is in keeping with the Nosferatu *modus operandi* in general and this character's concept in particular. Combat skills are not high on the list of priorities — this character sees all, hears all, and hides from most of it.

Roleplaying Tips: You revel in the shock and disgust which you inspire in "respectable" people. They judge so much by appearances, and scarcely ever regard you as a human being, so you seized on their image of you and made it into a shield and a weapon for yourself. Now you fling this image in people's faces whenever you can by being offensive, crude, crass and obnoxious whenever the opportunity arises. You are different with those who earn your respect, though, and your treatment of someone is often a reflection of their treatment of you.

Equipment: Sewer Haven (fully outfitted with cardboard box, carpet, a mattress — sans sheets — and decorations made from photgraphs torn from magazines), survival knife, filthy clothing, rope.

VAMPIRE™

Name: _____
Player: _____
Chronicle: _____

Nature: **Loner**
Demeanor: **Deviant**
Clan: **Nosferatu**

Generation: **13th**
Haven: _____
Concept: **Street Person**

Attributes

Physical
Strength _____ ●●○○○
Dexterity _____ ●●●○○
Stamina _____ ●●●●○

Social
Charisma _____ ●●○○○
Manipulation _____ ●●●○○
Appearance _____ ○○○○○

Mental
Perception _____ ●●●○○
Intelligence _____ ●●○○○
Wits _____ ●●●○○

Abilities

Talents
Acting _____ ○○○○○
Alertness _____ ●●●○○
Athletics _____ ●○○○○
Brawl _____ ●○○○○
Dodge _____ ●●○○○
Empathy _____ ●○○○○
Intimidation _____ ●○○○○
Leadership _____ ○○○○○
Streetwise _____ ●●●○○
Subterfuge _____ ●○○○○

Skills
Animal Ken _____ ○○○○○
Drive _____ ○○○○○
Etiquette _____ ○○○○○
Firearms _____ ●○○○○
Melee _____ ●●○○○
Music _____ ○○○○○
Repair _____ ○○○○○
Security _____ ○○○○○
Stealth _____ ●●●○○
Survival _____ ●●●○○

Knowledge
Bureaucracy _____ ○○○○○
Computer _____ ○○○○○
Finance _____ ○○○○○
Investigation _____ ●○○○○
Law _____ ○○○○○
Linguistics _____ ○○○○○
Medicine _____ ○○○○○
Occult _____ ○○○○○
Politics _____ ●○○○○
Science _____ ○○○○○

Advantages

Disciplines
Animalism ●○○○○
Obfuscate ●○○○○
Potence ●○○○○
_____ ○○○○○
_____ ○○○○○

Backgrounds
Mentor ●○○○○
Herd ●●○○○
Retainers ●●○○○
_____ ○○○○○
_____ ○○○○○

Virtues
Conscience _____ ●●●●○
Self-Control _____ ●●●●○
Courage _____ ●●○○○

Other Traits
Area Knowledge ●●●○○
_____ ○○○○○
_____ ○○○○○
_____ ○○○○○
_____ ○○○○○

Combat

Weapon	Difficulty	Damage

Humanity
●●●●●●○○○○

Willpower
●●●●○○○○○○
□□□□□□□□□□

Blood Pool
○○○○○○○○○○

Health
Bruised		□
Hurt	-1	□
Injured	-2	□
Wounded	-3	□
Mauled	-4	□
Crippled	-5	□
Incapacitated		□

Experience
[ ]

Attributes: 7/5/3 Abilities: 13/9/5 Disciplines: 3 Backgrounds: 5 Virtues: 7 Freebie Points: 15 (7/5/2/1)

TOREADOR DILETTANTE

Quote: *"Who called this rubbish art? There is nothing here — no soul, no heart, no feeling. Where is your inspiration? Maybe death would be a better muse!"*

Prelude: With the kind of money your family had there was never any reason to worry about what to do with your life. Art seemed interesting and you even appeared to have some knack for it. What you had more of a knack for, however, was appearing to be an artist and garning the praise and attention that came from such a pursuit. All the right people at all the right parties called you an artist, so an artist you were.

It was at one of these parties you met the individual who would prove to be your most important, and final, inspiration. For a month you created art as you never had before, and everything was done for him. At the end of the month he knew your genius had to live forever, and eternity was yours. One month later he left you, calling you a charlatan and a farce, undeserving of the

great gift he had given you. Now you live to prove him wrong.

Concept: The concept for this character is a stereotypical Toreador — a moneyed layabout who dabbles in the arts and loves to be thought of as a great connoisseur. Traits focus on socializing with a smattering of arts.

Resources are probably family money, and Retainers may well be carried over from breathing days.

As usual, Willpower could be built up, and the character would also benefit from a few more points in one or more artistic Traits, unless you want to keep the character as a patron of artists rather than an actual creator of art

Roleplaying Tips: Always speak in cultured tones, and never be neutral or non-committal about anything. You are always either wildly, gushingly enthusiastic or contemptuous and sarcastic. Sprinkle your conversation with words and phrases in various languages. Always seek to impress others with your culture — unless you decide to brand them as Philistines, in which case you can safely ignore them.

Equipment: Luxurious condominium (decorated with original art and sculpture), a new Miata, racks of designer clothing, credit cards.

VAMPIRE™

Name: Nature: Plotter   Generation: 13th
Player: Demeanor: Gallant   Haven:
Chronicle: Clan: Toreador   Concept: Dilettante

Attributes

Physical
Strength ●●○○○
Dexterity ●●○○○
Stamina ●●○○○

Social
Charisma ●●●○○
Manipulation ●●●○○
Appearance ●●●●○

Mental
Perception ●●●○○
Intelligence ●●●○○
Wits ●●○○○

Abilities

Talents
Acting ●○○○○
Alertness ●●○○○
Athletics ○○○○○
Brawl ○○○○○
Dodge ●○○○○
Empathy ○○○○○
Intimidation ○○○○○
Leadership ○○○○○
Streetwise ○○○○○
Subterfuge ●●●○○

Skills
Animal Ken ○○○○○
Drive ○○○○○
Etiquette ●●●○○
Firearms ○○○○○
Melee ○○○○○
Music ●●○○○
Repair ○○○○○
Security ○○○○○
Stealth ●○○○○
Survival ○○○○○

Knowledge
Bureaucracy ○○○○○
Computer ○○○○○
Finance ●○○○○
Investigation ○○○○○
Law ○○○○○
Linguistics ●●○○○
Medicine ○○○○○
Occult ○○○○○
Politics ○○○○○
Science ○○○○○

Advantages

Disciplines
Auspex ●○○○○
Celerity ●○○○○
Presence ●○○○○
_____ ○○○○○
_____ ○○○○○

Backgrounds
Resources ●●●●○
Retainers ●●○○○
_____ ○○○○○
_____ ○○○○○
_____ ○○○○○

Virtues
Conscience ●●●●○
Self-Control ●●●○○
Courage ●●●○○

Other Traits
Art ●○○○○
Carousing ●●●○○
Dancing ●●○○○
Game (Chess) ●○○○○
Art History ●●○○○

Combat

Weapon	Difficulty	Damage

Humanity
●●●●●●● ○○○

Willpower
●●●○○○○○○○
□□□□□□□□□□

Blood Pool
○○○○○○○○○○

Health
Bruised   □
Hurt   -1 □
Injured   -2 □
Wounded   -3 □
Mauled   -4 □
Crippled -5 □
Incapacitated □

Experience

Attributes: 7/5/3 Abilities: 13/9/5 Disciplines: 3 Backgrounds: 5 Virtues: 7 Freebie Points: 15 (7/5/2/1)

TREMERE OCCULTIST

Quote: *"Why do you ask me? Maybe I know, but I won't tell you. Even if I could, you're not worth it, for there is simply no gain in it for the risk I would take in telling such private details to the likes of you. Maybe after you have learned something of interest to me— then we can talk."*

Prelude: Years ago you studied the occult by corresponding with learned masters across the globe. There was no purpose to your quest; it was just part of your insatiable thirst for knowledge and your curiosity about the beyond. Somehow you came to the attention of one mystic in particular. After several years of correspondence, he invited you to meet him in Vienna, promising revelations of a sort you had never expected. Needless to say, you had never expected the conversion to Vampire.

Concept: The concept for this character is one of the great Tremere stereotypes — the occultist. Traits focus on arcane knowledge, with a reasonable level of general education and a fair proficiency in plotting schemes.

The character's Sire is around as a Mentor, for the Tremere are the most formal and structured of the Clans. The character's Sire may well be the Chantry head. Herd and Retainers may be mortal students of the occult, or others who have been provided by the Clan.

Again, Willpower is low, and Conscience needs improvement. Improving Thaumaturgy is expensive, but could be worthwhile. Increasing the overall level of education might also be useful.

Roleplaying Tips: You are privileged to have been shown some of the Inner Mysteries, and you now understand Truths which are beyond the grasp of simpler minds. When dealing with members of other Clans, always bear in mind their profound ignorance — either don't bother to explain anything to them at all, or go into labored and detailed explanations sprinkled with obscure terminology. Trust no one but your Tremere brothers, and always try to gain more information than you give in any conversation.

Equipment: Feathers, penny, wood splinter or Sire's locket; basement apartment, an old Volvo.

VAMPIRE ™

Name: Nature: **Traditionalist**   Generation: **13th**
Player: Demeanor: **Plotter**   Haven:
Chronicle: Clan: **Tremere**   Concept: **Occultist**

Attributes

Physical
Strength ●●○○○
Dexterity ●●○○○
Stamina ●●○○○

Social
Charisma ●●●○○
Manipulation ●●●○○
Appearance ●●○○○

Mental
Perception ●●●○○
Intelligence ●●●●○
Wits ●●●○○

Abilities

Talents
Acting ○○○○○
Alertness ●●○○○
Athletics ○○○○○
Brawl ○○○○○
Dodge ○○○○○
Empathy ○○○○○
Intimidation ○○○○○
Leadership ○○○○○
Streetwise ○○○○○
Subterfuge ●●○○○

Skills
Animal Ken ○○○○○
Drive ●○○○○
Etiquette ●○○○○
Firearms ○○○○○
Melee ○○○○○
Music ○○○○○
Repair ○○○○○
Security ○○○○○
Stealth ●○○○○
Survival ○○○○○

Knowledge
Bureaucracy ○○○○○
Computer ○○○○○
Finance ○○○○○
Investigation ○○○○○
Law ●○○○○
Linguistics ●●○○○
Medicine ○○○○○
Occult ●●●●○
Politics ●○○○○
Science ●●○○○

Advantages

Disciplines
Auspex ●○○○○
Dominate ●○○○○
Thaumaturgy ●○○○○
_____ ○○○○○
_____ ○○○○○

Backgrounds
Herd ●●○○○
Mentor ●●○○○
Retainer ●○○○○
_____ ○○○○○
_____ ○○○○○

Virtues
Conscience ●●○○○
Self-Control ●●●●●
Courage ●●●○○

Other Traits
Sense Deception ●○○○○
Hypnotism ●○○○○
Herbalism ●●●○○
Meditation ●○○○○
Alchemy ●●●○○

Combat

Weapon	Difficulty	Damage

Humanity
●●●●●○○○○○

Willpower
●●●●●●○○○○
□□□□□□□□□□

Blood Pool
○○○○○○○○○○

Health
Bruised   □
Hurt   -1   □
Injured   -2   □
Wounded -3   □
Mauled   -4   □
Crippled -5   □
Incapacitated □

Experience

Attributes: 7/5/3   Abilities: 13/9/5   Disciplines: 3   Backgrounds: 5   Virtues: **7**   Freebie Points: 15 (7/5/2/1)

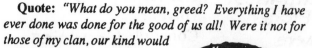

VENTRUE MANIPULATOR

Quote: *"What do you mean, greed? Everything I have ever done was done for the good of us all! Were it not for those of my clan, our kind would be no more, destroyed by your fractiousness and inefficiency!"*

Prelude: Nothing could stop your rise to the top. Starting off as the most junior of executives, your meteoric business career and incisive (often ruthless) decision-making

caught the attention of the corporate leaders. You may have been called a leech and a parasite by the bleeding-heart types, but they had no influence on your inevitable climb to power. Maybe it was because you had been marked for such great things that everyone was so horrified by your disappearance (that was very satisfying for you). To your great fortune, you had been noticed by another kind of leech, and now power has a whole new meaning.

Concept: This character was based on the concept of a business executive — someone experienced at organizing and manipulating others and running a business empire. Traits are geared towards gaining the obedience and cooperation of others, with a few business-related Knowledges thrown in.

Resources and Influence are relics of breathing days and they may well have been enhanced since the Change.

Low Willpower and combat skills are this character's greatest weaknesses. Existing Traits could be increased further to enhance the tycoon image, or other Traits might be bought to produce a more-rounded character.

Roleplaying Tips: You are used to being at the top or at least to being on your way there. When you talk, people listen, and when you give orders, they obey. You are dynamic and forceful, with a loud voice and no interest in other people's opinions or suggestions — unless you invite them. Your rise to the top was not bloodless, and you have no qualms about the means you will use to achieve your aims. Your ambition is by no means satiated, you have already plotted your rise to the top of Clan Ventrue, and your eventual establishment as Prince of the city. But you know you have many rivals, and you tread carefully.

Equipment: Large house, dozens of identical Business Suits, Glock-17, BMW.

VAMPIRE ™

Name: _____   Nature: **Director**   Generation: **13th**
Player: _____   Demeanor: **Traditionalist** Haven: _____
Chronicle: _____   Clan: **Ventrue**   Concept: **Tycoon**

Attributes

Physical
Strength _____ ●●○○○
Dexterity _____ ●●○○○
Stamina _____ ●●○○○

Social
Charisma _____ ●●●○○
Manipulation _____ ●●●○○
Appearance _____ ●●○○○

Mental
Perception _____ ●●●○○
Intelligence _____ ●●●○○
Wits _____ ●●●●○

Abilities

Talents
Acting _____ ○○○○○
Alertness _____ ●○○○○
Athletics _____ ○○○○○
Brawl _____ ○○○○○
Dodge _____ ○○○○○
Empathy _____ ○○○○○
Intimidation _____ ●○○○○
Leadership _____ ●●●○○
Streetwise _____ ○○○○○
Subterfuge _____ ●●○○○

Skills
Animal Ken _____ ○○○○○
Drive _____ ●○○○○
Etiquette _____ ●○○○○
Firearms _____ ●○○○○
Melee _____ ○○○○○
Music _____ ○○○○○
Repair _____ ○○○○○
Security _____ ●○○○○
Stealth _____ ○○○○○
Survival _____ ○○○○○

Knowledge
Bureaucracy _____ ●●●○○
Computer _____ ○○○○○
Finance _____ ●●●○○
Investigation _____ ○○○○○
Law _____ ●○○○○
Linguistics _____ ●○○○○
Medicine _____ ○○○○○
Occult _____ ○○○○○
Politics _____ ●●○○○
Science _____ ○○○○○

Advantages

Disciplines
Dominate _____ ●○○○○
Fortitude _____ ●○○○○
Presence _____ ●○○○○
_____ ○○○○○
_____ ○○○○○

Backgrounds
Resources _____ ●●●○○
Influence _____ ●●○○○
_____ ○○○○○
_____ ○○○○○
_____ ○○○○○

Virtues
Conscience _____ ●●●○○
Self-Control _____ ●●●●○
Courage _____ ●●●○○

✠— Other Traits —✠
Diplomacy _____ ●●○○○
Area Knowledge _____ ●○○○○
Economics _____ ●●○○○
_____ ○○○○○
_____ ○○○○○

✠— Combat —✠

Weapon	Difficulty	Damage

✠— Humanity —✠
●●●●●●●○○○

✠— Willpower —✠
●●●●●○○○○○
□□□□□□□□□□

✠— Blood Pool —✠
○○○○○○○○○○

✠— Health —✠
Bruised _____ □
Hurt   -1 □
Injured   -2 □
Wounded -3 □
Mauled   -4 □
Crippled -5 □
Incapacitated □

✠— Experience —✠
[   ]

Attributes: 7/5/3 Abilities: 13/9/5 Disciplines: 3 Backgrounds: 5 Virtues: **7** Freebie Points: 15 (7/5/2/1)

Permission is granted to photocopy this page, for personal use only.

Merits and Flaws are two new classes of Traits. Merits are things that work to the character's advantage, and Flaws are things that work to the character's disadvantage. They are ways in which you can describe your character in more detail than provided in the basic rules, but these new rules are optional. If you do not take Merits and Flaws for your character, you will not suffer for it; your character is simply different than who she might otherwise be.

When you create a character in **Vampire**, you are given 15 'freebie' points, to assign to whatever traits you like to give your character the finishing touches that make him unique. This optional system of Merits and Flaws expands that idea, allowing you to personalize your character even further.

Merits may only be bought with freebie points, and Flaws actually give you more freebie points to spend on Merits, or anything else you like. You can purchase as many Merits as you wish, up to the full amount of your freebie-points (though that would leave you weak in your other areas). Each Merit has a different cost, which is described in terms of freebie points, if you wish to take it you must spend that many of your freebie points.

Each Flaw that you purchase gives you additional freebie points. The amount gained is listed along with the Flaw. Thus, buying Flaws can allow you to buy more Merits. For instance Daredevil costs one freebie point, while Light Sensitive provides you with three additional freebie points. However, you can only take up to 7 points of Flaws (making it impossible for any character to have and spend any more than 22 freebie points). Additionally, Merits and Flaws may only be bought when the character is first generated (unless the Storyteller makes an exception for those who missed the opportunity earlier).

In some Chronicles, especially those where the horror is emphasized, Merits and Flaws will not be permitted, or may be restricted in some way. Make sure you have the Storyteller's permission before you start using these traits. Keep in mind that this system was not created to allow you to mini-max, it was designed to let you create a more fully realized character. The more you abuse the Merits and Flaws in an attempt to create a super-character, the less likely you will be allowed to take them again for your next character.

Psychological

These Merits and Flaws deal with the psychological make-up of your character, and may describe ideals, motivations, and pathologies. Some psychological Flaws can be avoided at the cost of a Willpower point, and are so noted. If you possess such a Flaw and do not roleplay the effects of it when the Storyteller thinks you should, then she may tell you that you have spent a point of Willpower for the effort. Flaws cannot be conveniently ignored.

Code of Honor: (1pt Merit)

You have a personal code of ethics, which you abide by strictly. Even when you are in Frenzy you will attempt to obey them (and thus get 3 extra dice to your self-restraint rolls when in danger of violating your code). You can automatically resist most temptations that would bring you in conflict with your code, and gain 3 extra dice to resist supernatural persuasions. You must construct your own personal code of honor in as much detail as you can, outlining the general rules of conduct by which you abide.

Higher Purpose: (1pt Merit)

You have a goal which drive and directs you in everything that you do. You do not concern yourself with petty matters and casual concerns, because your higher purpose is everything. Though you may sometimes be driven by this purpose and find yourself forced to behave in ways counter to the needs of self-survival, it can grant you great personal strength. You gain 2 extra dice on all rolls that have anything to do with this higher purpose. You need to decide what your higher purpose will be, just make sure you talk it over with the Storyteller first. (If you have Driving Goal, you cannot take this Merit.)

Berserker: (2pt Merit)

The rage is in you but you know how to direct it and make use of it. You have the capacity to induce Frenzy in yourself at will, and are are thus able to reap the benefit of acting without regard of your wound penalties. However, you must still pay the consequences of your actions while in Frenzy just as you normally would. Also, you still have the same chance of going into Frenzy, even when you do not wish to to do so.

Dual Nature: (2pt Merit)

You have two distinct Natures, both of which have an influence on your personality and behavior. When you pick these Natures be careful to choose Archetypes that are somewhat compatible (you can select one that's opposite on your Demeanor, however). Dual Nature does not mean schizophrenic (that is a derangement). You regain Willpower using both Natures.

Intolerance: (1pt Flaw)

You have an unreasoning dislike of a certain thing. This may be an animal, a class of person, a color, a situation — pretty much anything at all. You have a +2 difficulty on all dice rolls where the object of dislike is involved. Note that some dislikes may be too trivial to be reflected here — a dislike of WHITE WOLF Magazine or tissue paper, for instance, will have little effect on play in most Chronicles. The Storyteller is the final arbiter on what you can pick.

Over-Confident: (1pt Flaw)

You have an exaggerated and unshakable estimation of your own worth and capabilities — you display no hesitation in trusting your abilities in situations where you risk defeat. Becuase your abilities may still not be enough, this can be very dangerous at times. When you do fail in some task you are quick to find someone or something to blame other than yourself. If you are convincing enough, however, you can infect others with your confidence.

Mild Phobia: (1pt Flaw)

You have an overpowering fear of something, and instinctively and illogically retreat from and avoid the object of your fear. Common objects of phobias might include a particular type of animal, insects, crowds, open spaces, confined spaces, heights, crosses, garlic and so on. The things that normally frighten Vampires, such as fire or sunlight, cannot be chosen as the object of fear. You must roll Intelligence + Courage whenever the object of fear is encountered. The difficulty of this roll is determined by the Storyteller. If you fail the roll, then you must retreat in terror from the object, and if you get any less than three successes you will not approach it. Fear of the dark (scotophobia) might seem at first glance like a very challenging and interesting phobia to give to a Vampire, but it is not recommended as it can interfere too much with your operation in the game. The same is true of haematophobia, or fear of blood. The Storyteller, of course, has final say over which phobias are allowed in a Chronicle.

Prey Exclusion: (1pt Flaw)

You refuse to hunt a certain class of prey. This is tied up with your personality. For instance, an animal-lover might decide to hunt only humans, or a character might decide to spare a class of person she particularly admires: police,

teachers, medics, clergy, peace activists and so on. You are disturbed when others feed from this type of prey, and could possibly become enraged by it, or even drawn into a Frenzy (Storyteller's discretion). If you accidently feed upon this class of prey yourself, you will automatically go into Frenzy and will need to make a humanity loss roll (difficulty 8 or more). Note: This is not as restrictive as the Ventrue limitation, which limits you to a certain class of prey (therefore Ventrue cannot take this Flaw).

Speech Impediment: (1pt Flaw)

You have a stammer or some other speech impediment which hampers verbal communication. All relevant rolls are made with a +2 difficulty. Do not feel obliged to roleplay this impediment all of the time, like when you are just among your coterie, but in times of duress or when dealing with outsiders you should attempt to simulate it if possible.

Shy: (1pt Flaw)

You are distinctly ill at ease when dealing with people, and you will try to avoid social situations whenever possible. All rolls concerned with social dealings are made with a +1 difficulty, and any roll made while you are the center of attention is made at +2 difficulty. Don't expect such a character to make a public speech.

Compulsion: (1pt Flaw)

You have a psychological compulsion of some sort or another, which can cause you a number of different problems. Your compulsion may be for cleanliness, perfection, bragging, stealing, gaming, exaggeration, or just talking. This compulsion can temporarily be avoided at the cost of a Willpower point, but it is in effect at all other times.

Soft Hearted: (1pt Flaw)

You cannot stand to witness others suffering, not necessarily because you care about what happens to them, but simply because you dislike the intensity of emotion. If you are the direct cause of suffering, and you must witness it, it will bring you days of nausea and sleepless grief. You avoid situations where you might have to witness suffering, and will do anything you can to keep others away from it as well. When you feed you take care that it is not painful, and that the Vessel does not realize what is happening. You simply don't want to be reminded of it as you try to ignore the dark side. Whenever you must witness suffering, difficulties on all rolls are raised by +2 for the next hour.

Nightmares: (1pt Flaw)

You experience a horrendous nightmare every day, and memories of them continue to haunt you during your waking hours. Sometimes they are so bad that they cause you to loose one die on all your actions for a night (Storyteller's discretion). Some of these nightmares may be so intense that you will begin to mistake some of these unreal incidents for reality. A crafty Storyteller will be quick to take advantage of this.

Dark Secret: (1pt Flaw)

You have some sort of secret that, if uncovered, would be of immense embarrassment to you and would make you a pariah in the Kindred community. This can be anything from the murder of an Elder to former membership in the Sabbat. While this secret is on your mind at all times, it will come up in stories only once in a while. Otherwise, it will begin to lose it's impact.

Low Self-Image: (2pt Flaw)

You lack self-confidence, and don't believe in yourself. You have 2 less dice in situations where you don't expect to succeed (Storyteller's discretion, though the penalty might be limited to one die if you "help" the Storyteller by pointing out times when this Flaw might affect you). At the Storyteller's option, you may be required to make Courage rolls to do things that require self-confidence, or even, at times, use a Willpower point when others would not be obliged to do so.

Short Fuse: (2pt Flaw)

You are easily angered and put off kilter, so the difficulty of Frenzy rolls is always two higher no matter how you were provoked. This is a dangerous Flaw, don't choose it without thought.

Vengeance: (2pt Flaw)

You have a score to settle. This may be something from your breathing days, or it may be from after the change. Either way, you are obsessed with vengeance on an individual (or perhaps an entire coterie) and will make it your first priority in all situations. The need for vengeance can only be overcome with the use of Willpower points, and even then only temporarily. Someday you may actually be able to fulfill your vengence, but the Storyteller won't make it easy.

Hatred: (3pt Flaw)

You have an unreasoning hatred of a certain thing. This hate is total, and it is largely uncontrollable. It may be for an animal, a class of person, a color, a situation — anything. You must make a Frenzy roll against Self-Control whenever faced with the object of hatred. You constantly pursue opportunities to do harm to the object of your hatred or to gain power over it, so much so that your reason is clouded.

Severe Phobia: (3pt Flaw)

You have an overpowering fear of something: common objects of fear might include certain animals, insects, crowds, open spaces, confined spaces, heights, and so on. You must make a Frenzy roll using only Courage whenever faced with the object of fear, with the difficulty dependent of the circumstances. If you fail the roll, you must retreat in terror from the object of fear, if you get any less than three successs you will not approach it. The Storyteller has final say over which phobias are allowed in a Chronicle.

Driving Goal: (3pt Flaw)

You have some personal goal, which compels and directs you in sometimes startling ways. The goal is something limitless in depth that you can never truly accomplish. It could be to eradicate the Sabbat or achieve Golconda. Because you must follow its dictates throughout the Chronicle (though you can avoid them for short periods of time by spending Willpower) it will get you into trouble and may jeopardize your other goals. Choose your driving goal carefully, as it will direct and focus everything your character does.

Mental

These Merits and Flaws deal with the mind: its strengths, weaknesses, and special capacities.

Common Sense: (1pt Merit)

You have a significant amount of practical, everyday wisdom, and this can be of great advantage. Whenever you are about to do something counter to common sense, the Storyteller has the task of alerting you to what you are trying to do and how it might violate practicality. For novice players this is an ideal Merit because it allows you to receive advice from the Storyteller concerning what you can and can not do, and (even more importantly) what you should and should not do.

Time Sense: (1pt Merit)

You have an innate sense of time, and are able to estimate the passage of time fairly accurately without using a watch or other mechanical device. You can accomplish this whether you are concentrating or not. You can estimate the time of day to within a minute or two, and the passage of time with the same accuracy (down to the day and year). If you have just roused from Torpor, this can be an invaluable aptitude.

Concentration: (1pt Merit)

You have the ability to focus your mind, shutting out distractions and annoyances. Any negative modifier to a dice roll arising through distractions and other inauspicious circumstances is limited to 2, though no extra benefits are gained if one penalty die was imposed.

Lightning Calculator: (1pt Merit)

You have a natural affinity with numbers and a talent for mental arithmetic, making you a natural when working with computers or betting at the race tracks. All relevant rolls are made with a -2 difficulty. Another possible use for this ability, assuming that you have numbers on which to base your conclusions, is the ability to calculate the difficulty of certain tasks. In applicable situations, you may ask the Storyteller for the difficulty of some task you are about to perform.

Light Sleeper: (2pt Merit)

You can awaken instantly at any sign of trouble or danger and do so without any sleepiness or hesitation. The rules regarding how humanity restricts the number of dice usable during the day are waived.

Eidetic Memory: (2pt Merit)

You can remember things seen and heard with perfect detail. By gaining at least one success on an Intelligence + Alertness roll, you can recall any desired sight or sound accurately, even if you heard it or glanced at it only once (though the difficulty would then be higher) With five successes you can do so perfectly, the Storyteller relates to you exactly what was seen or heard.

Iron Will: (3pt Merit)

When you are determined and your mind is set, nothing can thwart you from your goals. You cannot be dominated, nor can you mind be affected in any way by spells or rituals, though the Storyteller may require you to spend Willpower points when extremely potent powers are being directed at you.

Calm Heart: (3pt Merit)

You are naturally a calm and well-composed individual, and do not easily fly off the handle. Reduce the difficulty on all your Frenzy rolls by 2 no matter how the incident is provoked.

Self-Confident: (5pt Merit)

Whenever you spend a point of Willpower to gain an automatic success your confidence in yourself may alow you to gain the benefits of that expenditutre without actually losing the Willpower. When you spend the point you will not lose it unless that success is your only one, i.e. you do not gain any additional successes from the dice you roll. This Merit may be only be used, however, when you need confidence in your abilities in order succeed. This means that you can use it when the difficulty of your roll is 6 or higher. You may still spend Willpower at other times, but when the difficulty is 5 or less, the Willpower will be spent no matter what you roll.

Deep Sleeper: (1pt Flaw)

When you sleep, it is very difficult for you to awaken. Raise the difficulty by 2 on any such roll, and roleplay out how you never seem to be on time when you have an appointment early in the evening.

Confused: (2pt Flaw)

You are often confused, and the world sometimes seems to be a very distorted and twisted place. Sometimes you are simply not able to make sense of things. You need to roleplay this out all of the time to some small degree, but the confusion becomes especially strong whenever there is a great deal of stimulus around you (such as when a number of different people talk all at once or you enter a night club with loud pounding music). Willpower is able to override the effects of the confusion, but only temporarily.

Amnesia: (2pt Flaw)

You are unable to remember your past, or anything of yourself, your family, or perhaps even your Sire. Your life is a blank slate and begins again now. However, your past may someday come back to haunt you... (You can, if you wish, take up to 5 points of Flaws without specifying what they are, leaving it to the Storyteller to detail them. Over the course of the Chronicle, you and your character will slowly discover them.)

Weak Willed: (2pt Flaw)

You are highly susceptible to the domination and intimidation of others; you are, in fact, unable to use your Willpower freely. You can employ your Willpower only when you survival is at stake, or when it is appropriate to your Nature (see the Archetypes section).

Absent-minded: (3pt Flaw)

This Flaw may not be taken with the Merit of *Concentration*. Though you do not forget such things as your knowledges or skills, you do forget such things as names, addresses, and even when you last ate. In in order to remember anything more than your own name and the location of your haven, you need to make a Wits roll or, as a last resort, use a Willpower point.

Awareness

These Merits and Flaws concern themselves with the doors of perception, or the lack thereof.

Acute Hearing: (1pt Merit)

You have exceptionally sharp hearing, even for a Vampire. Lower the difficulty by two on any dice roll that relies upon hearing (e.g. Perception + Awareness to hear a faint

noise, or Perception + Linguistics to overhear a conversation in a foreign language). Combined with Heightened Senses (level one Auspex) this Merit can provide vastly increased hearing acuity over mortals.

Acute Sense of Smell: (1pt Merit)

You have an exceptionally keen sense of smell. Lower the difficulty by three on any dice roll which relies upon smell (e.g., Intelligence + Occult to identify a ritual incense). Combined with Heightened Senses (level one Auspex) this Merit can provide vastly increased olfactory acuity over mortals.

Acute Sense of Taste: (1pt Merit)

You have an exceptionally keen sense of taste. Lower the difficulty by three on any dice roll which relies upon taste (e.g., Perception + Medicine to spot the taint of poison in blood or another substance). You are able to make distinctions in taste which others could not even be aware of. Combined with Heightened Senses (level one Auspex) this Merit can provide increased taste acuity over mortals.

Acute Vision: (1pt Merit)

You have exceptionally keen eyesight. Lower the difficulty by one on any dice roll which relies upon vision (e.g., a Perception roll to spot a clue, or Perception + Alertness to see the shadow of an approaching attacker). Combined with Heightened Senses (Level one Auspex) this Merit can provide vastly increased visual acuity over mortals.

Color Blindness: (1pt Flaw)

You can only see in black and white — color means nothing to you — although you are sensitive to color density, which is perceived as shades of gray. This makes it impossible to use the level two Auspex power, Aura Perception. Note: Color blind actually indicates an inability to distinquish between two colors, but we fudged a bit for the sake of brevity.

Hard of Hearing: (1pt Flaw)

Your hearing is defective. There is a +2 difficulty on any dice roll where hearing is important. You may not take this Flaw along with the Merit of *Acute Hearing.*

Bad Sight: (2pt Flaw)

Your sight is defective; there is a +2 difficulty to any dice roll where good eyesight is essential. This is neither near-sightedness nor farsightedness (which are correctable); it is a minor form of blindness, and is not correctable. You may not take this Flaw along with the Merit of *Acute Vision.*

One Eye: (2pt Flaw)

You have one eye — choose which one, or determine randomly, at character generation. Your blind side has no

peripheral vision, and two less die are rolled when a situation involves depth perception. This includes rolls for missile combat.

Deaf: (4pt Flaw)

You cannot hear sound, and automatically fail any rolls relying on hearing.

Blind: (6pt Flaw)

You automatically fail all dice rolls relying on vision. You cannot see — the world of color and sight is lost to you.

Aptitudes

These Merits and Flaws deal with special capacities and abilities of your character, as well as changing or modifying the effects and powers of your character's other abilities.

Crack Driver: (1pt Merit)

You have a natural affinity with driving motorized wheeled vehicles, such as cars, semi-trucks and even tractors. The difficulty is -1 for any roll requiring risky or especially difficult driving maneuvers.

Mechanical Aptitude: (1pt Merit)

You have a natural aptitude for dealing with all kinds of mechanical devices (note that this does not include electronic devices such as computers). The difficulty is 2 less on any dice roll when you are trying to understand, repair or operate any kind of mechanical device (but doesn't help with driving any sort of vehicle).

Computer Aptitude: (1pt Merit)

You have a natural affinity with computers, so the difficulty is 2 less on all rolls to repair, construct or operate computers.

Pitiable: (1pt Merit)

There is something about you which others pity. This concern causes them to behave, temporarily, as if they were caretakers caring for a child (see the Archetypes section of the game book). Some Natures will not be affected by this Merit (Deviant, Autocrat, Fanatic, Sycophant), and some Demeanors may pretend that they are not. You need to decide what it is about you that attracts such pity, and how much (or little) you like it.

Eat Food: (1pt Merit)

You have the capacity to eat food. It's an ability you developed at some point earlier in your undead existence, or perhaps it has been a latent ability all along. This is considered disgusting by other Kindred, but can be of great assistance in the Masquerade.

SERI 91·1112

Ambidextrous: (1pt Merit)

You have a high degree of off-hand dexterity and can perform tasks with the 'wrong' hand at no penalty. The normal penalty for using both hands at once to perform different tasks (e.g. fighting with a weapon in each hand) is +1 difficulty for the 'right' hand and +3 difficulty for the 'wrong' hand.

Natural Linguist: (2pt Merit)

You have a flair for language in all its forms. This Merit does not allow you to learn more languages than are permitted by your score in *Linguistics*, but you may add 3 dice to any roll involving languages, both written and spoken.

Daredevil: (3pt Merit)

You are good at taking risks, and are even better at surviving them. All difficulties are at -1 whenever you try something particularly dangerous, and you can ignore up to one botch result when you roll ones on such actions (you can cancel a single one that is rolled, as if you had an extra success).

Fast Learner: (3pt Merit)

You learn very quickly, picking up on new things faster than others. Gain one extra experience point at the conclusion of each story (not each game session).

Illiterate: (1pt Flaw)

Through lack of education or as a result of a condition like dyslexia, you are unable to read or write.

Inept: (5pt Flaw)

You are simply not attuned to your natural aptitudes, and therefore have 5 less points to spend on your Talents (so the most you could take on your talents would be 8, and the least would be 0). Of course you could still spend freebie points to take Talents. However, you cannot, at the start of the game, have any Talent at level 3 or higher.

Unskilled: (5pt Flaw)

You have never trained extensively in any skill or craft, and therefore have 5 less points to spend on your Skills (so the most you could take on your skills would be 8, and the least would be 0). Of course you could still spend freebie points to take Skills. However, you cannot, at the start of the game, have any Skills at level 3 or higher.

Uneducated: (5pt Flaw)

Because you have never been to school, you have 5 less points to spend on your Knowledge abilities (so the most you could take on it would be 8, and the least would be 0). Of course you could still spend freebie points to take

Knowledges. However, you cannot, at the start of the game, have any knowledge at level 3 or higher.

Supernatural

These Merits and Flaws are all some sort of supernatural benefit or detriment. They are highly abnormal, and not at all common. Because of the potential of these particular Traits, and the liberal way in which they deal with the "laws of reality," the Storyteller may not allow you to choose from this category — ask before you choose one. Furthermore, you should not select such traits, unless it firmly fits your character concept, and you have some way to explain why your character possess such a trait. In general, we do not recommend that anyone have more than one or two supernatural Merits or Flaws — they should be strictly controlled by the Storyteller.

Inoffensive to Animals: (1pt Merit)

Unlike as with most of the Kindred, animals are not distrustful or frightened by your mere presence. They treat you as they would any mortal and do not shy from your touch.

True Love: (1pt Merit)

You have discovered, but may have lost (at least temporarily) a true love. This provides joy in a torrid existence usually devoid of such enlightening emotions. Whenever you are suffering, in danger, or feel dejected, the thought of your true love is enough to give you the strength to persevere. In game terms this love allows you to automatically succeed any Willpower roll, and gives you a bonus of 2 extra dice on any Virtue roll, but only when you are actively striving toward protecting or coming closer to your true love. Also, the power of your love may at times be powerful enough to protect you from other supernatural forces (Storyteller's discretion). However, your true love may also be a hindrance too you, and require aid (or even rescue) from time to time. Be forewarned, this is a most exacting Merit to play out over the course of a Chronicle.

Danger Sense: (2pt Merit)

You have a sixth sense which warns you of danger. Whenever you are in danger, the Storyteller should make a *secret* roll against your Perception + Alertness; the difficulty corresponds to the remoteness of the danger. If the roll succeeds, the Storyteller tells you that you have a feeling of foreboding. Multiple successes may even be able to refine the feeling and give an indication of direction, distance or nature.

Clairaudience (2pt Merit)

You possess the natural affinity to sense and hear spirits, ghosts and shades. Though you cannot see them, you are able and speak with them when they are in your presence. It is even possible for you to summon them (through pleading and cajoling) to your presence. Spirits will not simply aid you or give you advice gratis — they will always want something in return.

Faerie Affinity (2pt Merit)

Your presence does not frighten faeries, indeed it attracts them, and you are naturally attuned to their ways. You are able, unlike most Kindred, to enter Arcadia, the mystical Kingdom of the faeries, provided you find an entrance.

Magic Resistence: (2pt Merit)

You have an inherent resistence to the rituals of the Tremere, and the spells of the magi of other creeds and orders. Although you may not learn the Discipline of Thaumaturgy, all such spells and rituals are +2 difficulty to cast when directed at you. Note: this includes all spells, beneficial and malign alike!

Occult Library: (2pt Merit)

You possess a library of Occult materials, which includes at least one version of the Book of Nod. You are not necessarily familiar with the contents of these volumes of knowledge (that is a function of your abilities), but in time of need it can be an invaluable source for research.

Unbondable: (3pt Merit)

You are immune to being blood bound. No matter how much blood you drink of other Vampires, you will never be bound to them.

Werewolf Companion (3pt Merit)

You have a friend and ally who just happens to be a Werewolf. Though you may call upon this being in time of need, it also has the right to call upon you (after all, you are friends). However, neither your kind, nor its, appreciate such a relationship, and will punish both of you if you are found out. Arranging for meeting places and methods of communication will be difficult. The Storyteller will create the Werewolf character, but will not reveal to you its full powers and potencies.

Luck: (3pt Merit)

You were born lucky — or perhaps the Devil looks after his own. Either way, you can repeat three failed rolls per story. Only one repeat attempt may be made on any one roll.

Spirit Mentor: (3pt Merit)

You have a ghostly companion and guide. This spirit is able to work a number of minor powers when it really struggles to exert itself (see the Haunted Flaw below), but for the most part its benefit to you is through the advice it can give. This spirit is like the unincorporated spirit of someone who was once living, perhaps even someone particularly famous or wise. The Storyteller will create the ghost character, but will not reveal to you its full powers and potencies.

Destiny: (4pt Merit)

You have a destiny to which your whole life is directed, though you may well not yet realize it. This culmination to your life will become more and more apparent as the Chronicle goes on, prophecies and dreams guiding your way, and granting you clues as to its nature. The sense of direction and security this feeling of destiny grants you helps you overcome fear, depression, and discouragement caused by anything not relevant to your destiny (and therefore, irrelevant to you). Until that Destiny is fulfilled, you may suffer setbacks, but nothing which will thwart you permanently. How this is played is up to the Storyteller.

Charmed Existence: (5pt Merit)

Your unlife if somehow protected, and you do not face the perils that others must. It could be that you are simply lucky. Because of this you may completely ignore a single one on every roll you make, thus making it far more unlikely that you will ever botch, and granting you more successes than others would obtain.

Guardian Angel: (6pt Merit)

Someone or something watches over you, protecting you from harm. You have no idea who or what it is, but you have the idea that someone is there looking out for you. In times of great need you may be protected from harm, though not always. This is not something to be counted upon. The Storyteller must decide why you are being watched over, and by what (it isn't necessarily an angel, despite the name).

True Faith: (7pt Merit)

You have a deep seated faith in and love for God, by whatever name you choose to call the Almighty. Perhaps your Faith came to you before your Embrace, and was strong enough to survive even this test; or, incredibly enough, the adversity you have experienced in your current condition has brought out what is best in you. On the back of your character sheet mark down that you have one point of faith (a trait with a range of 1-10). Your faith provides you with an inner strength and comfort that continues to support you when all else betrays you: your faith adds to all Willpower and Virtue rolls. The exact supernatural effects of this faith, if any, are completely up to the Storyteller (though it will typically have the effect of repelling Kindred). It will certainly vary from person to person, and will almost never be flashly or obvious — some of the most saintly people have never performed a miracle greater than managing to touch an injured soul. The nature of any miracles you do perform will usually be tied to your own Nature, and you may never realize that you have been aided by a force beyond yourself.

You must have a humanity of 10 in order to choose this Merit, and if it every drops below 9, then you loose all of your faith points and will only be able to recover them through extensive penitence and work (and only when your humanity is 10 again). No one may start the game with more than one faith point, additional points are only awarded at the Storyteller's discretion.

Cursed (1-5pt Flaw)

You have been cursed by someone or something with the supernatural or magical powers to do so. This curse is quite specific and detailed, it cannot be dispelled without extreme effort, and can be life threatening at times. Some examples follow:

• If you ever pass on a secret that was told to you, your betrayal will later harm you in some way — 1pt.

• You stutter uncontrollably whenever you try to describe what you have seen or heard — 2pt.

• Tools often break or malfunction when you attempt to use them — 3pt.

• You are doomed to always make enemies out of those to whom you become most attached too (so whatever you do, don't get too close to the other character's!) — 4pt.

• Every one of your accomplishments or achievements will eventually, inevitably, become soiled and in some way result in failure — 5pt.

Taint of Corruption (1pt Flaw)

Plants whither when you come near, and will die if you touch them. It is rumored that Caine himself possesses this Flaw.

Repulsed by Garlic: (1pt Flaw)

You cannot abide the smell of Garlic, the smallest taint of its scent will drive you from a room. The full force of its pungent odor will bring blood tears to your face and turn you nearly blind, while its touch can cause boils and even open wounds.

Magic Susceptibility (2pt Flaw)

You are susceptible to the magical rituals of the Tremere, as well as to spells of magi of other creeds and orders. All spells cast at you are -2 difficulty and have double effect on you.

Repelled by Crosses: (3pt Flaw)

You are repelled by the sight of ordinary crosses (just as if they were holy). Kindred who had the faith prior to their Embrace are the ones most likely to possess this Flaw as they perceive that God is judging them in their new form.

Can't Cross Running Water: (3pt Flaw)

You cannot cross running water, unless you are at least 50 feet above it. "Running water" is any body of water more than two feet wide in any direction, which is not completely stagnant. A Kindred with this Flaw obviously believes too much in old wives' tales.

Haunted (3pt Flaw):

You are haunted by a ghost which only you can see and hear (except those with Clairvoyance). It actively dislikes you and enjoys making your life miserable by insulting, berating and distracting you — especially when you need to keep your cool. It additionally has a number of minor powers which it can use against you (once per story for each power): hide small objects, bring a "chill" over others making them very ill at ease with you, cause a loud buzzing in your ear or the ear of others, move small object such as a knife or pen, break a fragile item such a bottle or mirror, trip you, or make eerie noises such as chains rattling. Yelling at the ghost can sometimes drive it away, but it will confuse those who are around you. The Storyteller will likely give a great deal of personality to the Ghost, so as to make it all the more frustrating for you.

Dark Fate: (5pt Flaw)

You are doomed to experience a most horrifying demise or worse, suffer eternal agony. Either way, no matter what you do, some day you will be out of the picture. In the end, all your efforts, all your struggles, and all your dreams will be as nothing. Your fate is certain and there is nothing you can do about it. Even more horrifying, you have some partial knowledge of this, for occasionally you have visions of your fate — and they can be most disturbing. The malaise that these visions put you in can only be overcome through the use of Willpower, and it will return after each and every vision (you may get them often). In terms of the story, someday you will indeed face your fate — when and how is completely up to the Storyteller. Though you can't do anything about that, you can still attempt to reach some goal before it occurs, or at least try to make sure that your friends are not destroyed as well. This is a most difficult Flaw to roleplay, and though it may seem as if it takes away all freewill, we have found that, ironically, it grants it.

Light Sensitive: (5pt Flaw)

You are more sensitive to sunlight than even other Vampires. Sunlight causes double normal damage, and even moonlight (which is, after all, the reflected light of the sun) causes you harm. Indeed, even bright lights can be painful, but that pain can be mitigated by wearing sunglasses. When the moon is shining, the light it casts will cause wounds in the same way sunlight does for normal individuals. However, the wounds caused by the moon are not aggravated, as are those caused by the sun, and can be healed by blood points normally. Remember, even on nights when the moon is full,

it may have already set when you venture outside, or be obscured by the clouds.

Kindred Ties

These Merits and Flaws deal with the place, position and status of a character within Kindred society.

Special Gift: (1-3pt Merit)

Your Sire gave you a valuable gift at the time of the Change. The Storyteller should choose one item from the *Mystical Equipment* list to give to you (though you can "suggest" something). The Storyteller will decide how much a particular item is worth.

Boon: (1-3pt)

An Elder owes you a favor, because of something either you or your Sire once did for him. The extent of the boon owed to you depends on how many points you spend, 1pt would indicate a relatively minor boon, while 3pts would indicate that he probably owes you his "life." See the rules for Prestation for more information.

Prestigious Sire: (1pt Merit)

Your Sire had or has great Status in the Camarilla, and this has accorded you a peculiar honor. Most treat you with respect as a result, while some have only contempt for you, believing you to be nothing compared to them. This prestige could greatly aid you when dealing with the Elders familiar with your Sire. Indeed, your Sire's contacts may actually approach you at some point offering aid. Though your Sire may no longer have contact with you, the simple fact of your ancestry has marked you forever.

Reputation: (2pt Merit)

You have a good reputation among the Kin of your chosen city. This may be your own reputation, or it may be derived from your Sire. Add +3 to all dice rolls for social dealings with the city's Kindred. A character with this Merit may not take the Flaw of *Notoriety*.

Pawn (3pt Merit)

You can manipulate and have some control over another Vampire, one of lesser generation than you. Your hold was likely formed through blood bond, but the force of your manipulations can also come from a variety of other sources, such as blackmail, bribes, or threats — you make it up. The pawn does not necessarily know that it is being controlled.

Clan Friendship: (3pt Merit)

For any number of different reasons — appearance, bearing, background, or demeanor — something about you appeals to members of a Clan other than your own (your choice). The difficulty is -2 for all rolls related to social dealings with members of this Clan. This can be a two-edged thing; you are also marked by others as a sympathizer with that clan, whether you like it (or deny it!) or not.

Enemy: (1-5pt Flaw)

You have an enemy, or perhaps a group of enemies, who seek to do you harm. The value of the Flaw determines how powerful these enemies are. The most powerful enemies (Methusalahs or Arch Mages) would be 5 pts, while someone nearer to your own power would be only 1 pt. You must decide who your enemy is and how you became enemies in the first place.

Sire's Resentment: (1pt Flaw)

Your Sire dislikes you and wishes you ill. Given the smallest opportunity, your Sire will seek to do you harm, and may even attack you if provoked. Your Sire's friends will also work against you, and many Elders will thus be ill-disposed toward you.

Twisted Upbringing: (1pt Flaw)

Your Sire was quite malevolent and taught you all the wrong things about Kindred society. Everything which you believe about how Vampires interact is wrong, and your faulty beliefs are likely to get you into a great deal of trouble. Over time, after many hard lessons, you can overcome this bad start (the Storyteller will tell you when). But until then, you will continue to believe what you were first told, no matter how others try to trick you into thinking otherwise.

Infamous Sire: (1pt Flaw)

Your Sire was, and perhaps still is, distrusted and disliked by many of the Kindred in the city. As a result, you are distrusted and disliked as well. It is a heavy load, and one not easily shed.

Insane Sire: (1pt Flaw)

Your Sire has completely lost his grip on reality, and has become dangerously insane. Any wrong that your Sire does may affected your standing, and some of your Sire's dangerous schemes may somehow involve you. Because their Sires are already assumed to be insane, Malkavians cannot take this Flaw.

Mistaken Identity: (1pt Flaw)

You look similar to another Kindred, and are mistaken to be them, much to your chagrin. This individual's allies will approach you and tell you things you do not want to hear, the enemies will attempt to do away with you, and others will treat you in strange ways. Ultimately you might be able to sort out things, but it will take tremendous effort.

Diabolic Sire: (2pt Flaw)

Your Sire is engaged in acts which could cause a tremendous uproar in the Camarilla. She could be wantonly breaking the Masquerade, or hunting down the Elders of the city and feasting on their blood. Archons are likely to come to you in order to discover where your Sire is, and they may not believe you if you tell them you do not know.

Clan Enmity: (2pt Flaw)

For some reason, something about you inspires contempt or hatred in members of a Clan other than your own. There is a 2 dice penalty to all dice rolls for social dealings with members of this other Clan. Select the 'enemy' Clan randomly or choose.

Notoriety: (3pt Flaw)

You have a bad reputation among the Kin of your chosen city. This may be your own reputation, or it may be derived from your Sire. There is a 2 dice penalty to all dice rolls for social dealings with the city's Kindred. A character with this Flaw may not take the Merit of *Reputation*.

Mortal Society

These Merits and Flaws deal with the influence, power and status of a character within mortal society. Some of them corrospond very closely with some of the background traits (such as resources, contracts, and influence), while others simply elaborate and expand upon them. In most cases you can choose what way you want to go to get the same result as a background, the Backgrounds give you more creative freedom, while the Merits provide you with exact details of what you possess. However, you cannot purchase a Merit from this section that has value greater than what you feel is the most closely related Background trait (e.g. you must have Resources of at least two in order to have a mansion, though if your Resources are only two then your mansion may not be in extremely good condition).

Mansion: (2pt Merit)

You own a large mansion, a home with 25 or more rooms, as well as the surrounding estate. The servants, if you have any, are provided for if you choose this Merit, though they cannot be used as herd or retainers unless you purchase the appropriate background. It is assumed that it has the most current electronic security available, as well as a fence around the perimeter. While the mansion can be in as poor or as good shape as you would like, the more lived in it looks the more attention it will garner. A ghost house won't attract IRS audits.

Nightclub: (2pt Merit)

You own a moderate-sized nightclub, perhaps one of the hottest nightspots in the city. This club brings in enough money to support you only in moderate luxury ($1000 a month, but it can grow), but more important than the money is the prestige. You may use the nightclub as your haven, or you may simply hang out there. The name of the nightclub, its style, design, and its regular patrons are all up to you. Variations on this theme could include: a restaurant, theater, comedy house, sports arena, or retail store.

Media Ties: (2pt Merit)

You have both influence over and contacts with the local Media. You can suppress and create news stories (though not always with 100% efficiency; journalist are a unruly bunch) and you have access to all the files and much of the street lore and rumor known by the staffs of newspapers and TV stations.

Police Ties: (3pt Merit)

You have both influence over and contacts with the local police department. You can, with a single phone call, cause an APB to be issued. However, the more often you use your ties with the Police department the weaker they become, and the more attention you raise toward yourself. Your grip is not solid (that is something that can be achieved only through game play), and it can let you down at times.

Political Ties: (3pt Merit)

You have both influence over and contacts with the politicians and bureaucrats of the city. In times of need you can shut off the power and water to a certain building (or even neighborhood), and can unleash many different means of harassment against your enemies. The more you use (and misuse) your political ties, the weaker they become. Total control can only be achieved through game play.

Underworld Ties: (3pt Merit)

You have both influence over and contacts with the local Mafia and organized street gangs. This provides you with limited access to large numbers of "soldiers," as well as extensive links to the underworld of crime. The more often you use your ties with the criminal element, the weaker they grow.

Corporate Ties: (3pt Merit)

You have both influence over and contacts with the local corporate community. You understand the dynamics of money in the city and have links with all the major players. In times of need you can cause all sorts of financial mayhem,

and could raise considerable amounts of money (loans, of course) in a very short period of time.

Judicial Ties: (2pt Merit)

You have both influence over and contacts with the Justice system. You know most of the judges as well as the prosecutor's department, and can affect the progress of various cases and trials with limited difficulty. Though it is highly difficult to actually intervene in a case, you can influence it in one direction or another. These ties can also make it easy to acquire search warrants.

Church Ties (3pt Merit)

You have influence and contracts with some local churches, and thus have the means to create protest rallies and raise money. The more you use your ties, of course, the weaker they grow.

Corporation CEO: (5pt Merit)

You have a particular influence and sway over a major corporation, and its associate companies, just as if you were its Chief Executive Officer. Indeed, you may have even

owned this company when you were mortal, and now continue to retain your control. Through this corporation you will know much of what is going on in the corporate community, and have the means of waging economic warfare. This Merit provides you with some amount of informal contacts, resources and herd, the exact extent of which is determined by the Storyteller.

Anachronism: (2pt Flaw)

You have been around as a Vampire for some time, and are not able (or willing) to keep up with the changing times. An Intelligence roll is needed whenever you have to deal with something from a later period than your own breathing days. If the roll is failed, use the net failures as a negative modifier to your attempts. *Example: Osric, a fifth-century Goth by birth, has this Flaw and is attempting to deal with a computer. The Intelligence roll results in two net failures. Osric now has a -2 modifier when determining the outcome of his attempt to make the infernal machine co-operate.*

Ward: (3pt Flaw)

You are devoted to the protection of a mortal who you may describe, though the Storyteller will actually create her. This character may be a friend or relative from breathing days, a descendant, or simply a mortal whom you admire and consider important. Wards have a way of getting caught up in the action of stories, and of course, are frequently irresistible to a character's enemies.

Hunted: (4pt Flaw)

You are devoutly pursued by a fanatical Witch-hunter. All who you associate with may begin to be hunted by the same individual as well. Though this Hunter seeks the destruction of all Kindred, there is something about you which drives the passion of this killer.

Physical

These Merits and Flaws deal with your health and physical composition.

Double-jointed: (1pt Merit)

You are unusually supple. Reduce the difficulty of any Dexterity roll involving bodily flexibility by two. Squeezing through a space which is normally too small is an example of a use for this Merit.

"Baby Face" (2pt Merit)

You look more human than other Vampires, enabling you to fit in the human world much more easily. Your skin is pink, you never really stopped breathing (even though you don't need to), and even sneezing comes naturally. You can even make your heart beat, as long as you have at least one blood point. This Merit can not be taken by Nosferatu.

Misplaced Heart (2pt Merit)

Your heart has actually moved within your body, no more than 2 feet from its original position near the middle of the chest. Those who stake you will find it very difficult to find the right location (which should be your most tightly held secret).

Efficient Digestion: (3pt Merit)

You are able to draw more than the usual amount of nourishment from blood. Each 2 Blood Points ingested increase your Blood Pool by 3 (round down so leftover 'halves' are ignored — for instance, taking 4 Blood Points raises the Blood Pool by 6, and so does taking 5 Blood Points).

Huge Size: (4pt Merit)

You are abnormally large in size, possibly over seven feet tall, and 400 pounds in weight. You therefore have one additional body level, and are thus able to suffer more harm before you are incapacitated. Treat this extra level as an extra hurt level, with no penalties to rolls.

Allergic (1-3pt Flaw)

You are allergic to some substance, in a manner not unlike mortal allergies. However, you do not get hives or sneeze but are actually incapacitated by your reaction. If the substance was in the blood you have drank, the reaction will be very strong, though touch alone is enough to disturb you. If it was in the blood, you will have 5 less dice on all your rolls for ten minutes — if you just touched it, it is only 2 dice. Choose from the list for which substance you are allergic too.

- Plastic: 1pt   • Illegal Drugs: 2pt   • Alcohol: 2pt
- Metal: 3pt

Short: (1pt Flaw)

You are well below average height, and will have trouble seeing over high objects and moving quickly. You suffer a -2 penalty to all pursuit rolls, and you and the Storyteller should make sure your height is taken into account in all other situations. In some circumstances this will give you a concealment bonus.

Disfigured: (2pt Flaw)

A hideous disfigurement makes you ugly and easy to notice as well as remember. You therefore have a zero appearance, much as those from the Nosferatu clan. This cannot be taken by Nosferatu characters.

Monstrous (2pt Flaw)

There is something wholly monstrous about you, something which makes you even more hidious than a Nosferatu. The change wrought in you by your Sire's blood warped more than just your insides, it warped your outside as well. You scarcely look human, in what manner you differ is up to you. Perhaps you have grown scales or warts all over your body, or perhaps the scream you issued when you died has been permanent frozen upon your face. Not only is your appearance a zero, much as it is with the Nosferatu, but you tend to make even other Kindred uneasy.

Selective Digestion: (2pt Flaw)

You can digest only certain types of blood. You can choose whether you can drink only cold blood (the blood of a dead person), blood with the taste of fear (found in blood only in moments of terror), or blood with the taste of joy, or perhaps only certain types (A, O, etc.) of blood. This Flaw may not be taken by Ventrue characters, since they already have something like it through their Clan weakness.

Permanent Wound: (3pt Flaw)

You suffered injuries at the Change which the Sire did nothing to repair. You start each night Wounded -3. This must be healed up each evening, upon wakening, or it will remain with you throughout the night. Each evening, after sleep, it will always return, even if healed the night before.

Thin Blooded: (3pt Flaw)

You have weak blood, and are unable to use it for anything but to sustain yourself from day to day and to heal your wounds. Blood cannot be used to add to your Physical Attributes, to power blood disciplines, nor does it have the power to create a blood bond. Moreover, you will not always be able to create a Vampire, half the time the Embrace will simply not work.

Child: (3pt Flaw)

You were a small child at the time of the Change. Although time and experience may change your outlook, you are stuck with a child's body. You have the *Short* Flaw (see above), and you find it difficult to be taken seriously by others (-2 penalty to all relevant rolls). Because you have never experience any sort of transformation change before (never having undergone the experience of puberty) you are ill-suited to withstanding the demands of the hunger (+1 to the difficulties of all such rolls). Additionally, certain clubs may not admit you, because you are "under-age."

Lame: (3pt Flaw)

Your legs are injured or otherwise prevented from working effectively. There is a -2 penalty to all dice rolls where movement is important. At higher levels, a character may need assistance, such as a pair of crutches, leg-irons or a wheelchair. A character may not take this Flaw along with the Merit of being Double-jointed.

Deformity: (3pt Flaw)

You have some kind of deformity — a misshapen limb, a hunchback or whatever — which affects the reactions of others and may inconvenience you physically at times. The difficulty on all dice rolls where physical appearance is important is raised by 2. It will also raise the difficulty of some Dexterity rolls by 2, depending on the type of deformity you possess.

One Arm: (3pt Flaw)

You have only one arm — choose which one, or determine randomly at character generation. Long before the Embrace you had lost it (otherwise you could simply regenerate it). It is assumed that practice will have accustomed you to using your one remaining hand, so there is no off-hand penalty. However, there is a 2 die penalty to any dice roll where two hands would normally be needed to perform a task. A character may not take this Flaw along with the Merit of being Ambidextrous.

Mute: (4pt Flaw)

Your vocal apparatus is incapable of functioning, and you cannot speak at all. Some other means of communication must be found, the most common being simply writing things down.

Paraplegic: (6pt Flaw)

You can hardly move without assistance, such as a pair of crutches, leg-irons or a wheelchair. Even then it can be painfull and cumbersome to do so. The Storyteller and you should take care to roleplay this Flaw correctly, no matter how difficult it makes things. A character may not take this Flaw along with the Merit of Double-jointed .

Chapter Three: The Expanded Character

"May I bring you up to date?
We are living in the 20th century, not the 18th.
May I bring you up to date sir?
We are not alive at all."
Wolfgang Press, "Louis XVI"

This chapter concerns itself with new Traits for your character, as well as expanded descriptions of Traits already described in the original rules. These are new Abilities, Archetypes, Disciplines and even Thaumaturgical rituals which you can now choose for your character. Nothing should be used out of this chapter without the permission of the Storyteller; some of these new traits may be inappropriate for some Chronicles.

SECONDARY ABILITIES

Following are a number of new abilities which you can use in any Storyteller game. They describe some of the limitless abilities a character can take to help describe who and what the character really is. In some cases, however, some of these abilities may seem less significant and useful that many of the more general abilities described in **Vampire** itself. In fact, some of them are subcategories of the other more general abilities. For instance, Sense Deception does much the same thing as Empathy, only more directly. This is why these traits are known as secondary abilities.

The Storyteller can deal with this in two ways. First of all, the difficulties can be made lower for the more specialized ability, making it more selective but more powerful. Alternately, the Storyteller can decide to let players purchase these secondary abilities for a lower cost. For instance, for every one point you spend on a secondary ability in Step Three of the character creation process (**Vampire**, p. 42), you gain two dots. They would only cost one freebie point to raise by one dot in Step Five. And finally, they would only cost the current rating in experience points to raise them one level after the Chronicle has begun.

It is not necessary for the Storyteller to take either course, but the option is certainly there and would be appropriate in many Chronicles. What we do in our own games is to take it on a case-by-case basis. The Storyteller may allow a certainly ability to be raised more cheaply than the others for reasons often tied to the character concerned instead of the ability. In other cases she might allow for lower difficulties. The Storyteller is always the final arbitrator.

Remember, this is your game, these are your rules, and you should to do with them as you see fit. What you find herein is only advice, nothing more, nothing less.

Talents

Artistic Expression:
You have the talent to produce works of art in various media. Even without a day's instruction, you are able to produce saleable works of two or three-dimensional art, and understand something of the technical aspects of paintings and sketches. You are also able to capture a reasonably accurate likeness of a place or person by sketching.

- • **Novice:** your work is simple, seen as charmingly naive by some and as amateurish by others.
- •• **Practiced:** your work could win prizes at local art-society shows.
- ••• **Competent:** you could get a showing in a minor gallery.
- •••• **Expert:** your work is widely admired, and galleries contact you about mounting exhibitions. You are invited to teach at local art colleges.
- ••••• **Master:** You are acknowledged as a driving force in contemporary art. Your work commands enormous prices, and is found in art museums as well as commercial galleries and private collections.

Possessed by: Artists, Commercial Illustrators, Cartoonists, Police Artists, Forgers, Woodworkers, Theatre and Movie Set-Builders, Special Effects Technicians, Model Makers.

Specialities: Oils, Watercolors, Mixed Media, Charcoal, Sketching, Caricature, Lighting Artist, Impressionist, Photo-Realism, Abstract, Miniatures, Stone, Resin, Wood, Metals, Classical, Kinetic, Models, Decoration.

Diplomacy:
You have the ability to deal with people of all types and creeds. Even when handling touchy subjects, you are able to get results without ruffling too many feathers. You are skilled at delicate negotiations and mediating disputes — getting along without others without overt manipulation or letting your own aims fall to the wayside. It is a knowledge of the formal rules of give and take, as well as the official cultural rules of conduct and politeness.

- • **Novice:** You can iron out schoolyard disputes.
- •• **Practiced:** Friends ask you to deal with things for them.
- ••• **Competent:** You could shine in management or personnel.
- •••• **Expert:** You could be a professional union negotiator or ombudsman.
- ••••• **Master:** You can do much to defuse nearly any situation from an industrial dispute to a religious war.

Possessed by: Schoolteachers, Union Negotiators, Politicians, Tycoons, Diplomats, Personnel Officers, Counsellors.

Specialities: Mediation, Negotiation, Etiquette, International Relations, Industry, Personal Relationships, Tact.

Intrigue:
You know the finer points of plotting and deal-making in the halls of power — including the subtle use of power in sometimes threatening but always non-confrontational ways to achieve your own ends. This can also be the ability to pick up important facts about others involved in the Elysium crowd by separating truth from the endless amounts of false and useless gossip.

- • **Novice:** Neonate
- •• **Practiced:** Ancilla
- ••• **Competent:** Elder
- •••• **Expert:** Prince
- ••••• **Master:** Primogen

Possessed by: Elders and Elder wanna-be's

Specialities: gossiping, feign ignorance, threats, plotting, rumor-mongering, alliances, betrayals.

Mimicry

Mimicry: You have a very versatile voice, and can imitate accents, people and sometimes other sounds. As well as being able to use this talent to entertain, you can use it to deceive. With enough talent, almost any sort of sound can be created — the larynx is an amazingly flexible organ.

- • **Novice:** You can manage a few accents passably, and do impressions of a couple of well-known personalities.
- •• **Practiced:** You can do a range of accents well enough to fool anyone but a native speaker, and imitate a range of celebrities and others.
- ••• **Competent:** You could do this on stage. As well as a wide range of accents and celebrity impressions, you can pick up someone's vocal mannerisms by studying them for a couple of hours, and imitate them well enough to fool someone who doesn't know them well. You can do basic birdcalls and some other sounds.
- •••• **Expert:** You can imitate a specific person well enough to fool someone on the phone, and pass as a native speaker in an accent which is close to your own. You can produce a range of animal and technological noises.
- ••••• **Master:** There is almost no accent, person or noise which you can't imitate.

Possessed by: Entertainers, Con Artists, Pranksters, Bird Callers.

Specialities: Accents, Celebrities, Birds and Animals, Mechanical Sounds, Vocal Impersonation.

Poetic Expression

Poetic Expression: You are able to put together words in ways which can evoke thoughts, emotions and reactions in those who read them. You can compose pleasing poetry in one or more styles, create short and long fiction, write essays, reviews and editorials, and invent advertising jingles. It is rare for one person to be skilled at more than one specialty at one time, so choose carefully.

- • **Novice:** You can write a short poem, and extemporize a limerick or couplet when the Muse is with you. A short story is not out of your reach.
- •• **Practiced:** You could publish your poetry or fiction in a local journal, or write basic hit-parade lyrics. You can extemporize simple *abab* and *aabb* type quatrains.
- ••• **Competent:** You could get your novel or anthologies of your work published and make a profit. You can extemporize more complex verse forms, and even make blank verse sound like poetry.
- •••• **Expert:** You are asked to do readings of your work for local societies nationwide, and aficionados snap up your works as soon as they are published. You can write lyrics which people will be quoting in ten years' time, and extemporize iambic pentameters without thinking about it.
- ••••• **Master:** Your work is already being taught in English classes, and you are recognized as one of the foremost writers of your day. Your lyrics are timeless, and you can extemporize in any form and any style.

Possessed by: Poets, Lyricists, Novelists, Journalists, Advertising Execs, Entertainers, English Teachers, Rappers.

Specialities: Limericks, Short Fiction, Novel, Scripts, Classical Forms, Extemporizing, Lyric-Writing, Jingles, Blank Verse, Deathless Art.

Search

Search: You are know how to best go about looking for someone or something in a small area, where you can concentrate your perceptions. This can be anything from searching for a lost ring in your bedroom to trying to uncover the assassin who is hiding in the garden.

- • **Novice:** Good at finding lost items
- •• **Practiced:** Tell-tale signs (e.g. broken plants) are apparent to you
- ••• **Competent:** You know where to look
- •••• **Expert:** Nothing escapes your glance
- ••••• **Master:** Spot the Purloined Letter in two seconds flat

Possessed by: Detectives, Maids, Policemen, Prison Guards.

Specialities: Sounds, Woodwork, Small Objects, People, Concealed Doors.

Seduction

Seduction: You know how lure, attract and command the attention of others in a sexual manner. By the way you hold yourself, how you look at someone and even by the tone of your voice, you are able to arouse and excite those upon whom you practice your wiles. Once you have fully seduced them, they will be willing to do nearly anything for you.

- • **Novice:** Teenager
- •• **Practiced:** The "older woman"
- ••• **Competent:** Heart throb
- •••• **Expert:** Movie Star
- ••••• **Master:** Vampire

Possessed by: Thespians, Escorts, Good-for-nothing men, Strippers

Specialities: Witty Conversation, Opening Line, Innuendo, Alluring look

Sense Deception: Over the years, you have
developed the ability to know instinctively when people
are not telling you the truth or not telling you the whole
truth. There is a way they look, a tone of voice, a
movement of the eyes — something you can't analyze,
but it's always there and your instincts rarely let you
down.

- • **Novice:** Sometimes you can tell, but you
  still get suckered — though it's more rarely
  than the average person.
- •• **Practiced:** It takes a silver tongue to pull the
  wool over your eyes.
- ••• **Competent:** Anyone who can slip one past
  you is a highly skilled con artist.
- •••• **Expert:** You could make a living screening
  people for security.
- ••••• **Master:** People whisper behind your back,
  and many are nervous talking to you. Your
  ability is almost supernatural.

Possessed by: Bodyguards, Reporters, Interrogators,
Security Personnel, Detectives, Mothers.

Specialities: Interviewer, Investigator, Courtroom,
Technical (Lie detectors).

Scan: You are practiced at noticing small details
and changes in the environment when you purposely
look or listen to what is going on around you. This

ability can only be used when you specifically say you
are attempting to notice if anything is amiss — if you
aren't concentrating, this ability will do you no good. If
you succeed in your roll you regain the Willpower
immediately.

- • **Novice:** If anyone notices police sirens, it's
  you
- •• **Practiced:** Police could use your detective
  abilities
- ••• **Competent:** The slightest motion draws
  your attention
- •••• **Expert:** Nothing escapes your glance
- ••••• **Master:** You can count the grains of salt on
  a pretzel — by taste

Possessed by: Detectives, GIs, FBI agents, Bodyguards, Nightwatchmen.

Specialities: Keeping Watch, Quick Scan, Listening, Smelling, Assassins.

Scrounging: You have a knack for finding
almost anything, under almost any circumstances. The
masters of your craft could find a hot spring at the North
Pole if they had to, or a mainframe computer in the heart
of the Amazon jungle. In the city, you know where to
find almost any kind of item or service — no questions
asked. It is amazing what you can find in dumpsters.

- • **Novice:** You can find basic equipment and services such as drugs, illegal weapons and hired thugs.
- •• **Practiced:** You can get hold of a vehicle, a forged passport or a skilled wiretapper.
- ••• **Competent:** You can find an aircraft and pilot or a hitman at an hour's notice.
- •••• **Expert:** You can find state-of-the-art military hardware, any vehicle you desire, and services better imagined than described.
- ••••• **Master:** You could probably find a rent-controlled apartment overlooking Central Park for $100 a month.

Possessed by: Criminals, Intelligence Operatives, Entrepreneurs.

Specialities: Illegal Goods, Vehicles, Services, Art, Technical Equipment.

Singing
: You have been blessed with a good singing voice and a natural feel for pitch and rhythm. Though you probably have a favored style of singing, you can probably use a variety of techniques. Singing is an extremely lucrative and popular talent in the modern age. Though most singers are amateurs, others make enormous amounts of money.

- • **Novice:** You stand out when the family gather around the piano.
- •• **Practiced:** You could get lead roles with local amateur societies, or become lead singer with a garage band.
- ••• **Competent:** You could get a chorus part on the professional stage, or get a recording contract.
- •••• **Expert:** You could get a lead on Broadway, or a record in the charts, any time you want.
- ••••• **Master:** They'll be playing your CDs twenty years from now.

Possessed by: Church Choristers, Rock & Rollers, Pop Stars, Opera Singers, Drunks.

Specialities: Opera, Easy Listening, Rock, Church, Musicals.

Instruction
: You have a talent for passing on information and skills to others. You might actually have worked as a teacher, or you might simply be the affable co-worker who shows newcomers the ropes. Either way, you can explain things and demonstrate techniques in such a way that anyone who listens to you can learn very easily. You can teach any of your Skills or Knowledges to another character, but you can never raise a student's score above your own: for example, if you have three dots in Computer, you cannot teach someone to raise them to four dots in that Knowledge. The time necessary to raise a skill is usually about one month per experience point, during which time the character may have to spend a number of Willpower points to keep at it. Interruptions can make this process extremely difficult (requiring a roll by both the teacher and the student, with a certain number of total successes needed).

- • **Novice:** You can take simple concepts (e.g., basic arithmetic) and present them in an interesting and digestible way. You can teach a Skill or Knowledge at the normal experience point cost.
- •• **Practiced:** You can teach moderately complex things (e.g. algebra) and make them straightforward and interesting. You can teach a Skill or Knowledge at the normal experience point cost.
- ••• **Competent:** You can teach any subject of which you have Knowledge, up to high-school level. You can make differential calculus sound like the simplest thing in the world. You can teach a Skill or Knowledge at the normal experience point cost.
- •••• **Expert:** Learning from you is scarcely any effort. You could teach irrational-number theory or Sumerian cuneiform to almost anyone. You can teach a Skill or Knowledge at three-quarters of the normal experience point cost (rounding fractions up).
- ••••• **Master:** You are an inspiring teacher, and leave a touch of greatness on anyone who studies with you. You can teach a Skill or Knowledge at half the normal experience point cost (rounding fractions up).

Possessed by: Teachers, Professors, Driving Instructors, Training Managers, People from All Walks of Life.

Specialities: Kindergarten, Grade School, High School, University, Skills, Knowledges.

Ventriloquism
: You have the ability to throw your voice, making it appear to come from somewhere else. As well as entertainment, this talent can be used for deception.

- • **Novice:** You could do a ventriloquist act at a children's party.
- •• **Practiced:** You could get a spot with a local amateur vaudeville club. You can make it look like someone standing next to you spoke.
- ••• **Competent:** You could almost make a living from your talent, with occasional TV variety shows breaking up the round of cheap clubs and theatres. You can make it look like someone (or something) within five yards of you spoke.
- •••• **Expert:** You could take your act to Vegas, and headline TV specials of your own. You

can make your voice appear to come from any spot within 30 feet of you.

••••• **Master:** Young hopefuls bombard you with questions, and *Variety* calls you the savior of a lost vaudeville art. You can make your voice appear to come from anywhere within earshot.

Possessed by: Entertainers, Con Artists, some Mediums.

Specialities: Distance, Clarity, Dummy, Inanimate Object (e.g. radio).

Skills

Acrobatics: You are a trained tumbler and

acrobat, able to perform feats of agility which are far beyond the abilities of an untrained character. For each dot in this Skill, a character can ignore one level of falling damage (see **Vampire**, p. 120) — so a character with two dots in Acrobatics can fall up to 10 feet without injury, and takes only one Health Level of damage from a 15-foot fall. This skill may be paired with Dexterity to roll for leaps and other acrobatic feats.

- • **Novice:** Grade-school gym class.
- •• **Practiced:** High school jock.
- ••• **Competent:** College team.
- •••• **Expert:** State champion.
- ••••• **Master:** Olympic gold medallist.

Possessed by: Professional Athlete, Jock, Martial Artist, Dancer

Specialities: Sport, Martial Arts, Dance, Enhanced Jumping/Falling

Animal Training: You are able to train an

animal of a certain species to obey commands and possibly perform tricks or other feats. Each species is a different specialty.

- • **Novice:** Heel, Fetch, Sit, Stay.
- •• **Practiced:** Local show standard.
- ••• **Competent:** Champion sheepdog standard.
- •••• **Expert:** Elite police dog standard.
- ••••• **Master:** Circus/Stunt standard.

Possessed by: Dog Handlers, Movie Animal Wranglers, Circus Animal Trainers.

Specialities: Dog, Horse, Elephant, Seal.

Archery: You know how to fire the bow, and may

be able to do so with great proficiency. Modern bows can be very complicated gadgets (especially crossbows), and this skill is essential if you hope to be able to use them correctly. Bows are able to fire wooden-shaft quarrels (without metal tips...).

- • **Novice:** High School Gym Practice
- •• **Practiced:** Forest Bow Hunter
- ••• **Competent:** Medieval Ranger

••••   Expert: Will hit a bull's-eye, usually.

••••••   Master: Robin Hood

Possessed by: Hunters, Hobby Enthusiasts, Competitors.

Specialities: Arched Flight, Forests, Target, Hunting, Moving Targets.

Artillery

Artillery: You have the ability to operate and shoot artillery of all varieties —anything from a mortar to a howitzer. Additionally, your knowledge of the weapons includes an ability to repair them

- **•   Novice:** young recruit
- **••   Practiced:** operator
- **•••   Competent:** Forward Observer
- **••••   Expert:** Gun Captain.
- **••••••   Master:** Can fire the thing by yourself if need be.

Possessed by: Weapons Designers, Armed Forces Personnel, Mercenaries.

Specialities: Aim, Forward Observation, Line of sight, Out of sight, Radar, Night fighting, Desert, Jungle, Friend from Foe.

Blacksmith

Blacksmith: You are skilled in the working of iron, and can make objects of iron and steel.

- **•   Novice:** You can make a horseshoe from a cut-iron bar.
- **••   Practiced:** You can make wrought-iron and mild-steel objects.
- **•••   Competent:** You can make different grades of steel and cast iron to industrial standards.
- **••••   Expert:** You can pattern-weld different grades of iron and steel to make a complex object such as a sword blade.
- **••••••   Master:** You can make a blade equal to any Japanese sword, or any other iron or steel object you please.

Possessed by: Artisans, Blacksmiths, Artists, Swordsmiths, Hobbyists.

Specialities: Wrought Iron, Cast Iron, Toolmaking, Blademaking, Art, Spot-welding, Pattern-welding.

Boat Handling

Boat Handling: You know your way around a boat, and can operate effectively in any crew position.

- **•   Novice:** Weekend sailor.
- **••   Practiced:** Serious enthusiast.
- **•••   Competent:** Competitor or semi-skilled professional.
- **••••   Expert:** Professional or Olympic standard.
- **••••••   Master:** Instructor or Olympic gold medallist.

Possessed by: Fishermen, Sportspeople, Hobbyists, Outdoors Enthusiasts.

Specialities: Sail, Power, Oared, Paddle, Inflatable.

Brewing/Distilling

Brewing/Distilling: You are skilled in the manufacture of alcohol and alcoholic beverages. You are familiar with the equipment used in brewing and distilling, and can maintain, operate and repair such equipment.

- **•   Novice:** Brew-kit user.
- **••   Practiced:** Home winemaker.
- **•••   Competent:** Moonshiner.
- **••••   Expert:** Commercial winemaker.
- **••••••   Master:** Chateau of Repute.

Possessed by: Hobbyists, Vintners, Moonshiners.

Specialities: Wine, Beer, Spirits, Industrial Alcohol.

Bribery

Bribery: You know how and where to grease palms in order to get the results you need. Coupled with Streetwise or Politics, this ability could get you a very easy life. However, you still need to decide who you are going to approach and who you are going to leave alone — remember, not everyone looks a blind eye.

- **•   Novice:** Get a bouncer to overlook the dress code.
- **••   Practiced:** Get the Building inspector off your back.
- **•••   Competent:** A policeman won't write you tickets.
- **••••   Expert:** The inspector from the EPA leaves you alone.
- **••••••   Master:** State politicians and local CEOs scratch your back.

Possessed by: Politicians, Lobbyists, Businesspeople, Criminals.

Specialities: Police, Bureaucrats, inspectors, Under-the-table, open "gifts"

Camouflage

Camouflage: You can change your appearance by a mixture of clothing, makeup and movement, so that you are difficult to spot in a variety of different surroundings. This is not the ability to look like someone else, but simply to hide. Your score can be added to many stealth rolls if you have had time to camouflage yourself or others.

- **•   Novice:** Boy Scout
- **••   Practiced:** Infantry Trooper
- **•••   Competent:** Marine
- **••••   Expert:** Special Forces
- **••••••   Master:** Ninja

Possessed by: Hunters, Military, Spies, Assassins, Poachers.

Specialities: Woods, Mountains, Urban, Open Country, Arctic.

Carousing

Carousing: This is the ability to have a good time at a party or other social occasion, and to make sure others around you also have a good time. Normally, it involves a mixture of eating, drinking and good cheer,

but for Vampires things are a little different. Carousing also includes the ability to *appear* to eat and drink normally, without actually doing so. Using this skill, one of the Kindred can attend, say, an opening-night cast party without arousing any suspicion — on a successful roll of Manipulation + Carousing, no one will notice that the character neither eats nor drinks. The difficulty of the roll depends on the social event: 3 or less for a houseparty with a buffet, 7 or more for a sit-down dinner. This skill can also be used to determine how entertaining and popular the character is at a party or event.

- **Novice:** You can plead a small appetite or recent illness.
- **Practiced:** Perhaps you're watching your diet.
- **Competent:** A charming dinner-companion.
- **Expert:** You obviously enjoyed the food.
- **Master:** You even called for seconds.

Possessed by: Actors, Dilettantes, College Students, Vampires.

Specialities: Sexual Innuendo, Lewd Jokes, Drinking, Exaggeration, Anecdotes.

Carpentry
: You are a competent woodworker, able to make a variety of objects from wood.

- **Novice:** Amateur handyman.
- **Practiced:** Professional handyman.

- **Competent:** Professional carpenter.
- **Expert:** Joiner and cabinet maker or night school teacher.
- **Master:** You have your own TV show; rich clients seek you out.

Possessed by: Carpenter, Furniture Maker, Handyman, Builder.

Specialities: Construction, Furniture, Quality Items.

Climbing
: You can climb mountains and/or walls, and seldom have any fear of falling. The technical skills of chimneying, spike setting and rapelling are all well known to you — though depending on your skill you may be good or indifferent at them. Remember, mountain climbing at night is far more difficult than a daylight climb unless you can see in the dark.

- **Novice:** Easy mountains or walls with handholds.
- **Practiced:** You go on mountaineering vacations. You can climb heavily-weathered stone or brick walls.
- **Competent:** You work in an outdoor pursuits center as a mountaineering instructor. You can climb moderately rough stone or brick walls.
- **Expert:** You've done at least a couple of famous peaks. You can free-climb a fairly smooth stone or brick wall.
- **Master:** Everest and K2 are mild hikes. You could free-climb the World Trade Center.

Possessed by: Mountaineers, Burglars, Enthusiasts.

Specialities: Cliff, Hiking, Ice, Buildings, Free Climbing, Rapelling.

Cooking
: You know how to prepare a variety of meals, and present them in an appealing manner. Although Vampires no longer eat, this can be a very useful social skill, especially if you like to lure potential Vessels to your Haven with the promise of a candlelit *tête-à-tête*...

- **Novice:** You give a reasonable dinner party.
- **Practiced:** You give an excellent dinner party.
- **Competent:** You could make a business of this.
- **Expert:** You could publish recipe books.
- **Master:** You could have your own TV show, or become chef in the finest restaurants.

Possessed by: Housewives, Chefs, Gourmets.

Specialities: French, Italian, Chinese, Thai, Cajan, Bread, Desserts, Pastries, Cordon Bleu.

Dancing
: You are a proficient dancer, socially and/or for the entertainment of others. You are familiar

with all the varieties of dance, but specialize in one particular style.

- • **Novice:** You can manage a waltz at a wedding.
- •• **Practiced:** You draw envious glances at weddings. You could perform on the local amateur stage.
- ••• **Competent:** You are the talk of the ball. You could perform on the local professional stage.
- •••• **Expert:** People ask you to teach them. You could perform on TV.
- ••••• **Master:** Nijinsky, Fonteyn, Nureyev, Barishnikov, Astaire, Rogers, Kelley — and you.

Possessed by: Socialites, Pop Stars, Music Video dancers, Ballet Dancers, Enthusiasts, Cruise Directors.

Specialities: Waltz, Polka, Two-step, Foxtrot, Jive, Disco, Latin, Show, Ballet.

Debate
: You are skilled at reasoned debate, and can put forward a convincing case through reason and logic. Combined with Diplomacy, this could make you a first-class negotiator.

- • **Novice:** Student.
- •• **Practiced:** Debate Team Member.
- ••• **Competent:** Union Negotiator.
- •••• **Expert:** Politician.
- ••••• **Master:** You could make Fundamentalists understand evolution.

Possessed by: Diplomats, Negotiators, Academics, Politicians, Intellectuals.

Specialities: Logic, Politics, Informal, Social Discourse, Morals, Low Brow, Low Blow.

Demolitions
: You have a knowledge of explosives and demolitions that allows you to set off and create (at higher levels) all types of bombs. You know how to handle nearly anything, whether it be dynamite, plastic explosive, nitroglycerin, black powder, blasting cord, nitrocellulose, or Napalm. Additionally, you know the techniques for disarming explosives, something that could come in very handy.

- • **Novice:** Guy Fawkes
- •• **Practiced:** Leroy Moody
- ••• **Competent:** Underground Chemist
- •••• **Expert:** Blows up buildings for a living.
- ••••• **Master:** Bye-bye World Trade Center.

Possessed by: Terrorists, Police Bomb Squads, Armed Forces Personnel.

Specialities: Dynamite, Plastic Explosive, Car Bombs, Disarmament, Detection.

Disguise
: You can hide your appearance — and even make yourself look like another specific person — by the use of clothes and makeup.

- • **Novice:** Good enough to fool someone who knows neither you nor the person you're impersonating.
- •• **Practiced:** Good enough to fool some of the people some of the time.
- ••• **Competent:** Good enough to fool some of the people most of the time.
- •••• **Expert:** Good enough to fool most of the people most of the time.
- ••••• **Master:** Good enough to fool nearest and dearest most of the time.

Possessed by: Actors, Spies, Undercover Cops, Criminals, Con Artists.

Specialities: Specific Person, Type of Person, Conceal Own Identity.

Escapology
: You are skilled in various techniques which enable you to escape from bonds and restraints. This skill has been used in entertainment, but can also be very useful in real life.

- • **Novice:** Children's party entertainer. Can escape from loose or poorly-tied bonds.
- •• **Practiced:** Amateur entertainer. Can escape from fairly well-tied bonds.
- ••• **Competent:** Professional entertainer. Can escape from handcuffs and chains.
- •••• **Expert:** Star. Can escape from a straitjacket.
- ••••• **Master:** Legend. Can escape from just about anything while tied in a sack underwater with a ticking time-bomb.

Possessed by: Entertainers, Spies, Special Forces, Amateurs, Pulp Detectives.

Specialities: Magic Tricks, Ropes, Boxes, Locks, Underwater, Handcuffs, Showmanship.

Falconry
: Once the sport of nobles, falconry is now a hobby practised only by a few enthusiasts. Combining this Skill with a Discipline like Animalism makes it possible to achieve truly impressive results.

- • **Novice:** The bird comes back — sometimes.
- •• **Practiced:** You can do small displays.
- ••• **Competent:** You work most of the local medieval fairs and outdoor exhibitions. You can catch enough to live on.
- •••• **Expert:** In a different time, you would have been a noble admired for your skill, or you could have worked for a noble.
- ••••• **Master:** In a different time, you would have been with the King's entourage.

Possessed by: Professional Falconers, Very Old Vampires, Enthusiastic Amateurs.

Specialities: Display, Hunting, History, Exotic Birds (e.g. Harpy Eagle)

Fast-Draw: This skill allows you to make a

weapon ready almost instantly. By rolling Dexterity + Fast-Draw (and getting three successes) a character can draw a weapon and have it ready for use just as if it had been ready in the character's hand all along. The difficulty depends on how securely stowed the weapon was — a gun hidden in a character's underwear is harder to reach than one in a belt-holster. This skill can be used with any weapon. When appropriate, the Fast-Draw score can be added to your Initiative roll.

- • **Novice:** You have good reflexes.
- •• **Practiced:** You're good, but not great.
- ••• **Competent:** You would have lasted a little while in the Old West. You could work Wild West shows.
- •••• **Expert:** Pretty fast. You could headline your own act.
- ••••• **Master:** Greased lightning. You might have been able to take Billy the Kid.

Possessed by: Gunfighters, Martial Artists, Cops, Special Forces, Vigilantes.

Specialities: Pistol, Knife, Sword, Arrow, Rifle/Shotgun, Sap.

Fast-Talk: This Skill allows you to convince

someone of something using a sincere expression and an avalanche of words, rather than reasoned debate and logic. It's a surprisingly effective technique, provided that the mark has no time to think and does not have a Wits score of 4 or more. The Storyteller should judge carefully whether this Skill is appropriate in a given situation, or whether it would be better to use some other Ability.

- • **Novice:** Vacuum-cleaner salesman.
- •• **Practiced:** Used-car salesman.
- ••• **Competent:** Professional con artist.
- •••• **Expert:** Teflon-coated politician.
- ••••• **Master:** You could sell sand to the Saudis.

Possessed by: Salesmen, Con Artists, Politicians, Televangelists.

Specialities: Sell, Confuse, Get Off Hook, Convince.

First Aid: This Skill allows a character to give

basic medical attention to another. It is not as comprehensive an ability as medicine, but does allow for a basic grasp of all the practices of first aid, and at higher levels, paramedics. Note that Vampires cannot benefit from First Aid for their wounds.

- • **Novice:** Mother of Small Children.
- •• **Practiced:** Boy Scout.
- ••• **Competent:** Office Safety Rep.
- •••• **Expert:** School Nurse.
- ••••• **Master:** Paramedic.

Possessed by: Mothers, Boy Scouts, Paramedics, Explorers, Outdoors Types.

Specialities: CPR, Broken Bones, Artificial Respiration, Diagnosis, Terminology.

Fishing: You can judge a body of water, and have

a fair chance of catching fish if there are any to be had. You are familiar with various kinds of fishing equipment.

- • **Novice:** Weekend angler.
- •• **Practiced:** Serious amateur.
- ••• **Competent:** Competition winner.
- •••• **Expert:** Professional fisherman.
- ••••• **Master:** Fish leap onto the shore as you walk by.

Possessed by: Weekend Warriors, Fishing Pros, Outdoors Types, Survivalists, Fishermen.

Specialities: Rod & Line, Fly, Deep Sea, Net, Big Game, Survival.

Forgery: You can make a copy of a document or

two-dimensional artwork which is good enough to pass casual inspection, and perhaps more detailed inspection as well.

- • **Novice:** Inter-office memos.
- •• **Practiced:** Signatures.
- ••• **Competent:** Commercial paper, passports.
- •••• **Expert:** Checks, bonds, bank drafts, some artworks.
- ••••• **Master:** Banknotes, old master paintings.

Possessed by: Criminals, Artists, Schemers.

Specialities: Handwriting, Drawings, Paintings, Bonds and Bills, Documents.

Gambling: You are adept at one or more games

of chance, and can play without too much risk of losing heavily. You can also increase your chances of winning without actually cheating.

- • **Novice:** Saturday-night poker with The Boys.
- •• **Practiced:** A couple of weeks in Vegas each year.
- ••• **Competent:** You are known in Vegas, Reno and Atlantic City.
- •••• **Expert:** You make a living from this. Your mother despairs.
- ••••• **Master:** You have to be careful not to tell people your name.

Possessed by: Professional Gamblers, Amateur Gamblers.

Specialities: Card Games, Dice Games, Roulette, One-Armed Bandits.

Game Playing: This Skill covers games of

strategy and skill such as chess, go, shogi, xiang qui, hnefatafl and so on. It does not cover card games (see *Gambling*), or simple games like tic tac toe and gomoku which are so much a matter of luck. Most board and war games are covered by this skill as long as they require some element of strategy.

- • **Novice:** You can beat your older brother.
- •• **Practiced:** You could get on a school team.
- ••• **Competent:** You could get on a college team.
- •••• **Expert:** You could get on a national team.
- ••••• **Master:** You could beat Karpov.

Possessed by: Enthusiasts.

Specialities: Chess, Go, Risk, Acquire, Stalingrad, Harpoon, Challenge.

Gunsmithing: You can repair firearms as

well as produce ammunition for a variety of different guns, including — if you are skilled enough — speciality ammunition such as caseless, hollow-point, mercury-tipped, and silver bullets. Given the time and the tools (and enough skill) you could build a gun from scratch — perhaps even one of your own design.

- • **Novice:** Black powder and paper cartridges.
- •• **Practiced:** Cased standard ammunition.
- ••• **Competent:** Magnum rounds.
- •••• **Expert:** Caseless and hollow-point rounds.
- ••••• **Master:** You name it.

Possessed by: Gun Nuts, Survivalists, Cops, Serial Killers

Specialities: Black Powder Weapons, Field Repair, Invention, Magnum and Supercharged Ammunition, Speciality Ammunition.

Haggling: You are skilled at bargaining and can

argue a price down or get some other concession from people under most circumstances. To bargain, make an opposed roll using your Manipulation + Haggling against the other character's Wits + Haggling (or Wits + Alertness). Each net success reduces the price by 5% if you are buying, or increases the character's offer by 5% if you are selling. Failure means the price does not budge.

- • **Novice:** Bargain Hunter.
- •• **Practiced:** Market Trader.
- ••• **Competent:** Horse Trader.
- •••• **Expert:** Con Artist.
- ••••• **Master:** Marco Polo.

Possessed by: Traders, Con Artists.

Specialities: Art, Weapons, Automobiles, Contracts, High Tech.

Heavy Weapons: You have the ability to

operate and shoot heavy weapons of all varieties — anything from an M60 heavy machine gun to a Dragon anti-tank weapon. Additionally, your knowledge of the weapons includes an ability to repair them.

- • **Novice:** Basic Training
- •• **Practiced:** Operator
- ••• **Competent:** Warrior
- •••• **Expert:** Killer

- ••••• **Master:** Rambo

Possessed by: Mercenaries, Armed Forces Personnel, SWAT officers.

Specialities: Desert, Jungle, Night Fighting, Friend from Foe, Loading.

Herbalism: You have a working knowledge of

herbs and their properties, medicinal and otherwise. You can find and prepare herbs, and know which herb or blend of herbs to use in any situation.

- • **Novice:** Read a book on it once.
- •• **Practiced:** Serious student of herb lore.
- ••• **Competent:** Local supplier.
- •••• **Expert:** Author of books on herbalism.
- ••••• **Master:** Herbal doctor.

Possessed by: Holistic Healers, New Agers, Wizened Old Women, Low-Tech Societies.

Specialities: Culinary, Medicinal, Poisonous, Narcotic/Hallucinogenic.

Hunting: You are skilled in finding and killing

animals for food or sport. In a type of terrain with which you are familiar, you are able to predict the likely type, number and location of food animals, and know the best way to go about finding and killing them.

- **Novice:** Weekender.
- **Practiced:** Enthusiast or Trooper.
- **Competent:** Survivalist or Marine.
- **Expert:** Special Forces.
- **Master:** Wild Animal.

Possessed by: Survivalists, Military, Pre-Industrial Societies, Outdoor Types.

Specialities: Temperate Forest, Jungle, Bush/Scrub, Mountain, Coast, Arctic, Desert.

Hypnotism:
You can place a willing subject into a trance, and use hypnotism to gather information or treat psychiatric problems. To place a willing subject into trance, make an opposed roll of your Charisma + Hypnotism against the subject's Intelligence (for an unwilling subject who is immobilized or Dominated to comply, use Intelligence + Willpower). The number of successes indicates the depth of the trance, and can be added to the character's Hypnotism to roll for the success of tasks such as gaining information. For example, a hypnotist with Charisma 4 and Hypnotism 4 hypnotizes a willing subject with Intelligence 5. The hypnotist rolls 5 successes and the subject 2 — a total of 3 successes in the hypnotist's favor, indicating a fairly deep trance. The hypnotist can now roll 7 dice (3 successes plus Hypnotism 4) to probe the subject's mind.

- **Novice:** You do it to entertain occasionally.
- **Practiced:** You are a skilled amateur.
- **Competent:** You could open a practice or go on the stage.
- **Expert:** You could write books on the subject.
- **Master:** Who needs Dominate?

Possessed by: Entertainers, Holistic Healers, New Agers, Police Specialists, Psychiatrists.

Specialities: Interrogation, Past-life Regression, Hypnotherapy, Behavior Modification.

Interrogation:
You are able to extract information from people by fair means or foul. Using a mixture of threats, trickery and persistent questioning, you can get the truth in the end.

- **Novice:** Nosey neighbor.
- **Practiced:** Movie cop.
- **Competent:** Talk-show host.
- **Expert:** Investigative journalist.
- **Master:** Spymaster.

Possessed by: Cops, Journalists, Secret Services, Inquisitors.

Specialities: Good Cop - Bad Cop, Threats, Trickery, Moral Blackmail.

Jeweler:
You are able to produce saleable pieces of jewelry (Dexterity + Jeweler), and appraise jewelry you see (Intelligence + Jeweler). You can determine the approximate worth of most jewelry by quick appraisal, but with modern technology it is easy to make a mistake without in-depth examination.

- **Novice:** You did a night-school course once.
- **Practiced:** A fairly serious hobby.
- **Competent:** A small business.
- **Expert:** This is your chosen career.
- **Master:** You are up there with Cartier.

Possessed by: Jewellers, Counterfeiters,

Specialities: Gold, Gems, Antique, Ancient, Mystical, Crystal.

Journalism:
You not only know how to write news stories, but also how to research and discover them in the first place. This skill also gives you with a working knowledge of the functioning of a news room and a newspaper as a whole. It can also provide a familiarity with television news reporting.

- **Novice:** Hack (TV reporter)
- **Practiced:** Features Reporter
- **Competent:** Sports Journalist
- **Expert:** Editor
- **Master:** Pulitzer Prize Winner

Possessed by: Free-lancers, Editors, Feature Reporters, Photographers, Foreign Correspondents.

Specialities: Politics, Sports, Corruption, Business, Deadlines, Editing.

Leatherworking:
You are able to produce serviceable items of leather, either for sale or for your own use.

- **Novice:** You got a craft kit for your birthday.
- **Practiced:** You make birthday presents for friends and family.
- **Competent:** You sell to local stores.
- **Expert:** People ask for your work by name.
- **Master:** Your picture appears in magazine ads.

Possessed by: Artisans, Survivalists.

Specialities: Clothing, Utensils, Horse-trappings, Special Interest Items.

Lip Reading:
You are able to understand speech without hearing it, just by watching mouth movement. Though you will not pick up on every word, usually you can figure out the sentence without too much trouble.

- **Novice:** If someone talks slowly and clearly, with exaggerated mouth movement.
- **Practiced:** If someone talks fairly slowly and you concentrate.
- **Competent:** Under most circumstances.
- **Expert:** Even under bad conditions, including foreign languages, bad light and distance.
- **Master:** Under just about any conditions.

Possessed by: Hearing-impaired, Spies, Detectives.

Specialities: Accents, Drunks, Poor Lighting, Fast Talkers, Surreptitiously.

Lock Picking: You are able to open locks

without having the correct key or knowing the right combination. Though this skill is certainly coming more and more irrelevant with all the new security devices in use, there are enough locks around to still make it worthwhile.

- •   **Novice:** Simple mortise locks.
- ••   **Practiced:** Cylinder locks and basic security locks.
- •••   **Competent:** Advanced security locks.
- ••••   **Expert:** Safes.
- ••••• **Master:** Fort Knox.

Possessed by: Burglars, Safecrackers, Spies, Locksmiths.

Specialities: Key-operated locks, Combination locks, Mag-card locks, Alarm systems.

Martial Arts Weapons: You know how

to use the different weapons of the marital arts, perhaps with great proficiency. These are complicated weapons to use, so this skill is essential in their correct deployment.

- •   **Novice:** White Belt
- ••   **Practiced:** Brown Belt
- •••   **Competent:** Black Belt
- ••••   **Expert:** Black Belt in more than one form.
- ••••• **Master:** Bruce Lee

Possessed by: Hobby Enthusiasts, Private Detectives, Instructors, Assassins, Ninja.

Specialities: Night Fighting, Group Fighting, Thrust, Sweep, Feint.

Masquerade: This Skill cannot be taken at

character generation, and is available only to Vampires. Masquerade reflects how skilled a character is at appearing to be mortal: appearing to breathe, creating a heartbeat, pink skin (produced by bringing blood to the surface), sneezing, masking Vampiric tendencies and so on. It may be paired with a Social Attribute to determine whether the character passes successfully as a mortal among mortals.

- •   **Novice:** Success in ideal circumstances.
- ••   **Practiced:** Able to pass casual inspection.
- •••   **Competent:** Success under most normal circumstances.
- ••••   **Expert:** Success under extreme circumstances.
- ••••• **Master:** Even a witch-hunter would be fooled.

Possessed by: Vampires only.

Specialities: Breathing, Heartbeat, While Sleeping, Sneezing, Hiccups, Skin Tone, Warm Skin.

Mechanic

Mechanic: You are a jack-of-all-trades with a particular affinity for mechanical devices, and can jerry-rig or repair just about anything mechanical, given the right tools and materials.

- • **Novice:** Fix a broken doorbell.
- •• **Practiced:** Fix a lawnmower, scratch-build a doorbell.
- ••• **Competent:** Fix a car, build an automatic garage door.
- •••• **Expert:** Fix a high-performance car, rebuild an engine.
- ••••• **Master:** Fix, build or improve almost anything.

Possessed by: Mechanics, Car Nuts, Hobbyists.
Specialities: Electrical, Cars, Domestic, Inventing.

Meditation

Meditation: You are able to enter a trancelike state at will, focussing your mind inward and dealing with a range of mental and physical problems. A successful roll of Willpower + Meditation is necessary to enter meditation; after each full hour, the character rolls Meditation against difficulty 9. Dice from the character's dice pool are subtracted if there are any distractions during that time. Each success on the second roll restores one point of Willpower, each botch result indicates that a Willpower is lost. If the meditation is interrupted and concentration is lost before the hour is up, no benefits are gained.

- • **Novice:** Read a book on it once.
- •• **Practiced:** Studied seriously.
- ••• **Competent:** Studied under a master.
- •••• **Expert:** Qualified to teach.
- ••••• **Master:** Just that.

Possessed by: Yogis, Mystics, Holistic Healers, New Agers, Old Hippies.
Specialities: Tantric, Transcendental, Yogic, New Age.

Orienteering

Orienteering: You have an excellent sense of direction, and generally know which way is north or which direction to go to reach some known location. Given a map, a set of landmarks, a compass or directions, you can get from here to there, even if you've never been there before. You can work out the shortest or easiest route, estimate how long it will take, and avoid surprises along the way. If you also have Astronomy, you can navigate by the stars. Most tasks of navigation are fairly straightforward, and within the reach of most people; the Storyteller will probably only ask you to use this Knowledge when a navigation task is difficult or unusual.

- • **Novice:** A Boy Scout. You can generally find a place a second time, or find your way home from somewhere.
- •• **Practiced:** You very rarely get lost, and can give accurate directions even in a place you don't know too well.
- ••• **Competent:** You hardly ever get lost, even in unfamiliar territory, rough terrain and bad weather.
- •••• **Expert:** You could walk a mile along a straight line blindfold.
- ••••• **Master:** You have a compass in your head — you always know which way is north.

Possessed by: Explorers, Scouts, Foresters, Trappers, Special Forces, Plane Navigator, Ship's Navigators, Explorers.
Specialities: Find North, Find Way Home, Air, Sea, Hiking, Road, Stars, Map Reading.

Parachuting

Parachuting: You know how to use a parachute, both for sport and for other purposes.

- • **Novice:** Weekend jumper.
- •• **Practiced:** Reservist.
- ••• **Competent:** Airborne regular.
- •••• **Expert:** Special forces or sport instructor.
- ••••• **Master:** Special forces instructor or sport champion.

Possessed by: Sport Parachutists, Military, Flying Enthusiasts.
Specialities: Skydiving, Mass Deployment, Escape, HALO (High Altitude, Low Open), Display.

Photography
: You know how to use a camera beyond pointing and shooting. You also know how to process photographic materials.

- • **Novice:** Local club member.
- •• **Practiced:** Local club prizewinner.
- ••• **Competent:** Semi-pro, you sell some pictures.
- •••• **Expert:** Professional photographer.
- ••••• **Master:** One of the best.

Possessed by: Artists, Journalists, Enthusiasts, Police Specialists.

Specialities: Art, Photojournalism, Portraits, Forensic, X-ray, Photolithography.

Pickpocket
: You are able to remove objects from someone else's clothing and person without their knowledge, even if it is in an inside pocket. Usually you bump into the person in order to distract them from your touch as you remove the object.

- • **Novice:** You can take wallets in a dense crowd.
- •• **Practiced:** You can take a wallet from an inside pocket.
- ••• **Competent:** You can take a keychain from a trouser pocket.
- •••• **Expert:** You can take a watch while shaking hands.
- ••••• **Master:** You can take anything from anywhere.

Possessed by: Criminals.
Specialities: Pockets, Watches, Chains, Get Aways.

Pilot
: You can operate a flying machine. Note that depending on your skill, you may be limited in what sort of aircraft you can fly. A glider pilot (level one Pilot) cannot fly a helicopter (a Level Four Pilot).

- • **Novice:** Club member. Hang gliders only.
- •• **Practiced:** Club champion. Gliders and Small aircraft only.
- ••• **Competent:** Professional or club instructor. Commercial Airplane License.
- •••• **Expert:** Military or display pilot. Any Type of Commercial Aircraft.
- ••••• **Master:** Elite military, top-notch stunt pilot, ace. Any type of Aircraft, commercial or military.

Possessed by: Enthusiasts, Pilots, Military, Police.
Specialities: Nightflying, Thermals, Dog Fights, Long Range, Take-off's and Landings, Glider, Helicopter, Light plane, Corporate jet, Commercial/transport jet, Fighter jet, Vintage plane, Autogyro, Blimp, Balloon, Hang-glider, Microlight.

Police Procedure
: You know the general police techniques and procedures of criminal investigation, and you have the ability to do them yourself (especially if you were once a police officer yourself).

- • **Novice:** Recruit
- •• **Practiced:** Patrol Officer
- ••• **Competent:** Detective
- •••• **Expert:** Police Lieutenant
- ••••• **Master:** Only a master criminal would need to know this much.

Possessed by: Police Officers, Attorneys, Reporters, Private Detectives, FBI
Specialities: APBs, Reports, Detectives, Autopsies.

Pottery
: You are able to make and fire ceramic items, either for art or for practical use.

- • **Novice:** Hobbyist.
- •• **Practiced:** Enthusiastic hobbyist, night-school student.
- ••• **Competent:** Professional, night-school instructor.
- •••• **Expert:** Craftsperson, growing business.
- ••••• **Master:** Household name.

Possessed by: Artisans, members of pre-industrial communities.
Specialities: Vessels, Sculpture, Models, Mouldings.

Psychoanalysis
: You are skilled in diagnosing and treating mental ailments without recourse to behavior-altering drugs. In a session of analysis, you roll Intelligence + Psychoanalysis against the subject's Intelligence + (5 - Empathy). Keep track of net successes; the Storyteller will decide how many successes are necessary to remove the Derangement. Even Freud couldn't do this in a single session, so be patient! Note that it is impossible to treat an unwilling patient this way.

- • **Novice:** Dutch Uncle.
- •• **Practiced:** Volunteer Counsellor.
- ••• **Competent:** Professional Counsellor.
- •••• **Expert:** Qualified Psychoanalyst.
- ••••• **Master:** Freud.

Possessed by: Psychoanalysts, Holistic Healers, Good Listeners, Counsellors, some Parents, some Teachers, some Priests.
Specialities: Freudian, Jungian, Humanist, Ericksonian, Holistic, Wiccan, Childhood, Psychosis, Neurosis, Self, Sympathy, Terminology, Research.

Public Speaking
: You are able to mold the emotions of a crowd by making a speech. This might be at a political rally, in a courtroom, at a lecture or even at the barricades once the revolution is under way. Whatever you want your audience to feel is what it feels.

- • **Novice:** Entertaining Speaker.
- •• **Practiced:** Compelling Speaker.
- ••• **Competent:** Inspiring Speaker.
- •••• **Expert:** Popular Champion.

Master: Churchill or Hitler.
Possessed by: Politicians, Revolutionaries, Actors, a few Professors.
Specialities: Entertaining, Moving, Rabble Rousing, Vote Catching, Lies.

Research: You are highly skilled at finding

information from conventional sources. Given time and a good library, you could assemble the sum of human knowledge on almost any topic.

- • **Novice:** Undergrad.
- •• **Practiced:** Grad Student or Research Assistant.
- ••• **Competent:** Professor.
- •••• **Expert:** Research Fellow.
- ••••• **Master:** Human Database.

Possessed by: Academics, Advertising Execs, Authors, Detectives.
Specialities: Any Knowledge.

Ride: You can climb onto a riding-animal and stand

a good chance of getting where you want to go without falling off, being thrown or having anything else unpleasant happen to you. When attempting something difficult, or when danger threatens, the Storyteller may require you to roll Dexterity + Ride to avoid trouble. This Skill can also be combined with Mental Attributes to reflect your working knowledge of the relevant trappings and equipment.

- • **Novice:** Pony club member, dude ranch vacations.
- •• **Practiced:** Pony club champion, weekend cowboy.
- ••• **Competent:** Pony club instructor, professional cowboy.
- •••• **Expert:** Showjumping champion, rodeo star.
- ••••• **Master:** Stunt rider.

Possessed by: Enthusiasts, Cowboys, Stunt Riders, members of pre-industrial societies.
Specialities: Horse, Mule, Camel, Elephant, Gallop, Tricks, No Hands.

Scuba: You are proficient in the use of an aqualung

(not a big deal for the Kindred), and are familiar with the many dangers of diving (such as sharks and the bends).

- • **Novice:** Once a year, on vacation.
- •• **Practiced:** Local club member.
- ••• **Competent:** Instructor.
- •••• **Expert:** Pro diver.
- ••••• **Master:** Navy SEAL.

Possessed by: Enthusiasts, Military, Treasure Hunters, Marine Biologists.
Specialities: Cold Water, Reef, Deep Sea, Recreational.

Sign Language:
You are able to communicate by using sign language with almost the same efficiency as a spoken language.

- • **Novice:** Basic ideas only.
- •• **Practiced:** Everyday conversation.
- ••• **Competent:** Moderately complex conversation, moderate speed.
- •••• **Expert:** Complex conversation, high speed.
- ••••• **Master:** As fluent as talking.

Possessed by: Hearing-impaired, some tribal societies.
Specialities: Lewd Expressions, Short Hand, Translation, Formal.

Skiing:
You can travel on skis for sport or transportation with little chance of a mishap. You can read snow, and know where it is safe and where it is not under most circumstances.

- • **Novice:** Vacation skier.
- •• **Practiced:** Enthusiast.
- ••• **Competent:** Ski bum.
- •••• **Expert:** Hot-dogger, ski champ, arctic forces.
- ••••• **Master:** Olympic medallist, elite forces.

Possessed by: Sportsmen, Military, Arctic and Mountain inhabitants.
Specialities: Cross-country, downhill, ski-jumping, snowboarding, stunts.

Sleight of Hand:
The quickness of your hands can deceive the eyes of others. You can perform magic tricks and other feats of legerdemain.

- • **Novice:** Card tricks at Christmas.
- •• **Practiced:** Children's parties.
- ••• **Competent:** Stage magician.
- •••• **Expert:** TV magician.
- ••••• **Master:** A legend in your own time.

Possessed by: Stage Magicians, Thieves.
Specialities: Produce Item, Conceal Item, Amuse.

Speed Reading:
Through practice, you have developed the ability to read and absorb large quantities of written material in a short time.

- • **Novice:** The *New York Times* in an hour.
- •• **Practiced:** A novel in 2-3 hours.
- ••• **Competent:** A textbook in 2-3 hours.
- •••• **Expert:** A fat textbook in 2-3 hours.
- ••••• **Master:** *War & Peace* in 2-3 hours.

Possessed by: Academics, Literary Critics, Journalists, Researchers.
Specialities: Technical, Fiction, Newspaper, Research, Skim.

Style:
You may not have been born good-looking, or possessed of a natural charm, but you know how to dress and make the most of your appearance. Even if you are not physically attractive, heads turn because of your dress sense and style. Note that this Skill only applies to people's reactions to your appearance; once you get closer, it's up to you.

- • **Novice:** Good Taste.
- •• **Practiced:** Socialite.
- ••• **Competent:** Celebrity.
- •••• **Expert:** Celebrity Advisor.
- ••••• **Master:** International Model.

Possessed by: Socialites, Celebrities, Fashion Professionals, the Gifted Few.
Specialities: Classic, High Fashion, Street Fashion, Retro, Ethnic.

Swimming:
You are able to swim enough to keep yourself afloat, and maybe a little more. Note that Vampires, unlike mortals, do not float naturally; if they do not swim, they will sink.

- • **Novice:** You can swim.
- •• **Practiced:** You can swim fast, or for extended periods.
- ••• **Competent:** Instructor/Lifeguard.
- •••• **Expert:** Swim team.
- ••••• **Master:** Olympic gold.

Possessed by: Athletes, almost anyone.
Specialities: Racing, Distance, Sea, Survival, Lifesaving.

Throwing:
You know how to throw things in general, as well as use various types of thrown weapons — anything from spears to hatchets to knives to baseballs (yes, if thrown hard enough, they make fine weapons).

- • **Novice:** Can throw a ball generally toward home plate.
- •• **Practiced:** High school baseball pitcher.
- ••• **Competent:** Deadly even in a food fight.
- •••• **Expert:** Bruce Jenner with a javelin.
- ••••• **Master:** Tom Glavine (Steve Avery!)

Possessed by: Hobby Enthusiasts, Competitors.
Specialities: Forests, Target, Hunting, Moving Targets.

Tracking:
You can identify the trail of an animal or person, and follow it under most conditions. Conditions will vary the difficulty of this task — following fresh tracks in deep snow is easier than following week-old tracks across a concrete sidewalk!

- • **Novice:** Boy Scout
- •• **Practiced:** Eagle Scout
- ••• **Competent:** Hunter
- •••• **Expert:** Indian Tracker
- ••••• **Master:** Grizzly Adams, Tonto.

Possessed by: Hunters, Survivalists, Special Forces, Detectives.
Specialities: Wolf, Deer, Rock, Urban, Identify.

Traps:
You know how to set a trap according to the type of game you want to catch.

- • **Novice:** Boy Scout.
- •• **Practiced:** Weekend Survivalist
- ••• **Competent:** Outdoorsman
- •••• **Expert:** Mountain Man
- ••••• **Master:** Grizzly Adams

Possessed by: Trappers, Special Forces, inhabitants of remote places.
Specialities: by quarry species.

Melee:
Though this skill has already been described, we have listed it here to provide you with an expanded list of specialties

Specialties:

Knife (any blade up to 10" long)

Shortsword (slashing/stabbing weapons up to 2 1/2ft long)

Broadsword (slashing weapons 3ft-4ft long)

Greatsword (slashing weapons 4ft-5ft long)

Smallsword (stabbing weapons 3ft and longer - includes foil and epée)

Saber (includes cutlass)

Club (anything from a pool cue to a mace)

Axe (one-handed, includes hatchet, tomahawk and kitchen cleaver)

Great Axe (two handed, includes wood axe and battle axe)

Polearm (anything 6ft or more in length)

Flexible Weapon (includes chain, nunchaku, flail, morning star)

Shield (adds to Dexterity + Dodge instead of Dexterity + Melee)

Knife

Spear

Sling

Short Bow (includes horse bow)

Long Bow (includes modern competition bow)

Crossbow

Knowledges

Accounting:
You can set up and keep accounts in the commercially-approved conventional manner, and you can also interpret accounts and find errors, tricks and embezzlement.

- • **Novice:** Night school.
- •• **Practiced:** Junior clerk.
- ••• **Competent:** Senior clerk or junior partner.
- •••• **Expert:** Senior partner.
- ••••• **Master:** Nothing escapes you.

Possessed by: Businesspeople, Specialist Investigators.
Specialities: Small business, Large corporation, Governmental, Taxes.

Alchemy:
You are familiar with the writings of the classical and medieval alchemists, and you also have some practical experience. This is related to the Knowledge of Chemistry, but indirectly — about the same relationship as is shared by Astronomy and Astrology. You can interpret alchemical texts, and understand the various symbols and ciphers used by the alchemists even when you find them in a non-alchemical context.

- • **Novice:** A mere dabbler.
- •• **Practiced:** Apprentice, probably still dependent on a master for instruction.
- ••• **Competent:** Journeyman, capable of making your own way, but with a long road still to travel.
- •••• **Expert:** Experienced alchemist, within reach of the greatest secrets.
- ••••• **Master:** Maybe that lead into gold thing can really work.

Possessed by: Occultists, Scholars, some Scientists.
Specialities: Transmutation, Cosmology, Lapis Philosophorum.

Anthropology:
You have studied the human phenomenon of society in many of its forms, and understand the basic rules and structures on a theoretical

level. You also have some specific knowledge of one or more contemporary pre-industrial societies.

- • **Novice:** Student.
- •• **Practiced:** Grad student or Research Assistant.
- ••• **Competent:** Professor or Veteran Fieldworker.
- •••• **Expert:** Head of department in major university.
- ••••• **Master:** Leading light of the field, your work shapes the future of the subject.

Possessed by: Scholars.
Specialities: Physical, Social, Ancient, Theoretical, specific cultures.

Area Knowledge:
You are familiar with an area — usually a city — and know a fair amount about its structure, history, geography and mortal politics. This Knowledge does not include Kindred affairs, which are covered by the Knowledge of Kindred Lore (below).

- • **Novice:** You know a fair amount for an outsider.
- •• **Practiced:** You may have lived there for a year or two.
- ••• **Competent:** You may have lived there for 5-10 years.
- •••• **Expert:** You're native born, and never left.
- ••••• **Master:** You could write the definitive book on the area.

Possessed by: Locals, Cops, Reporters, Cab Drivers.
Specialities: History, Geography, Politics, Transportation, Law.

Archeology:
You have studied the remains of the past and the processes by which they come to be preserved and discovered. You can interpret archaeological remains and identify the likely provenance of ancient artifacts; you also know a fair amount about one or more ancient cultures.

- • **Novice:** Undergrad or Amateur.
- •• **Practiced:** Graduate Student or Research Assistant.
- ••• **Competent:** Professor.
- •••• **Expert:** Research Fellow.
- ••••• **Master:** Doyen.

Possessed by: Scholars, Enthusiastic Amateurs, Popular Authors.
Specialities: Prehistoric Europe, Classical, Central America, Excavation, Underwater Archeology, Theory, Paleopathology, Paleoecology.

Architecture:
You are trained in the design of buildings, from both functional and aesthetic points of view. You can judge where the load-bearing elements of a building are and interpret architectural plans.

You know instinctively where the safest places are in the event of an explosion or earthquake.

- • **Novice:** Student.
- •• **Practiced:** Office Junior.
- ••• **Competent:** Junior Partner.
- •••• **Expert:** Senior Partner.
- ••••• **Master:** Head of Professional Body, Giant in the Field.

Possessed by: Architects, Structural Engineers.
Specialities: Houses, Office Buildings, Public Works.

Art History:
You have studied art as an academic rather than practical subject, and know a great deal about its history. You can look at a piece of art and have a good chance of identifying its place and period of origin, and in most cases you can name the artist without looking for a signature. You also have a fair idea of the current market price of a piece.

- • **Novice:** Student or Amateur.
- •• **Practiced:** Grad Student or Enthusiastic Amateur.
- ••• **Competent:** Professor or Auction House bigwig.
- •••• **Expert:** Research Fellow or Auction House Chief.
- ••••• **Master:** Head of Department.

Possessed by: Scholars, Enthusiasts, Auction House Personnel
Specialities: Classical, Renaissance, Masters, Impressionists, Primitive, American, Ethnographic.

Astrology:
You know how to compile and interpret a horoscope. Given the date and time (and, according to some systems, the place) of a person's birth, you can construct a personality profile and a set of predictions about the likely course of their life. Whether you actually believe these revelations is a matter of personal taste, but you can present them in a convincing and pleasing manner to those who *do* believe.

- • **Novice:** Dabbler.
- •• **Practiced:** Friends ask you to make horoscopes for them.
- ••• **Competent:** You could run a small astrology business.
- •••• **Expert:** You could have a syndicated newspaper column.
- ••••• **Master:** You could work for celebrities and politicians.

Possessed by: Astrologers, Amateurs, Mystics, New Agers, Old Hippies.
Specialities: Solar Horoscope, Ming Shu, Zu Wei.

Astronomy:
You know the heavens and their movements from a scientific rather than mystical standpoint. You can identify most constellations, oper-

ate an astronomical telescope, predict sunspots, eclipses and comets, and identify most heavenly phenomena.

- • **Novice:** Student or Amateur.
- •• **Practiced:** Grad Student or Enthusiastic Amateur.
- ••• **Competent:** Professor or Doyen of local society.
- •••• **Expert:** Research Fellow, TV host or NASA hotshot.
- ••••• **Master:** Renowned Scholar or NASA team leader.

Possessed by: Scholars, Amateurs, NASA operations staff.
Specialities: Planetary, Galaxies, Quasars, Novas and Nebulas, Black Holes, Big Bang Theory.

Biology:
You know about the nature of life, the forms it takes, and the way living organisms work. You have a reasonable chance of identifying a plant or creature, even from a fragment. You must have at least one dot in Science before you can acquire this Knowledge.

- • **Novice:** High School.
- •• **Practiced:** Student.
- ••• **Competent:** Grad Student.
- •••• **Expert:** Professor.
- ••••• **Master:** Research Fellow.

Possessed by: Scholars, Outdoors Types.
Specialities: Botany, Zoology, Ecology, Paleontology.

Chemistry:
You have studied the nature of substances and their interactions, and know how to prepare various chemical compounds and how to deal with various hazardous substances. You must have at least one dot in Science before you can acquire this Knowledge.

- • **Novice:** High School.
- •• **Practiced:** Student.
- ••• **Competent:** Grad Student.
- •••• **Expert:** Professor.
- ••••• **Master:** Research Fellow.

Possessed by: Scholars, Pharmacists, most Scientists.
Specialities: Organic, Inorganic, Analysis, Safety.

Criminology:
You have studied the nature of crime — when, where, how and why it is committed, the nature of the criminal mind and the history of famous cases. You are an expert on crime and law enforcement.

- • **Novice:** Amateur.
- •• **Practiced:** Enthusiast.
- ••• **Competent:** Scholar or Detective.
- •••• **Expert:** Criminal Historian or Senior Detective.
- ••••• **Master:** Eminent Authority. The Shadow.

Possessed by: Police, Authors, Enthusiasts, Criminal Psychologists.
Specialities: Serial Killings, Unsolved Crimes, Jack the Ripper, Criminal Psychology.

Cryptography:
You are skilled in the composition and interpretation of codes and ciphers. You can make a code which can only be cracked by someone scoring as many successes as you have dots in this Skill, and you can crack a code with a number of successes determined by the Storyteller to reflect its complexity.

- • **Novice:** Grade-School Spy Fan.
- •• **Practiced:** Word Puzzle Buff, Military Signals Officer.
- ••• **Competent:** Intelligence Officer.
- •••• **Expert:** Intelligence Cipher Specialist.
- ••••• **Master:** James Bond.

Possessed by: Spies, Puzzle Buffs, Military Signals Personnel.
Specialities: Letter Shifts, Mathematical Encryption, Obscure Character Sets.

Demolition:
You understand how structures such as buildings are made, where their weak points are and how to destroy them with the minimum of effort. You know how to rig a demolition charge, where to place it for maximum effect, and how to make a hole in

a wall or knock down a building neatly, without debris going all over and endangering the neighborhood.

- • Novice: Make a hole in a wall with a sledge-hammer.
- •• Practiced: Take down a detached house-sized building.
- ••• Competent: Take down one side of a du-plex without harming the other.
- •••• Expert: Take down a row-house without harming those on either side.
- ••••• Master: Take down a skyscraper with one explosion.

Possessed by: Demolition Engineers, Military.
Specialities: Houses, High-Rise, Military.

Economics: You know what an economy is

and how one works. Coupled with Area Knowledge, you will know where every penny comes from in the city and where it goes. You can study a city or country and gain a fair understanding of its economic condition and the reasons behind its condition.

- • Novice: High School.
- •• Practiced: Student.
- ••• Competent: Grad Student or Business Journalist.
- •••• Expert: Professor or Economic Consultant.
- ••••• Master: Research Fellow or Presidential Advisor.

Possessed by: Scholars, Economists, Businesspeople, Politicians, Bar-room Pundits.
Specialities: Private Sector, Public Sector, Stock Market, Taxes, International.

Electronics: You have studied the construc-

tion and operation of electronic devices. You can identify the function of an unknown electronic device, and diagnose and repair a malfunctioning or broken device given time and equipment. Note that electronic devices are not the same as electrically-powered mechanical devices — a hair-dryer is mechanical, a radio is electronic.

- • Novice: Tinkerer.
- •• Practiced: Radio Ham.
- ••• Competent: TV Repairman.
- •••• Expert: Computer Engineer.
- ••••• Master: Computer Hardware Designer.

Possessed by: Enthusiasts, Service Engineers, Inventors.
Specialities: Radio/TV, Control Systems, Information Systems.

Engineering: You can understand, design

and diagnose faults in mechanical systems of all kinds. You may not actually be able to build and fix them — that comes under the Mechanic Skill — but you can make a set of plans from which a skilled mechanic can build almost anything from a toaster to an airplane.

- • Novice: Amateur.
- •• Practiced: Student.
- ••• Competent: Junior Engineer.
- •••• Expert: Chief Engineer.
- ••••• Master: Ace Inventor.

Possessed by: Engineers, Model Makers, Inventors.
Specialities: Automotive, Air, Marine, Domestic, Maintenance/Repair, Invention.

Faerie Lore: You are knowledgeable in the

lore of the Seelie and UnSeelie Faeries, and know something of their great Kingdom: Arcadia. Because Kindred are unable to travel to this realm, most of your knowledge is hearsay, and it will be difficult for you to verify what you believe to be true.

- • Student: Speculation and hearsay.
- •• College: You know some relevant facts.
- ••• Master: Basic knowledge of their ways.
- •••• Expert: Expansive knowledge.
- ••••• Scholar: You think you know the secrets of these creatures.

Possessed by: Faeries, Lupine, Occultists, Vampires, Magi, Witchhunters.
Specialities: Enchanting Music, Faerie Food, Somniare, Atlantium, Antrum, Caelum, Barathrum, Tartarus.

Forensics: You are trained in the recognition

and interpretation of physical clues. You can examine the scene of a crime, for instance, and find out the race, sex, build, hair color, clothing type and probable social class of everyone who was there in the last three to four days. You can examine a body and discover the cause and probable circumstances of death.

- • Novice: Amateur sleuth.
- •• Practiced: Detective, FBI agent.
- ••• Competent: Police specialist.
- •••• Expert: FBI specialist.
- ••••• Master: Sherlock who?

Possessed by: Amateur Detectives, Police, FBI.
Specialities: Scene of Crime, Pathology, Ballistics, Fingerprints.

Geology: You have studied the physical compo-

sition of the earth, and know something about the physics and chemistry of rock, the formation of landscape features and related topics. You can identify the type and probable source of a piece of stone, tell a likely place to look for oil, precious metals and gems, identify ores and know how to refine them.

- • Novice: High School.
- •• Practiced: Student.
- ••• Competent: Grad student or oilman.
- •••• Expert: Professor or prospecting consultant.

•••••   **Master:** Research fellow.
Possessed by: Scholars, Oilmen, Prospectors, Outdoors Types, Mining and Structural Engineers.
Specialities: Petrology, Geomorphology, Prospecting, Paleontology, Engineering.

Heraldry: You have studied the art and language

of heraldry, and can interpret a heraldic device such as a coat of arms or a Japanese *mon* and design a new one which would be acceptable to the ruling authorities of heraldry. By successfully recognizing a heraldic device, you automatically know a little about the family or organization to which it belongs.
- •   **Novice:** Amateur.
- ••   **Practiced:** Enthusiast or Historian.
- •••   **Competent:** Grad Student or Genealogist.
- ••••   **Expert:** Professor or Junior Herald.
- •••••   **Master:** Research Fellow or King of Arms.

Possessed by: Enthusiasts, Historians, Genealogists, Heralds.
Specialities: British, French, German, Italian, Spanish, Scandinavian, Japanese, Modern, Mercantile.

History: You have studied the history of the

world or of a specific area or period, and understand what happened, when, why, and who was involved. You also have a fair idea of social, political, economic and technological conditions in various past times and places. Note that in the case of Vampire characters, this skill relates only to times and places which were outside their direct experience. For instance, a Vampire born in Ancient Rome would rely on memory for that history and culture, but would use History to uncover information about Classical Greece, which was before his time, or about Tokugawa, Japan, which was outside his experience.
- •   **Novice:** Amateur or High School.
- ••   **Practiced:** Enthusiast or Student.
- •••   **Competent:** Grad Student or Author.
- ••••   **Expert:** Professor.
- •••••   **Master:** Research Fellow.

Possessed by: Enthusiasts, Scholars.
Specialities: Political, Intellectual, Social, Economic, Technological, Classical, Medieval, Renaissance, Modern, Europe, Americas, Asia, Africa, Australia.

Kindred Lore: This Knowledge cannot be

taken at character generation; it can only come through direct experience. At the end of some Stories, the Storyteller will announce the maximum number of experience points a character can allot to the acquisition or improvement of this Knowledge based on what each character has actually found out during the course of the Story. Kindred Lore reflects a character's knowledge of the great secrets of the Kindred, of the Jyhad, Gehenna, the Antideluvians, Methusalah, Inconnu and the Book of Nod. Unlike the Occult Knowledge, most of what you learn about your subject is actually true (though certainly not all).
- •   **Novice:** But a whelp.
- ••   **Practiced:** Still mostly unfamiliar.
- •••   **Competent:** Broad familiarity with the legends.
- ••••   **Expert:** Knowledgeable of part of the great secrets.
- •••••   **Master:** Possessor of some of the great secrets.

Possessed by: Vampires, some Fearless Witch Hunters.
Specialities: Jyhad, Inconnu, Antideluvians, Caine, Book of Nod, Gehenna.

City Secrets: This describes a characters

knowledge of a particular city (you choose which); who is who, who has power, how they relate to one another and what is going on. In **Chicago by Night**, this Knowledge was called *Secrets*. No character may take this ability without the permission of the storyteller, and gaining experience in it works the same as with Kindred Lore. Note that each Kindred community is a separate Knowledge; knowing about the Kindred of Chicago gives a character no information about the Kindred of Los Angeles, for instance.
- •   **Novice:** Whelp.
- ••   **Practiced:** Naive or inexperienced.
- •••   **Competent:** You have an ear to the ground.
- ••••   **Expert:** Well-informed.
- •••••   **Master:** Seasoned intriguer.

Possessed by: Vampires, some Fearless Vampire Hunters.
Specialities: Prince, Primogen, Secret Powers, Anarchs, Influences, Sabbat Presence, Havens, Masquerade.

Literature: You are familiar with the literature

of one or more nations or historical periods, and know something of the general style and structure of literature — the things that set literature apart from mere fiction or entertainment. You can usually find a witty and apposite quote, or identify a quotation if you see one.
- •   **Novice:** High School.
- ••   **Practiced:** Student or Struggling Author.
- •••   **Competent:** Grad Student or Critic.
- ••••   **Expert:** Professor or Recognized Author.
- •••••   **Master:** Research Fellow or Celebrated Author.

Possessed by: Scholars, Authors, Critics, Culture Vultures.
Specialities: The Novel, Poetry, Drama, English, American, European, Classical, Mediaeval, Asian, Islamic.

Lupine Lore:
You are knowledgeable in the lore of Werewolves — what they eat, when they gather, their strengths and weaknesses. You can use this knowledge to discover how to best combat them, or how to bring about a peace between their tribes and you. Unlike the Occult Knowledge, most of what you believe about your subject is actually true (though certainly not all).

- •   **Student:** Speculation and hearsay.
- ••   **College:** You know some relevant facts.
- •••   **Master:** Basic knowledge of their ways.
- •••• **Expert:** Expansive knowledge.
- ••••• **Scholar:** You know as much about them as they do themselves.

Possessed by: Vampire, Magi, Witchhunters.
Specialities: Tribes, Totems, Spirit Guides, Packs, Ancestors, Genetive Disorder.

Magus Lore:
You are knowledgeable in the lore of magic and witchcraft. You know of the ancient orders of wizards: their cabals, covenants, and most secret rituals. Unlike the Occult Knowledge, most of what you believe about you subject is actually true (though certainly not all).

- •   **Student:** Speculation and hearsay.
- ••   **College:** You know some relevant facts.
- •••   **Master:** Basic knowledge of their ways.
- •••• **Expert:** Expansive knowledge.
- ••••• **Scholar:** You understand the theory of magic.

Possessed by: Vampire, Magi, Witchhunters.
Specialities: Rituals, Wicca, Astrology, Order of Hermes, Kabbalah, Order of Odin, Mystic Traditions.

Mathematics:
You have studied the science of numbers; you are able to perform complex calculations and understand mathematical concepts beyond basic arithmetic. Given part or all of a calculation, you can probably work out what it is intended to achieve.

- •   **Novice:** High School.
- ••   **Practiced:** Student.
- •••   **Competent:** Grad Student or Scientist.
- •••• **Expert:** Professor.
- ••••• **Master:** Research Fellow.

Possessed by: Scholars, Scientists.
Specialities: Pure Mathematics, Mechanics, Statistics.

Metallurgy:
You know about the properties and behavior of metals and alloys. You can identify almost any metal or alloy from a sample, given time and equipment, and know the melting point, stress limits and other characteristics of any common metal or alloy. You must have at least one dot in Chemistry or Physics to take this Knowledge.

- •   **Novice:** Student.
- ••   **Practiced:** Grad Student or Apprentice.
- •••   **Competent:** Professor or Engineer.
- •••• **Expert:** Engineer.
- ••••• **Master:** Chief Engineer.

Possessed by: Scholars, Engineers, Inventors.
Specialities: Iron and Steel, Copper Alloys, High-Stress Alloys, Conductors.

Meteorology:
Either through study or experience, you know a thing or two about weather. You can tell if it's going to rain this afternoon, tonight or tomorrow, or what the chance of snow is, or whether the skies will be cloudy or clear for the next few days. You can predict what the high and low temperatures will be, and so on.

- •   **Novice:** High School.
- ••   **Practiced:** Student, Weekend Camper or TV Weatherman.
- •••   **Competent:** Grad Student or Outdoor Enthusiast.
- •••• **Expert:** Professor or Farmer.
- ••••• **Master:** God calls you up and tells you.

Possessed by: Scholars, TV Weathermen, Outdoors Types, Farmers.
Specialities: Theoretical, Local Area, Prediction.

Naturalist:
You are a student of animal behaviour. Through study or experience, you know when and where to find certain animals, how to watch them without them running away or attacking you, and how they react to certain things. You can read natural signs and predict whether there is a predator or some other threat in the area, and interpret an animal's mood through its behaviour.

- •   **Novice:** Boy Scout.
- ••   **Practiced:** Outdoors Type.
- •••   **Competent:** TV Nature Show Host.
- •••• **Expert:** Seasoned Fieldworker.
- ••••• **Master:** David Attenborough.

Possessed by: Biologists, Outdoor Types, Hunters, Farmers, Wildlife Photographers.
Specialities: Temperate Forest, Jungle, Plains, Mountains, Coast, Arctic, Desert.

Physics:
You have studied the science of matter, what it is made of and how it behaves. You can calculate masses and velocities without even thinking about it, you know a little about why the universe is the way it is, and you might even understand the Theory of Relativity. You can understand and interpret physical data, the notes of other physicists, and experimental or lab equipment. You must have at least one dot in Science to take this Knowledge.

- •   **Novice:** High School.
- ••   **Practiced:** Student.
- •••   **Competent:** Grad Student.

••••   Expert: Professor.

•••••   Master: Research Fellow.

Possessed by: Scholars, Engineers, Scientists.

Specialities: Mechanics, Thermodynamics, Hydrodynamics, Aerodynamics, Astrophysics, Optics, Electronics, Nuclear, Theoretical, Applied.

Psychology: You have a formal education in

the science of human nature. You know the modern theories of emotion, cognative developement, personality, perception, and learning. Though this is largely a scholarly understanding of the human psyche, it can be used to better understand those around you.

•   Novice: High School.

••   Practiced: Student.

•••   Competent: Grad Student.

••••   Expert: Professor.

•••••   Master: Theorist.

Possessed by: Teachers, Researchers, Scientists, Councelors, Psychologists.

Specialities: Behaviorism, Freudian, Jungian, Humanist, Developemental, Experiemental, Animals.

Spirit Lore: You know of the spirit world, and

its structure and forms. Though you may not neccessarily have the abilty to astral travel, you understand how the process works. Neither is the world of Ghosts unknown to you. Unlike Occult Knowledge, most of what you

belive about you subject is actually true (though certainly not all).

•   Novice: High School.

••   Practiced: Student.

•••   Competent: Grad Student.

••••   Expert: Professor.

•••••   Master: Theorist.

Possessed by: Werewolves, Magi, Vampires, Psychics, Clairvoyants, Witchhunters.

Specialities: Benign Spirit, Malevolent Spirits, Mischievous Spirits, Astral Travel, Specific Site, Hauntings.

Theology: Religion is not an unfamiliar aspect

of human endeavor for you, and you understand fully its place in the world. At higher levels of knowledge, this skill lends an appreciation for all religious belief, while less skilled individuals tend to view their own beliefs as intrinsically superior to any others. This, of course, varies by individual. Possession of this skill in no way requires personal belief in the tenets of any specific religion.

•   Novice: Participant

••   Practiced: Alter Boy

•••   Competent: Priest

••••   Expert: Professor

•••••   Master: Theologian

Possessed by: Missionaries, Priests, Pastors, Nuns, Theologians, Atheists.

Specialities: Women's (often called Theaology), Comparative, Liberation, Agnostic, Christian, Buddhist

Toxicology: You have a working knowledge

of poisons, their effects and antidotes. You can analyze a poison to tell where it came from, and mix a poison or antidote given time and equipment. You must have at least one dot in either Chemistry or Biology to acquire this Knowledge.

•   Novice: Dabbler.

••   Practiced: Detective, Mystery Reader.

•••   Competent: Pharmacist, Mystery Writer.

••••   Expert: Forensic Scientist, Emergency-Room Doctor.

•••••   Master: Assassin.

Possessed by: Mystery Buffs, Detectives, Pharmacists, Medics, Assassins.

Specialities: Venoms, Chemical Poisons, Plant-based Poisons, Analysis, Antidotes, Instant Poisons, Slow-Build Poisons, Undetectable Poisons.

ARCHETYPES

The following new Archetypes may be added to those in the **Vampire** rulebook if desired. Before you choose one of these as your Nature or Demeanor, get your Storyteller's permission first.

- **Autocrat:** You must have complete control of the situation, complete control over those around you and as much control over fate as you possible can. Control is the only thing you understand; it is what you worship. Authority is what you desire, and it is what you gain when you have control. The more authority you have, the more control you have gained. One hand feeds the other. Others may consider you domineering, but they just aren't up for the job — you are the only one who can do it.

— Regain one Willpower whenever you achieve complete control over a situation involving other individuals.

- **Autist:** You must hide your secrets from others. Even more importantly, you hide your true self. Anyone who understands you can hurt you, so no one must ever see the real you, no one can come close. Give away as little of yourself as possible — adopt a false personality if you like — but just make sure no one gets hold of the truth about you. Knowledge is power, and those who know you can do anything they like to you.

— Regain one Willpower point whenever another character confesses they are unable to understand you, and whenever someone makes a false assumption about you which gives you an advantage.

- **Avant-Garde:** You must always be in the forefront, always the first with a piece of news, a new dance or fashion trend, or a new discovery in the arts. Nothing pains you more than hearing news second-hand, or being told of a hot new band by someone else. New discoveries are your life, and you devote a great deal of time and effort to keeping up with things. After all, if you're not in the forefront, you're nowhere.

— Regain one Willpower point whenever you are first with a piece of news or some other significant discovery.

- **Competitor:** You are driven by the need to win at all costs. The thrill of victory is the only thrill that you recognize; it is the thing that drives you on. You see life as a contest and society as divided into winners and losers, and believe *all* the macho business proverbs - *if you're not lead dog, the view never changes; there are no prizes for second place; eat or be eaten.* You try to turn every situation into a contest of some kind — it is the only way you can relate to anything. You are capable of cooperating with others, but only by turning the group interactions into another contest: you must be the leader, or the most productive, or the most indispensable, or the best liked — anything so long as it means you win in some way or another.

— Regain one Willpower point whenever you win a contest of any sort, formal or informal. For truly impressive victories, the Storyteller may award more points.

- **Confidant:** You understand people, and more importantly you like them. You are a facilitator who listens and gives advice. People confess to you and in return you give them advice, most of it good (though sometimes it is more for you than for them). You are very interested in other people, and who and what they are. Personality fascinates you, as does the sickness and the beauty of human nature.

— You regain a point of Willpower whenever someone confides in you on a personal and intimate level.

- **Critic:** Nothing in the world should be accepted without thorough scrutiny and examination. Nothing is ever perfect, and the blemishes must be pointed out in order for the good of it to be truly known. Your standards are high for everything, and you insist on their being met. You encourage the same ideals in others, because laxity and low standards reduce the quality of life for everyone. They'll thank you later, once they discover the purity of their perspective. You seek out and expose the imperfections in every person or thing you encounter. You are never satisfied with anything which is less than perfect, unless it is within yourself – after all, you're not a perfectionist.

—Regain one Willpower point whenever you are able to discover a significant imperfection in any person or thing which has escaped the attention of others.

- **Jobsworth:** You are dedicated to the unbroken routine of your existence, and will refuse to do anything which compromises your routine and established practices. No matter how urgent or deserving an individual case may be, the preservation of established practices and routines is more important. Individual decisions and considerations are fallible, whereas routines and established procedures are the distilled wisdom of years or decades of decision-making. Routines are what separate order from chaos. Make an exception once, and it sets a dangerous precedent; make an exception twice, and you open the door to anarchy.

— Regain a Willpower point each time you are able to preserve your routine, and each time you avoid re-evaluating anything or making a decision about a situation based on its individual merits. At the Storyteller's option, more points may be awarded for truly impressive feats of generalization.

- **Honest-Abe:** You have a moderate temperament, and refrain from telling lies and stealing from others at all cost. You were brought up to live honestly and openly, and to be good to others — simple truths by which you have lived your life ever since. You are not a dogmatist, you do not insist that others live as you do, nor have you constructed a complicated set of rules for yourself. You are flexible in your behavior, but always carefully look at what you are doing to do right by your beliefs.

— You regain five points of Willpower if you are completely honest and it harms you or your friends in some way, but later it turns out to help you. In other words, your honesty turns out to have been the proper way to do things, even from a pragmatic point of view.

- ## Masochist: You like to push the boundaries and try to see how much you can take, how much pain you can tolerate before you collapse. There is a certain satisfaction gained out of suffering humiliation, depravation and even mutilation — especially when you are the cause of it, and have some control over it. You know that it is somewhat perverse, but you know you aren't crazy — this is just the way you are.

— Regain two points of Willpower whenever you suffer in a manner in which you have not before.

- ## Mediator: The world is full of people who want things; sometimes people want exactly the same thing. Some people have what other people want and would be willing to talk about working out a deal, but just don't know how to start. Owing to some peculiar quirk in human nature, these people often have immense trouble finding and communicating with each other. That is where you come in. You are dedicated to mediating between people — fulfilling needs, smoothing over disputes, anything where people need help in talking to one another. You are the diplomat, the middle child, the perpetual person in the middle.

— Regain one point of Willpower whenever you are able to act as a go-between between two individuals or groups, and regain two points if you bring things to a satisfactory conclusion. The Storyteller may award more points for particularly outstanding mediation.

- ## Perfectionist: You can't stand imperfection, not in others and certainly not in yourself. Neither can you tolerate those who do not do everything they can to do their best, to make everything neat and proper and right in their lives. Though you may be strict with others, it is with yourself that you are most critical — everything must always be in its place, and you must always do the best and be the best.

— Regain a point of Willpower whenever you accomplish something flawlessly, without a single mistake, falter, wound, hesitation, confusion, hindrance or obstruction.

- ## Poltroon: Meeting trouble (or anything else) head-on is the tactic of fools and optimists. The sensible way to deal with trouble is to deny it a target. While some people might accuse you of sticking your head in the sand, they do have to admit that it has remained on your shoulders for quite some time, and looks like it will continue to do so indefinitely. You never confront when you can evade, and never face anything unless there is no other option. Courage is not high on your list of virtues, but then the line between courage and folly is virtually nonexistent to your eyes.

— Regain one point of Willpower whenever you are able to avoid a problem or situation without dealing with it.

- ## Optimist: Everything always turns out for the best; that is your simple motto of your life, and you know if you can just keep cheerful and stop worrying your problems will never be with you forever. Some call you a fool, but even they have to admit you're happier than they are. Certainly you'll encounter difficulties from time to time, but there's no sense in worrying yourself to death in advance. Don't worry, be happy, and have a nice day.

— Regain a Willpower point whenever things turn out for the best, just like you said they would. You must predict it, either out loud to the other characters, or to yourself (tell the Storyteller).

- ## Pedagogue: You've been a few places, seen a few things, and picked up a thing or two along the way — and you'd like to tell everyone about what you've learned. Teaching is your avocation, if not necessarily your profession. In your time you've seen inexperience and ignorance lead to all kinds of misery and misfortune, and it pains you too much to stand by and watch it occur. You are dedicated to passing on what you have learned for the benefit of others — not only skills and knowledge, but the less tangible assets of wisdom and experience as well. If given the chance you can go on for hours, relating to others of much of wisdom as you can.

— Regain one Willpower point whenever you see (or discover) that someone has benefited by something you taught or showed them.

- ## Penitent: You are unworthy. You are sinful. You are base, vile, and lacking in virtue. You have no right to exist and are utterly without hope. Either because of a low self-image or because of a spectacular trauma in the past, you have to spend your life making up for what you are, what you lack, what you have done. You owe it to Creation at large to make some kind of amends for the crime of your existence. Your daily struggle is to make up for your weakness, and your daily dream is to be able, at last, to overcome it. But you know you are weak and beyond hope.

— Regain one Willpower point whenever you are able to do a good deed for someone to whom (in reality or in your imagination) you have been an inconvenience, annoyance, or danger. For particularly outstanding acts of penitence or recompense, the Storyteller may award two or even three points.

- ## Praise-Seeker: You get your self-worth entirely from others. You crave approval and praise, and will go to extreme lengths to get it — even risking yourself and things you love if necessary. Unlike the Sycophant, you do not think of protection, and you have no thought of using others' good opinions to your own advantage — you simply crave their praise and approval for its own sake, so that you can feel good about yourself.

— Regain one Willpower point whenever another character offers unprompted praise, admiration or appreciation. If the appreciation is truly great, and/or the other character is powerful or particularly admired, the Storyteller may award extra points.

• Simpleton: You are a naive, unsophisticated thinker, and have no time (or ability) for subtlety, deceit or duplicity. You take everything at face value, have a tendency to believe everything you're told, and rarely see any hidden motives in others. Surprisingly to some, you survive very well without the plots, lies and stratagems which others seem to need.

— Regain one Willpower point whenever you are able to survive a set-up, plot or stratagem without even seeing it coming. If it's a particularly obvious or far-reaching plot, or if you never notice it at all (but suffer nothing by failing to notice it) the Storyteller may award extra points.

• Slob: It's not that you're lazy. But effort is a precious thing, and not to be wasted. A lot of people spend a lot of time and trouble doing things they don't need to do. Their houses are cleaner than a hospital (when's the last time anyone died of cholera or diphtheria in their home, for pity's sake?), they keep tidying (and they'll only have to get the things back out of the closet next time they need them), and they criticize you for not wasting your effort in this way. But answer this — who is it gets ulcers and stress-related angina? Things have a way of coming around, so why worry? Why stick your fingers in and risk making things worse? Relax — save your energy for when it's really needed.

— Regain one Willpower point whenever a problem or situation resolves itself without effort on your part.

• Sycophant: In the grand scheme of things, you are small and weak and not fit for survival. Your best hope is to find someone who is more powerful than you are and persuade her to take care of you. In return you will serve her, will admire her and follow her. You will do anything she says, unless it puts you in great risk. In any type of uncertain situation, you will attach yourself to the strongest-seeming person, siding with her, performing various barely-necessary services and generally trying to ingratiate yourself and earn some kind of protection. There is no limit to the depths to which you would lower yourself in order to be accepted, and you have no pride.

— Regain one Willpower point whenever a stronger character to whom you have attached yourself acts in your defense, be it siding with you in an argument or protecting you from physical harm.

DISCIPLINES

While the basic **Vampire** rules only allow characters to start eighth generation or younger, the evil of diablerie gives them the opportunity to drink the power of their elders. Though most Vampires, be they Neonate or Ancilla, have little chance (or need) for levels of power beyond the five included with each Discipline, the mere possibility of decreasing one's generation means that at some point someone, somewhere, will undoubtedly have a Discipline higher than 5th level.

It is also imaginable that some of you may be participating in Chronicles where the Storyteller wants you to start as Elders. For these Undead, the ability to have their disciplines go far beyond those of their younger Kindred is a necessity. Such characters would certainly have the chance to have 6th, 7th, or perhaps even 8th level Disciplines.

Higher levels of disciplines differ greatly from the earlier ones. As reflections of the Clan founder, the first five rankings are standard for all members of the Blood Lineage. When Kindred become powerful enough to go beyond these rankings, however, their disciplines begin to reflect their own inner natures. Thus characters capable of achieving each ranking from six to ten have a variety of abilities available to them at each level. When they have had the experience necessary to obtain these powers, they may choose whichever power of that level they feel best fits their character.

Also, as characters continue to progress in their disciplines, they may choose from any power of the rank they are achieving or lower. Thus when the fifth-generation Nosferatu Petrondon, with six levels of Obfuscate, has an additional 18 experience points available, he can choose any of the six or seven point Obfuscate powers or he can develop one of his own more suited to his inner being. Then, when he gets 21 more points, he can develop either a six, seven or eight-point power. He cannot spend just 15 points to continue to buy six-point powers.

There is something of a sadistic side to all this. In most Chronicles no player will ever come near to having a 10th level discipline, yet we list the 10th level powers to all the disciplines. For more than any other reason, we want to make you much more aware of what you might be going up against. You are indeed a creature of considerable power, but your elders are even more powerful, and that fact you must never forget.

These higher level powers are extreme, and as the level increases they grow even more grossly obscene. However, those of the early generations are vastly potent creatures, so these powers are not out of line. Only a very few individuals in the world would have Dominate ten, and you never want to meet one who does.

These are not all of the higher powers available. Indeed, the number of different higher level powers is limited only be the number of individuals who have reached such levels of power. Do not assume you will see these particular powers in use by characters who you meet, as your Storyteller will more than likely invent new powers for each character. You'll receive little advantage in knowing what powers your enemies may possess — but you will get a lot of frustration, as it will take you a long time to attain 6th level in any Discipline, if you ever do.

Note that higher levels of the physical disciplines (Celerity, Fortitude and Potence) do not have particular new benefits at higher levels. The potential to have up to 10 points added to one's strength is easily benefit enough.

Animalism

Level Six:

Species Speech: When using Song of the Beast, the character can only communicate with one animal at a time and must maintain eye contact for the entirety of the interaction. Species Speech allows the character to communicate with an entire group of creatures at once. A single success on a roll of Charisma + Animal Ken (difficulty of 8) indicates the character has established a level of communication similar to the one obtained through Song of the Beast.

1 success	May understand the animals' group dynamics (herd leader, basic motivations, etc.)
2 successes	May talk "baby-talk" with the animals
3 successes	Basic communication is possible and the character can expect responses to straight-forward questions.
4 successes	Complete communication up to the animals' potential is possible.
5 successes	Complete communication with the full trust of the animals. They will not mislead the character.

The character can only address one species at a time (i.e., she could talk to rats but not mice at the same time) and they must all be within ear-shot. Should she be interrupted by anything other than the group being communicated with, or voluntarily stop her sermon during this time, she will have to roll to reestablish contact with her former listeners, some of whom may well have run off by that time.

Shepherd's Innocence: While not all animals run away at the slightest approach from a Vampire, the relations between Kindred and most animals are far from the best. Dogs tend to bark in their presence, cats leave the room and horses will often throw them. On the other hand, animals find those Undead with Shepherd's Innocence not only inoffensive but extremely attractive. By using this power (Charisma + Animal Ken with the difficulty determined by emotional state of the animal), a character can quickly calm a charging lion, gain the trust of growling guard dogs and ride happily on the back of a wild elephant. If enough successes are obtained, the character may attempt nearly any sort of activity with the creature, supernatural or otherwise (this makes feeding from them absurdly simple).

Animal Succulence: The hunt for blood is one of the defining factors of a Vampire's existence. When first Embraced, many Kindred try to limit their feeding to non-sentient beasts, hoping to thus preserve their fast-fading Humanity. Most quickly find this mode of existence unsatisfying, and soon use nothing but humans for their Vessels.

Those with mastery of Animal Succulence, however, find animal Vitæ to be exceptionally nourishing. One of the few powers which does not require a roll, Animal Succulence allows a character to effectively double the Blood Pool size of an animal. Thus a cow would have 10 Blood Points for a character to drink. Note that this power is not transferable, and the cow would still only be worth five Blood Points to any other character.

Shared Soul: This power allows the character to momentarily share experiences with any one animal he can touch. While both beings maintain both freedom of thought and action, everything they sense, the emotions they feel and even their hopes and fears are felt by the other. Moreover, the memories of each are shared, and if enough time is spent in this state, both will know everything about the other (of course, much of one's experience will make no sense to the other, and may even cause temporary confusion once the experience is over).

Use of this Discipline requires a Perception + Animal Ken roll against a target of 6. Every turn after the first in this joint state requires the character to spend a Willpower point. It usually takes two turns to locate and extract a precise memory, and about five turns to completely share souls.

Level Seven:

Conquer the Beast: Those Kindred with the Animalism Discipline often have a greater understanding of the Beast within than do other Vampires, and those with the ability to Conquer the Beast seem to have the best understanding of all. With this power, the character can not only enter Frenzy at will, but maintain complete control throughout.

While the character no longer requires potentially deadly stimulus to enter this state, she must make a straight Willpower roll against a target of 7 to Frenzy. For every turn the character maintains this state, she must spend one Willpower point. When she runs out of Willpower, the Frenzy ends. The character can end it sooner if desired.

A failure on the targeting roll indicates Frenzy was not achieved, while a botch means Frenzy was entered but the character has no control over it and may not attempt to ride it in the normal fashion. More botches mean there is potential for Derangements (Storyteller's option).

Master's Voice: Like Species Speech, but the character can communicate with all animals within range of his voice no matter what their type. The difficulty and levels of success are the same as those with Species Speech, and the same interruptions will stop this power as well.

Level Eight:

Twin Spirits: Similar to the fifth-level power Sharing of Spirits, this power allows the character to take complete control of an animal as though he were inside it. While he controls the animal, however, he can also move about freely in his own form. Taking control of the animal requires a Manipulation + Intimidation roll, and the number of successes determine the amount of time the character can maintain this split personality.

1 success	up to one hour
2 successes	up to six hours
3 successes	up to one day
4 successes	up to one week
5 successes	indefinitely

Since the character maintains his own form while controlling the animal, he does not have to worry about taking on the animal's characteristics after the connection is broken. Since the character is maintaining two different forms, however, he does suffer distractions from the competing sensory input. In effect, the difficulty level of any roll he must make while controlling both forms is raised by one.

Mass Summons: This power allows the character to summon all animals around to her. While this does not place them under her control, the use of other Animalism abilities should be enough to ensure their aid. Even if this is not the case, the summoned animals will be unlikely to hurt the summoner. Additionally, the summoner can, if she desires, specify the types of animals she wants to respond, thus calling dogs and rats, but no cats.

Summoning these animals requires a Manipulation + Leadership roll against a difficulty of 7. Every success means a wider area has been affected. The distances are divided up depending on whether the summons is made in a city or wilderness area.

1 success	All summoned animals within one city block/half mile respond unless there is something actively preventing it (i.e., a dog's master says stay) or it is a ghoul.
2 successes	All summoned animals within two blocks/one mile respond unless it would be life threatening to do so or the animal is a ghoul.
3 successes	All summoned animals within five blocks/five miles respond unless it would be life threatening to do so or the animal is a ghoul
4 successes	All summoned animals within a half mile/seven miles respond unless it would be life threatening to do so.
5 successes	All summoned animals within 1 mile/10 miles respond.

Level Nine:

Flesh Bond: By the time a Vampire can develop this level of Animalism, they have formed an extraordinary bond with the "lower" creatures. Thus they can actually mesh their physical form with those of non-sentient beasts. With a roll of Stamina + Animal Ken (difficulty 7), the character can actually suck smaller animals into his very being and release them again at will. Each creature thus held uses up one of the character's blood points for every five points in its blood pool. Thus a character can bond with 10 rats (at 1/2 a blood point each) at a cost of one of his own blood points. This point of his blood pool will not be available for storing blood again until the character releases the animals.

While the character cannot physically absorb larger creatures, he can meld his body with theirs on a Stamina + Empathy roll (difficulty 7) at a cost of one Blood Point. Thus, he can slide his body into that of a charging Kodiak Bear and move around during the day within it. Those with Auspex can make a roll to see if they notice anything unusual about a character or animal that has "riders." Note that the character has no control over the animal in this state unless he has also used Shared Spirits on it and has it currently under his control.

Level Ten:

Army of Beasts: Not only can the character summon all the creatures within a certain area, but she becomes one with each of them. While her body remains stationary, she takes control of each animal summoned as though she were that animal. In effect she becomes both General and Soldier, seeing through the eyes of whatever horde of creatures she has called up, but requiring no special concentration to control them — they are her and she is them. The area of animals she controls is defined by the number of successes rolled on a Leadership + Survival roll. One success means the character can summon all animals within one mile. Each additional success doubles the previous level. Thus with five successes the character can summon and become all animals within sixteen miles.

Auspex

Level Six:

Telepathic Communication: While normal telepathy only allows a character to "read" someone's mind, Telepathic Communication allows her to read a target's mind, hold a conversation with it and even transmit images, emotions and sensory input to anyone she can see. Normally this form of communication requires the character make a Charisma + Empathy roll against the target's current Willpower, but if the target of the communication knows what the character is attempting, he can voluntarily waive his resistance and allow the character to engage in this communication without a roll.

Clairvoyance: The character can see and hear events at a distant place without the need for Astral Travel. This power is more-or-less instantaneous — like turning on a television — and the character need only concentrate on a familiar place or person to become a fly on the wall, seeing and hearing all that goes on with that place or person. The player must make a Perception + Empathy roll to 'tune in' successfully.

The character can also use other Auspex abilities in conjunction with Clairvoyance. Thus a character could look into a forest clearing and then read the aura of the werewolf hiding there. Each power is adjudicated separately, and may be rolled separately as well.

The Dreaming: The character can remain aware of events around him while asleep or in torpor. These dreams are filled with images of things which might affect the character, but they are often hard to interpret. The only distance limit for this power lies with the Storyteller's discretion. Essentially, the character should be able to dream about any event which would have a serious impact on his existence.

Eagle's Sight: This is a less-selective form of Clairvoyance. The character can mentally look down over a wide area as if from the air, allowing very rapid searches to be made or very large areas to be looked at. If the character also has Clairvoyance, it may be used to 'zoom in' to a particular location. The area covered is about 16 square miles (a radius of about two miles), and the apparent altitude is around 250 feet. It is not possible to look through solid objects using this power.

Prediction: This is the power to predict what people will say and sometimes do next. By making a Perception + Empathy roll against the target's current Willpower, the character can determine what the target will say next. With three successes, the character can also determine the other's next actions.

Sense Emotion: With this power, a character can extend her Aura Perception over an area. The character can sense the emotions of as many people as she desires within a 10 foot radius. A Perception + Empathy roll is necessary to use this power; the difficulty is 7, reduced by 1 for every dot above six in Auspex. The general mood, motivations and temperament of the crowd can be felt, and a sense gained of what direction it might be going. Most importantly, the emotional nexus of the crowd, its chief instigators and leaders will be identified by this power (the "hot" spots).

Level Seven:

Soul Scan: The character can discover the location of anyone he knows, wherever the target may be in the world. Roll a number of dice equal to Perception + Investigation with a target of 6 plus the quarry's Obfuscate.

Spirit Link: With Spirit Link, the character can engage in telepathic communication with a number of people. Every success on a Wits + Etiquette roll with a difficulty of 6 allows for one more person to be "hooked up." Everyone thus engaged can communicate at their leisure with all the others in the Spirit Link. Anyone else in the link can hear what is said as well. However, this power does not allow for mind reading.

Level Eight:

Psychic Assault: This aggressive form of Telepathy allows the character to force her way into the subject's mind and use telepathic force to cause actual damage. The telepath must make a roll of Manipulation + Intimidation, which is resisted by the target's Willpower (each of which has a difficulty of 8). The result depends on the number of net successes over the target's roll.

Botch	The target becomes immune to that Kindred's Psychic Assault for the remainder of the night.
Failure	The target is unharmed, and may make a Perception + Occult roll to realize that a psychic attack has taken place.
1 success	The target is shaken, but not physically harmed. The target loses one Willpower point and may need to make a Courage check, at the Storyteller's option. If Willpower is reduced to zero, the target is rendered unconscious.
2 successes	The target is badly scared, losing 3 Willpower points and needing to make a Courage check with a difficulty equal to the Vampire's Auspex score. If Willpower is reduced to zero, the target is rendered unconscious.
3 successes	The target loses 6 Willpower points and must make a Courage check with a difficulty equal to the Vampire's Auspex score. If Willpower is reduced to zero, the target is rendered unconscious and wakes up with a Derangement.
4 successes	The target loses all Willpower points, lapses into unconsciousness and gains a Derangement. The target's maximum Willpower score is halved permanently.
5 successes	The target must make a check against current Willpower or die; if the check is successful, treat the result as 4 successes.

This power cannot affect Vampires unless an extra Willpower point is spent.

Omniscience: The character immediately gains a complete understanding of the personality and identity of all those around him. On a Perception + Empathy roll against

a difficulty of 6 he understands emotions, hopes, fears, what individuals truly are (Kindred, kine, Werewolf, Magus, potential Magus, etc.), whether spirits are present, what type they are and anything else the Storyteller figures he should know. The cognizance of this information is immediate and absolute, he understands them as well as they understand themselves (at least in the moment). The limits of this extraordinary power can only be determined by the Storyteller, who should base the information gained on the number of successes that were obtained (only five successes or more would provide complete and fully accurate information, otherwise you may sense what they think they are, rather than what they truly are). Obfuscate can block the working of this power, as anyone of equal or greater level than the character's Auspex is automatically immune to it.

Level Nine:

Precognition: This power allows a Vampire to see through time as well as space. By making a successful roll of Intelligence + Alertness against a target of 8, the Vampire can see the place she is in, or a place she knows, as it will be in the future *provided no Vampire or other supernatural entity (or mortals controlled by such) takes direct action which alters that future (some exceptional mortals may also be able to change things).* The distance into the future depends on the number of successes rolled.

1 success	1 hour
2 successes	1 day
3 successes	1 week
4 successes	1 month
5 successes	1 year

As with all rolls, even more successes can mean even greater reach at the Storyteller's discretion. The information gained is usually fairly hazy, and is not self-explanatory. The character simply comes to understand what might take place in a specific place at a specific time. Keep in mind that this power is not exact. Rather than actually reading the future, this power identifies what might happen if all the current circumstances do not change. This power, however, can provide excellent guidance on where to focus one's actions, for it describes what factors will be of significance in the future.

Level Ten:

Pulse of the Canaille: A variation of the earlier Precognitive power, Pulse of the Canaille allows the character to sense not only what will happen in a certain place and time, but the current moods, trends and attitudes direction in which entire groups of mortals are heading. Even more valuable, is the capacity, with this power, to sense who influences or controls the groups of mortals and often the identities of these secret masters. The character must make a Humanity roll with a difficulty dependent on the size of the group being studied.

6 Difficulty	Organization
7 Difficulty	City
8 Difficulty	Region

anything of their person which they are in contact with and think of as their own) is effective.

Loyalty: Those whom the character has conditioned are made resistant to the Domination of others. Add five to their Willpower for resisting new Dominations.

Rationalize: Those whom the character Dominates are convinced their actions are entirely their own, and were right and proper under the circumstances. This requires a successful Manipulation + Subterfuge roll resisted by the target's Wits + Self-Control (difficulty of 7). The effects of this power depend on the number of successes obtained.

1 success	They will not believe that they have been dominated, at least at first.
2 Successes	They believe that their action are their own, but will begin to suspect something after time has gone by.
3 Successes	They will insist their actions were entirely their own, but can be talked out of it, given time.
4 Successes	They are convinced that every action they have taken was done of their own volition, and can only be talked out of it if shown absolute and convincing evidence.
5 Successes	Nothing can make them think that everything that they have done is not of their own volition no matter what evidence is presented. They will become enraged if the point is pressed too far.

The character may still choose that a victim should be aware of the Domination, if so desired.

Tranquility: This is a subtle power, unlike other forms of Domination. Only a few Kindred possess it, and your Storyteller may decide to restrict access to it. A character with this power may calm a Vampire who is in Frenzy without the Vampire losing Willpower. The Frenzying Kindred makes a Humanity roll against a target of 6. Each success lowers the difficulty of the Willpower roll the character must make as normal to end the Frenzy. Five successes means the Frenzy is overcome completely, and a botch leads them to attack the character who was trying to calm them. The power can only be attempted once on a character who is Frenzying.

9 Difficulty	Country
10 Difficulty	Entire world

The number of success obtained, indicates how much is known, and also how tightly, and in what ways, the groups of humans are controlled. If they are influenced by more than one supernatural creature, you will gain a sense of all of them.

1 success	You sense the mood and attitudes of the group.
2 successes	You also sense the group's future and potential.
3 successes	You know the extent to which they are controlled.
4 successes	You sense the aura of that which controls them.
5 successes	You know who is controlling them, and why.

Dominate

Level Six:

Obedience: The character may use the other powers of Domination without the requirement of eye contact. A touch is all that is required, and even the touch does not necessary have to be maintained (as long as the Domination does not last more than a single conversation). Skin to skin contact of some sort is not required, though touching their clothing (or

Level Seven:

Mob Rule: This power allows the character to attempt to Dominate more than one person at a time. For every extra success over the needed amount to Dominate the first victim, the character can Dominate one other person. This power does not require eye contact after the first target has been dominated.

Level Eight:

Far Mastery: This power is similar to the level six power of *Obedience*, except that even touch is no longer necessary so long as the character knows the location of the person to be Dominated. This power allows a Vampire to use any Domination power from a distance. The subject must be known to the Vampire, and a roll of Perception + Empathy must be made to establish contact. The use of Domination may then proceed as though the two were in eye contact. This power cannot affect Vampires, unless an extra Willpower point is spent.

Level Nine:

Best Intentions: Someone dominated through Best Intentions requires no specific commands. Instead, he will always act in the character's best interests until the domination is broken (see below). Similar to the Blood Bond, it differs in that the dominated individual does not have to guess at what the controller would want him to do in specific situations — he knows.

Best Intentions requires the character make a Charisma + Intimidation roll resisted by the target's Willpower roll. The hold is broken when the target gains either a permanent point of Willpower or a point of Humanity.

Level Ten:

Puppet Master: The character is able to Dominate another so completely, that they will act as if they are the character, taking actions just as the character would. They have become, in fact, the dominator, and his personality has been infused into them. A type of link is maintained between the two so that the Puppet is intuitively aware of what the Master needs and desires. A Charisma + Empathy roll must then be made, resisted by the target's Willpower (difficulty of 9). The number of successes indicates how much the target has subsumed the Puppet Master's personality into their own. This power can be attempted only once per year on a single individual, and failure does count as an attempt.

1 success	Confusion reigns, but on occasion they will take an action as the character would have them do.
2 successes	Schizophrenic, they are half and half (and very confused).
3 successes	With occasional (but severe) lapses, they think as would the character.
4 successes	They consistently behave and think as the character would, but not always.
5 successes	They are the character; it is as if there were two of them. The player can, in fact, play both characters as if they were one.

Obfuscate

Many of these Obfuscate powers can be seen through by another Vampire with Auspex even if they cannot be by mortals. Only those with an Auspex equal to or greater than your Obfuscate powers have any chance to do so. Those that are so fortunate must make a resisted roll using appropriate traits (as determined by the Storyteller).

Level Six:

Mind Blank: The character is able to conceal her mind as well as body. On a successful roll of Intelligence + Subterfuge, the Vampire becomes completely impervious to any sort of Telepathic contact (see *Auspex* above and in the **Vampire** rulebook). The blank may be overcome if the telepath successfully opposes the Vampire's initial mind blank roll with a roll of Perception + Empathy. Even if the telepath manages to penetrate the Mind Blank, he may use no more dice for his Auspex than he had additional successes in the penetration.

Conceal: The character may conceal a non-living object, up to the size of a house. The character must be touching the object or within 30 feet of it, and it must have some emotional attachment to her. The object is concealed as if by the power of Unseen Presence from the **Vampire** rulebook. Concealing an object such as a crate, casket or truck also conceals its contents. A concealed object may be discovered by accident if someone walks into it.

Soul Mask: Even with One Thousand Faces, Aura Perception can allow a Kindred to tear right through a character's disguise and see his true self. With Soul Mask, however, the character can choose an aura to hide his own. He can conceal his Vampiric nature, make himself seem completely innocent or more vile than he has any right to be. However, he can only choose one color to mask his true aura with unless he re-buys Soul Mask at a later level. Thus, with six points in Obfuscate the character could make his aura blue-white. With seven points he could make his aura blue-white or pitch black.

Level Seven:

Cache: This power allows a character to maintain any other power of Obfuscation while absent. The character must be present to conceal people, places or objects in the first place, but can then leave without the concealment being dropped.

Cloak: Just as Mind Blank allows a character to hide the psyche, so does Cloak allow her to conceal her aura from those using that Auspex power to search for her. The searcher must roll more successes on a Perception + Empathy roll with a difficulty of 8 than the concealer has on a Wits + Subterfuge roll with a difficulty of 6 in order to spot her. If spotted, the aura can be read normally.

Level Eight:

Old Friends: On a Manipulation + Acting roll, the character can cause someone else to believe she is someone different — someone the viewer would like to see. Not only will the viewer not question the character's presence, but he will likely divulge information he otherwise would not and will generally treat the character with a great deal of warmth.

Level Nine:

Create Name: Not only does the character appear as someone else using this power, but he almost actually becomes a new person by creating an entire new mindset and aura, thus allowing himself to masquerade in almost complete safety. Telepaths reading his mind will read that of the assumed identity unless six successes are obtained and aura readers will see the created aura unless they also roll six successes.

Level Ten:

Memories Fading Glimpse: With this power, a Vampire can erase all traces of her existence from the annals of time and mind, leaving absolutely no evidence that she ever was — everyone simply forgets about her. Once this power is taken, the character simply disappears from living memory, and not even her friends or family remember her. The effect is automatic and complete and affects everyone in the world (except for those with 10 Auspex, or its magical equivalent). The character is not invisible, but is simply not recognized and not remembered.

Though written references do not vanish and videotapes do not go blank, no one will actually read the references or see the Vampire on the film (though years and years later the images and words will return to their consciousness). When the character meets someone who once knew them, she must roll Manipulation + Stealth roll with a difficulty of 8, the number of success obtained indicates who successfully they have been forgotten.

1 success	Remember that they know you, but only remember one very mundane thing about you. However, that might be enough to active their other memories if they pursue it.
2 successes	They know that they know you, but know nothing about you.
3 successes	"Don't I know you?"
4 successes	They look at you funny, thinking to themselves, "there is something funny about her."
5 successes	They don't even see you, the effect is still so strong.

The effects of this power, of course, means no one else will ever come after the character. A botch is something like a beacon, it sends a signal to anyone interested in the character, letting them easily track her down.

Presence

Level Six:

Love: Similar to Compulsion by Attraction, only much more compelling, this power duplicates the effects of Blood Bond for as long as the target is in the presence of the character. It requires a Charisma + Acting roll against the target's Willpower, but if successful the power allows the character an immense amount of influence over the victim.

Enrage: The Vampire's very presence causes those around him to begin feeling irritable and hostile (but only when the Vampire wishes to cause such reactions). The slightest spark will generally be enough to cause arguments and fights. Enrage requires a Manipulation + Subterfuge roll against a difficulty of 8 and affects a number of targets depending on the number of successes. All Vampires who are affected by this power, must use a Willpower point or fall immediately into a Frenzy. If the roll is successful again, another Willpower point must be used. The only way to avoid having to use a Willpower point is to leave the presence of the Vampire.

1 success	two people
2 successes	four people
3 successes	eight people
4 successes	twenty people
5 successes	everyone in the character's immediate vicinity

Level Seven:

Mind Numb: While Presence generally creates emotions in people, Mind Numb actually removes them. When a character uses this power, those around him lose the impact of whatever emotions they were feeling and go numb. They lose all motivation or reason for action and will tend to do nothing. They will continue any rote task to which they have been habituated, and will even begin such tasks if left with nothing else to do (thus they might begin to vacuum if that is what they were doing a short time before). While this power does not lower their Intelligence, they have nothing to think about except whatever sensory input they are currently receiving. They will not react to anything but simple and immediate input (such as a hot object put in their hand) because they feel nothing about it. Therefore, they will not get angry at someone who yells at them, and will not become frightened if put in danger.

Mind Numb requires a Manipulation + Intimidation roll against the highest Willpower of the people being affected and the number of success indicates how many are affected. It lasts as long as the character remains in their presence. Other Vampires may resist the effect of this power by rolling Willpower (difficulty 8) if more success are obtained than the user received, then they are not affected.

1 success	three people
2 successes	six people
3 successes	fifteen people

Level Eight:

Invoke Frenzy: Like the sun or a flame, the character can send other Kindred into Frenzy at will. The type of Frenzy (Madness, Rage or Terror) must be chosen when the character uses this power, and is initiated on a resisted roll of Manipulation + Empathy (difficulty equal to the target's Willpower) versus the target's Virtue (difficulty of 7). A single success more on the character's part than the target's, indicates that the target has fallen into an immediate Frenzy

Level Nine:

Heart of the City: A character with this level of Presence has become so much a part of the life of the urban area she is in that she can affect the emotions of all who call it home. The character can make everyone in its confines feel whatever one way she wants them to (irritable, loving, trusting, hateful, etc.), though only in a subtle way. This power cannot cause everyone in a city to turn upon one another in rage — unless, perhaps, they were already in a state of great anger. Tourists are much less affected than the city's residents. Those with a close tie to the city, but living elsewhere, will be almost as powerfully affected as if they still lived there. The character must roll Charisma + Area Knowledge of the city being affected (difficulty of 10), and must spend a Willpower point before making the roll. The number of successes indicates how long the particular emotion that the character has broadcast will be felt. The character can end this affect at any time.

1 success	one minute
2 successes	ten minutes
3 successes	one hour
4 successes	one day
5 successes	one week

Level Ten:

Dream World: No longer merely tied to the cities, a character with this potent power can affect the dreams of everyone in the world (though she can focus on one city, or even one individual is she so wishes). The character can send symbols, themes, stories, images — anything she wants to, even nightmares. The broadcast is effective only on a successful Wits + Etiquette roll (difficulty 9). The number of successes indicates how profoundly people are affected by the dream.

1 success	Don't necessarily remember the dream, but it may affect them unconsciously.

4 successes	thirty people
5 successes	everyone in the character's immediate vicinity

Mask Empathy: Like Mind Numb, Mask Empathy removes emotions instead of creating them. However, where Mind Numb is a bludgeon, Mask Empathy is a scalpel, delicately cutting away at the ties between people. Essentially, it removes the links between people in the character's vicinity by cutting off emotional bonds. Lovers stop loving, friends care nothing for one another and alliances fade like fog. People will begin to behave like completely autonomous units, without any perception or desire for community. The character must make a Manipulation + Subterfuge roll against the highest Willpower of those being affected. Each success indicates the number of people affected. Other Vampires may resist the effect of this power by rolling Willpower (difficulty 8) if more success are obtained than the user received, then they are not affected.

1 success	one person
2 successes	three people
3 successes	six people
4 successes	twelve people
5 successes	twenty people

2 successes	They remember bits and pieces of the dream.
3 successes	It is firmly imbedded in their imagination, and parts of it emerge into consciousness over the day.
4 successes	The remember it all, and will brood upon it over the day.
5 successes	Many of them wake up screaming, the entire dream is forever engraved in their brains.

Protean

Level Six:

Flesh of Marble: Once this power is taken, the character's skin becomes as hard as stone while losing none of its flexibility. It is nearly impossible to cut or stake the character without proper equipment or preparation. Ten successes are needed to successfully stake the character in melee. The character suffers only half the normal damage from everything except fire and sunlight (in terms of total successes, round down) making soak rolls much easier to make.

Earth Control: No longer limited to just melding with the earth, the character can move through the earth as though she were swimming in water. The character must spend blood to enter the earth just like she does in Earth Meld, but can stay in and move around day or night. Chases under the earth can be resolved with characters making contested Strength + Athletics rolls.

Level Seven:

Homunculus: The character can create a three-inch-tall imitation of himself, by simply drawing it forth from deep in his mouth. This can only be done once a day, and the creature will only remain as long as it is fed one blood point per hour (it can only hold 3 blood points at a time). The Homunculus lacks disciplines, but it is in all other respects physically identical to its master. It is very loyal to the creator, doing anything asked of it (largely because it wants to live, and can only live if given its masters blood). Its personality is usually a warped version of the character's own, frequently expressing the most buried aspects of the character's true nature. It communicates in a small, pitiful voice, and is normally quite dutiful and doting. The Homunculus makes for an excellent guard while the character sleeps (though it cannot remain through the entire night, unless the character awakes at some point and feeds it more blood). The creature will be destroyed if it suffers 2 levels of aggravated wounds.

Form of the Ghost: While similar to Mist, this form lacks many of the disadvantages gained after transforming to air. In the Form of the Ghost, the character is still insubstantial, but she appears no different from her regular form. She can move as fast as she can in her regular form but is not affected by gravity, thus allowing for a version of flight. She does not require an opening to walk through barriers but passes through solid objects as though they were not there at all. Winds and storms have absolutely no effect on this form either.

Level Eight:

Movement of the Slowed Body: With this power, the character can move when he is not supposed to. Thus if the Vampire is in Torpor, has been staked or paralyzed, he can move. This movement is exceptionally slow, however, and any part of the body moved can only move at an inch per minute. This should be enough to allow the character to eventually remove that annoying stake, though it would take about an half an hour.

Level Nine:

Dual Form: Legends of Vampires being in many places at once are anything but rare, and may well be the result of a Kindred with the Dual Form power. When using this power, a character can split herself into two weaker forms, both of which act as though they were the original (thus allowing the player to control two identical characters).

The two forms are not as strong as the original, and all physical and mental attributes are reduced by one. Each form has half the Blood Pool of the original and can spend half as many Blood Points per turn. The two forms are not in contact with one another (unless the character has an appropriate Auspex power), but are intuitively linked — if one is in danger the other will know it.

The splitting of forms can be done more than once, thus it is possible for there to be four versions a Vampire, or even eight. However, the split cannot occur if it the character already has a zero in an attribute (thus it is not possible for Nosferatu to use this power).

The two forms can recombine only if they are touching, the process itself takes only a few minutes but can be quite grizzly to watch . The current blood pools of both are combined to form the complete character's blood pool. If the forms have spent a great deal of time apart from one another, it is likely that the weaker of the two will not want to recombine with the other as the weaker one always loses whatever unique identity it possessed. Thus the more powerful form may have to track it down, and force it to join (a most bizarre circumstance).

Level Ten:

Body of the Sun: With a great expenditure of Vitæ, the character can turn his body into an invulnerable ball of fire, burning and blinding all around him. With an immediate expenditure of three blood points and an additional two each turn, the character assumes the Body of the Sun. Anyone or anything touched by a Kindred in this shape reacts as though it had been burned by a bonfire with the heat of a chemical fire (difficulty 9, wounds of two on the resistance roll).

Almost anything around the character when she assumes this form is destined to be destroyed. Cainites, however, may have some chance to escape the deadly heat unless they are directly touched by it. It is almost impossible to combat it, and Kindred find it difficult to even look upon the character, (if they do so for more than a single turn they will be blinded for one hour).

While in this form, the character cannot be hurt by anything physical — whatever is not destroyed by the heat and flames passes safely through this gaseous form. The character maintains her old form and height, but her appearance cannot be determined. Finally, this form is completely resistant to any fire of equal or lesser intensity, and even sunlight will only affect the character if she botches a straight Stamina roll against a target of six.

Thaumaturgy

Thaumaturgy differs from other Disciplines in a number of ways, most notably the fact that none of the paths have more than five powers associated with them. Instead, the character can develop new paths and learn higher level rituals as they gain levels six to ten. Five of the more well-known paths are described here. Note: Paths only extend to the fifth level of power, and this is widely assumed to be their maximum, though only the most senior Tremere would know for sure.

Path of Conjuring

The ability to create things out of thin air is a traditional occult power, and those with Conjuring can do much more than pull a rabbit out of a hat. These conjured items differ from the real thing in a number of ways — most notably their lack of defects. Each item lacks defining characteristics. For instance, a wolf created using Summoning will have uniform patterns on its skin and a Mini Uzi brought to hand by Magic of the Smith will lack scratches, marks or personalized additions.

Note that nothing larger or heavier than the conjuror can be called into existence through this power, though the Tremere are said to have rituals allowing that. Also, the conjuror must have some familiarity with the object being summoned as it must be called out of her own memory. If the conjuror has never seen anything more than a picture of the thing to be made, then the Storyteller should increase the difficulty of the roll while intimate knowledge (conjuring your husband) may well have a decreased difficulty.

- • **Summoning the Simple Form:** With an expenditure of a Willpower point, the conjuror can summon up some simple inanimate object. The objects cannot have any moving parts and cannot be more complex than a flint dagger, a wooden stake or a featureless gold doubloon. The object requires the conjurer to spend a Willpower point per turn to keep it from disappearing. The object's quality depends on an Intelligence + Appropriate Ability roll (melee, metalworking, etc.) with a difficulty of 6. One success indicates an odd-looking, brittle object while five successes calls up one almost visually indistinguishable from the real thing and maybe even a little stronger.

- •• **Permanency:** At the cost of three Blood Points, the Vampire can conjure an object without a turn-by-turn expenditure of Willpower. The blood must actually be removed from the characters body and is then used up during the conjuration. This object is real, and will not disappear after a certain period of time — it is here to stay. Only simple objects, without moving parts can be conjured in this fashion. The object's quality depends on an Intelligence + Appropriate Ability roll (melee, metalworking, etc.) with a difficulty of 6. Once success indicates a flawed object while five successes calls up a nearly perfect one.

- ••• **Magic of the Smith:** This power allows the conjuror to create complex devices with movable parts. Guns, CD players or almost anything else can be called up using Magic of the Smith. The cost to conjure something using this power is five Blood points, and the object's quality and

reliability relies on an Intelligence + Appropriate Ability roll with a difficulty of 7. A gun made with only one success may well jam or even blow up in its creator's hand, while one made with five successes will work just as well as the real thing.

•••• **Reverse Conjuration:** This power allows the Vampire to attempt to dissolve someone else's conjuring. This requires the Vampire spend twice as much Willpower as the conjuror did to create the conjuring and to make a Willpower roll with a target of the creator's Willpower. As many successes are needed to reverse the conjuring as were gained in creating it, this can be done over a number of turns (as an extended roll).

••••• **Power Over Life:** While true life is still beyond the Vampire's capability, she can create simulacrums of the real thing through this power. The living beings thus summoned lack free will, emotions or creativity, but will intelligently follow the creator's instructions. Creating them requires an Intelligence + Empathy or Animal Ken roll, depending on what is to be summoned, at a cost of ten Blood points.

Even with Permanency, these creatures are too complex to maintain for long. Every day they are kept in existence they become a little more insubstantial, until by the end of a month they have faded into nothingness.

Neptune's Might

Vampire's generally have little to do with water as they no longer need to bathe or drink, but the liquid can still have a great effect on them. In legends, water has often had a restrictive effect on the Kindred, and some Thaumaturgists have duplicated some of these myths in magic.

• **Eyes of the Sea:** This power allows the character to look at past events which have occurred around a standing body of water as though he were that body of water. The number of successes made on a Perception + Occult roll determine how far back events can be seen.

1 success	One day
2 successes	One week
3 successes	One month
4 successes	One year
5 successes	Ten years

A body of water can be anything from a lake to a puddle. Obviously, oceans and rivers are not standing bodies.

•• **Jail of Water:** While this power must be used in the presence of a substantial amount of water, it can bind Kindred more effectively than steel chains. At the Thaumaturgist's command, enough water leaps from its resting place to completely cover the target, capturing Kindred and possibly drowning mortals. The character makes an Dexterity + Survival roll against a difficulty of 6. The number of successes she gets are the number of successes the jailed must make on a Strength + Potency roll with a target of 6 to break free. The target can only be held in one of these jails at a time. The Thaumaturgist can dissolve it at will.

- ••• **Dehydrate:** This path allows the character to cause wounds from a distance, pulling minute amounts of water from the victim's body. This power requires the character make a Willpower roll with a difficulty of 8 versus the target's Stamina + Survival (add in Fortitude if the victim has it) with a difficulty of 9. Every successes over the target's total number of successes causes the target to lose one health level. These wounds can be healed normally. Vampires do not loose body levels, but rather loose blood points at the rate of one for every success. The victim must also make a Courage roll against the number of successes rolled + 3 to take any action the next turn. Failure means the victim has been incapacitated by the pain.

- •••• **Flowing Wall:** One of the classic Vampire weaknesses of legend was their inability to cross running water. While this is only myth, those who can create the Flowing Wall have learned to create such barrier to the Undead. A standing body of water touched by the Thaumaturgist becomes impassable to Supernatural creatures (Vampires, Werewolves, etc.) on a Willpower roll plus the expenditure of three Willpower points. To break the barrier requires the intruder to make a Strength + Courage roll against a difficulty of 10. At least three successes are required, and they cannot be accumulated. Note that the Flowing Wall will also block its creator, though he can remove it at will.

- ••••• **Blood to Water:** This power allows the Vampire to turn an opponent's blood to water with but a touch. Fatal to many mortals, this can prove a great inconvenience to the Undead as well. It requires a roll of the Thaumaturgist's Willpower against the victim's Humanity + 3. Every success converts another Blood Point. This is almost immediately fatal to mortals. Besides destroying a Kindred's Vitæ, it causes a Cainite to lose the same number of dice to any rolls just as lost health levels do. The water is gone after the Vampire has slept, but the blood does not return.

Spirit Thaumaturgy

This Path of Thaumaturgy involves using spirits to do one's work, but if one fails, the cost is not only a point of Willpower, but also the enmity of the spirit. The Storyteller should decide what type of spirit the caster was attempting to use, and then have it plan to botch the character up sometime in the future.

This is the rarest path among the nine given here and in **Vampire**. Most commonly found only in the most primitive regions of the world, many who know this path learned the beginnings of it while they were mortal, for contact with spirits can be very hard for Kindred. There are also some Sabbat who know this Path.

- • **Evil Eye:** Similar to the first level ritual Curse, Evil Eye does not require a ritual. It only lasts for a Scene, but can be cast again and again on the same subject. The Storyteller should decide if cumulative bad luck can become permanent after enough castings — the character just has bad spirits following him around, and the spirits have become used to it.

- •• **Spirit Eyes ("The Sight"):** This power is very similar to Aura perception, but the character perceives spirits instead of auras. He sees them in the form they take: i.e. Fox spirits, Faerie plant spirits, etc. This includes Ghosts. He can also speak with them.

- ••• **Spirit Slave:** The character can demand a task of a spirit. The spirit has to be in the caster's presence. The spirit will perform the task, but not if it is beyond its powers. Recently dead can be forced into being Ghosts and haunt a location with this spell. However, in this case, it wears off after a while (Storyteller's discretion). For permanent hauntings, see Fetishes.

- •••• **Fetishes:** The character can force spirits to inhabit objects, or fetishes, she carries around with her. She can then use their powers anytime she wants, without casting this spell again. She can create Ghosts by first using Spirit Slave and then forcing the Ghost into an object which she buries or hides at the location. This will cost the caster an automatic Humanity loss.

- ••••• **Journey:** This spirit projection is similar to astral projection, but the spirit remains within the physical realm. The character's body remains in one place, generally guarded by a fetish, and her spirit travels about. The character can also be trapped into fetishes when in this state, and controlled by any spirit spell. Physical attacks have no effect on her. While the character cannot use any physical Disciplines (Celerity, Fortitude, Potence and Protean) while in this form, all the rest act normally. The spirit form is generally visible unless the character uses Obfuscate.

Elemental Mastery

Similar to Spirit Thaumaturgy, Elemental Thaumaturgy offers the Kindred control of the souls of inanimate objects. Often seen as control of the four elements (Water, Fire, Earth and Air), this path actually gives its followers the ability to manipulate all forms of insensate objects.

- • **Elemental Strength:** With this power, the Elementalist can increase all his physical attributes without the need of Blood Points. Instead he spends two Willpower and Strength, Dexterity and Stamina all increase by one. Each turn the heightened abilities are maintained, however, the Vampire must spend another Willpower point.

•• **Wooden Tongues:** While inanimate objects have only a limited concern in what goes on around them, Wooden Tongues allows a Vampire to at least get the impression of what the object has experienced. Its memory is limited and its feelings may be alien to the character, but it can give information of extreme value. This communication requires a Wits + Linguistics roll against a difficulty of 7. The more successes made, the more information received.

••• **Animate the Unmoving:** Chairs grab their occupants, doors swing open and closed and guns leap out of their owner's hands when this power is used. With a Willpower roll against a difficulty of 7, and at the cost of a Willpower point, the character may make an object within her line of sight come to life. An object cannot take action out of form (a door could not pick someone up and carry them across the street), but objects with legs can run, wooden stakes can twist out of hands and statues can mimic human life. The object maintains this mobility for as many turns as the character is willing to spend Willpower.

•••• **Elemental Form:** With this power, the character can take the form of some inanimate object of equal size and weight. This requires a Stamina + Repair roll against a target of 6 to see how good the change was. At least three success are required to allow the character to use any senses or Disciplines while in this form.

••••• **Summon Elemental:** Summon Elemental allows the character to summon one of the traditional Elementals of myth and legend. Beings of water, earth, fire and air come into existence within five feet of the character. These beings require the presence of some amount of their natural element in order to appear, and may or may not follow their summoner's instructions (generally a Charisma + Intimidation roll against a difficulty of 7). There are ru-mors of other Elementals which may be summoned other than the traditional four.

Corruption

The power to manipulate and warp others' forms and personalities can be looked upon as a natural one for the Tremere. Indeed, it is said one cannot be true master of this Clan without knowledge of this path, but then many things are said about the Tremere. The target needs to be within arm's reach of the caster for all of these powers.

• **Contradict:** The corruptor can make any individual say or do the opposite of what had been originally intended — but only in the moment. An arresting officer will let the prisoner go, a marriage proposal will turn into a bitter denunciation and a left turn will turn into a right turn. This requires a Manipulation + Subterfuge roll against the target's Willpower + 1.

•• **Disfiguration:** Just as One Thousand Faces allows a character to change his own appearance, so does Disfiguration allow a character to change someone else's. This requires a touch and an Intelligence + Disguise roll (difficulty 8). This will only change facial appearance, and the individual will otherwise remain the same. Nor-

mally this power is used to disfigure others, but it can actually be used to make them look better (or simply different). It is very difficult to make them look like someone else (raise the difficulty to 10)

Change Mind:
The number of successes achieved on a Manipulation + Empathy roll against the target's Willpower + 1 determines how long the corruptor can make the victim assume whatever one Demeanor is desired.

1 success	One turn
2 successes	One day
3 successes	One month
4 successes	One year
5 successes	Until some event occurs to make the victim change Demeanor involuntarily.

Cripple:
This power lets the corruptor effectively turn the target into a paraplegic on a successful Willpower roll against the target's Courage + 5. Note that Fortitude is also added to the target number if the victim has that Discipline. This effect lasts for a length of time according to the number of successes rolled

1 success	One turn
2 successes	One day
3 successes	One month
4 successes	One year
5 successes	Permanently

Corrupt Soul:
The number of successes achieved on a Charisma + Empathy roll against the target's Willpower + 3 determines how long the corruptor can make the victim assume whatever one Nature is desired.

1 success	One turn
2 successes	One day
3 successes	One month
4 successes	One year
5 successes	Permanently

THAUMATURGY RITUALS

Level One Rituals:

Purity of Flesh: This ritual allows the caster to cleanse his body of all foreign matter by sitting on the ground in a lotus position, surrounded by a circle of 13 sharp edged stones, and concentrating for 10 minutes. The ritual requires the expenditure of one blood point after which the caster's body and blood will be completely rid of impurities such as dirt, poison, alcohol and drugs (making it a good way to keep clean). It is important for the Kindred to be completely naked, including all jewelry, because the spell breaks all foreign substances down, leaving a nondescript ring of gray film around the place where he was sitting. If analyzed with the right equipment, the residue will show traces of the ejected material as well as the caster's blood. This ritual will clear the body of everything from slivers and bullets to prosthetic limbs and silicon implants, but is useless against diseases of the blood and any sort of mind control.

The Rite of Introduction: This is a method by which a Tremere announces her presence to the others of her clan in a city. When the caster recites a thirty minute incantation and speaks into a cloud of water vapor (such as steam or fog) a telepathic message is received by the Regent of the Chantry first and then by the others of the city's hierarchy in descending order. This ritual allows for a very short dialogue between the caster and each individual subject, but only the Regent of the Chantry is traditionally bound to answer. Thus, although the other Tremere will know of the caster's presence, the caster will only know of others at their discretion. This is a very old and formal ritual, and no longer as common as it once was; many of those of the newer generations aren't even aware of its existence. However, some Regents are very insistent that it be used when any Tremere enters "their" city, and tolerate no excuses if it is not done. This ritual can also be used as a distress call.

Engaging the Vessel of Transference: This is a ritual that empowers a container to draw blood from someone who touches it, replacing that blood with the Vitæ previously contained in it (generally that of the caster). Three hours are required, as well as the initial blood point to complete the enchantment. The container must be sealed after the caster's blood is deposited, and must be between the size of a cup and a gallon jug. The final step is to engrave an arcane symbol on the outside of the vessel; this rune can be understood to mean "change blood" with an Intelligence + Occult roll, difficulty 8, but it can be concealed with another surface. When someone touches the object, they simply feel a strange shivering sensation, and that is all. The object will continue to transfer blood each time someone (Kindred or kine) new holds it until it is broken open, so to keep a particular measure of blood inside it, it must be held with another object (gloves don't count). This ritual can be used to get a sample of blood from another for use in another ritual, or as an especially devious way of Blood Bonding someone.

Rebirth of Mortal Vanity: This ritual grants the caster the ability to grow her hair once again. It takes an hour of complex gesturing in front of a mirror for each inch that the caster wishes to grow, but such effort rewards the caster with immediate gratification. The only other requirement is a number of strands of hair from a different mortal child for each inch of hair to be grown. The caster can use this ritual on others, but they both must be in the mirror while the ritual gestures are made. The vampire's hair follicles again die after the ritual is finished, but the hair will remain at the new length until cut. If it is ever shorter than the length it was at the time of death, it will return to that length as normal. Those that were bald in their breathing days must remain so in undeath.

Incantation of the Shepherd: This is a ritual that takes a mere 15 minutes to perform. The caster needs to spin slowly in a circle while holding some sort of glass object over each of his eyes. He can locate all of his herd starting with the member who is closest to him and working out to the most distant. The Kindred must have tasted at one time or another the blood of each vessel to be located.

Level Two Rituals:

Blood Walk: This ritual allows the caster to trace the lineage of another Kindred. It takes a full three hours and a blood point of the subject to be traced. While the caster is in

a deep trance, the blood must be tasted, giving the caster knowledge not only of the Vampire's immediate Sire, but of successively older generations (a roll of Perception + Empathy, difficulty 6 is required, each success indicating a further generation discovered). Also, the caster automatically knows of any blood bonds the subject may have; Regnant or Thrall. Specific knowledge of each Vampire is obtained, including their true name, personality, and relation to the subject.

Ward Versus Ghouls: This ritual creates a mystic symbol that appears on an object that will protect it from ghouls, and transform it into a potent weapon that can be used against them. The caster must use a point of mortal blood, which is poured onto the object to be empowered — usually a small piece of treated parchment, a coin, or some other small object. In ten hours, the ritual is complete and the strange symbol appears, emblazoned on the object. Any ghoul who touches it will sustain a burning jolt (causing three dice of damage, at a difficulty of the ghoul's Stamina +Fortitude). As long as the ward is touching the ghoul, he will repeatedly take this damage, and once a ghoul has touched the ward, he must spend a Willpower point to touch it again. The warded object can be placed on an unbroken circle of any consistency and no ghoul will be able to cross into (or out of) the circle. One of the restrictions of the ritual is that the mystic symbol only wards *one* object. An example of this is when a Warlock places a ward on the side of a car; the ward would affect that panel of the door or fender and not the whole car. A final note: wards can be placed on bullets, but this should be done only to small caliber weapons (about .22 is a safe bet) so as to better the chance of the bullet not passing through the body (remaining in is the only way they will do extra damage). Even then, the ward symbol will probably be destroyed when the bullet is fired, because firing usually distorts the shape of the slug. In effect, a character must make at least five successes on her firearms roll for the ward to survive and be of use.

Donning The Mask of Shadows: This ritual enables the user to move about in a semi-visible shadow state that is perfect for night stalking. After a twenty minute chant, the caster can only be seen with an Intelligence + Alertness against the caster's Wits + Stealth. Auspex one reduces the difficulty of a person's chance to see the shady Warlock by three, and animals can automatically sense her. The ritual lasts the same number of hours as the number of successes in a Willpower roll.

Principle Focus of Vitae Infusion: This causes an object of the caster's choosing to corporeally alter in order to be infused with a point of his blood. The object must of a size that the Vampire can easily hold it in both hands, but can be as small as a pea. Of course one of the caster's own blood points must be used, and it takes four full hours to complete the proper series of incantations. Afterward, the object takes on a slightly more ruddy hue and is oddly slick to the touch. At any time when he is touching it, the Warlock who infused the object may release it from it's enchantment, causing it to begin disintegrating. In moments the object completely breaks down to an often disproportionate puddle of blood (the same blood point that went in), which can then be used in many ways. The best use of such a pea is to swallow it before allowing it to begin decomposition. Such an "infused focus" can be made for another Kindred, she simply must be present at the initial ritual (the blood point must still be the caster's). Many Tremere wear several pieces of infused jewelry as a safety measure.

Mourning Life Curse: This is a way to coax Vitae from a vessel without having to injure them in any way. The one hour ritual is performed ahead of time (it involves ingesting a small amount of crocodile blood), but is not completed. The spell is activated when the caster whispers the final power word in a hapless mortal's ear (the mortal needn't be pre-determined), causing them to begin crying tears of blood. Once it is done, the victim has no defense against the curse—they continue to cry/bleed until the caster looses sight of or removes his gaze from the subject. The effect is not very painful but is often quite traumatic, sleeping vessels will not necessarily awake because of it. The process is slow so it takes about five minutes to collect one blood point by this method. The only after-effect is slightly swelled capillaries around the subject's eyes, along with the normal effects of blood loss.

Level Three Rituals:

Ward Versus Lupine: This ritual works much the same as the Ward Versus Ghoul (level two ritual), but it affects werewolves. The only component needed is silver dust. Wards in general can be destroyed by most any normal means, but not by the being that it is versus; indeed, they can hardly bring themselves to come near it. There is no ward versus mortals.

Pavis of Foul Presence: This is sometimes referred to as "Our Ritual for the Ventrue" and is so tightly controlled a secret that it is supposedly unknown outside of the Tremere clan. This most specialized ritual was created (some say by Tremere himself) to combat the power of the Ventrue in the Camarilla. Any Presence discipline used against the caster is instead reversed to be felt by the offender. Thus, if the crafty Warlock was willed to panic and run, the Kindred who exercised his power will make whatever resisted roll is necessary against himself, more than likely turning the tables on the poor lick. Preparation takes a mere hour and the ritual will remain in effect until sunrise, but a blue silk cord must be tied around the neck of the caster for the spell to work and last.

Shaft of Belated Quiescence: This is a particularly vicious ritual that is cast on a stake that is meant for the heart of a vampire. In a five hour ritual, the caster must carve an ornate series of symbols onto a sharpened shaft of Ash wood, coat it with her blood, and blacken it in an oak wood fire. The darkened shard then becomes one of the most feared Kindred-slaying weapons known. A simple hit with the stake, even in the leg or arm, and the tip breaks off inside and begins burrowing into the defender's body, from where it will slowly begin working its way to the heart. The victim of this attack may not even know what is occurring until it is too late. The shaft will reach the heart in about one to ten days (roll a die) during which time the sufferer will only feel sharp pains now and then that grow closer together and more unbearable as the tip nears its un-missable target. Damage caused by the thing's journey isn't enough to remove wound levels from a Vampire, but it certainly will harm a mortal or ghoul. One of the only ways to be rid of the thing is to actually dig in for it — a very grisly process which won't necessarily work. The vile thing may actually seem to try to elude the operator, automatically burrowing away from the open wound. The "surgeon" does more and more damage as he digs deeper after it. Needless to say, it is a death sentence for a mortal and for a Kindred it may be as well, because who knows where they might be when they are immobilized...

Flesh of Fiery Touch: This ritual turns the caster's own skin into a protective trap. After the ritual is completed, any Kindred that touches the bespelled Warlock's flesh will receive a single point of aggravated damage in the form of a

searing burn. The damage can be resisted as normal with Fortitude, but if a Vampire continues to hold the caster, he will continue to take damage. The caster cannot do this damage by touching someone, however, he himself must be touched. Although this effect lasts until dusk the next day, it is not without its price; during the two or three hour ritual, the casting Vampire must consume a small burning coal, causing an aggravated wound (again, resist with Fortitude) as well as costing a Willpower point (to bring himself to do it). While the enchantment is in effect, the Kindred's skin takes on a subtle bronze tint (can be noticed by a straight Perception roll, difficulty 8, by a character doing some intense inspection of the Warlock) and is unnaturally hot to the touch.

Noncorporeal Passage: This allows the caster to become intangible and move about while still maintaining a slightly hazy image of himself. This means that the Kindred can travel unheeded through all obstructions, even walls. The caster is also impervious to most attacks as per the protean power "mist form." The drawbacks are: the caster must move in a straight line through objects and once she begins she must continue through; she cannot draw back. Thus, the vampire may not travel downward into solid ground — it would be a long walk. Also, the caster must have a piece of a broken mirror to hold her image as she moves noncorporeally. The ritual takes about an hour to prepare and will last a number of hours equal to the number of successes from a Wits + Survival roll; it can be canceled by shifting the mirror so that the caster can no longer see her reflection in it.

Level Four Rituals:

Ward Versus Kindred: This ritual works much the same as the Ward Versus Ghoul (level two ritual), but of course it affects vampires. The component needed is a point of Kindred blood.

Binding the Beast: This powerful ritual will pull a fellow Kindred out of Frenzy and even separate them from their Beast for a time. The ritual takes only ten minutes to perform, and the caster needn't see the subject, but the he must imbibe a full point of the Frenzied character's blood (it can have been drawn earlier) and push an iron spike through his own hand (causing two points of damage that can't be soaked). The subject suddenly emerges from Frenzy, often into an uncharacteristic passivity. In truth, his bestial side has been separated from his psyche for a time (equal in days to the number of successes in the caster's Manipulation + Empathy roll, difficulty being ten minus the subject's Humanity), during which the subject cannot Frenzy, may not regain Willpower, can only use one point of blood at a time regardless of generation, and cannot even feed without a Courage roll. In addition, the vampire must make a Willpower roll, difficulty 7, to use any Discipline. Legend is that some Kindred have been said to have starved into torpor upon undergoing this spell. The subject doesn't need to be in Frenzy, nor does she need to be willing, but can never be the caster himself.

Heart of Stone: This interesting ritual transforms the Thaumaturgist's heart to solid stone — completely stake proof. The rite consists of moulding a three-inch high earthen circle, about two meters in diameter on a stone surface (solid stone is preferred, flagstone is okay, concrete is unacceptable) with the caster then lying naked on her back in the center. A bare candle is placed on the chest, directly above her heart and allowed to burn until the wick is gone and the flame is smothered by the candle's own wax, which has melted all over the Warlock's chest causing one aggravated wound (can be soaked with Fortitude). The ritual takes a full seven to nine hours to complete, but lasts as long as the caster wishes. The effect has the following drawbacks and limitations: the caster cannot use Willpower, and if forced to use one (botching on a Thaumaturgy roll, for instance) the spell is immediately canceled; the caster's Conscience drops to one (zero, if it was already one); and the caster looses half her dice pool on all Empathy, most Social, and nearly any roll when she is trying to be nice.

Splinter Servant: This is one of the more horrific and bizarre of the rituals practiced by Thaumaturgists. This creation of another anti-Kindred weapon involves making a stake from the wood of a graveyard tree, or at least a tree that has nourished itself on the elements of the dead. After a two day gauntlet of incantation and preparation, the shaft is endowed with a form of limited, if dormant, life. At last, nightshade twine must be wrapped around the stake and sealed with wax to form a brittle sheath. If the sheath is torn off after that point, the enchantment is activated and whomever has released the servant must command it to attack someone, or it will attack the releaser. The stake then leaps into action, splitting apart and splintering to form makeshift limbs which it will use to propel itself toward its target at any cost. The little terror is relentless and will stop at nothing to impale its target's heart. It will continue trying until it has either succeeded or has torn itself to small pieces (which are inanimate — this will occur after three to five minutes). The splintering nature of the thing sometimes causes other side effects: often if it does impale its victim, it will continue splintering inside the heart, making it difficult to pull out, or maybe even leaving parts of itself behind (and still leaving the target immobilized). The Splinter Servant cannot be commanded to do anything other than attack, and it always goes for the heart, though it will not miss if it is not stopped.

Bone of Lies: This ritual requires a mortal bone, often a skull (it looks the most impressive), but even a string of teeth will do. The mortal must have been dead for at least two hundred years. The ritual can be performed in a single day, during which the bone must absorb ten full points of Kindred blood, leaving it a dark, dull red in color. Now the bone can be used to make whomever holds it tell the truth, much to her chagrin; every time she would have lied she tells the truth, like it or not. Each lie that the bone stops it absorbs, causing it to become blacker and blacker until all ten points of blood are used and it is completely black as sin (this is the reason that it is a "Bone of Lies" and not a "Bone of Truth"). The truth is, the ritual binds the spirit of the mortal to whom the bone belongs, and it is the spirit that forces the holder to tell the truth — a very degrading and cruel way to spend eternity. Although this fact is generally unknown, it is the reason that an anonymous bone is usually used; if the spirit is called forth it shall be a most malevolent and devious spirit as ever imagined, corrupted by the vile sins that have been forced upon it. This is also why the blackened bone is traditionally buried after use. The bone can never be reused for this ritual again.

Level Five Rituals:

Escape to a True Friend: This is a ritual that must be prepared ahead of time, but it can be of great use in a tight situation. A one meter circle must be burned into the ground, and many arcane symbols must be precisely placed about it. The entire process takes about three or four days and five of the caster's own blood points. Once this is accomplished, the caster alone may at any time step into the circle while repeating a friend's true name and be mystically transported to that friend. The Warlock will not suddenly appear before his friend, but will materialize someplace nearby where no one will be able to see him (usually within earshot of the friend's location). The enchantment will continue be reusable until the circle is broken or the symbols are marred.

Ward Versus Spirit: This ritual works much the same as the Ward Versus Ghoul (level two ritual), but of course it affects most ghosts and spirits. The component needed is pure sea salt. This is a basic ward and may not provide protection from some specific types of spirits.

Blood Contract: This ritual creates an unbreakable bond between the two parties of a contract. The contract must be written in the caster's blood and it takes about three days to complete. The ritual is finished when both parties sign the agreement in their own blood, after which they are impelled to abide by the terms as stated. The only way out is to complete your part of the bargain or burn the contract.

Stone Slumber: This ritual creates nearly impregnable protection for a sleeping Vampire. The caster must begin the ritual two hours before dawn at which time he will become solid stone. Just like a stone statue, the Kindred can be transported from place to place, even in direct sunlight, and will remain suspended in that state until the following sunset. Sleeping in this form does take three blood points instead of one. The Warlock is completely protected from staking and most types of flame and heat, but pieces can be broken off of him. Most kinds of mind communication and telepathy are impossible because the Thaumaturgist's mind is usually totally dormant.

One Mind of the Covens: This is a very exclusive ritual used by the Regent of the Chantry during a simultaneous communication between him and his equivalents across the world. He must engage in a one hour chant and make use of a silver mirror for the joining to be successful. This ritual is one of the main reasons that the Tremere clan is so controlled and organized — it allows the Elders to be supply current information of all the plots and schemes of and against the Clan.

Level Six Rituals:

Raise the Dead: This is a ritual that allows the thaumaturgist to do just that — bring the dead up to again dwell in the world of the living. This is not a "Resurrection" in the truest sense, however; the creature is not alive, nor is it undead, but it is in fact as dead as the day that it died. The corpse is animated by a spirit that the caster places within it in an eight hour ordeal involving black candle wax being poured over the throat and heart of the subject. The wax is what initially binds the spirit to the body, which must be branded on the forehead with a mystical symbol meaning "Debtor."

The entire ritual must take place in a circle of salt the diameter of the length of the corpse from head to toe, and in complete darkness, save for the candle light. The body used must be fresh enough to still have tissue remaining on the bones, for the bondage of the spirit lasts only while there is tissue (decomposition continues at the normal rate); thus the

Utter Destruction of Bonds: This is an incredibly powerful ritual, although many do not realize the extent of its potential, and must be used with discretion. This simple incantation takes a mere five to ten minutes to recite, but requires the caster's tongue to be removed, crushed and its blood and remains spread on the object to be affected. The tongue is removed at the very end of the ritual, so there is no point in cutting out and saving your tongues in your free time. This action unfortunately subjects the thaumaturgist to three aggravated wound levels that cannot be soaked whatsoever and he will not be able to speak for at least three days or however long it takes to regrow the tongue. It also costs the character a point of Willpower to bring himself to do it. However, this ritual will open any object and that object will never be able to be closed again. This includes manacles, hand cuffs, chests, boxes, windows, doors, safes, zippers, wounds, walls, books, eyes, mouths, throttles, holes in the earth, and the mouths of volcanoes. It will also open dimensional boundaries that are tied to physical objects and permanently destroy wards. Not included are blood bonds and mental domination or slavery. Storytellers must arbitrate in all cases.

Level Seven rituals:

Divorcing the Soul: This is a devastating ritual that separates one's spirit (the name is misleading) from their physical elements, although the spirit is kept imprisoned in the body. The affected individual cannot use or regain Willpower, all of her abilities drop to one, all Virtues drop to one, and she becomes almost incapable of creative thought. She has no motivation and little emotion (zero Empathy) and is twice as susceptible to mind attacks and control if Dominate, Presence or the like are used on her, and she has half the normal dice pool to resist.) She becomes lethargic, careless, depressed, and slow. The true strength of this spell is that it can be used on a nearly limitless number of people. During the ritual, the thaumaturgist drops dead pomegranate seeds in a ring around the target, saying an enigmatic chant with each one (it's a thirty-second chant). The target could be a single person, a house, an office building, a city block, or even a city. The caster must be walking (one seed per pace), so after the initial seven hour incantation it can take anywhere from ten minutes to several years to complete. The enchantment stays in effect until one of the seeds is displaced (burying them is a good idea). Still, even if the seeds are dispersed over a wide area, it is only a matter of time before one is disturbed.

Level Eight Rituals:

Chain of the Blood Line: This ritual grants the warlock power over another Vampires' extended brood, similar to a limited form of blood bond. This ritual takes three days and must end on the night of a new moon with the death of the Kindred whose brood the casters wishes to control. The subject is completely drained of blood until his life essence is sucked from his body by the caster. Thus, in addition to the

---

fresher the cadaver the better. This is a tortuous existence for the spirit trapped within the rotting frame, and most will wish release as soon as possible, which is the warlock's main bargaining measure to get the spirit to do her bidding, for only she holds the power to release the spirit. Other than that, the immured being may do as it wills with the new body that it has been forced into. Obviously, the spirit used must have been summoned or obtained somehow beforehand. Statistically, the creature has half the scores of the Physical traits of the body, and while the spirit is trapped within the corpses its traits are halved as well. A destroyed vampire cannot be raised by this ritual.

Ritual of Holding: This is simply a way of extending the effect of another ritual. It takes six hours added to the end of a ritual in order to hold its duration or enhance its effect. Of course, this spell has differing results with every ritual to which it is added. Examples: It will lengthen the reach of Blood Walk to include the subject's progeny, and perhaps those whose blood he has tasted as well. It will cause the container of Engaging the Vessel of Transference to exchange only one point of blood for two points that it takes. It may make a ward next to indestructible. It may make it impossible for Cleansing of the Flesh to eliminate the Shaft of Belated Quiescence. It may keep a spirit trapped by Raise the Dead and immured in the corpse indefinitely. The caster can make suggestions as to how it should work, but it will be up to the Storyteller to define the extent of the "holding."

normal effects of this act of diablery, the thaumaturgist learns all of the subjects' brood, and all of their brood in turn, down to the last of the bloodline. When these Kindred are encountered, the caster may command them in any way, impelling them to obey. The "enslaved" Kindred may resist this power by making a resisted roll of Wits + Self Control (difficulty is the caster's Willpower) against the caster's roll of Manipulation + Leadership (difficulty is the victim's Willpower). The difference between successes is the number of hours before the caster can attempt to command the defender again, or the number of hours before the defender can make a roll to resist again. In the latter case, the number of successes is cumulative, so the caster can easily bend the will of the weak-minded, and can command them for extended periods. In addition, the affected Vampires begin to feel goodwill toward the caster that must be resisted with a similar roll, and the same type of roll must be made before the commanded Kindred is able to attack the Warlock.

Bone of the Kindred: This is a two-day ritual that creates an enchanted weapon made of bone or ivory. The ritual requires the life blood of a Kindred. This blood is absorbed into the weapon and so cannot be used for any other purpose. The enchanted weapon will do the same amount of damage that it normally would, but in the form of aggravated wounds. When in use, the weapon may seem to "drink" any blood that is on it.

Level Nine Rituals:

Weapon of the Kindred Soul: This ritual creates an enchanted weapon much like a "Bone of the Kindred" weapon from the above ritual. The ritual requires the life's blood of a Kindred who is also an expert in the use of the weapon. As above, this blood is absorbed and may not be used in any other way. The weapon created by this ritual becomes the vessel for the slain Kindred's soul and willpower. The thaumaturgist conducting this ritual has a great deal of control over the weapon's new personality and goals, commonly giving the weapon an overriding desire to protect the thaumaturgist. The weapon will maintain all of the Abilities, Disciplines, etc. of the Kindred slain to create it, but all of the memories will seem to be distant and unimportant. The weapon is given a new name during the ritual, and will communicate with its user telepathically. In summary, the weapon is a free thinking being with its own goals, skills and mystical disciplines.

Level Ten Ritual:

Invulnerable Weakness: This is a jealously guarded ritual known only to a very few of the eldest Tremere. The rite demands the immense concentration of a year to cast and a massive number of complex components to complete. The most important component, however, is a large diamond bathed in the sun's rays for an entire, cloudless day and engraved with the symbols of life and death. This gem is then consumed on the final night of the ritual, when it will stay inside the warlock's body until it is slowly and mystically decomposed after a period of Stamina + Occult (difficulty 4) years. During that time (or until the stone is removed from the caster's body) the caster is immune to fire, heat and sunlight. Also, the vampire can remain awake during the day for Humanity + Fortitude (difficulty depends on the time of day) hours. It should also be noted that the elder's blood takes on amazing qualities because of the decomposing diamond — he that drinks a single point will not only gain the normal benefits of Elder Vitae (disciplines enhancement, increased blood pool) but will also be immune to the destructive powers of flame, heat, and the sun's light for an hour (that's one hour per point).

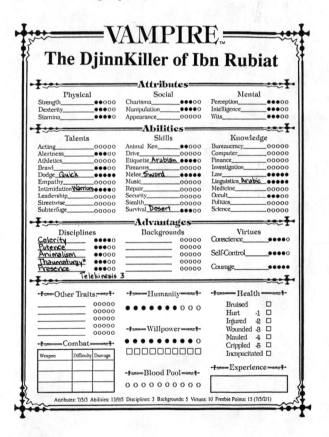

The Expanded Character

Chapter Four: Vampire Society

The world's as ugly, ay, as sin,
And almost as delightful.
Frederick Locker-Lampson, *The Jester's Plea*

This chapter describes the intricacy of the interactions of the Kindred in Vampire society, or the Camarilla. It also describes the function of Status, details a new background — Clan Prestige — and discusses how favors and promises are exchanged among the Kindred.

We also list four non-allied Vampire Clans — those neither of the Camarilla or the Sabbat — and one neutral blood line. While individual members of these groups may well be part of the Camarilla (your character perhaps), the Clan as a whole is outside the politics and intrigue of this august organization. These Clans, plus the Lasombra and the Tzimisces of the Sabbat, make up the 13 major Clans of Vampire lore. However, as illustrated by the Salubri, there are a score of minor Clans, most of them offshoots of the major Clans, and more can be created and used by your Storyteller. Do not think you know everything about the Clans just because you have read this chapter...

STATUS AMONG VAMPIRES

In general, a Vampire is expected to defer to Cainites of older generations. This is the primary hold the Elders have over the Anarchs, and it is how they maintain control over the Camarilla. Indeed, it is their most jealously guarded privilege.

Status is a measure of a Vampires standing in the Vampire community. It grows from the Vampire's generation and age, and cuts across Clan lines, but is largely a measure only in the city in which you reside (unless it is over 5).

The wider a gulf between Vampires, the greater the deference. In theory, this system is all that is needed to regulate behavior within the Camarilla. However, young Vampires sometimes distinguish themselves by a great accomplishment, and older Vampires sometimes suffer great setbacks and humiliating victories. In theory, the young are still required to bend the knee to their elders. In practice, they often use the goodwill their actions have generated to elevate themselves in Status and Prestige. This makes for some strange and deadly circumstances when relative Status is not exactly certain and confrontation is imminent. Vampires often disagree on the intangibles of Status, and the proper degree of respect due one another — it is the source of many hours of talk among Kindred.

Status is crucial among the Kindred, as it is the one mortal tradition to which they still cling, and the Anarchs' lack of respect for it creates much of the friction between them and the Elders. Though your characters may ignore the rules of Status, it is still wise to understand them. It is not difficult to snub your nose at the Elders, you just need to know how to get away with it, and when not to go too far.

The Harpies

Status is conferred and stripped by a consensus of those who haunt the exclusive halls of Elysium. Status is a function of those who concern themselves with such things, those who think of themselves as players in the major conflicts of the city, and those who collectively view themselves as princemakers (which they most certainly are). They are known as the Harpies, and though few would admit to being in such a group, all but the Anarchs are.

Anarchs have very little to do with, though they will often pay close attention to, who is currently in the limelight and who is in the outs. Even they feel free to humiliate and denigrate those who have lost favor; such opportunities for revenge are not often wasted.

Generally, when something occurs that would change people's opinions of someone, an intense period of gossip, rumor-mongering and intrigue takes place. No one wants to stick their own necks out, so they confer with others to see what the consensus is. When the group has made up its mind, its members feel free to make their judgement, knowing they are supported by "the city."

On the whole, the Elysium crowd tends to be highly critical and does not hesitate to punish those who trespass their customs or fail to meet their standards. Conversely, those who do well, those who best embarrass the current heroes, or those who have garnered an impressive amount of power in a short period are hailed by them and accorded much respect.

These vultures are the ultimate clique, and can be just as trite, blind, ignorant and treacherous as any high school peer group. Their judgements are total, and they are final. You can redeem yourself (or humiliate yourself) at a later time, but for the moment what they think determines your Status.

In short, they are the purveyors of Status.

While normally the Prince and the Primogen are not subject to the dictates of this group (they have too much power), even they can be toppled if they make too large a misstep. No one is beyond their reach. Status is too vital for anyone of influence to ignore, and in order to gain it, you've got to play by the rules.

Breaking the Rules

It can be a lot of fun to ignore the rules of Kindred society and tweek the noses of those who would lord over you. It is a dangerous sport however, and not to be considered without first understanding the risks. There can certainly be some gain from ignoring Status, not the least of which is gaining the respect and admiration of the Anarchs. Even some Elders might admire your courage — though most will be annoyed with your brazenness. Play it the way you want it, just keep in mind that every cause has its effect. Don't be surprised when things escalate out of control after you committed what you thought was a minor transgression.

One word of advice: if you are going to talk back to someone with higher Status, do not do it in public. You may make an enemy, but at least you will not lose Status.

Roleplaying Status: Low to High

A low-Status Kindred is expected to act in a respectful manner before a higher-ranking Clan member. You are to

speak in a respectful tone of voice, and use humble, deferential gestures. You should show every courtesy, deferring to the judgement of your superior in all things. If the you disagree with your Elder, you are entitled to politely express your point of dispute. If the higher ranking Vampire overrules you, you are to let the matter drop. It is not proper to make demands or question the judgement of the elder. The greater the gulf in Status between the two, the greater the respect you are required to exhibit. Of course if the difference is only 1 point, things are taken quite casually, but a difference of three or more requires the utmost of deference.

If you fail to meet the customs of your culture, you risk earning the enmity and wrath of the leaders of the city or your Clan. You must carefully weigh the advantages to be gained by antagonizing your superiors against the backlash of hostility you will incur from them. The rewards for keeping to your station in the hierarchy are many. Your Clan will continue to support your activities and bail you out when you are in danger. (Trouble- makers are often left to twist in the wind.) Earning the goodwill of high-ranking Kindred is like putting money in the bank. If you wait long enough, you'll have more than you put in. Some younger Vampires maintain these claims of rewards are exaggerated, and point to older, sycophantic Vampires who still have low Status despite an eternity of devotion and bootlicking. These young Kindred maintain that no one gets elevated in Status without stepping on a few toes, and therefore, the rewards are worth the risks.

Roleplaying Status: High to Low

A high-Status Vampire can expect a lower-ranking Vampire to act politely, listen often, answer when addressed, and behave in a deferential manner. If they are far apart in Status, the higher-ranking Vampire can expect the lower-ranking Vampire to carry out orders and instructions. The lower ranking Vampire is not a slave to the greater, but is is expected to never interfere with a superior's activities and to obey basic directives such as "leave my club!" The younger Vampire is also required to give a superior the benefit of the doubt in disputes, though in practice, low-Status Vampires often take whatever they can get.

Punishment:

The penalties for infractions of conduct within various cities and Clans vary widely, and there is no standard for enforcement. Usually, the higher-Status Vampire just points out the infraction. Often merely calling attention to the offense is enough to right it. Calling attention to the problem when the offender's close Kindred are present is also an effective response. At this stage an informal apology and improved behavior will set the situation to right.

If the disrespect continues even after a protest is expressed, the aggrieved party can lodge a formal criticism with the Sire of the offending party, and request the others of its line to discipline him. If that fails, the higher-Status Vampire often takes matters into her own hands, using whatever means of coercion she has at her disposal. She may end all contact with the other Vampire. She may end any favors or agreements she had with the Vampire and her immediate Kin.

At this time, the Harpies will likely make there displeasure known (that is if they still support and acknowledge the higher-Status Vampire). They will begin to shun the violator of their traditions and he may actually lose Status as a result (if he has any left to lose).

Failing that, she may take the matter up with the Prince. If the Prince straightens the matter out, the higher-Status Vampire will then be in the Prince's debt (see Prestation, below).

If that does not work, she take matters into her own hands, sabotaging the offending Vampire's plans, destroying his holdings and poisoning his "good" name with anyone who will listen. Many bitter rivalries have erupted over the proper amount of respect due because of Status. The Camarilla is still rent by some of these feuds, and some speculate that at the heart of the Jyhad is a fundamental struggle for preeminence and Status.

CLAN PRESTIGE

Clan Prestige is a new Background Trait designed to add color and fresh roleplaying possibilities to your stories by giving you greater understanding of and control over your place in the Clan. Your Prestige is a measure of your standing in your Clan, much as Status is a measure of your standing in a particular city. It grows from the goodwill, fear and awe you inspire in others of your Clan, and the extent to which you have mastered the rules, values and idiosyncrasies of you culture. In other words, it measures how well you've learned to play the games that are important to your Clan.

Clan Prestige can be invaluable in a number of different ways, being a major indication of how many of your Clan will respond when you call for aid, how many will stand up for you, and how well you are able to shape its internal politics.

Your Clan is the foundation and backbone of your character; without the backing of your Clan, it will be easy for others to abuse and misuse you.

Status vs Clan Prestige

Clan Prestige goes in a range of 1-5 as per normal (1-10 for some Elders). It is a Background Trait, and can be

Cobb 91

Prestige and the Clash of Generations

Status is often used by the elder Cainites to control the younger members of the Clan and direct their actions. Because Vampires start their undead existence with no Status or Prestige and gain these as they age, Status and Clan Prestige provide an effective means of generational control. It keeps the older Kindred (who have accrued more Status) dominant over the younger ones. Young Vampires often chafe under the rigid restrictions and tight control of the Status system, and seek to subvert, avoid and even over-throw them. This is understandable, since the system often rewards age and guile over youth, skill and energy.

Unfortunately, the young Kindred are too inexperienced, and have too little power in Clan society to really change the system. By the time they have learned to play the game well enough to gain power, they are firmly enmeshed in the machinery of Status generation, and have a vested interest in preserving the system that oppressed them. Thus, the system is maintained from generation to generation.

There are exceptions to this rule. Older Kindred can lose Status by making crucial blunders, like losing important territory, and younger Vampires can make rapid strides in Status through clever deeds and daring exploits.

Prestige Outside the Clan

Clan Prestige is rarely recognized across Clan lines. The actions so highly valued within the Clan are worth a lot less to outsiders. A low-ranking Ventrue is more likely to disdain a high-ranking Gangrel than defer to him.

Because most Clans do not acknowledge (or understand) the intangible, arcane criteria used by other Clans to confer Status, they prefer to judge Kindred from outside their own Clan by their actions and contributions to Vampire society in general. A Brujah would never concede that the system of honor and respect they use to keep the young, upstart Brujah in line bore any resemblance to the rigid, arcane, tyrannical caste system used by the Tremere. Likewise, the Tremere would be offended at the thought that the rude, violent manner in which the Brujah terrorize their young was in any way similar to their wise, sober system of hierarchical development. But in fact, the two systems function in a similar manner. The only difference is the criteria the Clans use to grant Prestige to their members.

Generating Clan Prestige

When you first create a character you can choose Clan Prestige (specify which Clan by describing it as Brujah

purchased using background and freebie points. Note that the Status system described in **Vampire** still holds true. The Clan Prestige system does not replace Status, it merely supplements it.

Clan Prestige grows from currying favor within the Clan, and sometimes, from betraying members of other Clans. It is measured across the width and breath of the Clan. Whereas Status is a measure of your character's standing in Vampire society and the degree to which you have made your mark on the lives of all other Kindred, from the local neighborhood to the global community.

A character who has made strong contributions to all of Vampire society by stopping a powerful Vampire hunter would increase in Status. A character who has helped organize the Clan against a common foe would increase in Clan Prestige.

Some Kindred trade overall Status for Clan Prestige or Clan Prestige for overall Status. By working with Vampires from other Clans, a Vampire can increase his standing among all his kind, at the expense of gathering resentment from his own Clan. By betraying members of other Clans, the Vampire can sometimes gain Status with his people, but be considered an untrustworthy traitor by the rest of the Camarilla. Sometimes the plan backfires, and the Vampire is despised by both groups. And sometimes it works so well she actually gains Status both within the Clan and without.

Prestige, Ventrue Prestige or the like) just as your would pick more general Status.

If your character has already been created, and you still would like to have Clan Prestige, you can do one of two things. First of all, with the Storyteller's permission, you can buy enough flaws to give you the freebie points to gain the background, or you can try to gain it as a result of the story. If you do things that would seem to raise your Prestige, the Storyteller may tell you that you have just gained it for the first time (to a level one) or that it has increased one level. It will continue to increase, or decrease, just as do other Backgrounds, as a result of what occurs in the Chronicle.

Intra-Clan Prestige

The Clan Prestige of each member is known to other members of the Clan. Low-Prestige Kindred are expected to defer to high-Prestige Vampires, high-Prestige characters demand courtesy and respect from lower-Prestige characters, and characters of equal Prestige jockey for a slight edge over each other. Sometimes Kindred of equal Prestige suspend further rivalry to work together harmoniously.

Refusing to acknowledge the Prestige of a "family" member is a great insult, and grounds for a feud.

Creating Prestige

Because Clan Prestige grows from so many disparate factors, it is more subjective than the other traits. Though all Clans use Prestige as a way of measuring the value of their members, they each use very different criteria for determining Prestige. The following section explains the rules and guidelines you follow in building your character's Clan Prestige. Each Clan description also lists a number of ideas you can pursue as a player to increase your Prestige.

CLAN ORGANIZATIONS

The Clans are listed here in order of complexity of social structure. They range from the most rigid and complex to the least-tightly organized. Each Clan is described in terms of how it organizes itself, not in terms of the individuals which comprise it. In general, the more formal a Clan is, the more codified its rules on proper behavior. (See Status and the Clans, above.) Even the less-formal Brujah and Nosferatu expect the lower-Prestige Vampires to defer to those of greater standing in the community.

The guiding principles, Clan structure, gaining power, gathering days, rumors about the Clan hierarchy, and some character ideas are listed for each Clan. All in all, we hope this provides you with a more well-rounded understanding of the seven Clans of the Camarilla.

Tremere

Though they are not the largest or the most powerful Clan, the secretive Tremere have a more rigid social structure than any Clan in the Camarilla. Absolute fidelity to the complicated and archaic Clan Law is demanded. Every member of the Clan is required to know his place in the Clan hierarchy, and to keep that place at all costs. The Elders impress on the young the belief that each member is but a stone in the great Pyramid, and one stone out of place can weaken the whole. It is little wonder that the Tremere as a whole are so dour and sober, since each feels the weight of the entire Clan firmly set upon his back.

Within their own Clan they abide by carefully defined codes of dominance and subordination and often expect others to fall into line as well. Their intense competition with one another makes them powerful as individuals, while their rigid structure makes them strong as a Clan.

Despite their rigidity, no other Clan, even the Brujah, actually rewards successful deviance as highly. Breaking the rules, and triumphing with exceptional success, is a sure way to earn respect and move up the ladder, gain control over a Chantry or even being offered the chance to start one's own. Doing so regularly is an equally sure way to die the final death.

Clan Structure

The insular Tremere have such an elaborate, well-regulated, and secretive global network that they are sometimes referred to as the "Illuminati." Indeed, in some ways they seem more like a sect unto themselves, much like the Followers of Set or even the Sabbat, than simply a Clan in the Camarilla. They call this world-wide structure the Pyramid, and within it, all in the Clan have their place. All Clan members are held in Thrall by the Clan itself. There are no free-agent Tremere.

Tremere are not, however, mere puppets and pawns. They are fiercely proud and highly competitive, and often pursue their own unique goals in addition to those of the Clans. For most Tremere, the Clan is the only place where they are understood and where they feel truly comfortable. It is not a cage, it is a haven.

The apex of the Tremere Pyramid is the Council of Seven, made up of all the Tremere of fourth generation. They are the leaders of the Tremere in Western Europe (including Australia and New Zealand), Eastern Europe, the Mideast, Africa, North America, Central America (and Mexico) and South America. There are no Tremere in the Asian nations, though it is rumored that a chantry has been created in Hong Kong.

The Council of Seven assemble once a decade in Vienna to chart and plan the Clan's growth. If a great danger threatens at any other time, they will call an emergency session to deal with the problem, but they resist scheduling anything other than their regular meetings, as they do not like to appear out of control on any issue. However, they are often in contact with one another via various communications rituals.

Directly under the Council of Seven is the Order of Pontifex. There are seven Pontifex under each member of the council, and their "domains" cross national lines, and are not geographical in bounds. They generally meet with each other once every seven years, in a special meeting convened by their Elder who sits on the Council. In North America there are two Canadian Orders, three United States Orders, one that concerns itself with multinational corporations, and one concerned with politics (and based out of Washington, D.C.). The U.S. is divided into Eastern, Midwestern, and West Coast Orders.

Below the Order of Pontifex is the Order of Lords. There are seven Lords under each Pontifex. They meet once every three years with their Elder. Some Lords preside over the Vampire communities of entire small nations. In the U.S., they each control the Chantries of a state or two.

Below each Lord is an Order of Regents. Each large city has a Tremere Chantry, and each Chantry has its Regent. The Regents all make a yearly pilgrimage to their Lord's Chantry for the meeting of the Order of Regents. There can be as many Regents in the Order of Regents as there are Chantries in the High Regent's area of dominion, but always more than seven.

After their Embrace, Neonate Tremere are held in Thrall and invested with the title Apprentice of the First Circle. They owe fealty to the Regent of the Chantry who is in turn commanded to follow his immediate superior, and so on up to the Seven Elders of the Clan. Neonates of the first circle meet with the Regent every week. As they progress through the ranks of the Chantry, they are initiated in six more sets of mysteries, until they become Apprentices of the Seventh Circle. Seventh Circle Apprentices rule the Chantry along with the Regent of the Chantry.

Each Neonate is bound in place below those who have been initiated into higher mysteries. They must listen to their Regent and defer to her in all things. Likewise, the Tremere who have only been initiated into lesser mysteries are bound beneath the Neonate, and must show the same respect to them.

The same procedure follows for Regents, Lords, and Pontifexes. Each of those three stations have a new set of Seven Circles of Mysteries, in addition to the Seven Mysteries for the Apprentices. All Regents, Lords, and Pontifexes must be initiated in a new set of Seven Circles of Mysteries to be promoted and gain power, just like the Apprentices.

Player's Guide

This pyramid of power does not follow strict geographic lines, however. In fact, in recent decades the geographic distinctions have blurred further. Even though each Chantry is made up of a small group of Tremere led by a Regent, the real flow of power cuts across the Chantries. A Regent in Chicago Chantry may have control over an apprentice in Los Angeles. A Lord in Angola may control a Regent and her Chantry in Sweden. The course of real power at all levels above the lowest Apprentices flows in mystical connections that span the Western World — connections which seem to change with bewildering frequency.

This is but a general overview of what is in fact an immensely complicated structure. The true map of Tremere power is a complete mystery to the rest of the Camarilla, and is unknown even to young Tremere. Only as the Apprentice advances in power does she begin to fathom the intricacies of this unique and complex web.

Gaining Power

The Tremere prize influence over other Kindred, and control over events in the mortal world. They prize competitiveness and those who best use their talents. They confer increased Prestige on Clan members who succeed at this, and have elaborate rules to determine which achievements are valid and worthy an increase in Prestige. (Prestige gains are rewarded by initiation in the next Circle of Mystery.) Clan members are expected to defer to the Clan Elders in all things, especially in the validation of accomplishments. It is the Elders, and the Elders alone, who award Prestige.

Moving up in rank within the Clan is almost always a difficult and torturous process — but it is the primary goal of most of its members. The competition is considered to be a means of keeping the most fit leaders atop the pyramid. Tremere Prestige can be considered a path to power.

Succession through these rigid ranks is supposed to be through recommendation and promotion by the Tremere's immediate superior, so absolute loyalty to Clan and Lord is vital for advancement. Because of this arcane system, it is difficult to gain Clan Prestige and easy to lose it. Most of the Tremere have great responsibility but little authority.

As a result, the members of the lower ranks are extraordinarily dutiful. As they slowly rise through the Orders they become fanatically obedient. They learn to place Clan goals over all other concerns, and to treasure any tiny, incremental gain in personal Prestige within the Clan.

They have considerable leeway in the conduct of their personal activities outside of the Clan. However, they must be willing to sacrifice themselves for the Clan when the need is clear, at least if they wish to advance.

There is little room for promotion based on maverick acts of individual brilliance or personal endeavor. And since very few of the Vampiric leaders ever die, change and advancement can be very slow.

The only time room officially opens in the great Pyramid is when a Tremere founds a new Chantry. When the Council of Seven concludes that an opportunity exists to expand into a new territory, they choose a highly loyal Tremere, and offer him the assignment. Tremere exist for such an endowment, and the possibility of it is one of the best reasons for them to be intensely loyal.

The Chantry regents are often petty dictators of the worst sort, and have considerable freedom to pursue Clan goals in their own fashion. Many outsiders believe there is a secret and quite arcane dueling process which the Elders use when they compete with one another.

During several expansionist phases in Tremere history, individual Tremere founded their own Chantries without permission from the Council of Seven. The Council struck against them, destroying most of the independent Chantries. A few survived the attacks, and became valuable enough to earn the right to exist. Their presence rankles some tradition-bound Lords and High Lords, and are a source of bitter, deep-seated division within the Clan. This ages-old schism is one of the few weak chinks in an otherwise solid Pyramid of power.

Of course, all is not paradise within the pyramid. There is another way to gain power and Prestige.

Breaking the Bounds

The leaders of the Tremere greatly fear losing their place at the top, but their dedication to the Clan prevents them from physically stopping skilled and ambitious newcomers. Since the Council of Seven assures its own safety through the Blood Bonds it holds over all Clan members, it feels safe enough to encourage neonates on the fast track to rise as fast as the system will allow them to. Not only do they see this as bringing the cream to the top, but they also like keeping those already on top on their toes. After all, after a few centuries on top even the best can become complacent.

So the Tremere have rewarded those who have gone against the wishes of their direct superior and won. Stories of the Neonate who stopped a Magi plot against the Tremere and was rewarded his Regent's Chantry warm the hearts of many apprentices. The few outsiders who know of such stories point out that nothing more is ever heard of the old Regent and pass whispers of Diablerie in the dark. Of course, Tremere Elders have never been known to look with favor on continued deviance or any swing from the party line.

Gathering Days:

Each Chantry assembles every Tuesday for formal council meetings called Convocations. These meetings are closed to all other Kindred, and even Tremere from other Chantries may only attend by special invitation. The topics discussed there are great secrets, and may not be mentioned afterwards to non-Tremere.

All Tremere in the Chantry are expected to be there, which puts a great strain on Tremere who are infiltrating other Clans or trying to launch autonomous projects. Missing a meeting is cause for loss of Prestige, and raises eyebrows within the Clan. Leaders provide exemptions in extreme circumstances, but repeat offenses meet with immediate censure and loss of Prestige.

These are mystical gatherings. Each Regnant chants a special incantation that joins him in telepathic contact with his Regent. They then join the rest in mystical communication. Convocation discussions revolve around recent accomplishments, and the Chantry's incremental gains toward fulfilling mystical prophecies necessary to seize control of all worldly systems. Note that this is not mind reading but merely communication.

The Tremere have a meeting every third month, on the third of that month. These are open meetings, and members of other Clans may attend. Petitions are heard, disputes resolved, and the Tremere put on a show of being a unified Clan that speaks with a strong, single voice. Deviation from the party line in such public circumstances can cause immediate loss of Prestige. At such meetings Tremere are quick to offer advice and aid (especially aid!) to non-Clan members who attend. The would like it if all Kindred were obliged to them in one way or another.

Once a year, at the end of October, the entire Clan connects in mystical union. They all chant the arcane mysteries and are joined as one mind. This Chant continues for two days, and reinforces the Tremere's understanding of his place in the mystical order. He understands that he is a weak brick in a mighty pyramid, and that all the strength he has stems from the whole.

While this union promotes a group consciousness, it does not allow for deep mental probes. The surface thoughts of all participating are turned to the same direction and focused together at the same point, but one cannot mind probe one's Elder this way.

Power Rumors:

Rumors have circulated for centuries that the true apex of the Tremere Pyramid is not really the Council of Seven, but a single individual who gives orders to the Seven. Some say this individual is Caine himself, but Kindred from other Clans say it is merely a insane and power-mad Tremere. A recent crisis in the Vienna Chantry fueled these rumors, and added a new twist; that the true leader is not even Kindred, but something far more powerful. If the rumor proves true, it would amount to rank betrayal by the Elders, and cause a

major schism in the Clan. The Tremere leaders indignantly deny these rumors, but the rumors persist nonetheless, perhaps because they have a certain logic to them. After all, each of the lesser councils has a single individual above them. The Council of Seven is the only exception, and some believe the Tremere would never be that inconsistent.

Some members of other Clans speculate that the Tremere trade followers like baseball cards. These rumors hold that the true reason for the trades is to build international, interlocking, cross Chantry loyalties, and freshen the magical mixture in each Chantry.

Some Vampires add that the trading has created a poisonous environment in which young Tremere try to backstab one another, citing the lack of a fixed, geographic-based power structure as the source of disloyalty. But others respond that the backstabbing is nothing more than a natural consequence of the rigid control and enforced loyalty exerted over all Tremere. Stripped of any chance for airing natural grievances, the Tremere end up gnawing at each other's underbellies wherever they can.

The infighting is rumored to be so intense that the Vienna Chantry set up a highly secret hit squad to carry out an inquisition within the entire Clan. According to the rumors, these inquisitors have absolute power to make or break any Elder. They are shuffled into a local Chantry in the usual

course of trading followers, and proceed to take notes on all rivalries. The backstabbing must be tearing at the heart of the Clan, or else Vienna would never resort to such drastic measures.

The annual Tremere Convocation is the source of great speculation among the rest of the Camarilla. Some say that it unleashes powerful magical energy across the world, and magical ceremonies performed at this time gain an unexpected boost. Some say that these two days are difficult for mortal institutions that debunk magic and attempt to fix reality to a single definition. Hard scientific principles are supposed to suffer, and weaken around the edges during this time.

Other Vampires maintain that the Tremere are highly vulnerable, and the annual convocation would be a great time to attack them. Others point out that were it so easy, it would surely have happened, since the Tremere are rumored to have many elemental enemies. The Tremere may actually be at their strongest during the convocation. Elder Vampires tell tales of inquisitive Kindred ripped apart just by the vibrations of the resonant, eerie Tremere chanting. Then again, this rumor may just be a smoke screen put up by the Tremere to distract attention from their annual Achilles heel.

Character Ideas:

A character from a properly founded Chantry can make his life's work the eradication of all independently founded Chantries. He believes this will strengthen the Clan. A character from an independent Chantry could be motivated by a desperate need to prove himself and his Chantry, by being twice as valuable to the Clan.

A character can decide to strain the bonds of tradition again and found his own Chantry, and force the Council of Seven to grant it full acceptance.

A character who hates her Regent suddenly finds herself inexplicably freed from the Blood Bond. Though she is not bound by arcane means, she is still bound by the tight strictures of the Clan rules, and must work within them.

Ventrue

The most rarefied members of a rarefied race, the Ventrue have a more formal social order than another other Clan in the Camarilla. Though they are not as well-organized as the Tremere, their rules and traditions concerning social conduct are much more formal and rigid. While they are free to squabble and fight among themselves, they are expected to do it by the rules

As the unofficial leaders of all Vampire society, they exert a great control over Kindred and mortals alike. They have the most to lose if the Masquerade is broken, and thus the greatest need to keep the others in line. As a result, they have created a very formal Clan structure and a very sophisticated means of advancement. Like urbane, old world businessmen, the Ventrue are bound by a long body of tradition, rules and heritage.

Clan Structure

The Ventrue are organized like a large, flexible, multinational corporation. They are far more integrated into the mortal world than any other Clan, and their organization reflects this. The senior members of the Clan sometimes meet, and this informal "board of directors" has members in thirty different cities. The main corporate directorates are in New York, London, Paris, Sydney, Moscow and Washington D.C.

All major cities have a Ventrue headquarters, called a Board. The Board is run like a business and is typically housed in a prestigious office building, country club or Gentleman's Club. (They will use men's clubs even when the Board is run by women). All Ventrue are members of all Boards, and may seek Haven in any of them at any time.

Because the Ventrue cherish control, they have infiltrated politics at the city, state and national level. Nothing goes on in local politics that the ghouls of the Ventrue do not know.

Gaining Power

The Ventrue prize sophistication and gentility. Gaining money, position, and influence in the world is important, but it must be done with grace and style. Boorish behavior in the pursuit of power is not acceptable.

Like the Tremere, the autocratic, sophisticated Elders insist on reverence from the younger Clan members. Following the Elders' rules and showing devotion and patience are sure ways to raise Prestige.

Unlike the Tremere, the Ventrue regularly value individual initiative and achievement over slavish devotion. A motivated neonate can make rapid strides up the Clan corporate ladder through bold, imaginative and decisive action. Gaining territory, strengthening relations with other Clans, ending an outside threat, and forging new connections with the world of mortals are all accepted means of gaining Prestige.

Though initiative is prized, competition within the ranks is not. In this sense the Ventrue emulate businessmen in the old-boy network rather than modern cutthroat capitalists. Young Ventrue interested in rapid advancement must be careful not to step on the toes of a higher-ranking Ventrue engaged in the same activity. Snatching territory or squelching a deal in progress is frowned upon, and is grounds for a loss of Prestige.

The Ventrue pride themselves on their courtesy toward one another, even to those with whom they feud. Such etiquette and personal pride is considered to be what best set apart the Ventrue form the "vulgurates" (the other Kindred).

On occasion, a young Ventrue has profited from snatching a deal from the hands of an Elder, but she must always be able to demonstrate that it was vital to the health of the Clan to do so. If it was not, she will loose considerable status.

Gathering Days

The Clan assembles regularly, on the first Tuesday of every month. Their meetings, called Directorate Assemblies, are conducted in exclusive clubs. Appropriately enough, they have the feel of a meeting of a Board for an exclusive, privately-held corporation. All Ventrue in the city are expected to attend, those who are not in attendance will likely be "fetched" by the retainers of the chairman (The eldest Ventrue present).

All business is conducted in a formal, though chummy, atmosphere. Any displays of passion or anger are frowned upon. Favored ghouls are often brought along as well, as the ghouls are essential for conducting business during daylight hours.

At the Directorate Assembly, the Clan is updated on recent acquisitions of power and wealth. New members are introduced, and all changes in Prestige are formally announced in the form of memberships to select committees or public humiliation by the Chairman. All Ventrue may speak, but are required to request a place on the agenda first, and it is possible for them to be turned down. Ventrue from other Boards may appear if they get special permission. Unlike the Tremere, the Ventrue sometimes grant members of other Clans permission to attend, but they can only be brought in after Clan business is concluded.

Ventrue have numerous informal meetings at concerts and museums, during which their business is conducted in public with careful codes. However, this differs little from the usual intrigue that takes place in Elysium.

Power Rumors

Some Ventrue believe that there is a schism going on in the upper ranks of Ventrue society. One faction wants to preserve the old-boy network which pervades the Clan's relations with the mortal world. The other faction believes all Clan resources are being inefficiently managed and unnecessarily hoarded. They want to open up the Clan monopolies to competition by other Ventrue (read: younger Ventrue). According to the rumor, this may allow for greater diversity of skill and ability and thus more influence for the Ventrue Clan as a whole. As a result, circumventing the old-

boy network may find more favor among the Elders than might be expected.

Character Ideas

You locate a high-technology business the older Ventrue have been slow to understand and exploit, and decide to penetrate that area to gain Prestige. You can pour all your cash resources into it, call home old debts, and use your own Domination to get a piece of the action. Thereby will your Prestige be increased, and your power expanded.

You see that an Elder Ventrue is mismanaging a vital Clan resource, and decide to risk a takeover. If you succeed, you still must show how your action was needed, and in the best interest of the Clan.

TOREADOR

Socializing is an art to the Toreador, and they take any opportunity to get together and jockey for eminence in Clan society. Social position is more fluid among the Toreador than any other Clan. An upstart can rocket to high Prestige and the mighty can be brought low like quicksilver.

The Elders are almost as prone to runaway passions as Toreador Anarchs, and have been known to make rash changes, granting huge boosts in Clan Prestige on a whim. Like the loud, flamboyant art types of the contemporary art world, the Toreador are caught in the grip of constantly shifting passions and crazes in a world where nothing is absolute, and all rules are as permanent as yesterday's trends.

Clan Structure

The Toreador have a very loose-knit, casual organization. They do not have the same sort of formal meetings and ambitious plans which characterize the Tremere and Ventrue. When they meet to track their organizational growth, they are more likely to discuss the merits of a new art movement as they are to discuss feeding grounds, local power, and threats to their community.

Though they are more informal than other Clans, their internal politics and social dynamic are as treacherous as any other, perhaps more. It is made all the more sinister because of the stakes they compete for — Prestige and Prestige alone. They do not view prestige as a means to an end, but an end in itself.

Their groupings are casual and flexible. A young Clan member is not required to stick with any one local group, but may switch allegiances at will. The national and international chapters are run like great conventions. Some of the larger and more prestigious art conferences around the world are actually disguised Toreador meetings. On the local level, the Toreador meet in city-wide groups called Guilds.

Artiste and Poseur

To the Toreador, nothing is greater than Beauty. The search for beauty is paramount in their minds, and those who discover new works of great aesthetic value, or even better, create them, are accorded increased Prestige.

This points out the fundamental division in Toreador society. There are two different and highly antagonistic factions of the Clan: the Artistes and the Poseurs. (Note: Artiste (pronounced Ar-TEEST) and Poseur (pronounced pose-ER) are derogatory labels used by each side to insult the other. All members of the Clan call themselves Toreador, and not Artiest or Poseur.

The Artistes are consistently engaged in the creation of new works of art, and often get intimately involved with the artists they patronize, demanding greater and greater brilliance and fanning the flames of inspiration.

The Poseurs pretend to be artists, but create very little. They are Vampires who were generally chosen because their great physical beauty rather than their talent. Often they were Embraced by a Toreador who was smitten by their beauty and suffered from clouded judgement. Others were Embraced by Poseurs who wished to validate themselves by creating more Toreador in their own image.

Some Poseurs reject the title and insist they are legitimate artists, pointing to substandard works as examples of their talent. Some Poseurs insist that their physical bodies are works of art in themselves. Others say their lifestyles stand as a stunning artistic achievements. Still other Poseurs make up for their own artistic limitations by becoming great patrons of the arts.

All Artistes reject the title, preferring to be called artists, or not to be labeled at all. Still the labels have stuck, much to the amusement of the rest of the Camarilla.

Gaining Power

Prestige is doled out in a different manner among Artistes and Poseurs. Artistes gain Prestige by creating new works of exceptional beauty, patronizing new art, and throwing great parties. Poseurs are limited to patronage and parties.

This has restricted the Poseurs from gaining Prestige as rapidly as Artistes, and has effectively confined them to the lower stations in Toreador society. It remains a barrier they bitterly resent. It doesn't help that so many of them fundamentally misunderstand the meaning and relevance of art.

To cope with this obvious handicap, some of the more daring Poseurs have adopted the role of performance artists,

indulging in baffling displays of incomprehensible activity, usually designed to show off their great beauty (or paradoxically, to disfigure it). Though it brought great Prestige to its most outrageous pioneers, this stratagem has otherwise met with only limited and short-term success. The Clan is in disagreement on whether it is a true art form or a passing fad.

In a more inspired move, some clever Poseurs compensated for their slower advancement by regularly throwing lavish parties at great personal expense. They gained Prestige by becoming crucial to the social scene. By toasting accomplishments of a few specific Toreador, and soundly criticizing others, they actually become kingmakers, usurping the Prestige-conferring role of the Elders.

Gathering Days

The Toreador love to meet together. All their meetings are run like parties or bizarre masquerades. Each Guild has a large meeting once a month on the night of the full moon. This gathering is called a Ball. By tradition, Toreador from other Guilds may attend at any time, and are often specifically invited. Non-Clan Kindred are not allowed except by prior invitation.

Once a year, on Halloween, the Toreador have a Grand Ball, in which several Guilds assemble for a great gathering. It is a highly political affair, though much of what is discussed and fought over would be uninteresting to anyone outside of the Clan.

Any Toreador can convene a special meeting of the local Clan. These impromptu Guild meetings are called Affairs of the Clan, and are used mostly for gaining Prestige. Attendance is strictly voluntary, but in practice everyone attends.

Once every 23 years, the Toreador hold a huge party which they call Carnivale. They rent a huge plot of land and throw a massive masquerade, with many of the great mortal artists of the day invited to attend. They release their inhibitions and unleash their animal natures. This celebration culminates in the coronation of the greatest mortal artist of the generation. They reward him with immortality. Literally.

Just like everything else in Clan life, however, this choice is subject to intense politicking and intriguing. More often than not, the chosen artist is unknown to the mortal world, and often has a mighty Toreador for a patron.

Power Rumors

Some say Toreador society only looks unstructured, but in reality is more strictly controlled than Tremere and Ventrue society. This rumor postulates the existence of an "Art Mafia" made up of Toreador Elders who control the art trends in mortal and Vampire society. They also control the artists who get promoted. Some say these secret movers are

really Tremere manipulators functioning through the Toreador.

Another rumor says that the Poseurs are conspiring to corrupt the Prestige-conferring process by secretly agreeing on the "next big trend," and lending the weight of all Poseurs to their decision.

Some Poseurs say they know of a plot to destroy them. They claim the Artiste Toreador Elders are presenting a petition to the Camarilla stating that the Poseurs were not selected to receive the Gift by conscious choice, but by overly sensitive Toreador driven mad with desire. Therefore, the Poseurs are all undeserving of life as Kindred, and should be killed.

Character Ideas

The character is a Poseur Toreador who resents his own lack of talent. He constantly concocts schemes to pass off outlandish ideas as heartfelt artistic creations.

The character is an anguished artist who only seems to be able to create great works when she has suffered profoundly. In order to gain Prestige, she is forced to seek out more and more reckless and dangerous situations.

Nosferatu

Ironically, the most anti-social of the Camarilla have a powerfully strong sense of community. Perhaps their ostracism from mortals and Kindred alike has forced the Nosferatu to seek consolation and companionship from their own kind. Like the cast-offs and misfits of the mortal world, they avoid mainstream society, and look to their own for understanding and community.

Clan Structure

The Nosferatu have a very loose world-wide organization. Their regional groups, called Broods, meet on a regular basis. The Nosferatu seldom have national or global meetings like the other Clans. Instead, local Broods often send emissaries to foreign Brood meetings.

Gaining Power

Nosferatu are far less Prestige conscious than their Kindred. They do not jockey with one another for a slight edge in Prestige. They do not seek Prestige for its own sake. Instead, they see Prestige as a way to honor those among them who have contributed to the Clan, and as a way to revere those who are valuable to their ongoing survival. Their approach to Prestige is unique among all the Clans, and may arise from their repudiation of all egotism and vanity.

The younger Nosferatu do not engage in cutthroat competition for favor in the eyes of the Elders, and the Elders do not actively seek to dominate or control the Neonates. A mutual respect pervades all their dealings with one another. Once a Neonate has survived the rigorous Embrace and transformation, she is considered worthy of respect.

Freed from the dissipating ordeal of competition, the Nosferatu have more time, energy and cooperative zeal to devote to their real business. Gathering information is a staple of Clan life. Their knowledge network is unmatched in all the Camarilla. High Prestige is accorded those who consistently provide fresh, accurate information which increases feeding grounds, helps with bargaining with other Clans, and contributes to the safety of all Nosferatu. But mostly Prestige is granted with age. The older the Vampire, the more he understands of the real workings of the world, and the more valuable he is.

Gathering Days

Nosferatu do not have regular Clan meetings. They do keep in regular contact and can quickly convene a council meeting, called a Hosting. The Vampire who calls the Hosting is responsible for providing a meeting place. They host one another with great respect and gentility. Other Clans have interpreted this respect as feigned politeness, but it is very real. Among themselves they generally believe in hospitality and consideration, if only because it is only by one another that they are ever fully accepted.

A Nosferatu may show up at another Brood's Hosting with little or no warning, and with no advance permission. This level of trust is unheard of among the other Clans, and accounts for much of the strength of the Nosferatu Clan.

Power Rumors

Some Nosferatu speak darkly and privately about a Tremere plot to infiltrate their ranks, learn their secrets, and try to manipulate their actions. No love is lost between the two Clans, the Nosferatu know too much about the Tremere Clans to feel comfortable with them, and the Tremere despise how much the Nosferatu know about them.

Oddly enough, unlike the rest of the Clans, the Nosferatu seem to have no rumors about suspicious, unseemly behavior by their Elders. Indeed, they seem to respect and admire the most aged among them.

Character Ideas

You are a Nosferatu who dislikes the cooperation within your Clan. Your ambitions include gaining Prestige through competition with others of her kind. You see the Nosferatu's lack of competition as laziness.

You wish to create regular meetings of your Clan, and convene a Hosting of the Brood at every waning moon. If you call for it, they will come, but they may not be pleased with your initiative, especially if you are younger than they.

You want to elevate the Prestige of all Nosferatu in the eyes of the Camarilla. You make it known that you will willingly undertake rigorous missions for the other Clans; missions only a hardened Nosferatu can perform. You do not seek payment or personal glory, but insists your Clan receive the praise. Other Nosferatu are irritated by this, and feel that what other Clans think of them is irrelevant.

Brujah

The rebellious, anti-authoritarian Brujah pride themselves on their free-wheeling, anti-social demeanor, and their rejection of the kind of the regimentation and rigid hierarchies that dominate most of the Camarilla. Brujah society falls into three distinct schools of thought, though individual Brujah often move from camp to camp during their life.

The first group of Brujah is called the Iconoclasts. They are wild, irresponsible, rebellious punks who aggressively lash out at anything they think helps prop up "the system." They are violent, aggressive, and tend to be younger than the others. Like mortal street punks, their social intercourse focuses on bragging, posturing, fighting, and insult contests.

They never make plans, have trouble agreeing on anything, and do not focus their efforts well. To them, the Brujah mission of anarchy manifests as violent outbursts and wild acts of destruction. They comprise the majority of the Clan.

The second group, called the Idealists, is less disorganized. The group consists mainly of older Vampires who are more contemplative and goal-oriented than any of the others. Though they believe in revolution as much as the Iconoclasts, they believe the only way to attain it is through discipline and planning. They often speak of the "Lesson of Carthage" and bitterly relate how the dream of a perfect society was destroyed by the other Clans.

They value cooperation, and try to create some sort of pecking orders within the Brujah. They indoctrinate new members into Clan rites and rituals, and zealously enforce the few Clan traditions. In this respect, they behave like the more structured Clans. Though their demands for order are often ignored by the other sub-groups, they do wield a degree of influence within the Brujah. They give the Brujah what little social structure it has, though they vigorously deny that they want to impose a governing system on the Clan. They carry out the Clan mandate of anarchy by formulating plans to overthrow mortal and Kindred systems, and by trying to get the rank-and-file Brujah to carry out their ideas. They are the second most numerous group in the Brujah.

The members of the third group, the Individualists, lie somewhere between the two others in age and in temperament. Like the Iconoclasts, they are often explosive and adventuresome. Like the Idealists, they often plan their actions and can work in concert. Unlike the other two, they do not lash out indiscriminately and they do not try to make the other Brujah execute their orders. Instead they craft a plan, and carry it out themselves. Or they announce a plan, and invite others along without dictating policy. They believe that anarchy requires individuals taking responsibility for all their own actions, and rejecting mindless conduct (like Iconoclast violence) and meaningless rules (like Idealist dictates). Though they are the least numerous subgroup of Brujah, they are the most effective in making measurable progress toward the group's goals through acts of rebellious, anarchic brilliance.

The difference between the Iconoclasts, Individualists and Idealists can be summed up as follows: the Iconoclasts try to be responsible for nothing, the Idealists try to be responsible for some personal goal, and the Individualists try to be responsible only for themselves. It is common for a Brujah to enter the Clans as an Iconoclast, grow to be an Individualist, and evolve into an Idealist as she becomes an Elder.

Clan Structure

The social lives of the Brujah Clan center around the hard-edged, rebellious, violent corners of mortal society. When the Clan assembles, they often do so in seamy punk bars or outdoors amidst industrial squalor. Idealists prefer to frequent University areas, libraries and think tanks.

Despite the efforts of the Idealists, the Brujah leadership structure is almost nonexistent. They are loosely organized, with no national or international meetings. Attempts by the Idealists to form international, national or state-wide councils have been shouted down by the fractious Brujah fledglings.

Though they never have formal meetings, the Brujah actually manage to disseminate information, argue about Clan policy (if any), issue warnings and threats, discipline Clan members and regularly accomplish tasks the official Clans can only handle through scheduled meetings. Here's how they do it:

The Brujah found that most of the Clan turns out for major concerts, block parties and counter-culture "happenings." The Brujah Packs that assemble usually stay in the immediate area long after the event. If they do not break into bouts of random violence, they usually argue about the issues of the day. These tense, spontaneous, late night showdowns evolved into informal meetings, called Rants. Any Brujah can attend, and can bring up any issue. The Rants are often long and heated, as some Brujah refuse to pay attention to others or take responsibility for keeping the meeting moving. Some even try to disrupt the Rants, claiming the meetings are too controlled.

Because the meetings are so informal, any Kindred can attend. Anarchs often show up to take part, and Tremere show up to take notes. (The Brujah have a great distaste for the Tremere "spies" and delight in harassing them throughout the Rant). Even some spirited mortals have found their way into Brujah Rants, attracted by the noise and high violence threshold, though few even begin to understand what is being discussed. Most are usually driven away in short order.

Gaining Power

Because there are three different Brujah subgroups, there are three different means of acquiring Prestige. (Note that Prestige itself is a very contradictory characteristic for this group.)

Brujah confer Prestige on their members for gutsy acts of recklessness and daring. The more anti-authoritarian the act, the more the Prestige conferred. Painting graffiti on an ancient, irreplaceable painting in Elysium is worth a little Prestige, though some members argue that the destruction of art contributes nothing significant to the advancement of Anarchy.

Telling off the Prince is better, especially if the Brujah gets away with it. Foiling a Tremere plot or shutting down the phone system confer far greater amounts of Prestige. The more an act contributes toward the overthrow of mortal or Kindred systems of rule, the more Prestige the Brujah receives.

There is a fundamental paradox in the manner in which the Elders confer Prestige on their young. Because they reward Brujah who bring low those in high positions of authority, they often find themselves obvious targets for younger Brujah looking to make their mark. This incongruity has kept this Clan divided and weak for centuries. Of course that is the way most Brujah like it — all the better to ensure the Clan is never used to support the establishment.

The younger ones also accuse the older Brujah of selling out on their anarchic mission by becoming as stuffy and structured as the Ventrue. The Elders, in self-defense, claim that the Neonates are not as wild as the Elders were when they were young, and the Iconoclasts are in no position to judge those who are older and more accomplished. Among the Iconoclasts, winning fights also confers Clan Prestige, as does triumphing over a rival Pack. Insulting a rival will also bring esteem and honor, as does toppling a valued member of the Clan. Iconoclasts who gain the respect of their peers often try to shed it quickly, before the double-edged sword of Prestige strikes them down. The Idealists are more comfortable with having high Prestige that the others. Many of them even crave it.

Individualists esteem other Brujah based on their value and contribution to the Clan and cause, but tend to treat all Kindred with a measure of respect, regardless of Prestige. Oddly enough, great Prestige is conferred when one individual or pack cooperates with other Brujah in a time of need. Most Brujah understand the need to support one another in time of need, and their pride in the Clan (paradoxical as it may sound) will always cause them to protect their "bloods" against outsiders.

Gathering Days

The Brujah have no gathering days. Small Rants occur on a regular basis, usually following concerts by underground bands. The better the band the larger the turnout, and the larger the Rant. Major Rants occur in each city following an appearance of the Grateful Dead. This is often the only time when Packs from all over the areas (and often several cities) get together.

Brujah sometimes hold their Rants in the concert hall or arena where the event was held. They Dominate the night watchmen to ensure privacy, and proceed to hash out their differences till morning.

Though the Brujah pride themselves on having no real Gathering Days, the Elders plan their activities around Rants they believe will be well attended, and use those large gatherings as an opportunity to dominate the Clan.

Power Rumors

Idealists are using the Rants as an opportunity to push their own agenda. The only thing a properly wild young Brujah can do is disrupt any Rant where any business is getting done.

The Rants are a good place to settle Clan business, but Malkavians disguised as Brujah keep disrupting them. They are spies for the Venture and Tremere, who still seek to wipe out the Brujah.

Some Brujah refer proudly to a secret Individualist plot to overthrow the government by turning important public officials to ghouls. They order their ghouls to blatantly magnify existing corruption to the point where it cannot be concealed any longer. They make corrupt politicians far less careful in concealing their chicanery and more flagrant in their flaunting of law and decency. The Brujah anxiously await the day that the public gets fed up with extreme government corruption and overthrows the system. The Individualists decided to institute anarchy this way because they want to make everyone into an anarchist, rather than imposing a system of anarchy on people who do not want it.

Character Ideas

You are a Brujah who wants to build your personal Prestige by challenging all members of other Clans to insult contests. If they do not agree to play along, you will follow them, harassing and disparaging them. Eventually they will give in.

You are a young Iconoclast who wants to join the Idealists by helping institute their plans among the rest of the Clan.

You are an Individualist who wants to contribute to anarchy in the world without resorting to meaningless violence, and without telling others what to do.

Gangrel

The Gangrel are loners and rugged individualists, preferring to assemble, even with each other, only rarely. As a result, Clan Prestige is of little concern to them. Still, they do look to Elders in times of crisis, and are concerned with keeping their young from getting out of hand. They live in horror of the intrigue and politics of other Clans and would do anything to avoid bringing such anarchy upon themselves. As a result, they create and uphold some minor social conventions, all of which revolve around maintaining "Clan Honor". Like rural farmers who live in isolated areas, they are suspicious of outsiders and acknowledge social niceties only when absolutely necessary.

Clan Structure

Because the Gangrel are essentially nomadic loners, they have little in the way of Clan organization. The largest social group they form are loosely confederated tribes. They do not get together, and are not very concerned with Prestige. They like wide open spaces, and are distrustful of, and uncomfortable in large groups. Because of the Lupines they are kept to the city, however, as much as they dislike its crowed, confined and polluted streets.

The Gangrel are a contradictory lot. On one hand they appear to be mellow forest dwellers who seem unconcerned with maneuvering with one another or betraying another to gain Prestige. On the other hand, they appear as fearsome, combative monsters, challenging and attacking one another to establish dominance.

Gaining Power

Gangrel seldom meet with one another, and consequently have little opportunity to jockey for Prestige. They have a strong respect for any Gangrel who survives their harsh life, and who do not use their powers to gain superiority over others.

When two Gangrel meet, they describe all they have witnessed, and tell all the tales they have recently heard. This spreads the Clan lore and history, and makes heroes out of some Gangrel. As a result, some Gangrel effortlessly raise in Prestige simply by being talked about. This uncomplicated network keeps the whole Clan well informed without requiring them to get together in large groups.

Sometimes Gangrel do clash. When they absolutely cannot agree, they resolve their differences by combats that other Clans consider very savage. The two tear into one another until one yields. The winner gains Prestige and the loser drops in Prestige. The loser can rechallenge the winner at any time.

Gangrel also engage in mock combat, which can seem very savage to other Kindred. They do this to get the full measure of the other, and see how the other has grown since they last fought. This mock combat, called the Ordeal, is another way to gain Prestige. Regardless of the outcome, it is a great honor to be selected by an older Gangrel for an Ordeal. The Clan believes that these mock combats keep them in fighting shape and make them all stronger.

Gathering Days

The Gangrel never have Clan meetings. Twice a year the Gangrel in a local area assemble for celebrations of the spring and autumn equinoxes. These are informal gatherings, and unless they are facing a direct threat, no business is done, it is strictly a celebration and social occasion. On May 8, the Gangrel celebrate Beltaine. They visit another Gangrel, or host a few Gangrel friends. This gives them an opportunity to show off their progeny (sometimes from afar, if they have not yet presented themselves to their Progeny), catch up on recent developments, and engage in recreational combat.

Power Rumors

Some Gangrel say the Gangrel Elders meet regularly in secret, and are trying to get the Clan to cohere and have regular meetings. Many Gangrel believe that this would compromise the independent nature of the Clan, though some say it would give them more strength.

Character Ideas

You are a Gangrel who lusts after Prestige. Rather than ranging your territory in the same fashion of your kin, you search them out, looking to challenge anyone you can find.

You are out to spread your fame far and wide. You try to spread false tales of your own glory to any who will listen.

You wish to get as far away from the other Kindred as possible, seeking to have nothing to do with such creatures. However, it is impossible to live in the country because of the Lupines, and until you can find some way to contact and befriend them, you must remain, miserably, in the city.

Malkavian

In rejecting the world, the Malkavians also reject standard social forms. When they meet, they choose parodies of human religious holidays and Kindred meeting times. They are so bizarre that it is impossible to describe any sort of consistent social structure among them. Though they do recognize one another as "family" it is not certain that they hold any sort of allegiance for the Clan. The sociability they do demonstrate for one another could be born out of a common delusion rather than any true feelings.

The truth is hard to decipher, as it always is with the Malkavians.

Clan Structure

The Malkavian have no apparent global, national or regional structure. Many do not even admit they belong to a Clan, insisting that they are Caitiff or that there is not such a thing as Clans. They do not attempt to control their young, and they do not rally behind the Clan in times of trouble. They are a collection of individuals who seem to have more in common with one another than with any other Clan or the Caitiff. For this reason, and the fact that they sometimes assemble, they are considered a Clan.

Gaining Power

The Malkavian system of Prestige generation seems to follow no visible pattern. Malkavians have been known to take the word of one of their Clan members as unquestionable law one day, and the next day do nothing but ridicule and humiliate him, and the next day completely ignore him. (But perhaps this is not really how they confirm Prestige since they treat all people in a strange and often inconsistent manner.) Members of other Clans have witnessed a Malkavian declare herself leader, and be followed unquestioningly by all other Malkavian. Then, several days, weeks or hours later, she inexplicably has no power at all. A Malkavian who once appeared to be greatly respected can suddenly be a pariah among his kind. Or a raving madman may suddenly

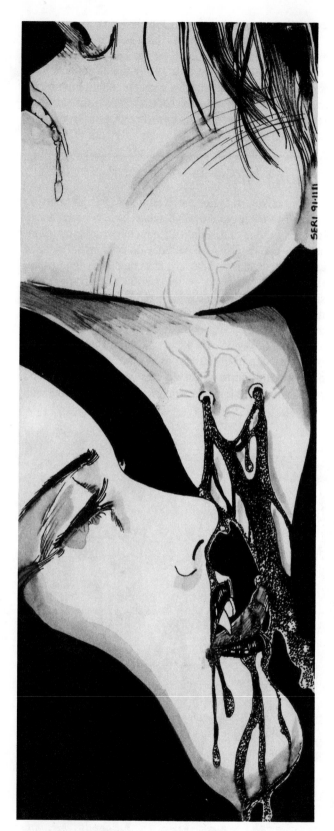

be heeded as if he was an emissary from Caine himself. In short, Malkavians rocket up and down the Prestige ladder with no rhyme or reason.

Any visible traditions designed to raise and lower Prestige appear to be nothing but parodies of the way other Clans behave. It is clear that the Malkavian themselves do not take them seriously. Though some take this as evidence that the Malkavian lack any sort of guidance, it may be more accurate to say they act on a form of guidance no one else can see or understand.

Gathering Days

Malkavian meetings are open to anyone, mortal or Kindred, who happen by during the meeting. Unfortunately, planning to attend a Malkavian meeting is difficult, and almost impossible. The Malkavian have inconsistent, shifting meeting days decided by long-standing tradition which only they seem to understand. Sometimes they meet on human holy days or days special or sacred to local mortals, like the Fourth of July. Sometimes they meet on days when Kindred Clans gather. Sometimes they won't meet for months on end. No one really knows what the pattern is. Some Kindred maintain that a common madness binds the Malkavian together and they all receive the same insight about where and when they should meet.

At any rate, Malkavian meetings are a mystery even the Tremere have not penetrated. When the Tremere discover that a Malkavian meeting has convened, they rush to attend. The Malkavian sometimes get together en masse for a few minutes just to watch the other Clans scramble to observe them.

At times, the Malkavian hold elaborate council sessions in destroyed churches, or abandoned buildings, complete with props and costumes. They mimic the behavior of other Vampires in their private Clan council meetings so thoroughly that the Ventrue and Tremere are alarmed about potential leaks. No one knows how the Malkavian know so much about other Clans' inner workings, but the other Clans deeply resent the revelation of their secrets.

The Malkavian call their meetings by a name that is a parody of another Clan council name, or sometimes by the real name. For instance, when they mimic Tremere meetings, they call their gathering the Circle of Seven Miseries. (For the purpose of the meeting, they organize into what they call the world-wide "Phyramid of Power" (pronounced FEAR-a-mid).

Power Rumors

Some Malkavians say that they are not a Clan, but that all Clans are really Malkavian. They maintain that the other Clans are subgroups that band together to avoid facing the inner demons to which the Malkavian surrendered. When other Clan members give up pretensions to sanity, or "Mortal Reasoning," they are truly free and can cross over to

Malkavian society. By this theory, Vampires Embraced by a Malkavian were simply fortunate enough to escape having to be Embraced by a deluded Clan.

Some non-Malkavians maintain that the Malkavians actually do hold real meetings, which are a complete secret to the rest of the world. The parody meetings which are open to other Clans are actually just part of an elaborate prank.

The Clan was not always disorganized and its members insane. In fact, it was once a power-mad, intrigue filled convocation, much as is the Tremere and the Ventrue. However, something happened, perhaps wisdom was finally discovered, and they began to take the path they are on now.

Character Ideas

You work at infiltrating another Clan to learn their secrets, and so as to be able to perform an exact parody of a high-ranking Cainite at the next Malkavian meeting.

You decide that you must have Prestige that will endure, and insist on being treated highly at all times.

Caitiff

The Caitiff have no structured society, and, as a result, no Clan Prestige. They do not assemble as a group, and have no customs that bind them together. Sometimes a small group of Caitiff will assemble to negotiate territory or address a common problem, but their meetings usually fall apart, due to their arrested social skills and innate suspicion of other Kindred.

However, there are a few rare Caitiff who have attained near mythic standing in their non-community. Caitiff who have performed an important service for the Prince, or saved other Caitiff from Vampire hunters, or generously yielded territory to newcomers may develop Prestige. Sometimes these unique individuals are looked to for leadership or advice, and serve as rudimentary Clan heads. But these are exceptions, and in general the Caitiff are most comfortable to remain loners.

Character Ideas

A Caitiff character may choose as her life's work the nearly impossible task of formally organizing the leaderless local Caitiff into a Clan as strong and diverse as any other.

A character may decide to make himself so useful to another Clan that they are forced to take him on as one of their own.

The character has become disgusted with his old Clan, and became a Caitiff by choice. He likes the freedom, and enjoys taunting his old Clan members at every opportunity. He feels truly "alive" to be free of their restrictions, and rejoices that he will no longer be manipulated by his dysfunctional Vampire family.

Gatherings of the Anarchs

Though they may be of differing Clans, Anarchs often have more in common with one another than with their parent Clans. Anarchs often work together to stop some local threat, investigate a mystery, gripe about the way the Elders run things, or just carouse. Within this sub-group, Prestige grows from wild exploits, acts of great daring, and from the stories and lies the Anarchs tell about themselves and others.

Brujah sometimes lead the Anarchs, encouraging them to disrupt the meetings of their own Clans, and subvert the Clans from within. The Anarchs are often eager to comply, and try to gain Prestige within the Anarchs community. (Note: Prestige among Anarchs is not measured with the Clan Prestige rating unless the Vampire severs all ties with his old Clan, and treats the Anarchs as his new family.)

Gatherings of the Camarilla

There are times when all of Kindred society needs to meet. This generally happens when a threat, like a rogue Methuselah, is looming. The Ventrue are usually responsible for assembling the Clan in a grand meeting called a Conclave.

Getting any business done is very difficult. The Tremere always appear, but give away little information, and seldom commit to anything. The Toreador love Conclaves, and use them as a chance to show off. Their participation is often limited to trivial matters. The Nosferatu emissaries listen well, but often do not take center stage. Brujah are often uncouth and disruptive. The Gangrel are easily bored if the meeting is not direct and to the point, and will leave if it breaks down into in-fighting. If a Malkavian shows up at all, his behavior is never predictable.

But if any business actually gets done, and the cause of the Kindred is furthered, the Vampire who convened the meeting is held in high regard by all his Clan and by many others outside the Clan as well.

BOONS AND FAVORS

The Rite of Prestation

Vampires gain status over individuals through an elaborate ritual of favors and boons called prestation. Prestation is based on the simple premise that when a Vampire receives an important gift or favor, he is beholden to its bestower and honor bound to return the favor. The greater the favor, the greater the debt. Until he pays back the obligation in kind, he is in the debt of the bestower, who has the right to call the debt due at any time. The bestower can call due the debt by requesting a service up to the size of the original favor, and sometimes more. On the surface this all appears little more than the straightforward commerce of mortals. But a lot more goes on under this polite facade. Vital issues of status and position are at stake.

In accepting the boon, the receiver automatically loses status. In some cases, merely asking for a favor causes the vampire to drop in status. The bestower in turn gains status by granting the boon (it is, after all, a demonstration of power). The status gained is commensurate with the magnitude of the favor, and the status of the vampire aided. Helping a neonate learn to survive provides less status than saving the Prince from certain destruction or embarrassment. The bestower rises in status in comparison to the receiver until the favor is returned and balance of status restored.

As a result of this curious system, many Kindred are not eager to call their favors due, especially when the one they granted the favor to is an eminent or influential member of the community. (A truly perverse example of how twisted relations between Vampires can become.) Instead they leave the beneficiaries of their largess to slowly twist in the wind, unable to regain their former status. A clever Kindred can milk the respect gained through prestation for far more than the original favor was worth. They can keep other Vampires in their place, and can even lord it over higher-status Vampires.

If a favor in return is not requested immediately, it leaves the receiver in the debt of the bestower. He cannot act against the bestower, and must maintain a courteous facade at all times. Meanwhile, the bestower can lord it over the receiver. However, the giver must be careful to avoid giving the receiver the opportunity to cancel the debt by incurring a like debt to the recipient.

In terms of the Status rules, you are considered to be the same status as the one who owes you a favor. While this change in the status rules only affects the bestower and the receiver (allowing you to treat as a peer the individual who formerly "outranked" you), others may pick up on it as well, and your over-all status might be affected. Though normally this is only temporary, sometimes through astute and clever ploys and moves it can be made permanent.

In general, how prestation affects status is completely up to your Storyteller. Play it how she calls it.

The Scope of the Debt

Prestation comes in different forms. Saving a life carries a great debt. Not only does the Vampire you saved owe you an immense favor, but all Vampires who depend on him or owe him favors are suddenly subservient to you. Saving the Prince's life means all the Vampires in a city owe you a debt (though in most cases a very small one).

Defeating an enemy will obligate all people who were threatened, and they owe you a favor in return. Protecting a Vampire from unmasking, or discovery by mortals, is worth a great favor. Helping out in the daily course of a Vampire's business is not worth much, unless the Vampire desperately needs the help.

Prestation works in minor ways as well, especially within Clans. If one Vampire gives a great party, the guests all feel an obligation to reciprocate, and always feel somewhat humbled in the presence of the party-giver, who is entitled to feel a certain smug self-righteousness until her guests reciprocate. The party giver cannot place herself above a high-ranking Vampire, or will it afford her major favors from all her guests, but she can expect them to act slightly deferential and respectful around her.

Because of prestation, small services are a great way for a Neonate to ingratiate herself with her betters. (Though it may earn her the contempt of her peers, who will accuse her of bootlicking.)

Granting a Boon

The ability to grant a boon is a demonstration of power. Thus many Kindred constantly search for ways to provide "assistance" to their fellows. This is especially true among the Tremere, who enjoy the reputation as the people you need to turn too if you are in need. Conversely, the inability to grant a requested boon can cause a serious loss of status.

Kindred are often offered favors by others, and when this occurs there can be a number of different reactions. It is dangerous to accept another's boon, especially from those of lower status, as you never know when it might be called due. Moreover, once the boon is given, its recipient has no say in what will be requested in return.

There are three different ways in which you can react when a boon is offered you. They are:

• **Acceptance:** You accept the boon, and are bound by prestation to the giver.

• **Refusal:** You immediately and forthrightly refuses the gift of the boon. This is often a case of one-upsmanship. You have just publicly announced that you do not need the other's boon. The other may lose status because of the humiliation.

• **Negation:** You refuse the gift of the boon, but in such a way so as to avoid insult (which can be very difficult). "Only that I may be of further service to you my Prince." In so doing you may gain status.

Returning a Boon

There are a number of different way in which a debt can be erased. It all depends on what the bestower wants from you, and when she wants it. Of course, if a Vampire can find a way to return the favor before being asked, it can be gotten rid of on your own terms and more quickly. The following are four different way in which a boon can be returned:

• **Trivial:** The bestower asks a trivial favor in return. e.g.: the other's presence at a party. The nature of the debt will affect whether a boon is trivial or substantial. Asking for a trivial boon will gain both parties some minor status, for being able to grant the boon and for requesting such a minor boon.

• **Balanced:** The favor returned equals the debt. Once it is paid, all is equal again and as it once was.

• **Substantial:** The bestower asks for a favor in return which is within the ability

of the lord to grant, but may cause the receiver some difficulty. Such a boon must be met, regardless of the cost, but may gain the receiver some status.

• **Overwhelming:** The favor returned exceeds the debt owed by an overwhelming degree. If it is too ridiculous, then the receiver may refuse without loss of status.

Oath-keeping

Most Kindred willingly adhere to the restraints of prestation. The Ventrue, Tremere and Toreador are scrupulous in how the hold to its strict rules. Some, like the Brujah, do so grudgingly (except for the Anarchs, who hold it in contempt). Some, like the Nosferatu, habitually ignore the proper etiquette when interacting with those to whom they are indebted (they are not obsequious enough). The Malkavian tend to ignore prestation entirely, though when they do play along, they find a way to corrupt the payback.

The Caitiff usually do not acknowledge the loss of status for a favor, though they usually do honor the debts. This is usually not an issue, as few Kindred will perform a service or grant a boon to a Caitiff. There is little status to be gained by assisting Caitiff.

The whole idea of Prestation hinges on whether or not the receiver publicly acknowledges the debt. This is a signal to others, demonstrating if you play by the rules or not. Those who do not play by the rules are distrusted ("Your word is not good enough for me!") and may lose status. In some cases the receiver may (however reluctantly) be forced to acknowledge the debt, no matter how it weakens them. For example, if a neonate risks Final Death for a Prince, then that Prince had better reward such behavior if he does not want to be humiliated.

Oath-breaking

Prestation is not enforced by any code other than the code of honor. A Vampire is no more bound by it than by any other promises she makes. No one will kill her for oath-breaking, but the friends and Clan of the aggrieved Vampire may make her life difficult. Those bound to the aggrieved Vampire by ties of prestation are also expected to snub and shun the Vampire who refuses to acknowledge the debt.

The Status lost by the offender will be considerable, but varies according to the circumstances and the numbers of individuals who side with the offender. Usually it will be at least one Status point, likely many more.

Sometimes a Vampire will swear vengeance against an oath-breaker. Ironically, those with great status, like the Prince, are the least likely to try to squirm out of returning a favor. They stand to lose a lot of Status if they break their word, and Status is what helps them hold onto their power.

Refusing to honor a boon often causes Vampires to strike back with all their ability. Refusing to honor a debt to a minor Vampire may earn you only personal revenge, but shafting an Elder can bring attacks from the entire Clan of the city. The injured party is still not allowed to kill the offender, but he can make life very difficult for the offender by sabotaging his feeding grounds, exposing his covert plots and attacking his ghouls.

Ostracism

The strongest revenge is ostracism. It is reserved for powerful acts of betrayal. If the wronged Vampire reports the oath-breaking to the other Kindred, and makes his case well, he may persuade his own Clan, the other Clans and sometimes the offender's Clan to ostracize the oath-breaker.

The offending Vampire is shunned by the Camarilla, and loses status with his peers. No one will work with him, or help him out. He is a pariah until he makes full restitution. No one will trust him, though Anarchs often respect those cast out of good society. In tight-knit Vampire circles, ostracism can be worse than the Blood Hunt (only a slight exaggeration).

NEW CLANS

Here are four new Clans, and one blood line (a type of minor Clan) which you can use to create characters. The inclusion of these Clans in this book covers all of the Clans, except the two Sabbat Clans. While you can use any of them to create a character, we hope these new Clans will provide you with some new concepts for characters and a broader range of character types to choose from.

Your Storyteller may create new blood lines or even Clans for her own Chronicle, so you should ask if their are any other Clans. In some Chronicles it might even be acceptable for you to create a blood line for your own character (with the help and supervision of the Storyteller, of course). If you do have the freedom to do so, we strongly encourage you to try it out — you will not find a more unique character.

Note: none of the Disciplines of these new Clans can be taken freely by characters from other Clans, though generally the Caitiff are free to do so. The express permission of the Storyteller is required before you can buy any of these disciplines during character creation (by using freebie points), or learn them during the Chronicle. The possessors of these Disciplines are very protective of them, and they do not readily teach them to outsiders.

Assamite

Nickname: Assassin

Vampires are the killers of the night, and none more exemplify this than the Assamites, slayers of both Kindred and kine. Called in regularly by the world's Justicars as Archons, and by Princes as assassins, there is nobody who is more feared by the Kindred. Secretive and clannish, Assamites will travel anywhere in search of their targets, accepting as payment the blood of their employers. Its members have gained a fearsome reputation as assassins of a most remarkable skill.

While Assamites spend much of their time in the same solitary pursuits of other Kindred, they are best known for their skills as hired killers. In exchange for using their unique talents against the enemies of Princes and Anarchs alike, the Assamites demand a portion of their employer's Vitæ. They do not accept every petition for aid, but once they have accepted a "contract" they consider themselves honor-bound to carry out the exact word of the agreement.

Founded more than a millennia ago in the hinterlands of the Turkish Mountains, this Clan has always fiercely protected its privacy. They are fundamentalists of a bizarre brand, a mixture of many Middle Eastern religions and Kindred mythology. They believe that the only way for Vampires to reach heaven to become closer to Caine — and the only means of doing this is to rise in generation.

For much of their early history they engaged in Diablerie, seeking always to bring themselves closer to "the One." They became the most feared killers among the Kindred. Clan legend claims their founder slew two of the second-generation Children of Caine by his own hand and at the behest of their brothers and sisters. It remains a mark of great distinction within the Clan to be hired to slay a Cainite of earlier generation, and to succeed single-handedly.

However, it is no longer possible for them to engage in Diablerie, due to an agreement made long ago. During the period of the great uprisings and the birth of the Sabbat late in the middle ages, the Assamites found it easy to hunt their prey. So many Elders were being killed that eventually the Camarilla declared a blood hunt against the entire Assamite Clan. After a period of seven years, Alamut, their ancient fortress sanctuary, was close to being discovered. For the first time in their history they sued for peace, and negotiated a complicated treaty.

The Assamites agreed to never again hunt other Kindred for their blood, and in exchange the blood hunt against them was called off. However, a great ritual was cast upon the entire Clan by the Council of Seven of the Tremere, which made it impossible for Assamites to drink the blood of other Kindred (see Clan weakness, below).

However, they managed to adapt some of the most ancient rites of their Clan into a means of reaching the same end as that of Diablerie. This was also the beginning of their role as hired assassins. The blood they take as pay from those who hired them is collected and then used in a ritual of creation. When they hold their five-year gatherings at Alamut, they are able to brew potions using the blood thus collected to raise the effective generation of a Clan member.

Any Assamite hoping to reduce her generation must gather 200 points of blood from Vampires of equal or lesser generation for the potion to be effective — it usually takes decades to gather that much blood. It is generally stored in vials and canisters, and is the most prized possession of any from this Clan.

Each Assamite gives a tenth of the blood which they gather to their Sires. While not Blood Bound or dominated into following the Clan traditions, individual Assamites are usually fanatically loyal to the Clan. No Clan has a stronger "Fight one, fight us all mentality." Should anyone try to cheat an Assamite, or attack her outside of an assassination attempt, then the whole weight of the Clan will be brought upon his head.

Should an assassin be killed by a target, however, the Clan will take no additional revenge. They will not accept any other contracts for the head of that individual, and will even honor him when they are given a chance. After all, it takes a very formidable Kindred to save himself from an Assamite assassination attempt.

Once a contract has been accepted, the assassin will not stop trying to fill it until the target is dead or she has proof the employer violated her trust (told her someone was ninth generation when he was sixth, or neglected to mention he was protected by a pack of Lupines).

Assamites also take contracts from mortals, and in this fashion have built up a vast amount of Clan wealth. This wealth is left at the disposal of the Clan, as individual members rarely have need of much money.

Appearance: Since most of them are of Middle Eastern heritage, they share the characteristics of peoples from that area — swarthy skin, aquiline features and black hair. Additionally, while most Vampires become paler through time, the members of this Clan become darker as the years pass by, until their skin turns a dark ebony.

Haven: The Elders of the Assamite Clan live at Alamut, located atop a mountain somewhere in Asia Minor. The neonates of the Clan spend very little time there after their initial seven-year initiation is over. They travel to different parts of the world seeking their fortunes and hoping to creating business. While away from the Clan haven, they seek the most inaccessible and private locations as their havens — luxury is not a concern.

Background: Assamites only create progeny when they have the permission of the Clan. Generally, the Clan will be watching a number of humans for a long time before allowing a member to initiate the subject. If permission is granted, the mortal must serve the Kindred for seven years, and only if she serves exceedingly well is she embraced (otherwise they are killed). They are then called Fidais and apprenticed for another seven years, during which time they are are introduced to the mysteries of the Clan and taught the techniques of assassination. During this entire period they are expect to be fanatically loyal to the Clan. Some time ago the Clan recognized the value of female assassins and keeps a 50-50 gender ratio as much as possible.

Character Creation: Almost all Assamites are still of Middle Eastern descent, and many are former soldiers, explorers, investigators or criminals. Their Natures and Demeanors are usually similar but almost never the same. Any attributes may be primary, but skills are usually the primary abilities. Popular backgrounds include Mentor (your Sire) and Clan Prestige (so you get plum contracts). All Assamites should have high combat skills.

Clan Disciplines: Celerity, Obfuscate, Quietus

Weaknesses: Assamites have two blood-related disadvantages. The first is the Clan requirement they tithe the blood they receive in payment to their Sire. The second is that they are unable to imbibe the blood of other Kindred, and if it is forced in them it acts as does poison to a mortal. Each blood point of another Kindred which somehow gets into them will do one health level of non-aggravated wounds before it is destroyed.

Organization: Far from the prying eyes of Kindred and kine alike, the Assamite leaders hold court in Alamut ("Eagles Nest"), their ancient mountain fastness. Here they receive assassination requests from the most powerful Kindred and kine, and assign assassins to specific contracts. Though it is always a request, you lose much Prestige if you refuse an assignment. Younger Assamites are spread across the world, and use their own judgement on accepting assignments from individuals other than Clan leaders.

Gaining Clan Prestige: The most obvious route for gaining Clan prestige is through successful assassinations, but there are other ways. Demonstrating loyalty to the Clan and one's Sire is an excellent means of gaining Prestige. Additionally, members of the Clan trade blood they have received as payment among themselves. For instance, a ninth-generation Assamite may trade two points of tenth-generation Vitæ to a tenth-generation sister in exchange for one point of ninth-generation blood. Being able to assist other Clan members like this gains one Prestige as well.

Quote: *"Their idiot games of power are not ours. What need have we for ruling a petty mass of squabbling sycophants when we are already on the true path? There are none who do not quake at the slightest hint of our presence, and that leaves a taste sweeter than blood in my mouth."*

Stereotypes:

• The Camarilla — A very useful pool of employers, but for us to join would be the height of stupidity. We gain far more acting outside their laws than we would within.

When you hear of one of these dogs in our city, beware! Watch them as you would a tiger poised to attack but never, never let them know of you. When you find who their victim is, do nothing to interfere—it is never worth it to draw their wrath.

Khalid, Nosferatu Elder of Chicago to his progeny

• The Sabbat — Useless Childer. They kill for no reason and with no grace — what good is a murder if it took the deaths of 20 of your Brothers and Sisters? It takes 100 of them to do what one of us can do.

Pretentious fools, they do our job for us. Who cares if they only kill those others want them to? In the end more of the Elders are extinguished. Their very presence spreads disharmony within the Camarilla.

Hook, Sabbat Scout

• The Inconnu — These Elders are the greatest challenge of all. If any fool requests you kill a member of this ancient group, send them to the mountain top.

They are murderous barbarians who care not what they destroy. They still seek after our blood, despite their oaths. All of it is a result of their twisted understanding of Golconda.

Mahatma, Monitor of Istanbul

Quietus

A quiet death is the goal of this discipline, and those who know it can kill without anyone knowing they were around. It is a discipline which all in the Clan seek to master. It is invariably the highest level Discipline any of them has. Assamite blood is nearly as poisonous to other Kindred as their blood is to the Assamites. Most of these powers reflect that all beings, in one way or another, are connected in the blood which is so central in their unlives.

Level One:

Silence of Death: With this power the Assamite can create a zone from which no sound may escape. For 20 feet around him in every direction there is complete silence. He could run at full speed, fire a machine gun or set off 100 pounds of dynamite right where he stands and no one would hear it as long as the sound was created within that zone. Note that the character can still hear things going on outside of this circle of silence, but cannot himself hear anything going on within the circle. This zone of silence costs one blood point to create.

Level Two:

Weakness: With but a touch of the hand and an expenditure of a Blood Point (which is actually brought to the surface of the palm), the Assamite can reduce her foe's Stamina by one point. This requires not only physical contact but also a Willpower roll with a difficulty equal to the target's Stamina + Fortitude. The number of successes gained on the roll determine how long the Stamina is lost.

1 success	One turn
2 successes	One hour
3 successes	One day
4 successes	One month
5 successes	Permanently (though Stamina can be bought back up with experience)

If a mortal is reduced to 0 Stamina by use of this power, he becomes very sick and has no immunities to disease. If one of the Kindred is reduced to zero Stamina by this power, she immediately enters Torpor and does not recover until one of their Stamina points have returned. If all their Stamina has been permanently destroyed, then they can only recover from torpor through mystical means.

Level Three:

Diseased: By once again touching a foe with the hand and spending Blood Points, the Assamite can reduce all his opponent's physical attributes by one. This requires a Willpower roll against the opponent's Willpower, and the number of successes obtained indicate how quickly the physical attributes return (if ever), just as they do in Weakness (see above). To use the Diseased power, the attacker must expend three Blood Points. If either Strength or Dexterity are reduced to zero, then the target cannot move until a point has been recovered. The effects on Stamina are the same as in Weakness.

Level Four:

Blood Agony: A character with this power can use his blood to cause aggravated wounds. The blood is used to coat a weapon like a sword, bullets or even fingernails. The weapon does damage normally, but each wound thus caused is an aggravated one.

Each extra blood point used on a weapon allows it to cause aggravated wounds on an additional hit. Thus if Absolom were to spend two Blood Points coating his broad sword, then he could hit once and do aggravated damage, miss and then hit again for aggravated wounds. No more hits would cause this sort of damage until he coated the blade again. Note that if a character hits but does no damage, the blood is used but no aggravated wounds are caused. The weapon must be large enough to accept all the blood a Kindred wants to smear on it. A bullet, for example, could not reasonably have any blood on it, and the blood would not cling during acceleration.

Level Five:

Taste of Death: The Vampire can effectively spit blood at her foes, doing aggravated wounds to those hit. This attack has a range of 10 feet for every point of Strength and Potence the character has and it does two dice of aggravated damage for every point of blood put into it. The attack is almost silent but the wounds it leaves cause horrible, permanent scars on mortals and Kindred alike.

Level Six:

Blood Sweat: By concentrating on the intended target, the character causes the target to bleed profusely from his sweat glands. This requires that the Vampire can see the target, and successfully roll Willpower with a difficulty of the target's Stamina + 3. The number of successes signifies the number of blood points lost. This happens at a rate of two per round. If it is a mortal target and he is reduced to zero blood points, then he dies as a result of blood loss. However, if the target is Kindred, she will enter Frenzy due to blood loss.

Blood Empathy: The character is able to leave traces of her feelings on the blood in a Vessel's system. If anyone drinks of this blood after the character has employed this power, the drinker will assume the feelings left by the character. This effect lasts for one day per blood point imbibed. To counteract this effect, the drinker must roll Willpower vs. a difficulty of 8. The number of successes needed equals the points of blood taken from the vessel.

Level Seven

Leech: The character no longer needs to bite a target to drink their blood. If the Vampire can make skin contact with the target, then she may take Vitæ in this manner. This power leaves no marks where skin contact was made. The Kindred may draw her Stamina in Blood Points per round with the expenditure of one Willpower point.

Foul Blood: On command, the blood in a Vessel forever becomes vile and undrinkable for anyone but the character. Anyone drinking this blood will take three damage levels of damage per point of blood imbibed. The character can continue to drink from the vessel without harm.

Level Eight:

Blood Clot: After touching the target with a blood-covered palm (and thus using 1 blood point), the character can cause the target's blood to clot inside the body. The character must roll his Willpower (with a difficulty equal to the target's blood points) with each success indicating the number of blood points that clot and cannot be used in any

fashion. The target must actually cut themselves open and bleed themselves in order to get rid of the "bad blood" which is now useless to them. This effect is cumulative, so the character can continue to clot the target's blood on successive turns. The character need not attempt to clot all of blood at once, and can clot as little as one Blood Point per turn (as long as at least one success is obtained). Note: using this power on humans to clot more than one point of blood makes them experience a stroke.

Level Nine:

Erosion: After touching the target with a blood-covered palm and using 5 blood points, the character can immediately reduce the target's Strength, Dexterity and Stamina to Zero. This will incapacitate the target as described earlier. In order to succeed, the character must win a successful Willpower versus Willpower opposed roll (difficulty 8) with the target. The target will only regain these points after the number of days equal to the number of successes the character received have passed.

Level Ten:

Immaculate Vitae: By using this discipline to alter his blood, the character is able to Blood Bond drinkers to him even if they drink one blood point of his Vitæ only once. This discipline will remove any Blood Bond previously held by the drinker in favor of the newly forged one only if the new bond is formed with a Kindred of an earlier generation than the first.

The Followers of Set

Nickname: Sand-Snakes

The Followers of Set, or Setites as they often call themselves, make up one of the most widely loathed Clans in the world. The Camarilla decision to ask the Setites to join came only after weeks of divisive debate, and the fact that few Setites responded to the call was met with a wave of relief from the young sect.

The explanation for this reaction lies with the very nature of the Setites. They are the masters of moral and spiritual corruption. They seem to have an uncanny ability to find the weakness in any organization or individual, and the uncommon urge to exploit it. Drugs, sex, money or power are their weapons of corruption and they take great delight in using them against Kindred and kine alike. The Setites believe that the power of decay and corruption is absolute and no one is immune. It is, in fact, a point of pride.

Although few Setites have become members of the Camarilla, this has not stopped factions within that group from making use of their special talents. Dealing with the Setites can be very risky as many a Prince and Elder have learned to their dismay. In the world of Kindred politics, the Followers of Set have the distinction of being regarded as a necessary evil. Some of the Elder Setites are rumored to be major instigators of various purges and Holy Wars which have plagued much of human history. Secretive and well hidden, their presence in a region is rarely known until an action or event reveals them. They are fierce and cunning manipulators.

The Followers claim to be able to trace their lineage back to the Egyptian Dark God himself. The truth of this, however, remains unrevealed. They are darkly powerful beings with unclear interests beyond the assumption of mortal and supernatural power.

According to legend, the Clan has its origins in Ancient Egypt. About 5000 B.C., a group of powerful Kindred gathered around the Nile River delta. Where these Kindred came from the legends do not say, but they are said to have established a thriving civilization with themselves as the ruling Gods. Among these Kindred was one named Sutekh. Sutekh, renowned as a warrior and hunter, stalked the darkness like a great beast and by 3300 B.C. was being worshipped by some mortals as the God of Night and Darkness. He was more than likely a member of the third generation, an Antediluvian.

For the next two millennia, Sutekh, now calling himself Set, enjoyed the worship of mortals and the respect of his fellow Kindred. But then a power struggle began when Osiris and several other Progeny began to claim absolute kingship over the rest of the Kindred. Set opposed Osiris, and for several hundred years a dark war was waged with savage intensity. By 900 B.C., the tide had turned against Set and his followers. Heru-Behutet and his warriors defeated Set and his allies in a great battle. Set was exiled and his followers slaughtered. In his anguish, Set vowed that if he was to be exiled into the darkness then that darkness would become all powerful.

In the centuries that followed, Set recruited new followers. Most came from Egypt but there were others as well. Greeks, Romans, Persians, and Semites all fell under the influence of Set, God of

Darkness. His message was carried to the far corners of the known world. From the mountains of Spain to the shores of the Black Sea, the seeds of darkness were planted. Finally, in 33 A.D., Set himself vanished from the world (likely to escape being a casually of the Jyhad). Before he disappeared, Set promised his followers that he would one day return in all his dark glory.

Even after his disappearance, this Clan grew in power. Always small in number, it exerted an influence that belied its size. Some say that they were partially responsible for forming the Inquisition, though there is no proof of this. Empires have come and gone and still the Followers of Set carry on their Master's dark traditions.

In modern times, the Setites found a new home in the Western Hemisphere. Both Jamaica and Haiti became fertile recruiting grounds for the Clan. Using the sophisticated science of modern times, the Setites became druglords extraordinaire. Their money and knowledge helped perfect crack cocaine and their love of perversity caused them to use modern marketing techniques to help flood European and American markets with it. There are several Haitian Secret Societies and Jamaican Posses rumored to be under their control, along with at least one Middle Eastern terrorist group. Wherever there is violence, corruption and misery, the Followers of Set can be found.

The first Follower into an area will establish a temple and prepare the way for the others. Once others arrive, they all stay at the temple until they have enough power to found their own. Each temple is at the center of a web of corruption, and is always controlled by a single Kindred (though she may have Kindred assistants — neonates who have not yet founded their own temple).

Appearance: The vast majority of the Followers of Set have very distinct Middle Eastern features, however, increasing numbers of members are taken from all races. Red hair is especially prized because it is considered a mark of Set. When the Followers are seen, they are usually garbed in deepest ebony robes of an ancient quasi-Egyptian style. Ritual disfigurement is also common, though the nature seems to vary from member to member.

Haven: The Setites prefer Havens deep underground, and they are often either caves or bunkers. Often, the walls of these Havens are decorated with Egyptian hieroglyphics telling the story of Set. These haven are known as Temples, and they are always under or near the headquarters for the Settites' criminal activities.

Background: Typically, the Followers of Set choose Neonates from their own human Retainers. They choose the ones who are the most devious and intelligent and have proved themselves over a number of years. Originally, only those of Egyptian descent were chosen as Retainers. Within the last century, however, a number of Europeans and Americans have been taken in.

Character Creation: Most Setites have an Outsider Concept although there are a small number of Dilettantes, Criminals and Politicians among them. They are often Curmudgeons or Deviants by Nature and will adopt whatever Demeanor suits them at the time. Social Attributes are Primary as are Talents. Most have the Background of Retainers and many have Contacts and Allies throughout various criminal organizations.

Clan Disciplines: Obfuscate, Presence, Serpentis

Weaknesses: Setites are extremely susceptible to sunlight. Double the dice for damage from any exposure to it. They are also susceptible to bright lights and take a -1 penalty to any die roll while in bright light (i.e. spotlights, nightclub strobe lights, searchlights, magnesium flares, etc.).

Organization: The Followers of Set have their own hierarchy loosely based on the temple structure of Ancient Egypt. Each city with a Setite presence has its own local Temple of Set presided over by a Kindred priest or priestess. There may be one or more sub-priests depending on the size of the Domain. There are usually three to five human Retainers per priest. The Grand Temple of Set is rumored to be somewhere in southern Sudan near the Ugandan border. There are monthly gatherings held in each temple at the dark of the moon. It is rumored that once every century there is a great gathering held at the Grand Temple.

It is also said that there once was a group known as the Children of Osiris who were opposed to the Followers of Set. Nothing is known of them, and the Setites claim to have literally consumed them. However, the Clan is fanatical in its attempts to discover if any of them remain, and take extreme precautions to protect themselves from the Children.

Gaining Clan Status: Gaining status within the Followers of Set is done through enslaving others through their own weaknesses. The more followers a Setite has, the more respected she becomes among her peers. Setites can also gain status by corrupting people and Kindred in high positions. The more respected the person being corrupted, the greater the status gained.

Quote: *"We are the small voice that whispers to you in the lonely hours of the night. We call to the Darkness within all of you. We came from the Dark and to the Dark we shall all return."*

Stereotypes:

The Camarilla — A group of arrogant fools who think they can use us when in truth it is we who use them. The Toreadors with their vain artistic pretensions and degenerate tastes are a special favorite. The Tremere and Ventrue Clans' love of power often leads them to us. The others all have their various weaknesses that make them easy prey too.

Dealing with the Followers of Set is, in effect, dealing with the Devil. Yes, they have their uses but then so does an Atomic Bomb and like said A-Bomb the Setites should be handled with extreme care and caution.

Galen, Elder of Clan Ventrue

The Sabbat — They belong to us already; they just don't know it yet. The darkness is strong in them but they love it in a different way than we do. They definitely do not understand the darkness as we do nor can they make use of it like we can.

Damned Snakes! The Camarilla is too weak and contentious to realize what a threat these bastards really are. You don't use a snake. You kill it before it kills you!

Malachaius, Elder of Clan Tzimisces

The Inconnu — Let sleeping fools lie. They think they're safe, but what they don't realize is that the darkness is everywhere. Like everyone else, they have their own weaknesses. Even they are not immune to us.

They are arrogant just like their Elder and like their Elder they too can and will be brought down. It is just a matter of time. Until then, we must do what we can to counter them.

Nefer-meri-Isis, Fourth Generation Ventrue

Serpentis (Gifts of Set)

This Discipline is derived and developed from the legendary powers of Set, and it is entirely unique to this Clan. Most of the powers work around the concept of corruption in one way or another.

Level One:

The Eyes of the Serpent: The eyes of the Setite appear to be gold with large black irises, and mortals around the character find themselves strangely attracted to him. These eyes are highly beguiling, and will immobilize mortals who look into them. Until the character takes his eyes off of them they are frozen in place. No roll is required for the use of this power, but it can be avoided if the mortal takes care not to look into his eyes. Vampires can also be affected by this power, but the Setite must succeed a Willpower roll (difficulty of 9) in order for it to work.

Level Two:

The Tongue of the Serpent: The Setite can transform her tongue into a long, forked, serpent's tongue. This tongue is generally about 18 inches long and can be used in melee combat. Its sharp forked ends do aggravated wounds (Difficulty 6, Strength damage), and if any damage is done, can suck out blood from the target on the next turn as though she had sunk her fangs into the neck.

Level Three:

Mummify: With this power a Vampire can assume an almost invulnerable form. The character enters a state similar to torpor, during which the only things which can harm him are sunlight and fire. However, the character is completely incapable of any action, including those disciplines which are normally active during torpor. The character can only be revived from this state by the taste of another's blood.

Level Four:

Form of the Serpent: The Setite is able to transform into a large, black Cobra — about six feet in length, half a foot around and the same weight as the character. When in this form the character benefits from all the advantages of it: slithering through small holes, poisonous bite (to mortals at least), and its rarified sense of smell. The character is able to use all of his other Disciplines while in this form.

Level Five:

The Heart of Darkness: This power allows the Setite to remove her heart from her body. Given a number of hours in which to operate, it can even be performed on other Kindred. This power can only be used at the dark of the Moon (the new moon). The heart must then be kept in a small clay urn, often buried underground. This effectively makes the Setite "stake proof," and also makes it easier to resist Frenzy (after all, the heart is the source of emotion). All rolls made to resist Frenzy are made at -2 to the difficulty.

The major danger of this power is that someone else will find the heart. If this happens, then the Setite is completely at the mercy of the finder. If the heart is cast into a fire or exposed to sunlight, then the Setite dies a horrible death. This is the only way that a Setite heart can be destroyed. Many Setites either carry their hearts with them or have several false hearts buried in different places. Most of them are too paranoid to visit their own heart, out of fear that they will lead someone to it, yet they live in fear because they are not sure it is still there. If the heart is impaled by a wooden stake then the Setite is put into instant torpor. There are

rumors that through possessing the hearts of their progeny the Elder Setites control their progeny. If this is true then it helps explain why the Clan is so tightly bound.

Level Six:

Temptation: The character can attempt to goad the target into doing evil simply by speaking with her and telling her about her weaknesses (roleplay it). This action will happen even if the target will lose Humanity because of it. To successfully goad the target, the character must roll his Wits + Manipulation against the target's Humanity (difficulty of 8 for both). If the amount of accumulated successes for the character equal or exceed the target's Humanity then she will begin to act in a highly corrupt and decadent manner as if she had no Humanity. The character is able to direct the corruption to some degree by making "suggestions." This effect is permanent, though eventually the target can overcome it by spending a variable number of Willpower points (often around eight), in the same fashion they are used to overcome a derangement. Willpower can be employed to resist the "suggestions" made by the character. The user of the Discipline must roll against difficulty 9 in order to affect a target who has achieved Golconda, while the target need only roll 7.

Obsession: This power creates an overpowering lust for whatever the character wills. The character need only speak with the target, telling him about this "lust." Whether it be money, sex or power, the target will crave it. Every day the target must possess or experience what he is obsessed with, or he will fall into a Frenzy when dawn nears. To successfully obsess the target, the character must roll his Wits + Manipulation against the target's Humanity (difficulty of 8 for both). If the amount of accumulated successes for the character equals or exceeds the target's Humanity, then he is overcome with the lust. This effect is permanent, though eventually the target can overcome it by spending a variable number of Willpower points (often around 8) in the same fashion they are used to overcome a derangement. See above for rules if this power is used against those who have achieved Golconda.

Level Seven:

Phobia: The target of this power can be given a fear chosen by the Vampire. The character need simply talk to him his fear. This fear can be as broad as cars to as specific as pink '79 Fords. Whenever the target is exposed to the object of his fear he must make three Courage rolls of 8 in order to stay in the area of the object. In order to come in contact with the object of the phobia, the target must spend Willpower points. The fear can be considered a powerful Derangement that can be removed by continued expenditure of Willpower points. To successfully implant the fear in the target, the character must roll her Wits + Manipulation versus the target's Humanity (difficulty of 8 for both). If the amount of accumulated successes for the character equals or exceeds the target's Humanity, then he is overcome with the fear. See above if the target has achieved Golconda.

Level Eight:

Corruption: By means of this discipline the character floods the target's mind with assorted memories of when the target let his Beast rule his heart and mind. As a result, the target becomes addicted to the feelings of sadism in the worst way. The target will lose Willpower at a rate of one per month until they sink into a murderous rage. To successfully corrupt a target the character must roll Manipulation + Empathy against the target's Humanity and accumulate as many successes as the target has Humanity. Anyone using this power who has more than three Humanity loses a Humanity point for causing the corruption. Note: this will not effect someone with 10 Willpower points or those who have achieved Golconda.

Level Nine:

Form of Corruption: This power is exactly the same as the Level 8 Discipline Corruption except that the corrupting evil can be "attached" to a specific object that will instill sadistic tendencies in anyone who touches it (perform an extended resisted roll of the creator's Manipulation+Subterfuge against the target's Humanity). The user of the power loses one point of Humanity for releasing such an object on the world, but no additional points are lost unless the creator learns of those who have been affected by the evil object. In this case, additional Humanity is lost only if those affected have a Humanity themselves of greater than three.

Level Ten:

Mark of Damnation: By placing her hand on the intended target's forehead, the user of this Discipline burns a hideous brand into the body and soul. Anyone looking at a target marred by this hideous disfigurement must accumulate five Self-Control successes (difficulty of 8) in three turns or less or wildly attack the target. This mark is so hideous that if the target looks at her own reflection she will attack the reflection until it is destroyed. The only way to resist this effect is to not be touched by the character. To communicate with anyone the target must remain out of sight, *in complete darkness*. The effects of this power can be overcome, but it requires powerful Tremere rituals or the caster's blessing in order to do so.

Giovanni

Nickname: Necromancers

No other Clan is more intent on maintaining a front of respectability than the Giovanni, and none are more repulsive at heart. Rich merchants, speculators and investors, Giovannis spend most of their nights manipulating their vast assets from skyscraper offices. They spend the rest of the night in crypts and mausoleums carrying out their dark and morbid rites.

Legend has it the Clan founder hoped to bolster his own power by Embracing a coven of Venetian Necromancers. This coven was actually a tightly knit family of Giovannis who had strong trade interests in the Mediterranean region. They repaid their Sire for his gift by slaying him and all his other descendants. The immediate reaction from Camarilla around the world was fear and horror, and many joined together to hunt these Devil Kindred. After almost a century of intermittent warfare, the Giovannis made peace with their foes by promising to maintain a low profile and keep out of Kindred politics, a pledge they have apparently maintained to this day.

Still, suspicion of this Clan has continued to the present day. By staying neutral in Cainite battles, the Giovanni have had free reign to build their merchant empires. Now the Clan's wealth is undeniable, but no one knows exactly what they use this wealth for. Few outsiders have ever taken part in their Necromantic rituals, so no one really knows the purpose of these. Instead, suspicions and innuendoes have taken the places of facts and truths.

Every member of this Clan is also a member of the Giovanni family. By long standing tradition they only Embrace those of their own family, and most of their retainers and ghouls are also of the family. Three members of each generation are chosen as children to be Embraced when they are ready, and are carefully raised to prepare them for it. Others in the family, as a reward for extraordinary service, may be Embraced later in their lives.

Because they are all related by blood (in both senses), they are extremely loyal to one another, and betrayal by one of them is unthinkable. Certainly they possess the most reliable retainers of any Clan in the world.

House Giovanni is one of the more rigidly controlled bloodlines, and contact is continually maintained between members of the line. It is still ruled with an iron hand by its patriarch, Augustus Giovanni, the original leader of the coven when they were first embraced. Augustus sees his control over the line much like a Prince rules over a city and requires those below him to adhere to the Rule Of Creation: his permission must be obtained before the Giovanni line can be gifted to anyone. However, some younger members of the Clan are given significant leeway and freedom to pursue new control over corporations. Because the Clan's influence in American is still limited, many have been sent to the "new world" in recent years.

If asked, most Giovannis would say they do what they do in order to gain a complete understanding and appreciation of the form they will have for all eternity. They believe this form to be of one use — gaining power. Others refer to the god-like feeling they get from having power over death.

Appearance: Despite (or perhaps because of) their horrid underground practices, Giovannis always try to maintain a front of respectability. Well-dressed in conservative styles, the women frequently look matronly while male Giovannis are often white-haired, bearded and look like a favorite uncle.

Haven: Mansions and condominiums in the finer parts of town, plus at least one hide-away in a sewer or graveyard.

Background: Giovannis will embrace only those from their own mortal family. Thus, all those in this Clan are of Italian descent.

Character Creation: Giovannis almost always come from a professional background, but split their most popular Natures between Deviant and Architect, though they take any Demeanor. Mental Attributes and Knowledge Abilities are almost always primary. They always have at least some Resources, but can have any other Backgrounds they desire. Most will also have retainers who are always siblings or cousins in the Giovanni family.

Clan Disciplines: Dominate, Necromancy, Potence

Weaknesses: Living creatures the Giovanni feed on take twice as much damage as they otherwise should. Thus if the Giovanni took one point of blood, her victim would take two levels of damage. For this reason, Giovannis are among the most prominent Bankers and take Vitæ from people who have died moments before whenever possible.

Organization: The Giovanni are based out of Venice, where the Clan headquarters are located. They work together in advancing the study of death, and can always call on others should they be in trouble. However, this is a small Clan, and physical assistance is usually hundreds of miles away.

Gaining Clan Status: The easiest way to gain status among the Giovannis is by accumulating the most wealth. The more difficult way is by creating new understandings of death either through art or magic.

Quote: *"None have as great an understanding of Death as we do. There is no great mystery and no facet of existence that affects every moment more than the fact that existence always ends. To understand this would be to be as a god."*

Stereotypes:

• The Camarilla — These suspicious busybodies are always putting their noses where they do not belong. If they truly wanted to know what we were up to, then they would kill themselves.

I have traced their corporate monies and found them to have a hand in almost everything that exists. They are planning something; what exactly is the only question.

Sovereign, Ventrue of Chicago

• The Sabbat — They have come the closest of anyone to grasping the Truth, but having stopped short they now will have a harder time reaching it than anyone else. They can be safely ignored.

A coven of old businessmen scurrying around the sewers? And you expect me to fear them?

Bishop Mark

• The Inconnu — They watch us constantly but understand nothing. If they did, they would not let us continue for we will be the end of them.

Nothing has confused me more than the existence of the Giovanni. How can I accept that some of the Earth's most ambitious businessmen have given up their lust for power to study dead bodies in graveyards?

Rebekah, Monitor of Chicago

Necromancy

This Discipline allows a Vampire to summon and converse with the spirits of the dead, possibly gaining advice and knowledge from them.

Level One:

Insight: It has long been believed by the superstitious that a dead person's eyes hold an image — the last thing they saw in life, or an image of the person's death or killer. This power allows a character to look into the eyes of a corpse and see the last thing those eyes beheld. A roll of Perception + Occult is necessary to use this power (difficulty of 8). This can even be done to Vampires (extinguished or not), in order to see the last thing they saw before they *died* (but the difficulty is 10). The number of successes indicates how much you learn about what was seen and heard at that moment, see below. This power cannot be used on Vampires who have reached Golconda.

1 success	Sense of how they died, of what caused it.
2 successes	See what happened in the minutes before their death.
3 successes	See and hear what happened in the minutes before their death.
4 successes	See and hear what what happened up to half and hour before the death.
5 successes	Completely understand everything that happened up to an hour before the death.

Level Two:

Summon Spirit: The trappings of a spiritualist seance are not necessary to use this power, although some Kindred find them pleasing. In order to summon a spirit, the following conditions must be fulfilled:

1) The character must know the name of the spirit to be summoned — although an impression of the spirit, obtained by the Auspex power of Psychometry, will suffice.

2) The spirit can be that of a dead mortal or extinguished Vampire. Destroyed Vampires who reached Golconda cannot be summoned. This power is not sufficient to affect a living spirit.

3) There must be some person or object in the room with a personal connection to the spirit in its life.

4) The Vampire must make a roll of Perception + Occult; if the spirit does not wish to be summoned, this roll may be resisted by the spirit's Willpower. The number of successes indicate how clear the contact is. For each question asked, roll one die for each summoning success — at least one success on this second roll is needed to maintain contact long enough to get an answer.

Level Three:

Compel: This power allows the character to master a summoned spirit. The character must make a roll of Manipu-

lation + Occult, which (difficulty is the spirit's Willpower). The number of successes indicate the degree of control, as follows:

Botch The spirit is enraged, and attacks the character.

Failure   The spirit is free to depart if it wishes. A hostile spirit may attack the character before departing.

1 success   The spirit is compelled to remain and not to attack any living creature without the character's permission.

2 successes   This spirit is bound to remain peacefully, and answer any questions truthfully.

3 successes   The spirit is bound to remain peacefully, and answer truthfully *and fully* — no half-truths, no leaving things unsaid.

4 successes   The spirit is bound to remain and answer, and to perform any task the character demands. If unwilling, it may do a bad job or willfully misinterpret instructions.

5 successes   The spirit is bound to obey both the word and the intention of the character's commands to the best of its ability.

Level Four:

Haunting: The character may keep a spirit from returning to the spirit world. A roll of Manipulation + Occult (difficulty is the spirit's Willpower if it is unwilling, or 4 if it wants to stay), keeps it in the world of the living for one day per success. For that time, it is not necessary to roll for severance of contact as described under *Summon Spirit* above.

Level Five:

Soul Stealing: The character summons the spirit from a living body. A roll of Manipulation + Occult is necessary (difficulty is the Willpower + Occult of the victim if they are unwilling). Success indicates that the spirit has been drawn from the body, and may be treated as a ghost. The body, meanwhile, begins to deteriorate and the victim must spend a Willpower point to return to the body in order to avoid death. The Vampire may use other powers of Necromancy to keep the spirit trapped outside the body if desired. Thaumaturgy may be used to cast another spirit into the vacant body.

Level Six:

Zombie: The use of this power allows a character to empower a newly dead body with motion. This will work as long as the body is not more than eight hours dead. The Zombie is not capable of independent motion and must be told what to do by the necromancer. The zombie will continue to function as long as it is given one blood point per day.

Zombies have one more point in Strength and Stamina than the body did at the time of death. They have an effective Dexterity of one. Also, Zombies can only move at a rate of 10 feet per minute.

Level Seven:

Torment: The character is able to mystically damage a spirit. Each success gained on an Empathy + Stamina roll against a spirit's Willpower causes the spirit pain as though a physical blow has been suffered. Needless to say, this can convince a spirit to behave. If the spirit suffers more than 10 such blows (wound levels), it is divorced from all contract with the physical world for a lengthy period of time (a fate considered worse that death by many spirits).

Level Eight:

Soul Exchange: The character is able to take two spirits from physical creatures and shift them into each others' bodies. Thus a bird can be transferred into a dog's body and vice versa. To succeed, the character roll Manipulation + Occult against a difficulty of 7. He must garner as many successes as the two targets have combined Willpower. Both targets must be no more than 10 feet apart at the time of the exchange and must be within eyesight of the necromancer.

Level Nine:

Possession: After summoning a spirit the character may place it in a recently dead body. The body must be no more than 30 minutes dead and the spirit must be willing to make the transfer. The spirit may then inhabit the body for as long as it pleases. This will allow the necromancer to place a spirit into a Vampire's body if she can achieve five successes on a resisted Willpower roll.

Level Ten:

Death Pact: This discipline allows the character to act as if he were the Prince of Darkness himself. By entering a written agreement with the character, the character agrees to serve as needed. This pact is then sealed by a drop of the target's blood. If character upholds his part of the deal, the victim's spirit becomes a complete slave to the character upon death. The character need not roll to summon or compel the spirit. The number of Intelligence + Occult success rolls made at the time of the pact signing determine how many times the character may call upon the spirit's services. The services, however, last until the spirit is dismissed.

Ravnos

Nickname: Gypsies

The Ravnos share many characteristics with the Gangrel, but there is no other Clan with which they more differ. Where the Gangrels are loners, the Ravnos love companionship. Where the Gangrels are combative, the Ravnos try to avoid direct physical confrontations. Where the Gangrels are honest and forthright, the Ravnos are masters of lies and deceit.

Their most obvious similarity with Gangrels is their life on the move. Few Ravnos would ever consider staying in one city for any extended amount of time. Those who have adapted to an urban lifestyle change their havens on a regular basis, never staying in one for more than a month.

Their other prominent similarity to Gangrels is their connection with Gypsies. However, where the Gangrels are widely accepted among Gypsies, the Ravnos are accepted only within their only family group (if they were of Gypsy blood). Though they live much like Gypsies, they are not accepted by them. While most blame this on the Ravnos' unquenchable compulsion to lie and steal from those around, others say the very aura of the Ravnos is repugnant to the sensitive Gypsy mystics.

Theft and con games are the most common aspects of the Ravnos lifestyle. Constantly travelling as they do makes it harder for them to be caught engaging in their favorite pastimes, and gives them an infinite number of marks and shills to take advantage of. There can be no greater pleasure than taking advantage of other Kindred, and a Vampire is advised to watch his wallet, gun and pants while these Licks are around.

Free movement is very highly regarded by the Ravnos. They freely move back and forth between cities controlled by the Camarilla and those controlled by the Sabbat. Anyone who attempts to prevent them entering a city is given the "treatment" — large groups of the Clan will enter the city and give it a thorough scouring. Few Princes have the courage to risk such, and though they may hate it, they will not prevent Ravnos from entering their city.

Ravnos take their personal and Clan honor very seriously, and it is one of their most prized possessions. However, the code of honor by which they live is quite different from the rules most folk follow. They do not place much pride in keeping their word unless they shake hands on it — after spiting into their palms (with blood, of course). They are honor-bound to avenge themselves if anyone besmirches their honor or "good name." They will not cheat or steal from others of the Clan, but do not feel such compunctions about outsiders. Friendship is held very highly, and they will always come to the aid of those who they think of as a "brother."

Appearance: Ravnos are almost always of Gypsy descent, and thus are often swarthy in complexion, with dark hair and black eyes. However, these traits are not universal. Not only have there been blonde-haired, blue-eyed Gypsies, oriental Gypsies and Gypsies of African heritage, but also in North America, where Gypsy culture has become more urban, Ravnos have been known to Embrace *gorgios* (non-

Gypsies). In Europe, however, all of this Clan are still of the Gypsy blood, and any gorgios Ravnos would be extinguished immediately.

Haven: Ravnos are constantly on the move, going from city to city. Though they may settle somewhere for a time, and even establish a Haven, after a few months they always hit the road again. Usually the Prince makes sure it is much sooner than that.

Traditional Ravnos make their homes in gaudily colored covered caravans which travel the countryside, stopping here and there to trade, celebrate holidays or just for a change of pace. In North America, where Gypsies have moved into the cities, the Ravnos have followed suit. Now they make their homes in the basements of fortunetellers' shops and in the backrooms of Gypsy houses (but always temporarily). Still, some Ravnos in the New World follow the old ways, while others have adapted them and travel across the continents in convoys of old luxury cars, vans and RVs.

Background: Ravnos generally Sire few Childer, and those they do embrace are generally the most promising members of their own family. Younger Ravnos have been known to be more willing to Sire, however, and neonate Ravnos of all backgrounds are beginning to plague the Kindred community.

Character Creation: Usually from Drifter and Outsider archetypes, Ravnos generally have Jester-type natures but are willing to change their Demeanors at a moment's notice. Social abilities and Talents are generally Primary and they almost always have a number of retainers in the form of family members. Some also have high Resources in the form of gold and jewels they have accumulated through the years. Such trinkets are highly-prized among them as symbols of success and expertise.

Clan Disciplines: Animalism, Chimerstry, Fortitude

Weaknesses Anyone around a Ravnos immediately feels suspicious and uneasy. Vampires know them from reputation, and these feelings are only intensified after any amount of time dealing with them. When dealing with the kine, treat a Ravnos as having half the Humanity she really does, thus limiting the amount of dice she can use in social interaction. Ravnos also have a code of honor, and though the character can break it freely, it will harm their Clan Prestige if they do.

Organization: There is no organization to this Clan as no Ravnos would trust another to keep his word. However, when two or more Ravnos meet somewhere, it is likely they will put on a great show of liking each other, pledging each other their undying loyalty — a vow which is quickly forgotten.

Gaining Clan Prestige: The best way to gain the respect of other Ravnos is to pull off wonderful cons which are then retold for years to come. Getting a Prince to trade her favorite vessel for a worthless knick-knack or stealing a Methuselah's coffin from his haven would earn a Ravnos a great deal of esteem within the Clan. The more souvenirs you can collect from your exploits the better; it is considered bad taste to talk about yourself unless you have something which you can show (the idea is, you're talking about the object, not yourself).

Quote: *"How could anyone take the form we have been given seriously? It's fun! We can do anything we want and all these others sit around trying to be statues. They act like they've been crucified on a trushul. That could never be the life for me."*

Stereotypes:

• The Camarilla — They died once and seem intent on dying again. They live unlives of quiet desperation, doing nothing and voluntarily jailing themselves in their cities.

These craven jackals lie and steal as though they had never heard of honor. Should another ever come to my city, I will declare a blood hunt at once on all their kind!

Wallace, Prince of Birmingham

• The Sabbat — Humorless brutes. They kill for no reason and have even less of an appreciation of comedy than do the stone-faces of the Camarilla.

These clowns may seem to be the least of our troubles, but do not underestimate them. With their control of illusions, there is little they cannot seem to do. Were they to turn against us in large numbers, we would have a most unwelcome and painful fight on our hands.

Karina, Sabbat Assassin

• The Inconnu — As boring as these musty old fogies may seem, they are really the only group which seems to understand what we do. They are never what they seem.

The neonates are amusing little Childer, but beware the Elders. They use their tricks to cover something far deeper.

Elijah, fifth-generation Gangrel

Chimerstry

Masters of trickery and deceit, the Ravnos utilize their ability to create illusions and hallucinations in much of what they do. The most basic illusions can fool storekeepers into taking one dollar bills in the place of hundreds, or scare Kindred with a fake stake. At higher levels, the fake stake could actually hurt the Vampire and make her believe she was paralyzed.

These illusions involve few resistance rolls since no one in our day and age goes around expecting to see illusions. Still, if someone were to create a Flying Purple Vampire Eater out of thin air, then she could expect a certain amount of disbelief from those who would notice it. The less believable an illusion is, the less it will be believed by the skeptical minds of modern mortals.

Illusions cannot be created if the Vampire making it could not sense it. Thus a blindfolded Cainite could not use Ignis Fatuus to create an image of a gun, but she could use Fata Morgana to create one in her hand if she were blindfolded since she would be able to touch it. Other people would see, smell, feel, taste and smell the gun if the Vampire so desired.

Level One:

Ignis Fatuus: These minor, static illusions affect one sense. Anyone in the area can detect the illusion using that sense, but not with any others. Note that even if an illusion can be detected by touch, it is not really there and thus an invisible Ignis Fatuus wall could be walked through (you need merely push — if you slap an illusion you would feel it, but your hand would go through it). These cost one point of Willpower to create and last until the character can no longer sense it, decides to end it or it is seen through in some way. Ending an illusion takes no time or effort and happens whenever the creator wants it to.

Level Two:

Fata Morgana: These major illusions can be detected by any or all senses, as decided on by the Vampire when he creates the illusion. Once again, the illusion is not really there, and can be passed through. Like Ignis Fatuus, these too are static and cannot be moved once created. They cost two Willpower points to create and disappear as per Ignis Fatuus.

Level Three

Apparition: This power is used in conjunction with either of the above powers and allows them to move. The creator spends one Willpower point to make an illusion move in one specific way and can only change or stop this motion if she has done nothing but concentrate on the illusion after creating it.

Level Four:

Permanency: This power, also used with Ignis Fatuus or Fata Morgana, allows the illusion to continue even when the Vampire cannot see it. All he has to do is expend a point of Willpower and the illusion will stay until dissolved.

Level Five:

Horrid Reality: This illusory power is only effective against one person at a time. Essentially, the victim of Horrid Reality believes completely and totally that the illusion exists. A fake fire will burn him, a fake wall will stop him and a fake bullet can wound him. If the Vampire is trying to damage a foe with this power, it requires a resisted Manipulation + Subterfuge roll against the victim's Perception + Self-Control. Every success causes the victim an additional level of damage, though the character can do less then the dice offer if she announces there is a maximum amount of damage she wants to do before the dice are rolled. Normally the roll's difficulty is 6, but attempting to cause aggravated wounds makes it 8. You cannot kill a person in this manner, and all injuries will disappear once the character is truly convinced that they have not been harmed (which can and will take a considerable amount of time — psychological therapy might even be required).

Level Six:

Fatuus Mastery: The Kindred no longer needs to spend a Willpower point in order to create illusions. In addition, the Kindred no longer needs to sense them to have the illusion continue, though the character must be within 1 mile of the illusion. This power only works with Ignis Fatuus, Fata Morgana and Apparition.

Mass Reality

This power causes more than one person to experience a Horrid Reality. Anyone in the same general area of the illusion will sense it as if it was actually present. Thus if an illusion of a machine gun was created, then the gun could shoot a number of people if the character so wishes.

Level Seven:

Far Fatuus: This allows the character to create illusions at a distance. The only provision is that the character be able to mentally picture the destination of the illusion. This usually means that the character must have personally been to the place in question. However, the character could have the location described in detail by someone who has been there or see a photograph. The difficulty of the Far Fatuus depends solely on the familiarity of the location. Use other powers of this discipline as normal to create the illusion.

6	Place as familiar as one's Haven.
7	Visited three or more times.
8	Visited once.
9	Described in detail.
10	Never been there, but have a photograph.

Level Eight:

Pseudo Blindness: Characters who possess this discipline are incapable of viewing falsehoods. This means that the character is unaffected by any Obfuscates or Chimerstries below level nine. They simply cannot perceive them (even if they wanted to) and are thus not affected by them. Also lies cannot be heard by those who possess this discipline. If a lie is told, the character will hear it but will know it to be false.

Level Nine:

Sensory Deprivation: This discipline denies the target's access to all five senses. For the duration of the effect the target cannot see, hear, smell, taste or feel anything. This effectively makes the target lose contact with the world. If the character has any power that involves these senses they are inoperable (i.e. Auspex, Clairvoyance, Clairaudience). The difficulty number is the target's current Willpower. This effect last for as long as the table below indicates.

1 success	1 turn
2 successes	1 hour
3 successes	1 day
4 successes	1 month
5 successes	1 year

Level Ten:

Reality: This allows the illusion master to create his own version of reality for someone else to stumble around in. Use of this power requires a Wits + Intimidation roll against the target's Willpower + 2. Three successes are needed to send the target into this reality, and the victim must spend a number of Willpower points equal to the total number of successes to escape. Until the victim thus escapes or is let free, she will wander around in a universe where everything from how it looks to its physical laws are defined by the character. Note that the target really does leave her previous reality and cannot be found with any discipline.

Salubri

Nickname: Cyclops

More of a blood line than a Clan, this widely hated group has far more enemies than they really deserve. Only seven of these Cainites exist at a time, for after they finally attain Golconda they end themselves and pass their blood on to the individual they have chosen to take their place. Few survive for more than a few hundred years, for it is considered agony to exist in such a state.

Among other Clans they are known as murderers and diablerists of the worst kind. In human society they can usually pass for normal until someone notices that they possess a third eye (yes, you read correctly). Princes have been known to call a blood hunt at the merest suggestion one might be in their domains and the Tremere are especially known to hate them.

The reason for this lies far back in the legends of the Salubri, once part of a small Clan of the same name. The members of this Clan involved themselves very little in the affairs of other Kindred and were thought by some to be nothing more than a myth. They believe it was Saulot, the founder of this Clan, who was the first of the Kindred to reach Golconda. It is considered fact that when he returned from his journeys to Asia, a third eye had opened in his forehead, giving him access to new powers no other Kindred had ever developed.

Some in the line say their third eye is a sign of the ease with which they achieve Golconda, while others say it is merely an opening which allows them to see more than others might. In any case, for the next several millennia, the Clan founder spread rumors of this state through Kindred society and is thought to have had a hand in the development of Carthage and the creation of the Inconnu, though he never joined this august group.

During this time Saulot Sired very few new Kindred, but those he did Sire followed him on his path to redemption. It is said he created his last Vampire during the reign of Caligula, and then removed himself from the company of both Kindred and kine. This voluntary separation lasted until the Middle Ages, when an order of magi managed to find the Clan founder lying in torpor. The Salubri say the order's founder himself tracked down the Antediluvian and sank his teeth into the ancient's neck. The Salubri also claim their founder did not resist. After this the order methodically tracked down Salubri descendants and slew them.

They could not slay them all, however. The older ones were actually the easiest to kill, while the ones created after Saulot reached Golconda proved somehow resistant to the order's magics (for they possessed the and knowledge of Golconda). Thus the order did everything in its power to turn the world against the Salubri, leaving them hunted and terrorized, unable to use their healing powers without fear of being sought out and killed.

Still, the only force which manages to kill most Salubri is themselves. When a Salubri Sires, she takes great effort to teach her Childe the ways of the lineage and how to best protect oneself. She also prepares the neonate's path to Golconda, and then commits suicide by forcing the Childe to drink her blood.

They believe the spirit of a Vampire to be tortured, and to have no hope for peace unless Golconda is attained. In fact, they think that if anyone, Kindred or kine, should be extinguished before reaching Golconda, then it will be eternally condemned to be a bound spirit (a ghost which is restricted in location or temperament, and can be summoned and controlled by mortals). Their sole goal is to pass from this existence and to be free.

They consider it to be their duty to pass along their beliefs to others, and take great efforts to explain "the facts of things" to others. Since they cannot imagine living an eternity of pain, they cannot imagine that others would not like to listen to their words. This is perhaps part of the reason why they are so widely disliked.

These Kindred find the path to Golconda easier than do most, but even for them it is no automatic thing. Their Sire will have hidden clues in books, people, and places for the Vampire to find. Once the Salubri has reached Golconda, they find life easier in many ways. Other than not giving into the Beast, Golconda lets Kindred open themselves to Disciplines with ease. Instead of having to become an older generation learn Disciplines higher than five, a Vampire in Golconda can learn new powers with but the expenditure of experience. Thus the Salubri ready to Sire are able to use the precognitive powers of Auspex to determine their Childe's fate and work to aid them along the path to Golconda. The spirits of Vampires who have attained Golconda cannot be summoned or controlled in any way.

Appearance: The members of this lineage come from all varieties of people. Children, old men, teenagers and middle-aged women have all been chosen. Once they have been Embraced, however, they begin to develop the clan's third eye. While it is not always noticeable (when it is closed, only an eye slit, which appears like a small scar, can be seen), the third eye is extremely prominent when in use.

Haven: Anywhere, but their havens are usually far from other Kindred and protected by mortals.

Background: The Salubri only pass on their gift to those who have proven themselves to be of the highest Humanity. Healers, holy men and women and true philanthropists have all been chosen at one time or another. Most have also had some background in the occult.

Character Creation: Nearly any concept will make for a good Salubri, but it is exceptionally rare for them to come from the criminal or soldier concept. Almost all have a Caregiver archetype but they can have any Demeanor. Mental Attributes and Mental Abilities are usually Primary, but this is not always the case. All Salubri must take five points in the Generation background to represent their Sires' sacrifice for them, and because of their problems with feeding (see Weakness), many have herds of faithful followers.

Clan Disciplines: Auspex, Fortitude, Obeah

Weaknesses: Whenever one of the Salubri takes blood from someone who resists the Kiss, the Salubri loses one level of health for every Blood Point taken. This is not so much physical damage as psychosomatic. It must be healed normally (with blood). The Vampire must know the target is not resisting and is at peace in order to not take the damage. This is why most of this Lineage are either Casanovas or Sandmen. Additionally, the character must continually persevere towards Golconda; any straying from this path will lead to dire consequences (like the inability to regain Willpower). When Golconda is finally reached, an end must come to this existence when a successor is ready.

Organization: There is no organization to this Lineage — indeed there is little contact — but they will do anything within their power to help others of their line. This extreme loyalty is part of the reason the Tremere have not done more to wipe this Clan out — the cost would be just to high. All Salubri are of eighth generation, and it is usually believed the Elders were all wiped out years ago. However, rumors frequently surface that one Elder or another was seen in some far place.

Gaining Lineage Prestige: In general they do not spend enough time with one another to make Prestige important. When it is a concern, it depends entirely on how far along the road to Golconda one is. If one has actually achieved that state, then continued existence loses all of its meaning, and while others of your lineage will still do anything for you, they expect you to extinguish yourself soon.

Quote: *"Nothing can be considered more important than the freedom of souls. Not just your soul and mine, but the souls of everyone on Earth. Thus we should consider our trials and tribulations a gift, for such freedom is impossible without overcoming adversity."*

Stereotypes:

• The Camarilla — These pitiful pawns of the Tremere have no idea of the harm they are doing the world and themselves. They want to live lives of evil but have given no thought to what that really means.

These soul suckers enjoy nothing more than tricking us into believing they mean no harm. Those who believe them are lost, for they want nothing less than our very souls for their own twisted pleasure.

Andark, Tremere Chantry Leader

• The Sabbat — These murderers are a more traditional evil than are the members of the Camarilla, but this makes them no better or no worse. They are blind, and in their blindness they destroy things of great value — their souls.

These quacks are not healers. The one time we might want to actually help the Camarilla is in snuffing this scourge from the planet.

Clifton, Probationary Sabbat Pack Member

• The Inconnu — Many of these powerful elders know the truth about us and are willing to help us. This is not true for all, but it seems to be true for most.

We kept an eye on the Tremere when it first began and know what crime its founders committed. Our sorrow is that we did not act then. Now we can but act and protect the children of my friend Saulot.

Mahatma, Monitor of Istanbul

Obeah

The power to heal is nothing to scoff at, for the might of Obeah has saved many lives. However, there is more to it than just healing. It provides a form of control over other people's bodies and spirits. The ability to steal souls comes when five levels have been gained, and may well be at least part of the reason Vampires so easily believe the Tremere's propaganda.

Obeah seems connected to the Clan's third eye, and any Kindred learning this Discipline will also start to develop the eye.

Level One:

Panacea: Just as a Vampire can lick a wound he has made and cure it, so can those with Panacea lick a wound someone else has made and heal it. For every blood point expended during the licking, the character can heal one health level. Note that the character must be able to lick the wound to heal it.

Level Two:

Anesthetic Touch: A way of ending the pain many people feel, a Vampire using Anesthetic Touch may lay her hands on someone and stop their body from feeling any pain. This also paralyzes the target and requires a Willpower roll against the target's current Willpower after the touch has been made. The numbness and paralysis last for a length of time dependent upon the number of successes.

1 success	One turn
2 successes	Two turns
3 successes	Five turns
4 successes	One hour
5 successes	One day

Level Three:

Neutral Guard: This power allows a Vampire to protect both himself and those under his care. After the character spends two Willpower points, no one not already within 10 feet of him can come that close to him until he voluntarily drops the Neutral Guard. Anyone trying to come that close must gain at least three success more than the Vampire in an extended and resisted Willpower versus Willpower conflict. If the Vampire who put up the Neutral Guard gets three more successes then the intruder, then the intruder is paralyzed for five turns.

If the Vampire voluntarily drops the Guard, then he must spend another two Willpower points to reestablish it.

Level Four:

Treat the Sick Mind: By the time a character has learned to treat the sick mind, then the Third Eye has become completely developed. Using the Third Eye on an unmoving target allows the Vampire to sense the target's derangement(s) and cure him. Sensing the Derangement requires a Perception + Empathy roll against a target of 7. Actually curing the Derangement requires a Charisma + Medicine roll against the target's Willpower + 3 (remember, the Derangement is a survival mechanism and the subconscious will not be willing to let it go). During the cure, the Vampire gets one extra die to roll for every success made on the diagnosis.

During the treatment, the target's body is bathed in a soft golden glow from the Third Eye, and anyone in the area will more than likely notice both the glow and the eye. Also, if the target moves during this time, the difficulty of both the diagnosis and the treatment increases by one. If the target gets beyond five feet of the healer, then the treatment ends.

Level Five:

Unburdening of the Bestial Soul: This power allows a character to pull someone's soul from his body and store it within himself while working powerful healing magic upon it. Meanwhile, the target's body must be kept as a mindless zombie. The character must use her third eye to look into the eyes of her target, and then make an extended Willpower roll against the target's Willpower to take the soul. The character must accumulate three successes, and if interrupted, the process must start all over again. No roll is necessary when a willing target is involved. However, Tremere propaganda about the use of this power means that there are few willing targets. The Tremere hold this power up as an example of the "soul stealing" evil of the Salubri.

The soul becomes a part of the stealer's being, and can be released back into its host body anytime the character desires. Until this happens, the body remains a mindless slave, following whatever simple orders it is given. The body can still die, however, and must be told to eat, move out of harm's way or anything else that requires voluntary action. If the target's soul is not returned to his body in a reasonable amount of time, then the character will automatically lose a point of Humanity for such a heinous act. Use of this power in such a way has been to send at least one Salubri spiralling away from the path of Golconda.

Once the soul has joined with the character's own, the character may begin to restore health to a soul that may have been overcome with the Beast. On a point for point basis, up to the character's Empathy rating, the character may spend Willpower to restore Humanity to the target. A character may unburden the ills of any soul only once, even if the character's Empathy rating later increases or if the character did not restore Humanity equal to his current Empathy. Once flaws have been passed over, they cannot be cleared later.

Level Six:

Renewed Vigor: By touching the target's bare skin a character using this Discipline is able to remove any health levels lost. This requires an expenditure of one Willpower point. This will mend aggravated wounds as well.

Pain for Pleasure: By making a successful Willpower roll against a difficulty of 8, the character is able to dull the senses of the target so that they feel intense pleasure instead of pain, and lose no dice due to wound results. Unfortunately, this also results in the target not knowing he is injured. This experience is very sensual and some targets may actually go out of their way to endanger themselves so as to achieve the pleasure.

Level Seven:

Repulsion: This power makes the Vampire's spirit unsightly, causing people to avoid contact with her. This repulsion does not raise attention to the character, but it simply makes people avoid the character as best they can manage, without really realizing what they are doing. This sensation is something like an unpleasant deja vous. Although the experience is not actually painful, there is no urge to search out the source. In this manner, people and Vampires can be avoided without attracting undue supernatural attention.

Level Eight:

Vitæ Block: Successful use of this power requires an Intelligence + Occult roll with a difficulty equal to the target's current Blood Pool (maximum difficulty of 8). The number of successes indicates how many of the target's remaining Blood Pool are rendered unusable. Used multiple times in succession, this power can cause even older Vampires to regret the effects. The effect lasts until the affected Kindred spends a number of Willpower equal to the Blood Pool points so "blocked." None of the blocked pool is available until the entire blocked amount has been forced free.

Level Nine:

Spirit Marionette: This discipline allows the character complete control over the target's body and spirit. To be successful the character must win a Willpower versus Willpower contest (difficulty of 6 for both) and accumulate as many successes as the target's Willpower. The character then can bend the will of the target to do anything the character wills. There is only one provision — the character must pantomime all of the actions of the target. This means if the character wills the target to walk, then he must also walk. Unless the character can make a Empathy roll against a difficulty of 9 to move on his own for a turn, the target continues to mock him. This Discipline also allows the target access to any Disciplines, Talents or Skills of the character.

Level Ten:

Resurrection: This power allows the character to summon the soul of a recently dead human back to its body. The target cannot be more than an hour dead for each Willpower spent bringing the target back to life. The minimum Willpower spent to perform this ritual is one. The body must be at least 80 percent complete. Even if the head is missing, the corpse will grow a new one. The third eye will shed such a bright light during this process that it will blind anyone looking directly at it . Note: This power will *not* work on Vampires.

Chapter Five: Roleplaying

This chapter provides you with some ideas on how to enjoy and roleplay **Vampire**. These ideas may not be appropriate to your own style of play, but the essays herein may at least provide a means of helping you explore this game. **Vampire** is a unique roleplaying game, and it requires new ways of doing things. We hope this chapter will broaden your awareness of the different styles you can use with it.

Each of these essays is written by someone who has worked with Vampire intensely at some stage of its creation and developement — whether it be with design, art or layout. Each of the writers has played Vampire, some for quite a while now, and understand what works for him and what doesn't. Every one of us also possesses a unique perspective on how **Vampire** "ought" to be played, and we don't always agree. Our opinions are not neccessarily those of White Wolf (White Wolf can't have an opinion, it's not alive) but you can't get a better idea of what we, as a group, think about our baby than by reading what follows.

Just don't take it too seriously. After all, no one ever said we were the experts. In the end, we're just players like you. Enjoy!

LIFE'S NOT THAT SIMPLE

By Graeme Davis

Man: An animal so lost in rapturous contemplation of what he thinks he is as to overlook what he indubitably ought to be.

Ambroce Bierce, *The Devil's Dictionary*

I've always felt vaguely uncomfortable when people have asked me how to be a better roleplayer, because there isn't a right or wrong way. Provided everyone's having a good time, everything's fine — and there is such a diversity of gaming styles that the right thing for one player or group would be the worst thing in the world for someone else. But then, **Vampire** isn't just another roleplaying game; it has its own personality and peculiarities. It's also quite possible **Vampire** will be your first game of this kind.

There are two areas to look at: roleplaying in general and roleplaying **Vampire** in specific.

Roleplaying has a lot to do with acting and a little to do with statistical simulation. Statistically, your character is a piece of paper with a few numbers on it and some scribbled notes on personality. Artistically, your character is a complete alter ego, potentially as powerful as the greatest character ever penned by a novelist or playwright. The game rules give you a start, but it's up to you to make that difference.

You need a clear idea of what your character is like and how this will be reflected in play. The Archetypes give you some help, and more can come from the character's Traits. Don't be afraid to spend a few minutes before each gaming session just looking over your character sheet and getting back in touch with your character.

Always remember that your character is not yourself. Your character will probably have different strengths and weaknesses and areas of knowledge than you do. Perhaps the hardest thing is ignoring something you know, because *your character* doesn't know it. You'll be tempted to act out of character, to gain an advantage. Be true to your character at all times.

You must also pay attention to the characters of the other players and those run by the Storyteller. Without selling yourself and your character short, try to fit harmoniously into the group. Expect the same courtesy from your fellow gamers, and tactfully discuss any problems between games. If you really find yourself out of sympathy with the style of the group you're in, then perhaps you should look elsewhere for more congenial gaming.

Most important of all, you should know yourself and your preferences, and know what you want out of gaming. Is it to build a more powerful character than anyone else? Is it to face and overcome challenges? Is it to explore the world of the Kindred at first hand? Or is it to get away from your own life and into a more interesting situation for a few hours a week, and just have a good time? Think about this, and about how the game can provide you with what you seek.

But enough of generalities. What's special about playing **Vampire**?

This game presents you, the player, with a range of challenges that can't be found anywhere else. The core of this lies in a series of dynamic tensions which are built into the setting and the game system. **Vampire** is a game which gives with one hand and takes away with the other — everything has a price, and every gift is boobytrapped.

For example, **Vampire** characters are immensely powerful compared to the world in which they operate. In most roleplaying games, a character must be nurtured through months and years of play before being able to throw a compact car across the street, shrug off a hail of bullets or do many of the other things which are child's play to the average Neonate. Some players might be tempted to go on the rampage, relying on force alone and trashing everyone and everything that gets in the way — the "Terminator Syndrome."

But in **Vampire**, life's not that simple. The more you act like a monster, the stronger the Beast becomes within your character, and before you know it, it's all over. You have enough power to achieve your goals easily and quickly, but do you dare *use* the power? You need a pocket-knife and Fate has given you a nuclear bomb.

And then there are the limitations of your Vampiric existence. You have to be under cover the moment the sun rises, and you have to stay there till it sets. Mortals can hunt you by day in almost perfect safety. You must hide your Haven well, cover your tracks carefully, and make sure you are well-guarded during the daylight hours when you are helpless. It's a good thing no one believes in Vampires these days. The Masquerade is a vital protection for you and your kind, and you must not jeopardize it. Another limitation on your freedom of action.

Finally, there's the Hunger. You might as well admit it, you are enslaved by your thirst for blood. If you try to fight it, you invite the Beast to break through your waning self-control — but you must be a clever predator, and leave no tracks. You must kill regularly without losing your soul. Without detachment, your existence can drive you insane, but become too detached and you lose your Humanity; the Beast wins again.

And as if it weren't enough trouble simply existing as a Vampire, you have to face the society of the Kindred. In many ways, other Vampires are your most dangerous foes. There are the insane games of the Jyhad, in which many Kindred are sacrificed daily. There are any number of inter-Clan and inter-fief rivalries and feuds. And there are those who would destroy you like unwanted kittens. The right to make Progeny is jealously guarded in Kindred society, and every Neonate is an unwelcome strain on the Masquerade and the food supply. You will always have enemies.

To top it all off, many of the problems you'll have to face in **Vampire** are human problems — rivalries, jealousies, misunderstandings and disagreements — but they are writ large because they affect powerful Vampires rather than puny mortals.

Good luck, Neonate. Keep your wits about you, trust no one and check everything you see at least twice. To think that some poor, misguided mortals actually *envy* your condition...

EXPLORING A HEART OF DARKNESS

by Stewart Wieck

"No man is an island, entire of itself; every man is a piece of the continent, a part of the main . . ."
John Donne, *Meditation XVII*

I have different goals in roleplaying depending on the function I am performing on a given evening. As a player you have only one tool to work with — your character — and thus you must learn to use that tool adeptly. The responsibilities of a Storyteller go well beyond playing a character, even if in the end the character is the focus of everything the Storyteller hopes to accomplish. Though a Storyteller's primary task is to create entertainment for the players, his other goals in roleplaying are no less personal. However, no such barrier or ulterior motives separates a player and his character, so a powerful connection is created. I believe it is this connection that provides roleplaying with its unique power and flavor.

Because of the way the rules in **Vampire: The Masquerade** were established to govern the behavior of Vampires, these creatures of night are time-bombs waiting to explode. When will the Beast be unleashed? However, it is not the Beast itself that I find as interesting as exactly what makes these bombs tick. What in a person (or in a "character" to maintain a respectable distance) makes him deny or accept the Beast? Search for Golconda or merely continue to exist? Of course, it's more than simply a matter of how people react to these game terms. It's mostly a matter of what these things can represent in the real world.

One of the most fascinating aspects of creating a character, whether it is for a piece of fiction or a roleplaying game, is considering his motivations. Goals are an important signpost in our society, and I do not dispute the need to have something on the horizon for which you assemble your resources and drive forward, but isn't the more interesting facet what motivates a person to move in that direction in the first place? When a person determines his goals, isn't this really just a matter of exploring why something is important to him. You may want to be wealthy, but why? A character, therefore, is marked primarily by why he does what he does.

Transferred to real life, the only place where fictional characters can tell us anything, motivations are important to consider for a couple reasons. First, by finding a new way or reason to act, a person can explore part of himself that may have been lost or not developed in the past. It's amazing to realize these other parts of yourself, and they are all Backstage at the Theatre of the Mind (ah . . . yes, that other essay — see below).

Understanding motivations that are not your own also allows you to tap into the guiding forces in the lives of others. This is the flip-side of exploring yourself, and it's the aspect I would like to briefly explore. At first this may seem to be a paradox, for how can exploring others be a personal experience?

We have to realize that dealing with others is almost as personal as dealing with ourselves. Beyond the truly personal benefits gained by exposure to new ideas, it's healthy to learn how others think and why they behave as they do. There are such diverse opinions and ideas in the world that it can be honestly overwhelming to try to accommodate them all, and Ray Bradbury's classic **Fahrenheit 451** is all about yielding to a thousand differing voices. The answer to the seeming paradox is personal growth.

This awareness of and possible intimacy with other ways of thought is bound to influence a person. Perhaps it's an influence that is undesirable or limited, but it may also be a path or idea that had yet to be considered. The latter variety of path may lead you not only to new thoughts, but perhaps understanding. Assumptions made as we grow up are inevitably a result of a worldview imposed upon us by innumerable factors like genetics and education, but I contend that the step beyond what may be a limiting view is often a step outside of your current self.

So how is this accomplished in a roleplaying game? Use your alter-ego not so much as an extension of yourself (for it can be dangerous to make such an intimate assumption), but as a tool for discovering how others would respond in a situation. If you were transformed into a vampire, you might respond by trying to tell your friends and family about it and look for support. Even though the circumstances are bizarre, many of you might find that support. But what if you were a person with no personal ties? Where could you find support? Without such support how would you survive in a world where murder is commonplace. And more than "simply" murder, but cannibalism as well.

In the real world we hear the voices of thousands of different races, cultures, social classes, education levels, religions, governments, and more. It's probably impossible to listen carefully to them all, but they are the chorus of mankind. However, individual voices are bound to slip into and out of harmony and that's the time to explore the significance of their ideas. Characters in roleplaying games can be efficient sounding boards for such investigation.

Roleplaying

YOU PLAYED YOURSELF, KID

By Josh Timbrook

*"This thing of darkness I
acknowledge mine"*
Shakespeare, *The Tempest*

If you're playing **Vampire**, then you are already familiar with the unique aspects of roleplaying that a Storytelling chronicle allows you to experience. The basic concepts and ideas of **Vampire** encourage an introspective style of roleplaying; you must battle the Beast within as well as the conflicts without. This style lends itself to some interesting methods of creating and developing your player character. It provides opportunities for your character to grow in depth as aspects of his personality are revealed. This is what I have found to be the most interesting things about playing **Vampire**, and it is of this which I will write about.

To move away from these generalizations, one aspect of character development that I've found myself delving into with **Vampire** is that of playing myself. I don't really mean *myself*, but somehow it seems that branches of my own personality seem to always squeeze into my characters. Some small facet of me is amplified to create their core personality.

This same phenomenon has happened to you as well, whether you realize it or not. Think back — your first roleplaying experiences probably involved chopping at evil creatures as you navigated through labyrinths of doom, all while you collected treasure and experience points and a place in the heroes' hall of fame. If you are honest about it, you know there wasn't a whole lot of characterization going on. Still, you played the game that way because it was something you always wanted to do while you watched Conan slay or read about Frodo's adventures. But all along, your different characters had similar ways of dealing with situations; this was what your friends referred to as your "style."

Subconsciously (or perhaps consciously) this was your own method of solving problems. Perhaps later you scoured the stars for new forms of life, or better yet, looked for the clues that would lead you down the final path to insanity while tracking the being that had swallowed the sanitarium whole. The stories grow in depth and you found the time to discover that your character liked to drink hot cocoa in the mornings, or had a constant sniffle, or had a tendency to blow a bubble pipe now and then.

These exaggerated traits were the best way to begin your character's development, and during an extended campaign they began to take a smaller role in the playing of your character alongside other traits that were there before, but were never explored fully. It was here that you may have begun to truly allow pieces of your own personality to slip into your character. Now you were able to play characters of completely different concepts, ideals, and walks of life. Perhaps there were parts of you that, however minor, wanted to be more this way, or more like that kind of person.

Now that you are playing **Vampire**, a game that examines the inner workings of your character, why not use roleplaying as a tool to explore your own mind on a conscious level?

Express that part of you that finds heavy metal to be intriguing, even though you are straight R & B, in a character that is a headbanging band member. Play someone who really enjoys working with her hands, an area in which you've only dabbled (yes you, with the 10 thumbs). Even better, create a character that exemplifies a representation of what you aspire to be. If you'd want to be hip or cool, have your character remain silent at all times, absorbing the comments and threats of others without providing your own input. This is what you'll act on anyway. This would be especially challenging and interesting if you normally are very vocal in your opinions.

For a most challenging role, play the personality of someone you know, or a friend that's sitting across the table from you (if you don't overdo it, chances are they won't even notice). Try an amalgamation of two or more people who you know and alter them as you go — by the time you're done you'll have created a unique persona.

By playing others, you can come to understand them better — you will learn about how they feel in situations where they are uncomfortable and why they react in certain ways to certain things. It can be a very illuminating psychological exercise; there is certainly no better way to hone your empathy.

Let us not forget the game which you are playing now. The setting and storytelling approach associated with **Vampire** provides you with the opportunity to explore aspects of life and fantasy normally completely inaccessible, aspects which you normally would not be able to, or might not want to experience. For instance, the influence of evil on your character is a primary theme in the game, but that is probably the only place that you'd want to come close to it. In any case, the vile grasping fingers of corruption are a most interesting subject to toy with; will your character fall into the pit of bestial, murderous rage, persevere and overcome the evil urges, or try to mold and use the evil for his own purposes or even for the cause of good. Unfortunately, such temptation often ends in disaster, but it can be, nevertheless, very compelling to play such a tragic and debased figure.

Horror is a major element of The Masquerade, both the personal terror so relevant in the life of the Kindred, and that of everyday life in a hellish world. At times it can be enjoyable to play into the hands of the insanity around you, or go along with the Storyteller's cruel plans for your violent end. A story of death and failure may not be as uplifting as a one of life and success (aka Spielberg), but it can be just as incredible an adventure. For a concept that isn't as grim, but just as out of reach, play a character of the opposite sex — a difficult task to perform perfectly, but one that can provide you with a new perspective on life.

Vampires are extremely sensual creatures, but loving is difficult for them, and such a story could prove either destructive or fulfilling for a character, and is an excellent way to contribute to the atmosphere and plot the Storyteller is trying to get across.

The important thing to remember is that this is a game and any of these things you have imagined are a part of you which can be experienced from the safety of your dining room table. Roleplaying is not only entertaining, but educational in ways that nothing else really is. There is more to it than that though, for just as novelists or poets are considered artists, so to is the creation of a story by a troupe of roleplayers a work of art. So go to it with style and flair; embellish the story with a fascinating character — it doesn't matter if it comes from you or from the world you observe, for it's yours.

BACKSTAGE AT THE THEATRE OF THE MIND

by Daniel Greenberg

Those who do not fight their demons within themselves are destined to fight them outside themselves.
-Ancient Chinese Proverb

The neonate struggled up from the dank earth, the stink of the sewer still clinging to her tattered clothes. She pulled her worm-white body free of the crumbling soil and shook the dust from her raven hair. With an unnatural burst of speed she took off across the graveyard, running like a woman torn from sanity. She gibbered and laughed, flailing her ivory arms as she ran, exalting in her newfound freedom and eager for a taste of fresh, sweet blood. The Hunger was so strong she could almost taste the blood trickling down her bone-dry throat, filling her with a warmth and solace unknown in her cold and desiccated tomb.

She darted into a darkened alleyway, grateful for sheltering walls after the dangers of the open field, even deserted as it was. With a slower, more confident gait, she loped toward the Rack. Within minutes she could see the colorful bursts of neon glittering harshly across the cold, dark and silent street.

Idly she wondered who the next donor would be. Would he be beautiful? Would he cry?

Sound like fun? If so, why? Who would want to do such a thing? Who would want to become a Vampire, even in make-believe? Who would want to open his mind to all that lurking, brooding unsavoriness? And worst of all, how do you explain the attraction to someone who only plays standard, conventional roleplaying games, or worse, has never played a roleplaying game at all?

Well, it's easy to explain. It's because.... hmmm. What is it, anyway? What is it about this stuff that fascinates us so? What is it about these flawed, doomed and tragic monsters that draws us to them with such compelling force? Given the choice, none of us (OK, very few of us) would voluntarily wish to become Vampires, and live a stifling half-life subsisting on the vital essence of people who are fully alive. So why is it so damn much fun to play?

After all, we're talking about Vampires here. Creatures that prey on a living people, engaged in parasitical relationships of the most frightening order. Hideous undead that lack all human desires save an undying lust . . . for blood. Beings whose mortal passions are a sham; a masquerade adopted so the Vampires can feel less like the Beast they are slowly and inevitably becoming with every drop of fresh human blood that passes their lips.

So why are we so captivated? Are our tastes so jaded that this is the best way we know to get our thrills? Or could there be more to it?

Maybe it's the same reason that Vampire tales have endured down through the centuries and across every continent. Because they teach us something about ourselves. About passion. About cravings. About the insatiable quest for influence over others. About giving and receiving.

Roleplaying games take place in the Theatre of the Mind. They happen only in that unique universe created at the juncture of several shared imaginations working and playing in harmony. They are a backdrop against which our creativity cuts loose.

Very often players find their characters begin to take on a life of their own, determining their own course of action and doing things very differently than the player had planned or could have anticipated. There have been many times that I have been so "in character" that my characters have said and done things I could never have imagined saying or doing. But in retrospect, their actions were more in keeping with their persona than the actions I had planned. I have witnessed this phenomenon so often it no longer strikes me as odd.

This is very similar to the way many authors say their fictional characters behave. Many times writers have been forced to rework chapters and entire plots because their characters refused to behave. Once the author had wound them up, they determined their own course of action. Actors also report that the characters they bring to life also take on a life of their own, inventing gestures, phrasing and actions beyond anything the actor had planned. It's called "getting into character" and happens to Method actors and traditional actors alike. So it's not surprising that the same thing happens to roleplayers, who are like actors that write their own parts.

Mary Shelly said that she wrote her immortal story **Frankenstein** to "speak to the mysterious fears of our nature." She found her inspiration in this, as well. She wrote,

"I did not make myself the heroine of my tales. Life appeared to me too commonplace an affair as regarded myself. I could not figure to myself that romantic woes or wonderful events would ever be my lot; but I was not confined to my own identity, and I could people the hours with creations far more interesting to me... than my own sensations...My imagination, unbidden, possessed and guided me, gifting the successive images that arose in my mind with a vividness far beyond the usual bounds of reverie."

So where does this stuff come from? Where are these very real, very "alive" characters and stories born? I suspect they spring from that very source that generates our strange attraction to Vampires and Vampire stories. I think it comes from the vast pool of human potential.

Every human being has the potential to be a Hitler, a Gandhi, or something in between. Every decision we make defines us and also limits a bit of this potential. The sum total of these decisions defines our personality.

So what happens to all those other decisions? What happens to the roads not taken after we have moved on? Are they pruned from our psyches like dead branches? I don't think so. I suspect that they linger on in the lower chambers of our minds, always ready to be called upon. When people regularly act out of cruelty and spite, options advocating respect and love call out across the gulf like a conscience. In people given to consistent acts of kindness and compassion, the hurtful and wicked options lurk like naughty sprites, tempting us to dark choices.

But a roleplaying game is a safe haven for drawing new options from our vast storehouse of human potential. It's a chance to lower the water level of our unconscious just a bit and see what's there. To act out those untried choices in a safe, secure environment, where the choosing will not cause difficulty or harm. It's a chance to shine a little light on the dark corners of our minds, and live out possibilities we could not and would not exercise in real life.

The choices we make in our waking lives are a serious business. We choose them carefully, knowing that they impact not only what happens to us, but define who we are. For the most part we think of ourselves as moral people, and strive to choose actions that benefit everyone.

Many actors find it very fulfilling to play villains. Writers find it refreshing to write about corrupt people. And audiences of all sorts love to see and read and hear about the exploits of evil characters. They find it a cathartic experience, and very often feel cleansed after it, as if the excursion into the darker parts of their psyche paradoxically left them cleaner.

So is it any surprise roleplayers should be any less drawn to creatures of the night like Vampires? By fearlessly giving expression to dark ideas which normally go unexamined, and are sometimes violently repressed, we can deal with them openly and honestly. By acknowledging that we have dark thoughts in the corners of our minds we can expose them to the light of day. By examining them, and playing with them as we would a less threatening idea, we can come to truly understand them. And when we put them down, perhaps their pull on us will be a little less strong. The only thing we truly fear is the unknown, and exploring malevolent ideas in books, movies and roleplaying games makes them less unknown.

I believe it's a mistake to suppress our fears and dark desires. Anything we repress grows until it seeks expression outside ourselves. Impulses we express in a healthy manner are purged and lifted from our psyches.

Vampires are symbolic of some of the conflicts that we are trying to work out in ourselves. They embody issues of belonging, ostracism, otherness, hurtful and helpful relationships, the struggle for identity, and the price of love.

I suspect that this is why the **Vampire** game is so much more compelling than straightforward roleplaying games. In most other games the central conflicts are all external to the character. They involve struggles with dragons and fearsome monsters. In **Vampire**, the real struggle is internal, mirroring the inner conflicts that lie at the heart of humanity.

TIN WREATH

by Andrew Greenberg

What god, man or hero
Shall I place a tin wreath upon!
   Ezra Pound, *Hugh Selwyn Mauberley*

Heroism is anything but easy in **Vampire**. Aside from the fact that you commit all kinds of horrible acts for the sake of (and at the sight of) the Vitæ so essential to your very existence, there are the thousands of years of tradition which conspire to leave you anything but a hero.

The myths and legends of almost every people on Earth have a name for you, and none of them are good. You are the drinker of blood, corruptor of innocence, stealer of souls and terror of the night. With all this against you, how can there be a desire to be a hero and for what reason would you possibly want to be good?

Aside from the very basic statement that being good is the correct thing to do, there are the very basic advantages which come with heroism. Admiration, support, friends, rewards and, most importantly for **Vampire**, freewill are just some of these.

There can be no shortage of powerful beings who would like nothing more than bend your character to their wills. Those characters who revel in their evil become pawns of greater powers while heroes maintain their freewill. The reason for this is simple: villains become what they are by giving in to their base desires. No one is easier to manipulate than one who exists primarily to fulfill such wishes. Just give him what he wants and he will do whatever you say. Even if the character has his own vile agenda, it is sure to intersect the schemes of more powerful, equally horrific creatures more than happy to use you for their own ends.

Being the hero, on the other hand, means you operate your own agenda. You may end up working in harmony with someone else for a short time, but your will remains your own. Elders interested in using you find it harder to do because your basic wants and desires have nothing to do with theirs. Those with whom your goals do coincide are far less likely to be interested in manipulation and subverting your freewill than are those with goals of evil.

Becoming a hero is not easy for Kindred. Doing good and helping others for the sake of helping them is difficult when you might go mad at any moment and rip their throats out. The only way to safeguard against this is by raising your Humanity, and you cannot raise your Humanity if you commit horrendous acts. Caught in this vicious cycle, a character seems destined to end up nothing more than a murderous, blood-thirsty slave to the Beast.

There are ways to prevent this unsatisfactory end, however. Being a hero requires a lot more involvement in the Chronicle than does just going out and running roughshod over the town. The first and most obvious step to becoming a hero involves heroic action. Stopping the Tremere plot to take over Chicago, running the Sabbat out of town or just doing your best to protect innocents are nice ways to start, but you run the risk of becoming predictable. When the evil ones know you will go out of your way to protect the infant child, then they can stop you every time you move to end their plans. When you become predictable, others learn to control you for their own purposes, and heroes are not another's pawns.

Thus merely reacting to Storyteller initiatives and stopping the heinous plots other Kindred have implemented is not enough. The time has come to truly take the initiative, to stop reacting and start acting. Doing this does not even require the approval of your Storyteller. Begin by gathering information. Tell the Storyteller your character is making an effort to meet with other Kindred. Script the Chapters of the Story yourself. Talk about who you are visiting and what you plan to discuss. Even just making friendly conversation with Neonates and Ancillas can reveal all sorts of clues as to what the Storyteller is planning, even if she does not realize she is giving such clues away.

Now act on this information. Track down leads you develop and act to stop growing dangers before they get out of hand. Far too often an adventure takes the role of somebody's great plot coming to fruition. What would happen if you stopped the plot before it came to a head? You would still get the experience but the whole Story would be run on your terms, not the enemy's. For once the odds would be in your favor.

BRIDGES '91

THE ANCIENT ART OF ROLEPLAYING

By Sam Chupp

Some stories are magical, meant to be sung
Song from the mouth of the river
When the world was young
And all of these spirit voices rule the night
Paul Simon, *Spirit Voices*

Roleplaying isn't anything new. It is a new name for a very old activity — that of storytelling. Those of us who dream and dare to tell our own stories are forever changed. We are lifted out of our lives by it, and are made able to see potential futures and transform our current perspectives. Whether we realize it or not, we are taking our places beside our ancestors who helped keep myths, lore and wisdom alive from generation to generation. We share skills with the shaman, the wise one, the bard and the philosopher when we will our minds to work telling a story. We are tapping into something mysterious and ancient — our own creativity.

It is not surprising that there are many people who cannot understand what roleplaying means to us because creativity is so often drained out of us in our early childhood. Tragic misunderstandings, followed by ignorance and fear, have led many to ignorant assumptions about our activities. People have always been terrified of what they do not understand.

In **Vampire**, the stories we tell confront the darkness in our lives and force us to try to understand the balance we walk precariously between Life and Death. These stories often contain the same characters and plots as the stories we were told as children. Because the myths we deal with in storytelling are a fundamental part of our nature, we are brought to these same themes again and again. They are part of our human condition, inherent to our lives and help us understand the vast mystery that we carry around with us. In helping us to understand the mystery, they help us to no longer fear it. We are then free to explore even deeper than we have gone before.

Storytelling, like any talent, can be practiced, explored and developed. It is a talent that is not only important for the Storyteller, but for the players. Every member of the troupe is responsible for adding and building on the story that is being told.

One of the best ways to connect yourself more deeply with the story is to get in touch with the stories of the past. Go to the library and read myths, legends, folklore, and faerie stories. The descent and return myth of Inanna, Queen of Heaven is fundamentally appropriate to the Vampiric point of view. Read the classics of literature and poetry. Shakespeare's **Macbeth** explores the darkness within — the

Being a hero does not stop here, however. Share the information you gather. Even a hero sometimes needs backup, and allies from a number of clans and backgrounds (i.e., the other players' characters) can prove invaluable. Continue to aid other, preferably honorable, Kindred and you should always have friends ready to come to your rescue.

This course of action can be even better when you have all the players involved in it. A group of heroes dedicated to a common cause can accomplish far more than can one. Just look at Tolkein's fellowship to see the truth in this. It gets even better when you're the one deciding which direction things go.

If your Storyteller is the type who likes to have your character constantly find out that everything he has done for a Chapter was scripted by some malevolent Elder, then the time has come to take over the show. She may well work to stop it, just as the characters she runs would. Becoming a hero in a Vampire is not easy; however, it was never meant to be.

The rewards are worth it, though. Everyone gets to decide what direction the Chronicle will go in and everyone will be able to get into the give and take of free individuals, not controlled pawns. Enjoy it.

same inner recesses Vampire explores. Talk to your grand-parents and ask them what it was like when they were your age. You never know when you'll need detail about any period in history from a personal point-of-view (after all, Vampires live a long time! One glance at **Chicago By Night** will tell you that it is important to understand the history of an area when you are dealing with Kindred.) Our grandparents also have stories of their own to tell, stories which you can use to get more into the stories that are being told by you and the Storyteller.

Another way to connect with the stories in **Vampire** is to get in touch with the stories of the present . . . the stories you hear about on the evening news, the anecdotes your parents or friends tell you over a meal. And most importantly, the stories that your own brain tells every night as you sleep — your dreams. Keep a journal next to your bed and write down your dreams and your nightmares. These are "postcards from the unconscious" as Chris from **Northern Exposure** says. Your dreams and especially your nightmares, once translated into the context of you character's psyche will make for some strange, powerful, and frightening roleplaying.

The stories of the future are also important — talk to the visionaries and children of today and they will tell you these stories. Science fiction will also deal with this subject, but so will poetry, new music, and art. Set your stories "five minutes into the future" and you'll also be connecting to the same thing the prophets and philosophers of yesterday did.

The storytellers of the past utilized makeup, masks, music, drums, puppets, costumes, props, lighting, illusion and mimicry. Which of these tools do you use? Picking up one or all of these will enhance your storytelling experience and, at the same time, help you get closer to the mysterious ancestral storyteller that you are unconsciously following. It can certainly bring you more deeply into the story if you use such props. Don't wait for the storyteller to supply you with them, bring them yourself, for your own character.

As a player, it is your duty to help tell the story. The referee can only do so much. It is the players who take the mental scenery, props, and costumes the referee has provided and use them to transcend the setting. You are the flesh and blood of the story, you make things happen, you are the only one who can decide to have a good time and in the process get in touch with a fundamental human need ... the need to create. Only when you are actively participating in the telling of a story can true "roleplaying" be accomplished.

In order to do this, you must know what part your role plays in the story. Actors are constantly asking "What's my motivation?" Learn the motivations of the protagonists of the past and you will find yourself slipping into the role. Another way to do this is to take the characteristics of a friend you admire and "play" that friend into your character. I myself do this and on occasion I find myself asking "Now what would Gary (or Leigh Ann, or Dean, or Lauren) do in this situation??" Because you see your friends in a rather

mythic way — really as characters that you know well — you will be better able to play the role.

Roleplaying is fun — plain entertaining amusement. Roleplaying is also an innate part of the human condition. If there were no roleplaying, something else would come to take its place for it is imperative that we tell the stories within us. Stories about ourselves and our place in the universe. Stories which we have recreated from the vast tapestry of human experience.

Our modern myths and legends will be revised by our sons and daughters just as we tell our adaptations of the stories of our ancient mothers and fathers. The cycle will continue on into the future, as it does today, and as it has in the past.

Like the shaman, the philosopher, and the bard, the play we do is work, vital work that, even if it doesn't change society and the world, will change our lives for the better and make us feel like we are part of a continuing story all our own, and recognizing our origins and looking to our horizons.

A ONCE FORGOTTEN DREAM

by Mark Rein•Hagen

Welcome, O life! I go to encounter for the millionth time the reality of experience and to forge in the smithy of my soul the uncreated conscience of my race."

James Joyce, *Portrait of an Artist as a Young Man*

I have always been in love with roleplaying. Slap-happy mad over it. Ever since that first Sunday afternoon when my father and I sat down with the church intern and played **Dungeons & Dragons**, it has been my passion

It was one of those joyful, melodic January afternoons that you only find in Minnesota (or so the myth goes), when, though it might be 20 below, the sun still gleams off the the vast wilderness of snow as if it were still summer. With a huge lunch tucked under out belts, we tried out this strange new game he'd been telling us about for weeks.

In short order we'd created our characters and begun our adventure. I rolled up a Dwarf and my father made a Cleric (appropriately enough, as he is a Lutheran minister). We were prepared to encounter all manner of fell beasts and sinister mysteries, but not to be caught up by it in the way we were. The adventure was called *In Search of the Unknown*. How apropos that title was I was not to realize until much later.

After a few hours of play we found ourselves hopelessly lost due to a magic portal we accidently entered, wandering blindly through a very dangerous section of the dungeon desperately trying to find our way out. We were running

very low on spells, supplies and hit points. Our lives were in great peril. Suddenly my father, while exploring a side corridor, somehow got trapped in these sticky spider webs. By having the good sense (luck) to put my torch to the flames, I was able to rescue him. The cleric was slightly injured but it was enough to free him and to kill the spider. It was my idea, I had come up with it on my own and I had saved the day.

I was so excited that I couldn't sit still whenever the gamemaster rolled the dice after that, and when we finally got out of the dungeon with our treasure and our lives intact, I raced around the house screaming with relief and exaltation.

It was wonderful. It was exhausting. It was miles beyond any other experience I'd ever had.

In that afternoon I was transformed, elevated to a new plane. I had a profound, almost spiritual, experience and the memory of it has never left me. I had discovered roleplaying.

Even since that day, I have been searching to recreate the intensity of that experience. My entire goal in roleplaying has been to once again visit that mystical garden in which I so enjoyed myself, and discover a means by which I might remain there.

This sort of experience is not unique, and I would wager that you have memories of something similar. Indeed, the same sort of thing happened to me when I first read the **Hobbit** in the hall loft of my grandfather's barn, was introduced to **Star Wars** from the front seats at the Excalibur, and first fell in love (but that's another story).

It is the sort of thing that changes a life.

But the trouble is, it didn't happen every time I played. In fact, it didn't happen again for a very long time. The journey to the garden is hard to make, even if you have been there before — experiences cannot be created on command. It was years later, only when I was in college, when it happened again.

For nearly seven years, roleplaying was something else, and though I enjoyed what I was doing it wasn't really what I was after. My friends and I became experienced dungeon crawlers, we collected magical swords like they were swizzle sticks, and used up wish rings as if they were glazed donuts.

Our characters were great heroes, our adventures were fantastically imagined, and the monster we slew were loathsome and foul. We were having fun, but it wasn't what I was looking for.

Yet it was engaging enough that after a while I forgot why I was roleplaying. Sometimes the dream still compelled me, but I really didn't think about it very much. After a while we began to grow a little tired of dungeon crawling, so we started exploring new avenues of adventure. Though collecting treasure lost some of its charm, I found satisfaction in trying to steal the other players goodies. Though becoming the heroes of the realm became old hat, we still had fun rescuing the Elven princess (about seven times, all told) and restoring her to the crown. After we had played for a long time, the mechanics became interesting to figure out . . . and to beat. Mini-maxing was an intellectual exercise of quite profound proportions.

Sure, we had fun, but it wasn't exhilarating, it wasn't transforming, and it wasn't what I really wanted. For many years, however, this sort of roleplaying was enough to bring me back Sunday after Sunday.

Eventually, it grew altogether too wearisome, and I began to roleplay less and less. Roleplaying became a hollow experience, a sad reenactment of the rites of youth.

Then it suddenly it happened again, while playing Runequest and exploring the ruins of Pavis. An experience just as intense and transforming as the first. All of a sudden I realized what I had been missing, and I was horrified. A skilled and intense gamemaster had brought back the magic (the snake is still in my dreams Jonathan).

These two experiences are what, for me at least, define what roleplaying is about. It is what attracts me, and continues to compel me. And it is this experience around which I design all my games and stories. Roleplaying intensely is how **Vampire** is meant to be played. Helping others to find and have this experience is the central theme of my work — simply because it is what has so captured my imagination.

Vampire is a very personal game, as intensely self-reflective as anything I have ever done. It is meant to allow you to create a character as personal and real as a character in roleplaying can possibly be.

The other part of roleplaying you already know about, the stuff about magic swords and Elven princesses, and figuring out the rules. I don't need to tell you how to do that, because we all know how to roll dice and have fun. It comes pretty naturally. What I do want to tell you about, is how to find the experiences — because they aren't always easy to find (especially if we've been warped by some of our earlier experiences with roleplaying). There are a number of things you can work on:

First of all, long before the game begins, you should try to make your mind as open and receptive as you possibly can. I try to get myself ready by thinking about my character in terms of his or her emotions, I try to feel what my character feels, I try to think the way my character thinks, I even try to say things the way my character would. Sometimes I experiment a little bit with it hours before the game begins. It's a type of meditation, I suppose.

I can't tell you how important it is to believe in the world and the story created by the Storyteller. You need to believe in the Storyteller with all your heart to wholly imagine and understand what the Storyteller describes. The tapestry that is woven cannot be fully imagined without your cooperation, and you must trust that what is being told is true, and that the decisions made are real. You should not challenge the Storyteller, for each time you do so, you tear away a little bit at the magic being created.

You need also create a compelling character, someone who you can identify with as strongly as possible. In **Vampire** you need to be able to sympathize with the situation of your character and the horrible dilemma of this protagonist. The character is the most important element of **Vampire** — make sure you create someone who you can explore your dark recess's of your own psyche with. Don't flake out and play someone easy, or nice. Play some other game if you want to do that.

Lastly, and most importantly, it is vital you exercise your imagination boldly. If you can dream in color, you are ahead of the game, and if you can imagine a face from only a description you are fortunate indeed. If you imagine a whole world in motion and color, then you are ready for the experience.

You can't train this talent, but you can awaken it, and once you have it again, you can practice it.

It is vitally important that you add to the story whenever you can, using your imagination to add details and descriptions that breathe life to what the Storyteller has created. You need to build upon the world that is slowly being created.

For **Vampire**, I often take scenes from movies, settings actually, and simply use them to jumpstart my imagination. For instance, I imagined a night club out of **The Hunger** when I first encountered the Succubus Club, and the vividness of my memory helped to bring it to life. When Josh described it in more detail, I simply modified my own version of it to suit his (and I threw a few of my ideas into the fray, hoping part of my vision would become part of the reality).

In this way, I practice my imagination, and provide it with solid foundations. The imagination is key to the experience, so I am constantly working on visualising everything described by the Storyteller.

When the moment does at last come, when the story suddenly blossoms in its full glory, then you need to let go. You need to close your eyes and enter the story without reservation (metaphorically speaking). You need to be ready for it, and then you need to grab it by the horns.

There would be nothing better than to have an "experience" every time I roleplayed — but that is an unrealistic expectation. In fact, even now, playing regularly with some of the finest roleplayers I have even known, I still only have "the experience" every once in a while. While the frustration is hard to deal with sometimes, I still get a kick out of some of the more mundane aspects of roleplaying, the Vampire princesses and all that.

But I live for the experience.

Chapter Six: Equipment

"When the going gets tough, the tough go shopping"
Shopping mall mantra

Vampires have uses for almost as many things as do humans, and shopping can be as great a pleasure for them as for any member of the Canaille. However, it is not as easy for the Undead to walk into a Wal-Mart or shopping mall as it is for us, partly because the lights are a little too bright in such places. Certainly the advent of mail order catalogs and shopping via television have been godsends.

The equipment list that follows should be used as a guide. The Storyteller or a catalog will provide the details for items not on this list. It is important to note that given enough money and time, there is almost nothing that cannot be purchased in today's world. However, when dealing with the black market, there are no guarantees or warranties, and prices tend to escalate sharply as items increase in illegality.

Finding something on the black market requires a Wits + Streetwise roll against a difficulty based on what is being looked for. In today's world, drugs and cheap (hot) jewelry may be only a difficulty of 5, handguns a 6, automatic weapons an 8 and anti-tank weapons a 10. Every criminal-oriented contact the character has decreases the difficulty by one, while contacts specifically described as smugglers, arms merchants or explosives experts might eliminate the need to roll whatsoever.

Finally, you should feel free to ignore this chapter or portions of it as you (or your Storyteller) sees fit. Some of the number-crunching rules presented here can limit the storytelling atmosphere Vampire creates. For example, your Storyteller may find the rules for determing the difficulty of hitting with thrown weapons to be a little too exact and finicky. The Storyteller, of course, has the option to declare a difficulty number without regard for what the rules state it "should" be.

"Weapons are tools of ill omen."
Sun Tzu, *The Art of War*

FIREARMS

This section is meant to supplement, not eliminate the original weapons chart. For many Storytellers, it may well be too much bother to decide which police officer is carrying a S&W M640 instead of an M686, and just rule that they all have revolvers. For those who are interested in expanding their campaign's guns, this section includes a variety of both common and rare weapons to spice up your Vampires' nights. Following the weapons chart are short descriptions of all the guns included.

Firearms

Firearms Chart by Type

Name	Caliber	Difficulty	Damage	Rate	Capacity	Concealment	Range
Revolvers							
Smith & Wesson M640	.38	6	2	3	5	P	12
Smith & Wesson M686	.357	6	3	2	6	J	30
Colt Anaconda	.44	7	4	2	6	J	50
Colt Python	.357	6	3	2	6	J	30
Ruger Redhawk	.44	7	4	2	6	T	65
Light Pistols							
Glock 17	9mm	7	2	4	17	J	17
Walther PPK	.380ACP	7	2	3	7	P	15
Heckler & Koch P7M13	9mm	7	2	4	13	P	20
SigSauer P226	9mm	7	2	4	15	J	20
Hammerli M280 Target	.22LR	6	1	5	5	J	30
Heavy Pistols							
M1911	.45ACP	8	3	3	7	J	25
Glock 22	.40S&W	7	3	3	15	J	25
SigSauer P220	.45ACP	8	3	3	7	J	30
Glock 20	10mm	8	3	2	15	J	25
Heckler & Koch P7M10	.40S&W	7	3	3	10	P	20
The "Big Boys"							
Desert Eagle	.50AE	8	5	1	7	J	30
Cassull	.454	7	5	1	5	J	40
Linebaugh	.475	7	5	1	6	J	40
Light Submachine Guns							
Ingram MAC-10 *	9mm	7	2	18	30	J	25
Mini-Uzi *	9mm	7	2	21	20/30	T	25
Heckler & Koch MP-5 *	9mm	7	2	21	30	T	40
Skorpion	.32ACP	7	1	15	15/20	J	20
TEC9	9mm	8	2	18	20/32	T	20
Spectre *	9mm	8	2	18	30/50	T	25
Calico 950 *	9mm	7	2	21	50/100	T	25
TEC22 *	.22LR	6	1	15	30	J	20
Heavy Submachine Guns							
Uzi *	9mm	6	2	21	25/32	T	50
Heckler & Koch MP-5 *	10mm	6	3	15	30	T	45
Thompson M1928 *	.45 ACP	6	3	15	20/100	T	50
Machine Pistols							
Glock 18 *	9mm	7/8	2	19	17/19	J	20
Beretta 93R *	9mm	7/8	2	15	15/21	J	20
Steckin *	9x18mm	7/8	2	15	18	J	18
Heckler & Koch VP-70z *	9mm	7/8	2	9	18	J	20/30

Firearms

Firearms Chart by Type

Name	Caliber	Difficulty	Damage	Rate	Capacity	Concealment	Range
Rifles							
Remington M700	.30-06	8	6	1	5	N	300
Ruger 10/22	.22LR	6	2	4	10/50	N	100
Browning BAR	.30-06	8	6	2	4	N	275
Remington M740	.223	8	5	3	5	N	275
Weatherby Mark V	.460WM	8	9	1	3	N	300
Assault Rifles							
Steyr AUG *	.223	7	5	21	30/42	T	200
M16 *	.223	7	5	20	20/30	N	200
Famas *	.223	7	5	25	25	T	200
AK-74 *	5.45mm	7	5	20	30	N	200
SA-80 *	.223	7	5	20	20	T	200
Mini-14 *	.223	7	5	15	30	T	200
Battle Rifles							
M-14 *	7.62mm	7	6	10	20	N	275
AK-47 *	7.62x39mm	7	6	10	30	N	250
Heckler & Koch G3 *	7.62mm	7	6	10	20	N	300
Fn FAL *	7.62mm	7	6	10	20	N	275
Pump-Action Shotguns							
Ithaca M37 (Stakeout)	12 gauge	5	6	1	5	T	15
Remington 870	12 gauge	5	6	1	8	N	20
Mossberg M500	12 gauge	5	6	1	5	N	20
Automatic Shotguns							
Fianchi Law 12	12 gauge	6	6	3	8	T	20
Benelli M-3 Super 90	12 gauge	6	6	3	7	T	20
SPAS 12	12 gauge	6	6	3	8	N	20
Remington 1100	12 gauge	6	6	3	8	N	20
USAS 12 *	12 gauge	7	6	6	10/20	N	20

Difficulty: The Difficulty to hit

Damage: The base damage done on a successful hit

Rate: The maximum number of bullets a gun can fire in a turn

Capacity: The number of bullets the gun can hold

Concealment: P = can be hidden in a pocket; J = can be hidden in a jacket; T = can be hidden in a trench coat; N = cannot be hidden on your person

Range: This can be doubled, but anything above what is listed here is considered a long-range shot.

* indicates the gun is capable of three-round bursts

Smith & Wesson M640: This small revolver, sometimes referred to as the Detective's Special, is one of the most popular snub-nose guns. Hammerless, meaning the gun can hold no more than five bullets, its barrel is two inches long.

Smith & Wesson M686: A popular police magnum in the United States. It can also chamber .38 special caliber ammunition.

Colt Anaconda: This powerful magnum is primarily used for hunting and silhouette target shooting. It can also chamber .45 special caliber ammunition.

Colt Python: Similar to the Smith & Wesson M686 and also popular among police. Can chamber .38 special ammunition. It is also being challenged in popularity by Colt's own less-expensive King Cobra.

Ruger Redhawk: Made in the United States, this sizable revolver is used primarily for hunting. There is an even larger version, the Super Redhawk, with a scope mount and an effective range of 100 yards. This huge pistol even comes with its own sling.

Glock 17: Featured in the worst mass killing in the United States as of November 1991, this Austrian-made pistol gained a notorious reputation even before it was widely distributed. Concerns its plastic polymer frame would prove invisible to metal detectors proved groundless.

Walther PPK: Made famous by James Bond and British Intelligence, this gun has since been replaced by the VP-70z, and is now considered antiquated and underpowered.

Heckler & Koch P7M13: This recently developed automatic has become popular among police in the Northeast United States as well as in its homeland of Germany.

SigSauer P226: This high-capacity pistol came in second during U.S. Army trials for a new universal sidearm. It makes up a quarter of U.S. police 9mms, and is used by police in Germany where it is produced.

Hammerli M280 Target: A custom-made target pistol, this very expensive gun has a contoured grip made expressly for its user. Should anyone else try to use the gun, they would suffer an additional +1 to the difficulty to hit.

M1911: A mainstay of the U.S. Army for years, this gun was replaced in 1985, but many are still in use. It has also been a popular model in civilian markets.

Glock 22: Featuring a new caliber introduced in the late 80s, the Glock 22 is a lightweight pistol with more stopping power than a 9mm. It has found acceptance among some police, but is moving slowly towards wider popularity.

SigSauer P220: This double-action automatic has become renowned for its reliability. Anyone of these guns is likely to remain around for a long time to come.

Glock 20: Essentially a Glock 22 featuring 10mm caliber ammunition. This ammunition has is heavier than 9mm and has greater stopping power.

Heckler & Koch P7M10: Also featuring a new caliber, this gun has also been slow to gain wide acceptance.

Desert Eagle .50 AE: This huge pistol has found little acceptance among those who would really rely on it in combat, but is popular with armchair soldiers. Made in

Israel, this pistol has great stopping power and can also be found in .357 and .44 magnum calibers.

Cassull: This is a highly expensive custom-made gun. Cassull is the name of the man who develops these from Ruger Redhawks.

Linebaugh: Also custom made, these pistols are often used to hunt Cape Buffalo in Africa.

Ingram MAC-10: Extremely popular when first introduced, this submachine gun has been surpassed by more recent guns. Comes with a folding stock, a flash suppressor and muzzle brake are also highly recommended.

Mini-Uzi: The Israeli line of Uzis have become the best known submachine guns in the world, and includes not only the Mini-Uzi and Uzi, but also Micro-Uzis and Uzis in other calibers. While the Mini-Uzi is not as popular a combat weapon as its larger brother, it has been known to be carried by troops operating in tight confines.

Heckler & Koch MP-5: This popular German-made submachine gun is a mainstay of SWAT teams, counter-terrorist forces like England's SAS and even some U.S. Special Operations troops. The MP-5 is arguably the best SMG currently on the open market, known for its reliability and fast handling. There is also a more concealable model — the MP-5K.

Skorpion: A pistol-sized submachine gun, the Skorpion has been a mainstay of intelligence services and terrorists for 30 years. Not thought to be in active service with governments anymore, these Czech-made weapons are still popular in espionage novels.

TEC9: The TEC9 is a very cheap automatic pistol easily changed to full auto. Available readily in the United States, anyone with one rating in both Firearms and Security can convert it to full auto. The reliability of such a weapon should be considered questionable.

Spectre 9mm: An American-made submachine gun, the Spectre saw consideration by a number of SWAT forces but has yet to be adopted by many.

Calico 950: Also under consideration by a number of U.S. SWAT teams, the Calico's innovative top-feeding tube allows it to carry 100 rounds. They eject from the bottom, thus making it easy for the user to collect the spent cartridges in a bag attached underneath.

TEC22: Called the Scorpion (not to be confused with the Czechoslovakian gun of the same name, the TEC22 is small, easily controlled but not known for its reliability or durability.

Uzi 9mm: Possibly the most commonly known submachine gun in the world, the Uzi has found users in military, terrorist and criminal organizations around the world. Anyone from an Israeli tank crew member to a West L.A. gang member may be found carrying it. It was made for desert warfare and is especially known for its reliability.

Heckler & Koch MP-5 10mm: The MP-5 in 10mm was developed by H&K as a potential submachine gun for use by the F.B.I. It can be considered to still be in trial usage.

Thompson M1928: The Thompson M1928 is the classic Tommy gun of gangster movie fame. It is an especially

heavy submachine gun, and becomes even heavier with the addition of its well-known 100-round drum.

Machine Pistols: These guns are commonly fired both in their semi-automatic setting at a rate of 3 or in their full automatic setting at the rate listed. Note that these guns are all manufactured outside of the United States and are very rare in that country.

Glock 18: The Glock 18 is a full-auto version of the Glock 17. It was developed for the Austrian counter-terrorist units. Its import into the U.S. is severely restricted.

Beretta 93R: This Italian machine pistol comes with a folding grip for the user's off-hand. The gun was popularized in the Executioner series of books.

Steckin: The only East bloc machine pistol listed here, it is uncommon in the West. It chambers its own special, smaller 9mm ammo and cannot use the Western-style 9mm.

Heckler & Koch VP-70z: Used by British intelligence, this pistol can only achieve its full-automatic setting with the attachment of a stock, which also increases its range.

Remington M700: An extremely popular bolt action hunting rifle, a version found use in the Vietnam war as the Marine's preferred sniper weapon.

Ruger 10/22: Used primarily to hunt small game, Ruger has supported this weapon with a wide variety of options. Users can choose from a number of stocks, magazines, flash suppressors and other attachments.

Browning BAR: Another popular U.S. hunting rifle, often used in deer hunting.

Remington M740: Also popular for hunting, it chambers the same size ammunition as does the M-16 assault rifle.

Weatherby Mark V: A British-made hunting rifle with a magnum round, this gun can be used to hunt anything from deer to small helicopters. However, its recoil is likely to break the arm of people who use it without being properly braced. Ignore if the character has a combined Strength + Potence of 5.

Steyr Aug: The Steyr Aug is made in Austria and is the most up-to-date assault rifle currently in service. It is also used by the armies of Australia and Saudi Arabia.

M-16: A very common assault rifle is the M-16 of the United States. Sold around the world by Vietnam, U.S. military personnel and the C.I.A., it can be found almost anywhere. Its most recent version, the M-16A2 is the current assault rifle of the United States.

Famas: The Famas currently has the highest cycle rate of any assault rifle in service. It is standard issue to the French Foreign Legion.

AK-74: The AK-74 replaced the older AK-47 as the assault rifle of the Soviet Union. It is still not very common in the United States.

SA-80: This British-made assault rifle was made to be compatible with the M-16 and can use the other weapon's magazines. Since being introduced, a diversity of opinion has arisen as to its quality, and a love-hate relationship similar to the one the M-16 inspired when it was first introduced is now prevalent.

Mini-14: Made by Ruger and commonly available in the U.S., the Mini-14 is a lightweight assault rifle with limited military usage. Amongst its many options are a folding stock, a 90-round magazine and special sight mounts.

M-14: This was the main U.S. Army weapon prior to adoption of the M-16. A version, the M-21, found continued use as a sniper rifle.

AK-47: The AK-47 is quite common in Third World countries and is now becoming popular in the United States. Once the main weapon of the Soviet Union, it was replaced by the AK-74.

Heckler & Koch G3: This heavy German battle rifle has become extremely popular in South America.

FN FAL: This battle rifle finds little use in developed countries outside of its Belgian homeland, but it has been adopted by a number of Third World forces, especially in Africa.

Ithaca M37: The Ithaca M37 is a fairly common shotgun, but the Stakeout version can be considered illegal. In this form, the stock has been removed, thus allowing for easier concealment. It can also be sawed-off, reducing the difficulty to 4 and the range to 7.

Remington 870: A popular U.S.-made hunting weapon, this shotgun can be found almost anywhere.

Mossberg M500: Not as much a hunting weapon as it is a police firearm, it is smaller than the Remington but not much more concealable.

Fianchi Law 12: This Italian-made shotgun is very expensive, and generally comes with intricate detail work to make it look more attractive.

Benelli M-3 Super 90: Another commonly used police shotgun, this model is especially popular among SWAT teams.

SPAS-12: A military weapon, the SPAS-12 has been adopted in Europe.

Remington 1100: This American-made shotgun is popular with both hunters and police in the United States.

USAS 12: The USAS is a full-auto shotgun. Its appearance is that of a very large M-16. It is now being purchased by SWAT teams inside the United States and found some use by Special Forces during the invasion of Panama.

MELEE WEAPONS

Clubs

Staffs: A traditional quarterstaff is "as tall as the wielder, and as big around as her fist", but any pole, pipe or board that is long enough will suffice. In general, the heavier the object the more damage it does.

Difficulty: 4 **Damage:** Strength +1..+3 **Ability:** Melee **Weight:** 7-10 lbs

---

Special Maneuver: *Sweeps*

Staffs can be used to "sweep" an opponent's legs out from underneath him in a fight. Treat this maneuver like a throw ending with the opponent falling in place — but with the added advantage that the character does not need to close in with the opponent.

Quarterstaff: Any pole or board from four to eight feet long fits this category. The Japanese staff is called a Rokushakubo (meaning "six feet of wood"). This name is usually shortened to "Bo-staff."

A staff purchased at a Martial Arts Supply will be a Bo-Staff from 5 - 6 feet long, 1.5 inches in diameter, and will cost around $35.

The 2"x 4" "studs" found on most construction sites are just the right length for quarterstaves, but are generally soft pine that breaks quite easily. During every round of combat, keep track of the total successes rolled (both yours and your opponents). If the total number of successes rolled is over five, then the 2"x 4" "stud" breaks.

Example: While a cop is chasing her, Val ducks through an apartment complex still under construction. When the cop is just a few feet behind him, Val grabs a 2" x 4" and swings at the cop's head. Val rolls her Dexterity 3 plus her Melee 3 for six dice total against a difficulty of 4. Val gets 4 successes. The cop strikes back with his nightstick, rolling 5 dice and getting 2 successes. Val received more successes than the cop, so the cop takes a shot to the head. More than 5 successes were rolled, however, so Val is left holding a short staff.

Jo-Staff: Any pole or pipe two to four feet in length makes an excellent short staff. As with a long staff, the heavier it is, the more damage it will cause. At a Martial Arts Supply a Jo-Staff will be 3.5 - 4.5 feet long, 1.5 inches in diameter, and will cost $25.

Difficulty: 4 **Damage:** +1..+3 **Ability:** Melee **Weight:** 3-7 pounds

Special Maneuver: *Block*

Due to the ease with which a trained attacker switches the Jo-staff from hand to hand and integrates blocking and striking into one smooth motion, a character with a specialty in Jo-Staff (short staff) may roll one extra die to soak his opponent's successes. This die does not count toward causing damage or hitting.

Example: The cop rolls to his feet and he and Val strike at each other again. The cop wins this combat by one success, and manages to get three successes on the damage. Val, now using the longer part of her broken 2"x4" as a Jo-staff, rolls her Stamina 3 plus Fortitude 2 as well as one extra die for the Jo-Staff against a difficulty of 8. She gets two successes, and is only bruised by the cop's attack.

Clubs: Saps, blackjacks, nightsticks, bats, etc. and all sticks, poles or pipes no longer than four feet can be considered clubs. The heavier they are the harder they hit.

Difficulty: 4 **Damage:** +1..+3 **Ability:** Melee **Weight:** 0-5 pounds

Special Maneuver: *Haymaker*

Clubs are big levers to increase the force of a blow. A trained attacker may choose to put even more effort into a blow and cause tremendous damage, but this will leave them open to attacks they may otherwise have defeated. A character attacking with the Haymaker specialty loses a die from her dice pool to hit. However, when rolling damage she rolls two extra dice.

Example: Sharon rolls four successes to hit Don. Don, using his Haymaker specialty, rolls Dexterity 2 plus Melee 3 for a total of 5 dice against a difficulty of 4. Because he is swinging a Haymaker, he loses one die and only gets three successes, and Sharon will now roll for damage.

Baseball Bat: A quality wooden Baseball Bat will cost $25, and would do damage of Strength + 1. Bats are also available in double-weight practice models for $35 and do damage of Strength + 2. Aluminum bats cost about $10 more than wooden ones of the same quality.

Cane: Canes can be light but effective clubs and cost $10.00 - $50.00 depending on decoration and quality.

Special Maneuver: *Hook*

An expert with a hooked cane (the traditional kind), can use the hook in combat to snare an opponent's arm or weapon. This increases the difficulty of the attack by one in addition to all other modifiers. The results vary depending on what the attacker desires:

Snared opponent's weapon: Strength vs Strength roll to jerk the weapon out of his hand.

Snared opponent's arm: Strength vs Strength roll to jerk the opponent off balance (he can take no actions next turn), or Dexterity vs Dexterity roll to grapple with the opponent held at the end of the cane.

All these rolls have a Difficulty of 6. The last option can allow a skilled attacker to grapple and immobilize a character at a range of three to four feet.

Example: Tim (who is a cane fighting expert) is confronted by a knife-wielding street tough with an attitude. Tim attempts a strike using the hook specialty. The Storyteller rules that the knife is too small to hook, so Tim tries for the arm. The street tough rolls four successes. Tim rolls his Dexterity 3 plus Melee 3 against a difficulty of 5 (Cane 4 plus one for the hook specialty). Tim rolls 5 successes. Tim has now hooked the tough's arm, and he wants to grapple. Tim rolls his Dexterity, 3 dice, against a Difficulty of 6, rolling two successes. The tough rolls his Dexterity, 3 dice, against the 6 Difficulty, rolling two successes. The round is inconclusive. The stalemate will continue until one of the combatants receives more successes than the other. If the tough wins out, then Tim's hook will have become dislodged. If Tim wins out, then every success of his will lessen the number of dice that the tough may roll the next turn (Grapple — **Vampire** p. 149).

Knives

Knives come in all shapes and sizes, the two main classes being weapons and tools. Knives designed as weapons almost always have a cross guard to protect the fingers. Knives that are tools tend not to have this guard because it gets in the way.

Difficulty: 4 **Damage:** Strength+1
Ability: Melee **Weight:** 0-2 lbs

Special Maneuver: *Double Strike*

Knife fighting is based on speed and reflexes. A character using this specialty can split her dice pool between two attacks against the same target (without the use of Celerity). Each attack pool receives one additional die. The difficulty for each attack is 5. Damage is determined normally for each attack. The character's Dexterity + 1 (plus Celerity) is the maximum number of dice that may be used for each attack.

The number of additional attacks possible is determined by dividing your skill by 2, so if you were of seventh generation and had a skill of 6, you could attack three times in one turn by dividing your dice pool three ways. Dexterity + 1 (plus Celerity) is still the maximum number of dice for any attack but the first. Also, the difficulty of all attacks would increase to 7.

Steak Knife: A set of eight costs $10 new, while a single one might cost $.50 at a thrift store. Weight and size are negligible, but they only do a character's Strength in damage and have a tendency to snap under pressure.

Butcher Knife: Good knife sets cost from $30 to $50 new, half that used. A single Butcher Knife costs $10. Butcher knives have single-edged blades from 8" - 12".

Fighting Knife: These knives cost $40 to $200 for one off the shelf, but triple that for custom made. A fighting knife will have a blade 6" to 14", and a handle 6" to 10". Thus a fighting knife is 12" to 24" long.

Many fighting knives are double-edged. In many states (California and New York, for example) simply possessing a double-edged knife is a felony offense.

Swords:

Roughly speaking, any weapon with a blade longer than a foot or so can be used as a sword. Some specialties include: Rapier, Rapier & Main Gauche (both variants of Fencing), Broadsword, Sword & Shield (or club and shield, as modern riot police), Two-Handed Sword, Scimitar, Kendo or Kenjutsu (Japanese Sword Fighting), Escrima (Filipino Stick Fighting), Kalinda (Caribbean Stick Fighting), Short Sword or Nightstick (many of the moves are identical), and Two-Sword.

Fencing Sword: A very lightweight sword used for thrusting. Modern fencing weapons have no blade and cannot be sharpened, although a true Rapier has a very sharp blade. A good foil can cost $50, and a rapier $200, though used equipment would be much cheaper.
Difficulty: 5 **Damage:** Strength+3
Ability: Melee **Weight:** 2 - 3 lbs

Special Maneuver: *Lunge*

Properly speaking, the only time to lunge is to finish off the opponent in one final move. The lunge as written here includes a "cross-step" to increase the range. A character with this specialty may attack an opponent up to five yards away. The difficulty is 7 and the damage is Strength+4. No dodging is possible for the character making this maneuver, either before or afterwards. The best way to use the lunge is against an opponent who is charging. A lunge will enable the character to attack the opponent before he can attack her.

Example: As Karl charges at Sandra with a butcher knife, she lunges at him with a fireplace poker. Karl dodges while attempting to close to knife range. Sandra rolls five successes, and Karl only rolls four. She has hit him and may now roll for damage. If he still desires, next round he can attack her, although she will still be able to attack him normally.

Cavalry Saber: A cavalry saber has a gently curving blade 2 1/2 to 3 feet in length. A reproduction cavalry saber costs around $40.00.
Difficulty: 6 **Damage:** Strength + 4
Ability: Melee **Weight:** 2-3 lbs
Medieval Broadsword: A simple sword with a three foot straight blade and a long (9") handle. Broadswords tend to be quite heavy for their size and cost $100.
Difficulty: 6 **Damage:** Strength + 5
Ability: Melee **Weight:** 5-10 lbs
Two-Handed Sword: A two-handed sword, or greatsword, has a blade from four to six feet in length and a handle one to two feet in length. A two-handed sword requires about six feet on each side of the user and six feet of overhead clearance. They cost around $250.
Difficulty: 5 **Damage:** Strength + 6
Ability: Melee **Weight:** 10 - 15 lbs
Wooden Swords: Any of the above swords are available in wooden, practice versions but are treated as clubs. Many practice swords are filled in with lead slugs to weight the same as the "real" sword. Some practice swords are weighted twice as much. They only do Strength + 1 for damage (+2 for Two-handed). Note that they can be sharpened and used as long stakes.

Martial Arts Weapons

At the Storyteller's discretion, the use of martial arts weaponry is a separate skill from Melee. These weapon styles have developed over centuries as unique and powerful martial arts in their own right.

Many of the traditional martial arts weapons developed on the island of Okinawa, near Japan. When the Japanese invaded Okinawa during the middle ages, the Japanese samurai ordered all the weapons on the island confiscated. The Okinawan farmers learned to fight with the farm tools ready at hand. Other martial arts weapons were developed by the Japanese Ninja, clans of assassins trained from birth at fighting and stealth.

Tonfa: Tonfa developed from rice grinders used on Okinawa. A tonfa is simply an L-shaped piece of wood, with the long part of the L being 18" and the short part about 6". These weapons are used to block (protecting the forearm), to strike (as a nightstick), and to hook (as a cane). Tonfa are so effective that many police forces (especially on the West Coast) are now using them as nightsticks.

A character using tonfa may block melee weapons without taking damage. This requires a Dexterity + Martial Arts Weaponry roll against a difficulty of 6. The successes are applied both against the attacker's roll to hit and roll for damage.
Difficulty: 6 **Damage:** Strength +1
Cost: $15 ($25 a pair) **Weight:** 1 lb each.

Nunchaku: Nunchaku, or Numchuks, developed from Okinawan grain threshers. A pair of Nunchaku is made of two sticks tied end to end with a short cord. In use these sticks are twirled rapidly, flipped over the shoulders and across the back, striking out unexpectedly at one or more opponents. A character with a Martial Arts Weaponry skill may do a double strike as per knife fighting (see above) or grapple, causing one extra die of damage during such combat.
Difficulty: 7 **Damage:** Strength+1
Cost: $10-$20 **Weight:** 1.5 lbs
Manrikigusari: Gusari is a Japanese suffix meaning "of (or with) a chain." A manrikigusari is a fighting chain, originally developed by the ninja to help defeat samurai in combat. A manrikigusari is normally about an inch in diameter and six to eight feet in length, with a fist-sized weight on each end. In the hands of a master these weapons are truly frightening. The chain will wrap around a block to strike the opponent from behind, will entangle arms and legs, or crack like a whip directly into the target.
Difficulty: 8 **Damage:** Strength+1
Cost: $100 (very rare) **Weight:** 25 lbs

Special Maneuver: *Attack against Dodge*

After an opponent has declared she is dodging, a manrikigusari wielder may declare "Attack Against Dodge." Before rolling, the wielder may "soak-up" the dodge successes by removing dice from his dice pool one for one. An attack against dodge may be either an entangle or a strike.

Special Maneuver: *Entangle (per hook)*

An expert can use the chain in combat to ensnare an opponent. This increases the difficulty of the attack by one in addition to all other modifiers. The results vary depending on what the attacker desires.

Snare opponent's weapon: Strength vs Strength roll to jerk out of hand

Snared opponent's arm: Strength vs Strength roll to jerk off balance (victim must abort all actions)

Sai: Sai are sword catchers developed by the Okinawans from pitchforks. A Japanese variant of this weapon, called a Jitte, exists. Sai are used to block, strike as a heavy nightsticks, and catch blades or disarm sword wielders.
Difficulty: 7 **Damage:** Strength **Cost:** $50 for a set of two
Weight: 10 lbs each.

Special Maneuver: *Disarm*

A sai wielder may make any attack an "attack to disarm." The difficulty of this attack is an eight, and he must receive **four** more successes than his opponent. If he succeeds, then the opponent's weapon is torn from her grasp. If he only succeeds by three successes, then the opponent's weapon is immobilized in the forks of the sai. Roll Strength vs Strength to determine who breaks the other's hold.

Miscellaneous

Brass Knuckles A set of large rings have the same effect as these weapons. They increase the damage pool for punches by one die. They cost $10 a pair.

Bottle: This improvised weapon does Strength for damage but will break on the first blow.

Broken Bottle: This does damage as a small knife, but will break if blocked, becoming useless.

Chains: A chain used without the Manrikigusari skill does Strength + 2 in damage and has a difficulty of 8. Chains can also be wrapped up and used as a club.

Straight Razors: As small knives.

Melee combat example

Example of Play

Gordon, a skilled martial artist, is visiting his Sire's lands in Zagreb, Croatia. He is out alone taking a relaxing stroll by the waterfront when the peaceful evening is shattered by screams from a nearby alleyway. Before Gordon can decide what to do, four burly men with clubs and knives rush out of the alley. Seeing Gordon, they attack him!

The four attackers rush towards Gordon, taking a few seconds to close with him. Gordon uses this time to size up his opponents, draw a knife, and move a few steps so that his back is against a wall. Just before the four reach him, Gordon throws his knife into the chest of the first. The man gasps and falls, forcing the others to step around his body. As the second man does so, Gordon whips out his nunchaku and strikes at him, but the man blocks with his club and steps back. The remaining two attackers both swing at Gordon with knives, and one of them succeeds in slashing his arm.

Gordon, realizing that he cannot hold off three attackers for any length of time, presses an all-out attack and hits two of his attackers, forcing them back. Then he makes a break for it, running back towards his Sire's turf. The unwounded thug glares after him but does not follow.

Example of Melee Mechanics

(Gordon is played by Steve, Cindy is the Storyteller)

Cindy tells Steve that while Gordon is walking along minding his own business he must make a Streetwise plus Perception roll. Steve rolls 3 dice for perception plus 2 dice for Streetwise for a total of 5 dice. Cindy tells him he is rolling against a difficulty of 8. Steve rolls only one success, but he also rolls a 1, and so cancels it out, meaning Gordon fails the Perception roll and did not hear the mugging taking place in the nearby alley, nor did he see the thug at the end

of the alley acting as lookout for the others. All Cindy tells Steve is that Gordon hears a scream from a nearby alley, and four thugs run out of the alley and spot him.

At this point, Steve asks for information about what Gordon can tell about the thugs from looking at them. Cindy tells him the thugs are charging at Gordon, (Gordon did not run or attempt to talk to them) but she also tells him that two of them are carrying knives and two have clubs made from pipes. Gordon can also see that they all are dressed in faded workclothes and they all look muscular.

Steve has Gordon draw his knife. Cindy tells him that the nearest thug is still 15 feet away from Gordon. Thinking quickly, Steve realizes Gordon has another weapon on him, so he throws his knife at the first assailant, using his sidearm specialty.

Steve rolls Dexterity (2-1=1) plus Throwing 4 for a dice pool of 5 against a difficulty of (5 yards divided by 2 Strength) 3. As the dice pool is superior to the difficulty, Gordon has an automatic success. Steve rolls anyway, and rolls 3 successes. For damage, Steve rolls Gordon's Strength+2 (2+2=4) plus 1 for the knife plus one for the success, a total of 6 dice against a difficulty of 5 (the thugs Stamina of 2 plus the constant 3 (rulebook pg. 148). With great luck, Steve rolls six successes! Cindy states that attacker is out of the fight with a knife near his heart.

Steve breathes a sigh of relief and states that Gordon is drawing his nunchaku and stepping back so that his attackers will be forced to maneuver around their fallen comrade.

Cindy agrees that this will allow Gordon to deal with them one at a time for one more round, while they step around the body.

As the three remaining attackers close, Steve has Gordon attack the first one near him, who is armed with a club. Cindy also has the thug attack. Gordon rolls Dexterity 2 plus Nunchaku 4 for 5 dice against a difficulty of 7. The thug rolls his Dexterity 2 plus Melee 2 for four dice against a difficulty of four. Both Gordon and the thug roll 3 successes, an inconclusive round. Cindy states that the thug is hanging back, waiting for his friends to close in.

The other two thugs are now within knife range and Cindy has them both attack. Steve decides that he should only defend this round and not try to attack. Steve also decides that the time has come to spend a blood point on Celerity. Gordon's roll is Dexterity 3 plus Dodge 3 for five dice against a difficulty of 3 (the thugs are Dexterity 2, + 1 [rulebook pg 149]). The thugs both attack with five dice against a difficulty of 4. One thug rolls three successes, but Gordon rolls five successes to dodge him. The other thug rolls five successes and Gordon rolls only 3 to dodge. Cindy rolls the thug's damage of Strength 2 plus 1 (for the knife) plus 2 (for the additional successes) for a total of five dice against a difficulty of 6 (Gordon's Stamina 3 plus 3). Cindy rolls three successes, but Steve states that he wishes to "soak" some of this damage if he can. Steve rolls Gordon's Stamina of 3 against a difficulty of 8 and achieves 2 suc-

cesses, thus taking only one health level of damage. Cindy rules that Gordon has a nasty slash on the arm.

Steve, realizing Gordon cannot hold off three determined attackers, commits to an all-out attack using his double strike specialty in combination with his inhuman speed. Steve says Gordon will Strike Twice with his nunchaku on each action, attacking both the knife-wielding thugs. Steve also has Gordon spend another blood point, this one on Strength. Gordon's dice pool for the nunchaku attacks will be Dexterity 2 plus Celerity 1 plus Melee 3 for 6 dice, which Steve will split evenly. The Strike Twice specialty will give each attack one additional die, or a total of 4 dice for each attack, against a difficulty of 7. Against the first thug Gordon rolls 3 success for the first attack and none for the second. The thug rolls only one success. Against the second thug Gordon rolls one success for the first attack and 2 for the second. The thug rolls two successes on his attack, and Cindy elects to use them in counteracting Gordon's more successful attack. The third thug strikes with his club — but rolls only two successes.

Against the first thug Gordon has a damage pool of Strength 3 plus 2 successes equals 5 dice against a difficulty of 5. Steve rolls 3 success. Against the second thug Gordon has a damage pool of 4 dice against a difficulty of 5, and rolls 2 successes. The third thug has a damage pool of 3 dice. Cindy rolls 2 success, but Steve is able to roll to soak the damage.

Cindy states that the knife wielders have both ducked back away from Gordon, and Steve takes the opportunity to have Gordon flee, preferring flight as the better part of valor.

THROWN WEAPONS

The Throwing skill can cover a number of different weapons, including: knives, hatchets, spear, bola, shuriken (throwing stars or blades), and rocks. The difficulty of hitting a target with a thrown object or weapon is determined by dividing the range in yards by the Strength of the character (Range in yards/Strength). Thus, if the character has a Strength of three and is throwing a rock at a doorway 16 yards away, the difficulty would be six (always round up). If they roll more failures than successes, then assume each failure moves the point of impact 1 yard from the target. The maximum range a character can throw a small object is Strength multiplied by 10 in yards. The weight that can be thrown is one pound per point of Strength. The dice pool to hit is made up of Dexterity + Throwing. Strength determines the difficulty, and, of course, the number of dice in the damage pool.

At the Storyteller's discretion, a character can make one for one trade-offs in range and weight. Thus a character with a Strength of 5 could throw a four-pound object as though his Strength were 6, or a six-pound object as though his Strength were 4.

Also at the Storyteller's discretion, if a character misses a knife attack by two successes or a hatchet attack by one, then the weapon struck the target with the handle or haft. The dice pool for damage should be reduced by five dice, very possibly causing no damage.

Rocks: Found almost anywhere, rocks are the basis of the thrown weapon system.

Shuriken: Shuriken are too light to be thrown far or to cause much damage. The maximum effective Strength usable when throwing Shuriken is two. Shuriken are frequently thrown in groups, though, and for each extra Shuriken, increase the difficulty to hit by one but add one die to the dice pool for both hitting and damage. The character's skill is the maximum number of shuriken she can throw at once. Damage for shuriken is based solely on the character's Strength + the number of successes from the attack roll. Each success adds one die to the dice pool for damage. Also, shuriken are often poisoned (see poisons, below). Shuriken cost $5 each, and weigh almost nothing.

Knives: Knives use the throwing rules above with one exception. Always treat a thrown knife as being one pound heavier than it really is due the control required in striking the target with blade first. Throwing Knives cost $20.

Hatchets: Hatchets use the rules above except that a hatchet is a natural lever for multiplying force. Add one to the Strength of a thrown hatchet attack made by someone with the Hatchet skill. This increase applies to both range and damage. However, hatchets are harder to control than knives, so always increase the difficulty of a thrown hatchet attack by one in addition to all other modifiers. Hatchets cost $15.

Special Maneuver: *Sidearm Throws*

This is a powerful but difficult technique is used in throwing weapons of all sorts. Rather than using an overarm throw as normally seen in circus or rodeo knife throwing competitions, this technique involves swinging the arm around to the side of the body when throwing, releasing the weapon in an underarm style. This uses many more of the large muscle groups of the body (even the legs and hips, when done correctly), resulting in a longer, harder throw. This is the style of throwing that the German army used during WWII with their specially made long-handled grenades (the "Potato Masher"). The disadvantages to this style are that the character must have room to swing the arm widely, and that accuracy is much harder to achieve. When a character is using a sidearm throw, her effective Strength is increased by two, but her effective Dexterity is decreased by one.

Spears and Javelins: A javelin is a short spear about four feet in length. Spears meant for throwing are also generally around this length. They cost $25.

Difficulty: As above **Damage:** As above+3
Ability: Spears **Weight:** 3- 4 lbs

Special Maneuver: Spear Thrower

A spear thrower, or Atlatle, is a four to six-foot stick with a notch at the end to hold a spear. The Atlatle effectively makes the arm much longer, increasing the strength usable for the throw by two. This cannot be used with sidearm throws.

Bola: A bola is made up of three to five weighted cords joined in the center. The bola is used to entangle an opponent. As the weapon is whirled around before being released, the character using a bola must have 2 yards of clear space on all sides. Treat a bola as a any thrown weapon, but a bola will cause no damage. Instead, it will entangle the opponent, decreasing the number of dice used next turn by the number of successes achieved on the attack roll. They cannot be used with sidearm throws.

ARCHERY

Shooting a bow follows the same procedure as shooting a gun. Roll Dexterity + Archery with a difficulty of 8. The maximum range for a bow is the minimum Strength for that bow multiplied by 30. Bows cause very little damage by impact. They cause injury by creating a slash or puncture wound. An arrow with any style of sharp point will cut through many types of "bullet-proof" cloth and kevlar in particular.

Because of the relatively low velocity of an arrow, the arrowhead must be as sharp as possible. If the Storyteller feels there is a reason the arrows are not sharp, he should reduce the number of dice in the damage pool by anywhere from one to three.

Small Bow: 30 lb
Minimum Strength: 2 **Range:** 60 yards
Damage: 2 (-1 die per five yards)
Weight: 10 lbs **Cost:** $30
Large Bow: 60 lb
Minimum Strength: 3 **Range:** 90 yards
Damage: 3 (-1 die per five yards)
Weight: 15 lbs **Cost:** $60+

Compound Bow: Compound Bows are more efficient and accurate than "simple" bows. A compound bow has a system of cables that reduces the "pull" of the bow by 50 percent once the string has been pulled half way. Thus a character pulling a 60-pound bow would only hold 30 pounds on the string while aiming.

Minimum Strength: 3 **Range:** 180 yards
Damage: 3 (-1 die per five yards)
Weight: 15 lbs **Cost:** $100+

Bow Sights: Decrease difficulty by one for aimed shots.
Weight: Negligible **Cost:** $50

Silencers: The difficulty to hear an archer is normally 8. These small soft pieces of plastic attach directly to the bowstring and eliminate the "twang" of the released string. Increase difficulty of hearing the bow twang to 10.
Weight: Negligible **Cost:** $20

Releases: A trigger release for a bow is a device that holds the string, enabling the archer to grip a large handpiece. This makes it much easier to hold the string for any length of time and so gain an aiming bonus. It also provides a clean release of the string, essential for an accurate shot. Increase skill by one and increase difficulty of hearing the bow "twang" by one.
Weight: Negligible **Cost:** $30

Arrow Types

Arrows come in all shapes and sizes. All arrows can be purchased with either aluminum or wooden shafts. A wooden arrow makes a serviceable stake through the heart, but aluminum arrows are harder to break.

Target: Target arrows have a point with no blades. Increase the attack dice pool by one but decrease the Damage dice pool by one.

Broadhead: Broadhead arrows are hunting arrows. They are designed to kill by creating a deep, broad wound. Due to the weight of the arrowhead they are less accurate than target arrows. Decrease the attack dice pool by one but increase the damage dice pool by one.

Fishing: A "fishing rig" consists of an arrow with a trident-like head (three or four prongs) and a reel of fishing line attached to the bow. Reduce the attack dice pool by one die for the weight of the arrow, by one for the drag caused by the fishing line, and by one if the character is shooting at a target underwater (refraction), for a total reduction of three dice to the attack die pool. For bowfishing without a fishing rig, reduce the dice pool by five dice.

Bird: Bird arrows are trident-shaped like fishing arrows, but they end in blunt points. The idea is to stun the bird. Increase the attack die pool by one and decrease the damage die pool by four dice.

Crossbow

A crossbow can be cocked and held ready to fire indefinitely. Crossbows typically have a "pull" of over 100 lbs. Many crossbows fold in the middle to create a lever for cocking the bow. Others require the use of a small windlass (called a cranequin) to cock the bow. Still others use a lever (called a goat's foot). If you do not have a mechanical aid of some sort to help in cocking the bow, then the Strength needed to cock the bow is 4. Anyone can fire a cocked crossbow. Crossbow arrows are properly called "quarrels" or "bolts" and can be found in the same types as longbow arrows. Note that crossbows can be fitted with most gun accessories.

Range: 100 yards **Cost:** $80+
Damage: 3 (-1 die per 10 yards over the Maximum range of 100 yards)
Cranequin-style
Minimum Strength: 2 **Cocking Time:** 1 minute
Goat's Foot or Folding
Minimum Strength: 3 **Cocking Time:** 15 seconds
No aid
Minimum Strength: 4 **Cocking Time:** 10 seconds

An Arrow Through the Heart

In order to shoot an arrow through the heart of a vampire, and so stake him, raise the difficulty of the shot by 5. This is the equivalent to shooting a man with "only part of head exposed". Remember: in order to stake a vampire, you must achieve at least five success on this roll (**Vampire p.** 121).

HEAVY WEAPONS

It is unlikely that Kindred will ever stand and fight with or against the armies of the kine. However, military power is too often used by governments or rebels, and it's easy to become caught in the crossfire.

Few who have not witnessed it understand the destructive power of high explosives or heavy weapons. To illustrate the damage ratings in the sections that follow, some examples:

•A home-made black powder bomb weighing 10 lbs will make a crater 10 feet deep by 20 feet around. (This crater is probably larger than the room you are now sitting in.) The bombs aircraft drop use a higher grade of explosive and weigh from 50 to 1000 lbs.

•One medium-sized artillery shell landing in the center of a block of brownstone rowhouses would level half of the block, and shatter every window for five blocks. An artillery barrage consists of hundreds of such shells.

•.50 cal machine gun bullets retain lethal force after passing completely through a stone house. Such machine guns commonly fire 600 rounds per minute.

Military grade field weaponry is almost always illegal for civilians to possess. At best, registration of each weapon will be needed along with a Class C firearms permit (Licensed Collector) from the federal government. State and local governments may also want a permit and/or a tax. While such weapons might be owned legally, firing them within city limits, even on private property, is always illegal. There is probably no faster way to call lots of police than firing full automatic weapons in the city.

Grenades

Fragmentation Grenades: A fragmentation grenade has a damage pool of 12 dice if it goes off in your hand. For every yard between the grenade explosion and the character, reduce the damage pool by one die.

Example: A fragmentation grenade detonates five yards away from Terry. He will take 12-5 = 7 dice rolled against his Stamina+3. If Terry chooses to try and soak this damage, the difficulty of the roll will be 7+3=10. If Terry had been one yard closer to the grenade he would have taken 8 dice of damage, but the soak roll would still be a 10, as that is the maximum difficulty.

Weight: .6 lbs **Cost:** $20-$200 **Size:** A 6" x 4" cylinder

Concussion Grenade: A Concussion grenade has a dice pool of 8 if it goes off in your hand. Reduce the damage pool by one die for each yard between you and the explosion. Since these are more commonly used by police, they are easier to acquire on the black market and thus cheaper than are fragmentation grenades.

Weight: .5 lbs **Cost:** $10 - $100 **Size:** A 6" x 4" cylinder

Smoke Grenades and Tear Gas Grenades: Smoke grenades emit a dense cloud of white or colored smoke. Tear gas grenades emit a cloud of irritating gas (see poisons). There is no blast from these grenades as the smoke is released through holes in the canister. The cloud will fill a 10 by 10 yard area in one minute and will last 10 minutes in still air.

Weight: .6 lbs **Cost:** $5-$50 **Size:** A 7" x 5" cylinder

White Phosphorus: White Phosphorus grenades generate a temperature of 2700° F when they explode. A WP grenade has a dice pool of 12 if goes off in contact with you. Reduce the dice pool by one per **two** yards. **This is aggravated damage because of the burning.** WP grenades will set most common materials on fire if they are at all flammable.

Weight: .6 lbs **Cost:** $20-$200 **Size:** A 7" x 3" cylinder

Explosives

High explosives are regulated by state and federal permits and licenses, although anyone can buy black powder. Explosives are rated in terms of Blast Power. Every point of an explosive's blast power is worth 1 die per pound of the explosive. Each explosive also states what is needed to detonate it, and whether or not it will burn non-explosively.

Black Powder: One of the few cheap, legal and readily available explosives, gunpowder will not explode unless it is "packed" into a bomb. Loose gunpowder will only flare and burn.

Blast Power: 1 **Cost:** $12.00 per lb
Detonate: Heat, Flame **Burn:** Yes, but very hot

Blasting Powder: This modern gunpowder is as that used in commercially-sold small arms ammunition. It is also called "smokeless powder," in comparison with Black Powder. Frequently sold under the brand name "Pyrodex," it is legal to purchase in small quantities.

Blast Power: 2 **Cost:** $18.00 per lb
Detonate: Flame, Heat **Burn:** Yes

Nitroglycerine: Nitroglycerine is an oily, clear liquid that can be easily made in a home workshop. It is very unstable, though quite powerful. These facts combine to make Nitro unpopular. Rules for the detonation of liquid nitroglycerin are left up to the Storyteller, and capriciousness is advised as it mimics best the nature of this fickle explosive. Nitro may be "safety packed" by a character trained in explosives handling. This will significantly reduce the dangers.

Nitrocellulose (gun cotton) is manufactured by soaking cotton (cellulose) in nitroglycerine (nitro). This stabilizes the nitroglycerin.

Blast Power: 3 **Cost to make:** $50/lb (approx. one pint)
Detonate: Varies **Burn:** No

Nitrocellulose (Gun Cotton)

Blast Power: 3 **Cost:** Same **Detonate:** Heat, Flame, Impact **Burn:** Yes, makes an excellent fuse

Dynamite: Dynamite (also called TNT) is nitroglycerin stabilized in charcoal. Dynamite that goes through changes of temperature over a fairly long period of time will "sweat" pure nitroglycerine crystals. Dynamite in this state will appear shiny, not waxy as is normal (see nitroglycerin for rules on detonation of deteriorated dynamite).

Blast Power: 3 **Cost:** $5.00 per lb **Detonate:** Fulminating Primer only **Burn:** Yes, can safely be used as emergency flare.

Plastique (C-4): Plastique (Plastic Explosive) is manufactured in varying strengths. It is similar to modeling clay in consistency, and is extremely stable. Most military explosives are plastique.

Blast Power: 1-20 **Cost:** $25-$1,000 **Detonate:** Primer Only **Burn:** Yes, safe to cook on.

Primacord: Also called instant fuse, Primacord is an explosive manufactured in string form. It is used to detonate widely separated explosives at the same time. It can also be used as a "main charge" by an expert.

Blast Power: .5 **Cost:** $10-$100 **Detonate:** Primer Only, Open Flame **Burn:** No

Napalm: Napalm is jellied gasoline. When it burns it tends to cling to whatever it is burning. Napalm will continue to burn underwater. The only way to remove burning napalm is to scrape it off, invariably removing the skin as well. All damage done by Napalm is aggravated. Roll one die to see how much of your body is covered by napalm (The Storyteller may modify this roll as she sees fit). Roll that many dice in the damage pool every turn for 10 turns. Napalm can be made in home laboratories and placed in glass bottles for throwing.

Napalm bombs will have a Blast Power of 6 - 12 to spread the napalm out. Modern jets drop napalm canisters with no explosives in them, as they rely on the speed of the jet to spread the napalm when the canister ruptures.

Blast Power: 0 **Cost:** $50/lb to make **Detonate:** Open Flame **Burn:** That's the point

---

Support Weapons

Support Weapons provide heavy or sustained firepower and require a separate skill of either Heavy Weapons or Artillery to use. Machineguns are the only exception to this, requiring the Firearms skill. The cost of all these items is left

off as anyone selling these to a Vampire will demand whatever she believes the market will bear.

Holding and firing any weapon listed as normally requiring a tripod requires a minimum Strength + Potence of 6.

LAW: LAW stands for Light Anti-tank Weapon. The LAW is a disposable, one-shot rocket and launcher. The launcher is a tube about 2.5 feet long and about 4 inches in diameter. The rocket is about 14" long.

Difficulty: 7 **Damage:** 12 **Range:** 200 yards
Ability: Heavy Weapons **Weight:** 5 lbs

Stinger: A shoulder fired anti-aircraft missile with a heat seeking guidance system. This is a "fire and forget" weapon, requiring nothing further from the user after aiming and shooting.

The LAW (above) and the Stinger produce "backblast" when fired. That is, flames and rocket exhaust emit from the rear of the firing tube. Because of the backblast, there is a two-yard danger zone directly behind the firer of any such weapon. Anyone in the danger zone when the weapon is fired will take four dice of aggravated damage from the flames.

Difficulty: 7 **Damage:** 14 **Range:** 2 miles
Ability: Heavy Weapons **Weight:** 25 lbs

Grenade Launchers: The M-79 grenade launcher looks (and operates) like a stubby shotgun with a 2" diameter

barrel. The grenades explode on impact. There is no magazine to this weapon as the weapon fires one shot, then must be reloaded.

Difficulty: 6 **Damage:** grenade **Range:** 400 yards
Ability: Heavy Weapons **Weight:** 6 lbs

Flame Throwers: A backpack carries tanks of napalm, and a hose connects to a rifle-like launcher. It weighs 50 lbs with all 3 tanks, but only one tank is needed. Each tank is good for 5 minutes of constant spraying.

Difficulty: 6 **Damage:** per napalm **Range:** 60 yards
Ability: Heavy Weapons

Mortars

Indirect fire weapons like mortars send their projectiles in an arc, rather than line of sight like a gun. Because of this, no mortar can be fired inside a building. Mortar shells fall vertically onto their targets and do damage like explosives, losing one die for every yard of distance from where it landed. The smallest mortars fire grenade-sized shells. Large mortars break down into 3 man-portable loads (the barrel and two halves of the baseplate). Some large mortars are towed on small trailers.

Small Mortar
Difficulty: 8 **Damage:** 12
Range: 3/4 mile (1320 yards) **Ability:** Artillery
Weight: 50 lbs. (breaks down into barrel and baseplate, each 25 lbs.) **Ammunition Weight:** .5 lbs per shell

Large Mortar
Difficulty: 9 **Damage:** 24
Minimum/Maximum Range: 600 yards/2 miles
Ability: Artillery
Weight: 660 lbs (splits into three nearly equal pieces)
Ammunition Weight: 1.5 lbs per shell

Small Howitzer (105mm): This weapon requires a crew of four — two loaders, one aimer and one "trigger-man." Guns of this size are normally fired at targets are miles away by using radio communication with a forward observer. The forward observer tells the gun crew which direction to correct their aim, thus zeroing in on the target shot by shot. Reduce difficulty by one per shot with a forward observer correcting fire. The minimum difficulty is 5 (after five rounds of having the targeting corrected). A successful hit immediately drops the difficulty to 5.

Difficulty: 10 **Damage:** 30
Range: 10 miles **Ability:** Artillery

.30 Caliber Machine gun: This weapon is often found on vehicles, or as a squad support weapon among Third World armies. It comes with a bipod and the ammunition is belt fed.

Difficulty: 6 **Damage:** 6
Rate: 21 **Capacity:** 100 **Range:** 800 yards

.50 Caliber Machine gun: This weapon is often found on vehicles, or as a squad support weapon. It comes with a tripod and the ammunition is belt fed.

Difficulty: 7 **Damage:** 8
Rate: 30 **Capacity:** 200 **Range:** 1000 yards

30mm Cannon: Found only on vehicle mountings. Belt-fed, the high rate of fire allows the gun to "drill into" a target. Consider all successes during one turn cumulative for defeating armor thickness.

Difficulty: 7 **Damage:** 10
Rate: 42 **Capacity:** 100 **Range:** 1200 yards

M-19 Grenade Launcher: This fully automatic 40mm grenade launcher rests on a tripod and can either fire from its belt or individually chambered rounds.

Difficulty: 6 **Damage:** per grenade
Rate: 21 **Capacity:** 50 **Range:** 600 yards

TOW: This is a wire-guided anti-tank missile that is vehicle or bipod launched and produces backblast like a LAW.

Difficulty: 6 **Damage:** 16
Rate: 42 **Capacity:** 2 **Range:** 2500 yards

2.75" Rocket: These rockets are used as vehicle-mounted artillery. They are found mounted in clusters of 6 to 60.

Difficulty: 8 **Damage:** 15
Rate: 1 **Range:** 3000 yards

105mm Gun: This type of gun is found mounted on tanks. They normally fire armor-piercing ammunition, either "shaped charge" or solid shot. Armor-piercing ammunition (of either type) does not have a blast effect. There is damage only to whatever the shell strikes.

Difficulty: 7 **Damage:** 20 **Rate:** 1
Capacity: 1 **Range:** 1200 yards

120mm Gun: See above.
Difficulty: 7 **Damage:** 30 **Rate:** 1
Capacity: 1 **Range:** 2000 yards

Other Ranged Weapons

Lasers: Current lasers do blinding damage only, and they must hit the eye to do this. In clear air, day or night, range is about 1 mile. A character looking in the direction of the laser will be blinded for 1 die minus Stamina in minutes. Double this if the victim was using Auspex at the time. Rain or fog significantly decreases the range of the laser. A laser requires some kind of power source.
Difficulty: 10 **Damage:** blind
Weight: 10 lbs **Cost:** $1000 **Ability:** Firearms

Tasers: These are electric shock stunners. A "Taser" consists of a battery pack (hip-mounted) and a pistol-like launcher. The launcher uses CO_2 to fire two probes which must both "ground out" on the target. Mortals heal the damage within a day and Vampires need only sleep for a day.
Difficulty: 3 **Damage:** 4
Range: 10 yards **Weight:** 2 lbs **Cost:** $100
Ability: Firearms

ACCESSORIES

Swordcanes: These weapons are concealed within the cane itself, and when removed the cane can be used for parrying, increasing the opponent's difficulty to hit by one. All statistics are the same as a fencing sword.
Cost: $60+ **Weight:** 10 lbs

Gun Canes: A "one-shot" gun hidden in a cane (normally a break-open shotgun).
Cost: (Must be custom made) $150

Weapon Holsters: Holsters cost $15 and up, depending on the fanciness. All of the holsters described here can be found at security goods stores.

Hip Holster: These either come in standard gun or knife holster varities, which are available with its own belt or it slips onto a belt. Most holsters are worn snapped shut to keep a gun or knife inside in case of a fall. This also prevents any "quick draws."

Shoe or Boot Holsters: These are hard to see, but also difficult to reach in some common situations (sitting in a car, for example). They are also normally worn snapped shut.

Inside Thigh: Impossible to see, yet the holster remains easy to reach with slight modification to the clothing. This type of holster is often worn without safety straps.

Hat: Small items may be hidden in a hat, but they will become obvious if the hat is removed.

Back of Neck: Used mainly with throwing knives, this sort of holster is difficult to see underneath a jacket — unless you bend over too sharply.

Underarm: This variety is the second-most common after hip holsters. Small weapons are almost invisible, but they can be spotted if the viewer has training.

VEHICLES

"You wanna' survive? Well here's what you do.
Get yourself a good fast bike,
learn to ride like a bat out of hell,
and pray it's not raining on doomsday."
— Anonymous Biker - 1978

Wheeled Vehicles

Brake, a new statistic for vehicles, is the number you multiply current speed (in miles-per-hour) by to figure stopping distance in feet. Below 30 mph do not use the "Brake" number. Instead assume that any vehicle can stop within its own length.

Bicycle: Maximum speed on a good racing bike is eight times Strength in miles-per-hour, but a character can only maintain that speed for Stamina + Fortitude minutes. A normal pace for a bicycle is about 3 times Strength in mph, and can be maintained for Stamina plus Fortitude in hours. Halve these speeds and times if the character is traveling uphill, and double the times (not the speeds) for downhill travel.

Safe: 3 x Strength   **Maximum:** 8 x Strength
Maneuver: 5   **Brake:** 2   **Cost:** $50+

Compact: Exemplified by a Yugo or Toyota — two-door, maybe hatchback or sedan.

Safe: 70 **Maximum:** 90 **Maneuver:** 5
Brake: 2 **Cost:** $6000

Mid-Sized: Including the Ford Taurus, these include four-doors and station wagons.

Safe: 70 **Maximum:** 120 **Maneuver:** 5
Brake: 2 **Cost:** $12,000

Large: This class includes luxury cars, mini-vans and pick-up trucks.

Safe: 70 **Maximum:** 110 **Maneuver:** 4
Brake: 3 **Cost:** $20,000

Sports Car: Almost always two-door, this class includes hard-tops and convertibles.

Safe: 100 **Maximum:** 190 **Maneuver:** 6
Brake: 2 **Cost:** $22,000

Vans: These classic cargo vehicles have sheltered many Kindred during their travels.

Safe: 60 **Maximum:** 100 **Maneuver:** 5
Brake: 3 (empty) 4 (loaded) **Cost:** $ 19,000

RVs: Recreational Vehicles, or RVs, are one of the best ways for kindred to travel, especially if retainers must be fed and sheltered.

Small: A small RV will provide living space for four, although it will be crowded.

Safe: 60 **Maximum:** 80 **Maneuver:** 3
Brake: 3 **Cost:** $10,000

Medium: Living space for six (crowded).

Safe: 60 **Maximum:** 80 **Maneuver:** 3
Brake: 3 **Cost:** $20,000

Large: These fifth wheel models require a tow vehicle, typically a six-wheel pickup. Living space for 8 (crowded).

Safe: 60 **Maximum:** 80 **Maneuver:** 3
Brake: 4 **Cost:** $30,000

Jeep: Jeeps have exceptional off road mobility.

Safe: 60 **Maximum:** 80 **Maneuver:** 4/8 (off road)
Brake: 2 **Cost:** $15,000

Motorcycles: Motorcycles are very difficult to control on roads in inclement weather. Triple the brake in rain (or gravel or sand), and halve the maneuverability. A motorcycle cannot be ridden in snow without chains or spikes on the tires. Half maneuverability at the very best.

Small: Honda CB-1
Safe: 75 **Maximum:** 130 **Maneuver:** 8
Brake: 1 **Cost:** $5,000

Medium: BMW R-75
Safe: 85 **Maximum:** 130-170 **Maneuver:** 7
Brake: 1 **Cost:** $10,000

Large: Yamaha Venture
Safe: 90 **Maximum:** 170 **Maneuver:** 5
Brake: 2 **Cost:** $15,000

Sidecars: While it is possible to mount a sidecar on any motorcycle, it is normally done with the larger bikes.

Safe: -40 **Maximum:** -20 **Maneuver:** 1/2
Brake: 2 **Cost:** $15,000

Off-Road Bike: These bikes avoid the problems regular motorcycles suffer on bad terrain.

Small: **Safe:** 40 **Maximum:** 70 **Maneuver:** 10
Brake: 1/2 **Cost:** $5000

Medium: **Safe:** 50 **Maximum:** 80 **Maneuver:** 9
Brake: 1/2 **Cost:** $9,000

Large: **Safe:** 60 **Maximum:** 90 **Maneuver:** 9
Brake: 1/2 **Cost:** $14,000

Trucks: These high-capacity vehicles can be extremely valuable for Kindred on the run, even though they lose a great deal of maneuverability at high speeds.

Small Truck: Vehicles in this class are no longer than 15 feet.

Safe: 70 **Maximum:** 110 **Maneuver:** 5-8
Brake: 3-5 (depending on load)

Large Truck: This class of vehicle can be up to 28 feet long.

Safe: 60 **Maximum:** 110 **Maneuver:** 5-8
Brake: 3-5 (depending on load)

Tractor-Trailer: These 18 wheelers measure up to 60 feet long. Note that the normal "dry van" hauled by this truck cannot be opened from the inside.

Safe: 70 **Maximum:** 110 **Maneuver:** 4-8
Brake: 3-5 (depending on load).

Boats

Boats do not have any brakes, per se. A boat has a listed amount by which it can decelerate each turn. Also, their speed is measured in knots per hour.

Canoes: **Cruise:** Strength in kph
Maximum: 2 x Strength in kph **Maneuver:** Dexterity
Deceleration: 1/2x Strength in kph
Capacity: 2 people + gear or 3 people. Some canoes are much larger.

Rowboats: **Cruise:** Strength + 3 in kph
Maximum: 3 x Strength in kph **Maneuver:** 6
Deceleration: 2 x Strength in kph
Capacity: 4-6 people and some gear

Johnboats: Flat-bottomed fishing boat with small electric motor.

Cruise: 8 kph **Maximum:** 10 kph **Maneuver:** 7
Deceleration: 3 **Capacity:** 2 people and fishing gear.

Small Sailboats: **Cruise:** Wind in kph
Maximum: Wind+Boating **Maneuver:** 4
Deceleration: Dexterity
Capacity: 2 people with minimal gear

Large Sailboats: **Cruise:** 2 x Wind in kph
Maximum: 2 x Wind+Dexterity **Maneuver:** 3
Deceleration: Dexterity **Capacity:** Sleeps 6-8 people

Small Powerboat (Ski Boat): **Cruise:** 30 kph
Maximum: 50 kph **Maneuver:** 5
Deceleration: Dexterity **Capacity:** 4 people + Gear

Medium Powerboat (Cabin Cruiser):

Cruise: 20 **Maximum:** 30 **Maneuver:** 3
Deceleration: Dexterity **Capacity:** Sleeps 6-8 people
<u>**Large Powerboat** (Yacht):</u>
Cruise: 20 **Maximum:** 30 **Maneuver:** 2
Deceleration: Dexterity **Capacity:** Sleeps 20+ people

Aircraft

Stall is the minimum speed for an aircraft. Stall x 100 is the minimum length of runway in yards the plane requires to land. Note also that flying at night is considerably more difficult than flying by day, though a pilot may take a specialty of Instrument Flying if she has more than three points in Piloting.

<u>**Small:**</u> **Stall:** 60 mph **Cruise:** 110
Maximum: 170
Maneuver: 5
Capacity: 4 adults
<u>**Medium:**</u> **Stall:** 90 **Cruise:** 180
Maximum: 230 **Maneuver:** 4 **Capacity:** 8 - 20 adults
<u>**Lear Jet:**</u> **Stall:** 100 **Cruise:** 350
Maximum: 450 **Maneuver:** 4 **Capacity:** 8 - 20 adults
<u>**Large:**</u> **Stall:** 180 **Cruise:** 270
Maximum: 380 **Maneuver:** 3 **Capacity:** 50 adults
<u>**Large Helicopter:**</u> **Stall:** 0 **Cruise:** 150
Maximum: 240 **Maneuver:** 6 **Capacity:** 30
<u>**Hot Air Balloon:**</u> **Stall:** 0 **Cruise:** Wind
Maximum: Wind **Maneuver:** 0 **Capacity:** 4
<u>**Parachutes:**</u> A parachute takes 30 minutes for a skilled person to pack, and one full turn to don. A normal (one-person) parachute can support 600 lbs in an emergency, but everyone relying on it will have to make Dexterity rolls (difficulty dependent on terrain) upon landing to avoid injury.

Armored Fighting Vehicles; Tanks and Armored Personnel Carriers

These vehicles all require a crew of two (a driver and a gunner) at a minimum, though one person could drive the vehicle without firing, or vice versa. Armor is rated by its toughness and its thickness. The toughness is the Difficulty for the damage roll and the thickness is how many successes need to be achieved before the armor is penetrated. This is always written Toughness/Thickness.

M-60: This is the U.S. Army main battle tank from the early 60s until the early 80s. It mounts a 105mm main gun (63 shells), a .50 Caliber co-axial machine gun (6000 rounds), and a .50 Cal. anti-aircraft machine gun in a swiveling cupola (1000 rounds). It has a driver's vision port to the front and gunner's sights in turret. It is equipped with smoke dispensers, radio and can be sealed against NBC contamination. The main gun is gyro-stabilized to allow firing while in motion. Anti-aircraft machinegun cannot be used when the vehicle is buttoned up (no occupants visible). It has a telephone on the rear of the hull to allow supporting infantry to talk with the tank crew.

Height: 3.6 yards **Weight:** 50 tons
Crew: 4 **Range:** 310 miles
Safe: 20 **Maximum:** 30 (on road only)
Maneuver: 2 **Brake:** 3 **Armor:** 6/16 (2/3 on sides)

T-72: This is the Soviet Army main battle tank from the early 70s until the early 80s. It mounts a 125mm main gun (50 rounds), a .50 Cal. co-axial machine gun (5000 rounds), and a .50 Cal. machine gun (1000 rounds) for anti-aircraft purposes. There is a driver's vision port to the front and a gunner's sight in turret. It is equipped with smoke dispensers and radio, it can be sealed against NBC contamination. The main gun is gyrostabilized to allow firing while in motion. Treat it as a 120mm gun for firing purposes. Anti-Aircraft MG cannot be used when the vehicle is buttoned up.

Height: 2.7 yards **Weight:** 40 tons
Crew: 3 **Range:** 300 miles
Safe: 20 **Maximum:** 40 **Maneuver:** 2
Brake: 4 **Armor:** 6/14 (1/2 on sides)

M-1 Abrams: The U.S. Army main battle tank from the early 80s onwards. Mounts a 120mm main gun (48 shells), a .50 Cal. co-axial machinegun (6000 rounds), and two .50 Cal. machineguns (1000 rounds). There is a driver's vision port to the front and gunners' sights in turret. It is equipped with smoke dispensers and radio, it can be sealed against NBC contamination. The main gun is gyrostabilized to allow firing while in motion. Top mounted machineguns cannot be used when the vehicle is buttoned up. A telephone on the rear of the hull allows supporting infantry to talk with the tank crew. The vehicle can snorkel under water up to 30' deep.

Height: 2.7 yards **Weight:** 59 tons
Crew: 4 **Range:** 300 miles
Safe: 30 **Maximum:** 45 (on road only)
Maneuver: 2 **Brake:** 3 **Armor:** 8/18

T-80: The Soviet Army main battle tank from the early 80s until present. Mounts a 125mm main gun, a .50 Cal. co-axial machinegun, and a .50 Cal. anti-aircraft machinegun.

Height: 2.7 yards **Weight:** 59 tons
Crew: 4 **Range:** 300 miles
Safe: 30 **Maximum:** 45 (on road only)
Maneuver: 2 **Brake:** 3 **Armor:** 8/18

M-113: The U.S. Army Armored Personnel Carrier from the early 60s until the late 70s. Mounts various weapons (generally heavy machineguns) in a cupola.

Crew/Capacity: 13 troops **Safe:**30
Maximum: 45 **Maneuver:** 3 **Brake:** 3 **Armor:** 10

Bradley: The U.S. Army Armored Personnel Carrier from the early 80s until present. Mounts a 25mm cannon (treat as a 30mm cannon) and two heavy submachine guns with ports for four other weapons.

Crew/Capacity: 13 troops **Safe:**30
Maximum: 45 **Maneuver:** 3 **Brake:** 3 **Armor:** 10

BMP: The Soviet Armored Personnel Carrier from the late 60's until present. It mounts a 30mm cannon and a .50 cal. anti-aircraft machinegun.

Crew/Capacity: 11 troops **Safe:**30
Maximum: 45 **Maneuver:** 3 **Brake:** 3 **Armor:** 5/10

Military Aircraft & Boats

UH-60A (Blackhawk): A U.S. Army general utility helicopter used for troop transport and resupply. It can be armed with .30 cal machine guns firing from the sides of the vehicle.

Crew: 3 **Passengers:** 11 **Range:** 450 miles
Stall: 0 **Safe:** 180 **Maximum:** 280
Maneuver: 7 **Deceleration:** 30 **Armor:** 3/5

AH-64 Apache: The current U.S. Army attack helicopter. It can land on a 15 degree slope. It is equipped with a radio and can be sealed against NBC attacks. It is armed with a 30mm chain gun, four rocket launchers or 16 TOW missiles, and two 2.75" rocket pods.

Crew: 2 **Passengers:** 0 **Range:** 450 miles
Stall: 0 **Safe:** 180 **Maximum:** 300
Maneuver: 9 **Deceleration:** 20 **Armor:** 6/9

MI-8 Hip: This is the standard Soviet combat helicopter. Instead of dividing helicopters into assault and transport models, the Russians make heavily armed transports. The "Hip" is the most common military helicopter in the Eastern block, while the "Hind A" is its more modern replacement. It carries four Sagger anti-tank missiles and two .30 caliber machineguns. Treat the Sagger anti-tank missile as a TOW.

Crew: 3 **Passengers:** 24 **Range:** 300 miles
Stall: 0 **Safe:** 180 **Maximum:** 250
Maneuver: 5 **Deceleration:** 20 **Armor:** 4/4

MI-24 Hind A: The standard Russian combat helicopter, it is armed with four Sagger missiles and two .30 caliber machineguns.

Crew: 4 **Passengers:** 8 **Range:** 400 miles
Stall: 0 **Safe:** 180 **Maximum:** 300
Maneuver: 7 **Deceleration:** 20 **Armor:** 5/6

F-14A Tomcat: This multi-role jet fighter carries four Sidewinder air-to-air missiles (Difficulty 8 Damage: 15 Rate: 1 Range: 3000 yards), six Sparrow air-to-ground missiles (Difficulty: 8 Damage: 20 Rate: 1 Range: 3000 yards), and 14 250-lb bombs (Difficulty: 8 Damage: 40) as well as a 20mm cannon (Difficulty: 7 Damage: 8 Rate: 42 Capacity: 200 Range: 1000 yards.

Crew: 2 **Passengers:** 0 **Range:** 400 miles
Stall: 300 **Safe:** Mach 2 **Maximum:** Mach 2.5
Maneuver: 7 **Deceleration:** 50 **Armor:** 3/3

Coast Guard Cutter: A typical coastal patrol craft, this ship could be met anywhere within 200 miles of the shore. It generally mounts nothing more than a .50 caliber machinegun.

Crew: 35 **Passengers:** 5-10 (70 in emergency)
Range: 900 miles **Cruise:** 10 **Maximum:** 20
Maneuver: 3 **Deceleration:** 5

Combat Example

After spending several pleasant years in Zagreb, Gordon is distressed at the destruction caused by the Yugoslavian civil war and becomes involved in the fighting when Serbian troops march on the city. One day, just after sunset in late November 1991, Gordon is sneaking through the alleyways toward a meeting with an arms supplier. Suddenly, up ahead in the street at the end of the alley, he hears voices, footsteps and the distinctive sound of a treaded vehicle on pavement. He dives into a trash pile seconds before a powerful searchlight beam illuminates the narrow, unpaved alley. Luckily, the APC passes by. Gordon sees a few footsoldiers dog-trotting beside the vehicle.

"I knew I was lugging this thing for some reason," Gordon thinks to himself as he fingers up the iron sights on a LAW rocket he was carrying. Gordon sneaks to the end of the alleyway and peers out. Lady luck has given him a perfect shot at the rear of the APC. He takes a breath, exhales slowly while he aims, and then fires. The rocket blazes a trail straight into the thin rear armor of the APC, exploding with a muffled flash, followed by a second, louder explosion as the APC bursts into flames, lighting the streets with a fiery glow. The foot soldiers dive for cover and fire back randomly, but Gordon flees back down the alleyway.

Mechanics Example

(Cindy is the storyteller, Gordon is played by Steve.)

Steve has rolled four successes for Gordon to sneak along the alleyways toward his meeting when Cindy asks him to roll Perception + Streetwise. Steve rolls five successes and Cindy tells him that he hears an armored personnel carrier moving down the street he is about to enter. Steve has Gordon hide in the closest place, and rolls Dexterity + Stealth for four successes. The foot soldiers roll Perception + Alertness plus three dice for the spotlight but minus two dice for jogging, and none of them rolls more than 3 successes.

Steve has Gordon sneak to the end of the alleyway, readying his LAW. The APC is only 50 feet away when Gordon fires. Steve rolls Gordon's Dexterity 2 plus Celerity 1 plus Heavy Weapons 2 for 5 dice against a difficulty of 7. The target is well within range for a LAW so there is no range penalty. Steve rolls 3 successes, a hit! Steve now figures out the damage that Gordon has caused. Steve rolls 12 dice against a difficulty of 5 (from the vehicle description), and gets 10 successes. The armor of the APC has been breached. Since the shot was to the rear of the vehicle (where the fuel and engines are) Cindy rules that the APC bursts into flames. Cindy rolls Intelligence + Firearms to determine what the soldiers will do. She reasons that 4 successes will be needed for any of the soldiers to return fire before Gordon escapes. Luckily for Gordon, none of the soldiers roll well.

CAMPING SUPPLIES

While Vampires have little need for many of the comforts mortals require and feel the effects of nature less, camping supplies can make any extended stay out of doors much more pleasant. For the Kindred spending time in the wild, comfort is the first concern. Camping supply stores can be found in every large city.

Tents: Tents are made of lightweight nylon treated with silicone. They are light and waterproof but hardly light-tight. It would be almost impossible to opaque a nylon tent. For Kindred caught where they must camp, a much better idea is to lie in a body bag or other light-proof container inside the tent, hopefully with ghouls on guard outside.

One-Person Tent: A one-person tent is three feet wide, two feet tall and eight feet long and is merely a shelter around a sleeping bag. It could hold two in an emergency, but they had best be close friends.

Weight: 2 lbs   **Size Folded:** 1 Quart   **Cost:** $75

Two-Person Tent: Two-person tents are domes about five feet in diameter by four feet high.

Weight: 5 lbs   **Size Folded:** 2 Quarts   **Cost:** $110

Three-to-Five-Person Tents: These tents are larger domes, seven feet in diameter by six feet high.

Weight: 8 lbs   **Size Folded:** 3 Quarts   **Cost:** $150

Sleeping Bags: As long as the temperature is above freezing, there is little reason for Kindred to worry about insulation. Below freezing, a sleeping bag alone will not suffice as warmth must be generated somehow. Blood points can be used to generate body heat (which Kindred usually do not have), and usually one will provide warmth for about an hour.

Down: Down sleeping bags are lighter, warmer and less bulky than their artificial counterparts, but they are more expensive and lose ALL of their insulating capability when wet.

Lowest Temperature: -10 F   **Weight:** 4.5 lbs
Size: 6 quarts   **Cost:** $125

Insulite: Insulite sleeping bags remain warm even if soaked.

Lowest Temperature: -10 F   **Weight:** 5.5 lbs
Size: 8 quarts   **Cost:** $100

Backpacks: Anyone doing serious hiking will need packs. While rucksacks will do to haul things a short way, for long-distance packing a padded, internal-frame backpack is the only way to go.

Rucksack: The basic bag with straps
Weight: 2 lbs   **Size:** 15 quarts   **Cost:** $30

Basic-Frame Pack: This pack has a tubular aluminum frame that a rucksack attaches to, allowing weight to be distributed across the shoulders and hips.

Weight: 3 lbs   **Size:** 20 quarts   **Cost:** $80

Internal-Frame Pack: The frame on this pack is inside the seams of the rucksack, and is made of thin slats of alloy instead of tubes. This enables the wearer to adjust the pack like an article of clothing to distribute weight evenly and comfortably.

Weight: 3 lbs **Size:** 23 quarts **Cost:** $120

Electric Warmers: This is essential equipment for prolonged exposure to below freezing temperatures. If the temperature is below 20° F or so, a Vampire will freeze and become immobile after Stamina + Fortitude hours if she has no protection. However, she would be perfectly comfortable with the temperature set at 33° F.

Thermal Underwear: Like an electric blanket made into clothing, this is worn under winter clothes. Requires a battery pack of eight D cells for six hours. **Cost:** $100

Electric Blanket: A camping version that runs off batteries (eight D Cells) or can plug into a car cigarette lighter. **Cost:** $50

Heat Packs: About the size of a full quart freezer bag, these chemical-filled packs generate heat after being activated. Activation is usually by slapping, but some require a tab to be pulled. One is good for 1 hour of low heat. **Cost:** $10

Stoves: Small camping stoves are available for $40.00. Expect to pay more for a model that will burn any fuel. Most stoves require either propane or special liquid fuel. **Cost:** $40 - $200

Coolers: Perfect for storing blood or other perishables, some can plug into cigarette lighters and will act as small refrigerators. For more money, you can buy a small refrigerator with a tiny freezer or icemaker, but these must normally be wired into a vehicle. **Cost:** $60+ for plug in cooler, $200 for small fridge (installed)

Ice packs: These work the same as heat packs, above, but are cold. **Cost:** $10

Water Bottles: Hold one quart to one gallon. **Cost:** $5

Fishing: Basic fishing gear (Rod, Reel and Line) costs around $30 for simple, but quality gear.

Climbing Equipment: Basic climbing gear will cost $100 per person outfitted. This includes 100 feet of good rope, a nylon web harness, a set of 20 chocks, five pitons, a helmet, and other basics. **Cost:** $40 - $200

TOOLS

Tool Sets: Tool sets have a rating from one to five like attributes. Tool sets vary too much to give exact rules for all possible tools. In general, a simple tool set fits into a single carrying case, a medium tool set is still transportable, but requires two or three large trunks, and a complete tool set is a permanent workshop.

Examples:

Woodworking
- • Hammer and nails, screwdriver, $50
- •• Level one + carpenters belt, $200
- ••• Level two + Circular Saw, Drill, Miterbox, $1000
- •••• More Power Tools, $2000
- ••••• Complete Woodshop, $3000

Auto Mechanic
- • Locking-Pliers, Crescent Wrenches, Duct Tape, $50
- •• Level one + Socket Wrenches,$200
- ••• Level two + Power Tools, $1000
- •••• More Power Tools, $2000
- ••••• Complete Shop, $300

SURVEILLANCE AND SECURITY

Visual

Binoculars: Binoculars will magnify view from 4x to 20x depending on the model. Add 1 die to vision rolls for each "10x" of magnification.

Weight: 3 lbs **Cost:** $70+ **Size:** 6" x 8" x 10"

Telescopes: Telescopes will magnify the view from 20x to 500x or more. Treat each multiple of 10 as a plus one to vision Perception rolls.

Weight: 10 lbs **Cost:** $150+ **Size:** 6" x 30" tube

Damage Resistance	(Difficulty / # Successes Barrier absorbed in	Structure	(Difficulty / # Successes Barrier absorbed in
Structure	piercing)	Interior Ceiling/Floor	5/5
Exterior Frame Wall	5/5	Bullet Proof Glass	6/2
Exterior Brick Wall	7/5	Car Door/Body	5/3
2' Thick Stone Wall	7/12	Car Engine	6/12
Exterior Door	4/4	Wooden Desk	3/6
Security Door	8/8	Metal Desk	5/6
Security Gate	6/6	Empty Filing Cabinet	5/4
Interior Door	2/2	Full Filing Cabinet	5/8
Interior Wall	3/5	Bar Counter	3/6

Still Cameras: Cameras come in a wide variety of forms. All cameras require film except for some new cameras that store images on computer disks. These cameras do not require a darkroom to produce printed pictures, but they do require a computer. Special items for the 35mm camera include:

A telephoto lens which will act as a telescope;

Infrared film takes a picture based on the heat radiation of objects (Thermal Radiation), as opposed to the visual light used by normal film. Vampires are typically room temperature (unless they fed very recently) and so do not show up well on infrared photographs or equipment.

Ultraviolet film uses light of shorter wavelength than the human eye can see. Vampires will photograph normally on this film.

Flash bulbs which blind everyone around for 6-Wits turns (double this if the character was using Heightened Sight or Gleam of the Red Eyes)

Video: Video cameras record images onto a magnetic tape. The tape may be reused, albeit with some loss of quality. The following statistics are for camcorders.

Weight: 2 lbs **Cost:** $1000 **Size:** 5" x 8" x 7"

Light Enhancing Goggles: "Starlight" scope or "Owls Eye" device. It gathers and enhances available light. Useless in total darkness. In any but total darkness will give a plus 3 to the dice pool for visual perception.

Audio

Shotgun Mike: Also called a directional mike, this device will allow the user to listen in on (or record) a conversation up to 200 yards away. Loud noises will interfere with the mike, as will a sufficient volume of background noise. It is very difficult to eavesdrop on a conversation on a crowded dance floor. The chart below lists some sample difficulties using a directional microphone.

Location	Difficulty
Alone in the center of a field	2
Alone in the light woods	3
Mostly empty restaurant patio	4
Crowded patio	7
Alone in heavy woods	7
Alone in field with radio	7
On crowded dance floor (no band)	10
On crowded dance floor with rock band	impossible

Cost: $300 **Weight:** 10 lbs **Size:** 2' long x 2" around

Area Mike or Pressure Zone Microphone (PZM): These will pick up all sounds in a given area. They can be tuned to pick up only certain frequencies or patterns of sound, for example, the sound of breaking glass.

Cost: $50 **Range:** 50 feet

Bugs: Any radio transmitter (a cheap CB, for example) can be used as a bug, if hidden properly. Any voice activated recorder can also be used as a bug — but you have to go back to get the tape.

CB	$40
Voice activated Tape	$30

Multi Band Radio $120

Small self contained "bugs" cost $100+. They are radio transmitters with very short ranges, typically 50 yards or less.

A Word about Doors, Windows, Walls, and Hinges.

People who really want in and do not care at all about your rights will blast a hole in the wall and walk in. Armies, vice police and organized crime syndicates favor this method. Windows are, of course, the second best way in. Windows are also the best place to shoot out...

When soldiers or SWAT teams come to a locked door, a common tactic is to shoot out the hinges with a 12-gauge shotgun, then knock the door in with a 16-pound sledge hammer.

Lockpicks: A set of metal tools somewhat similar to a dentist's picks. They are of negligible weight. While not illegal to own, they will certainly cause suspicion. **Cost:** $35

Security Systems

Audio Visual security systems involving cameras, closed circuit television, and microphones. Often the mikes are tuned to pick up certain sounds (breaking glass, voices, etc.) The cost of security systems varies widely, from $200 for self-installed, up to the thousands for professionally installed systems. Despite the sophistication of technology, the single best piece of security equipment is still a loyal ghoul standing over your bed.

Sensors: Security systems are based on sensors, which come in two flavors, On/Off and perception-based.

On/Off sensors do not have a roll to detect something; they either trigger or they do not. For example, a window breakage sensor will go off only if the window is broken, and an electric eye will go off only if the light beam is broken. There is no roll for these sensors, the Storyteller must have the players describe their actions very carefully and have the sensors respond accordingly.

Perception-based sensors have a perception attribute used in the same manner as a character's. For example, a thermal sensor might have a Perception of 8. The sensor will roll eight dice against a difficulty of six to spot a character and trigger an alarm.

The most basic security system is an intercom with one box outside the door and one inside. These systems usually include a remote control for the door locks so that you can "buzz someone in." This costs $200 installed, and includes one deadbolt lock

A slightly more advanced system might include a video camera and a monitor in addition to the intercom. This would cost an additional $300. Each additional station on the intercom will cost $50. To add a magnetic card type lock to a security system costs around $300, while adding a keypad and code number type of lock costs around $500.

Additional options are presented in the table below.

Option	Cost
Intercom	$200
Additional Stations	$50 each
B&W Video Camera	$100
Monitor	$50
Cheap Deadbolt Lock	$30
High Quality Deadbolt Lock	$200
Magnetic Card System for Lock (Lock not included)	$300
Keypad System for Lock (Lock not included)	$500
Police Bar (floor brace)	$75
Police Bar (across door)	$75
Iron Security Gate	$300
Steel Security Door	$400
Burglar Bars	$80 per Window

Sensors

Window sensors (for breakage)	$25 per Window (on/off)
Electric Eye	$150 each (on/off)
Ultrasonic Sensor	$200 each

	(Perception 6)
Thermal Sensors	$175 each (Perception 8)
Airport X-ray Machine w/monitor	$2000 (Perception 12)
Siren (90 decibel)	$50 (adds +1 to Awakening)

Firefighting Equipment

Smoke Alarms	$20 (Perception 6)
Sprinkler System	$1000 per room
Foam System	$2000 per room
Fire Extinguishers (type ABC)	$25 - $100

For rules on waking up when an alarm sounds during the day, see rulebook pg. 143

PET GHOULS

Animals are described using only the physical and mental attributes. Animals also have Talents, reflecting innate or trained abilities. Example: An attack trained dog might gain 3 points of Brawling, though it could only be used with its bite — using it to throw is a bit improbable.

Trained animals can also gain Willpower. This is especially true for animals that have lived a long time, as they become much harder to intimidate. Just as with human Ghouls, animal ghouls automatically have the Discipline of Potence, and may be able to learn other Disciplines.

Dogs and Cats

Dogs: Dogs are frequently made into ghouls due to their loyalty and intelligence. Also, dogs rarely attract attention, and can be easily trained.

Small: Chihuahua, Toy Poodle.
Strength: 1, **Dexterity:** 3, **Stamina:** 2
Perception: 3, **Intelligence:** 2, **Wits:** 3
Willpower: 3 **Health Levels:** 2-3
Attack: Bite/1 die
Talents: Alertness: 3, Athletics: 2, Dodge: 3
Weight: 10 - 15 lbs
Medium: Beagle, Border Collie
Strength: 2, **Dexterity:** 3, **Stamina:** 3
Perception: 3, **Intelligence:** 2, **Wits:** 3
Willpower: 3 **Health Levels:** 4-5
Attack: Bite/1 die; Claw/1 die
Attack: Bite/2 die; Claw/1 die
Talents: Alertness: 3, Athletics: 2, Dodge: 3, Digging 3, Tracking 3 (Smell)
Weight: 15-40 lbs
Large: Great Dane, German Shepherd
Strength: 4, **Dexterity:** 3, **Stamina:** 3
Perception: 3, **Intelligence:** 2, **Wits:** 3

Willpower: 5 Health Levels: 4-5
Attack: Bite/2 die; Claw/2 die
Talents: Alertness: 3, Athletics: 2, Dodge: 3, Brawl: 3, Smell: 3 (Drugs and Explosives)
Weight: 40+ lbs\

House Cat:
Strength: 1, Dexterity: 3, Dexterity: 3
Perception: 3, Intelligence: 2, Wits: 3
Willpower: 3 Health Levels: 4-5
Attack: 1 damage, major distraction
Talents: Alertness: 3, Athletics: 2, Dodge: 3, Brawl: 3, Climbing: 5 (trees)
Weight: 10-15 lbs

Bobcat
Strength: 3, Dexterity: 3, Stamina: 3
Perception: 3, Intelligence: 2, Wits: 3
Willpower: 3 Health Levels: 4-5
Attack: Bite + Claw/2 dice
Talents: Alertness: 3, Athletics: 2, Dodge: 3, Brawl: 3, Climbing 7 (trees)
Weight: 30-40 lbs

Lion
Strength: 4, Dexterity: 3, Stamina: 3
Perception: 3, Intelligence: 2, Wits: 3
Willpower: 4 Health Levels: 10
Attack: Claw/2 dice;Bite/4 Dice
Talents: Alertness: 3, Athletics: 2, Dodge: 3, Brawl: 3
Weight: 200-300 lbs

Tiger
Strength: 7, Dexterity: 4, Stamina: 3
Perception: 4, Intelligence: 3, Wits: 3
Willpower: 3 Health Levels: 12
Attack: Claw/5 Dice; Bite/7 Dice
Talents: Alertness: 3, Athletics: 2, Dodge: 3, Brawl: 3
Weight: 600-800 lbs

Birds

Parrot
Strength: 1, Dexterity: 3, Stamina: 2
Perception: 3, Intelligence: 2, Wits: 3
Willpower: 1 Health Levels: 3
Attacks: Harassment
Talents: Alertness: 3, Mimic: 3

Hawk
Strength: 2, Dexterity: 3, Stamina: 3
Perception: 3, Intelligence: 2, Wits: 3
Willpower: 3 Health Levels: 4-5
Attacks: Claws/2 Dice (When Flying), Bite 1 die (only in desperation)
Talents: Alertness: 3, Athletics: 2, Dodge: 2, Brawl: 1, Hunt: 3

Other

Horses
Strength: 6, Dexterity: 3, Stamina: 3
Perception: 3, Intelligence: 2, Wits: 2
Willpower: 3 Health Levels: 5-6
Attack: Kick/3 Dice
Talents: Alertness: 3, Athletics: 2, Dodge: 3, Brawl: 3

Camels
Strength: 6, Dexterity: 3, Stamina: 3
Perception: 3, Intelligence: 2, Wits: 3
Willpower: 3 Health Levels: 4-5
Attack: Kick/3 Dice; Bite/2 Dice
Talents: Alertness: 3, Athletics: 3, Dodge: 3, Brawl: 4

Chimpanzee
Strength: 6, Dexterity: 4, Stamina: 3
Perception: 3, Intelligence: 3, Wits: 4
Willpower: 3 Health Levels: 4-5
Attack: Bite/2 Dice, Claw/2 dice
Talents: Alertness: 3, Athletics: 2, Dodge: 3, Brawl: 2, Climbing 8
Weight: 130-200 lbs

Snakes
Strength: 1-2, Dexterity: 3, Stamina: 3
Perception: 3, Intelligence: 1, Wits: 2
Willpower: 4 Health Levels: 2

Attack: Bite (see drugs and poisons) or Constrict/4 dice per turn

Talents: Alertness: 3, Athletics: 2, Dodge: 3, Brawl: 3, Strike: 5

Spider

Strength: 0.1, **Dexterity:** 3, **Stamina:** 3

Perception: 1, **Intelligence:** 1, **Wits:** 1

Willpower: 3 **Health:** 1

Attack: 0, Bite may be poisonous (see Drugs and Poisons)

Note: You must make a Alertness + Perception against a difficulty of 7 to notice a spider crawling on you.

Ants

Strength: .2, **Dexterity:** 1, **Stamina:** 3

Perception: 1, **Intelligence:** 1, **Wits:** 1

Health Levels: 1-2

Attack: 0, major distraction. Some ants are very poisonous.

COMPUTERS

The new literacy is computer literacy. Those who can comprehend even the lowliest computer have touched a vast potential machine of information. A computer is a tool for accessing information, a tool for analyzing that information, and a tool for acting upon that analysis — all at the same time.

Computers in the real world are a very complex subject. For the sake of simplicity, we describe four types of computers and offer some rules for using them in a storytelling game.

Laptop: The smallest of the computers, laptops are designed primarily for portability. Although small, these computers will still run most software. **Cost:** $2000

Personal Computer: A desktop computer like that found in most offices today. These computers are quite powerful and software is available for many different tasks. **Cost:** $1000

Minicomputer: Typically used by a smaller office or organization, minicomputers are multi-user. More than one person can use the computer at once. **Cost:** $10,000

Mainframe Computer: Used by banks, governments and large institutions, mainframes are like minis, only much larger and more powerful. **Cost:** $100,000+

Computers Equal Information

Computers normally become involved in a game because information is on someone else's computer and the characters want it, although computers do have other uses (writing and addressing form letters, for example). The characters may be keeping information of their own on a computer (this should give a healthy bonus to a recollection roll).

Computer Security

Computer security comes in two forms: physical security and "software" security. Physical security is the denial of physical access to the computer — no access, no data, no data theft. A physically secure computer is one that is not connected to the phone lines. Turning a computer off is a good way to add to physical security.

Software security is any program that keeps unauthorized people from looking at certain information stored on a computer. Unless the person using a computer has purposefully hidden or encrypted information, anyone with **any** computer skill will be able to retrieve **all** information on that computer — given enough time.

In the real world, someone hiding information on a computer either does it right or they don't. If it is done correctly, and that means using security software, then getting the information without the correct password is very difficult. This makes passwords a valuable commodity.

The basics of computers are as follows:

In order to use (or abuse) a computer system, you must have both physical access to the computer (in person or by telephone), and software access to the information that you desire. Software access could mean the correct password, or it could mean a skill roll to break through ("crack") the security system.

How to determine skill and time to crack any system:

System	Time(Hours)	Difficulty
Laptop	1	5
PC	2	6
Mini	3	7
Main	4	8
Security	+1-6	+1-6
Poorly Organized	+1-6	+1-3 (9 max)
Cracking Software	-1-8	-1-8

Example*: A laptop (1) with moderate security software (3) will require four hours for each roll to crack the system, while the difficulty will be an 8. The number of successes must be set by the Storyteller.*

Time: The number of hours used by each roll.

In order to write a security program, make 3 rolls (Intelligence + Computer) with a difficulty of 7. The total number of successes accumulated from the rolls is the difficulty of the security program. Security software can push the difficulty factor over 10. The only way to crack such a system is to use "**Cracking Software**" (created the same way) to reduce the difficulty to 10 or lower.

Poor Organization will never push the difficulty over 9. A poorly organized computer makes it hard to find information on (takes more time), but not much more difficult. Also note that "poor organization" may be a perfectly logical filing system the characters do not understand!

Before introducing a computer into the Chronicle a Storyteller should decide the following things:

- What Chronicle-relevant information is on the computer?
- What other information is on the computer? (for descriptive purposes)
- How well (or poorly) organized is the information?
- Was any attempt made to hide information? If so, how much time/difficulty will this add?
- Taking all of the above into account, how many successes must the characters have to retrieve the information?

Computer Uses

Dedicated computers: A dedicated computer system is a computer designed to do only one task. A bank ATM machine is a good example, as are the Fire-Control systems on modern naval vessels. These computers are normally PC or mini-sized systems, but they are typically very hard to break into. Add two to the difficulty.

Dedicated computers store a record of everything that the computer does. For example, an ATM stores a record of all transactions that have taken place, and it also stores a record of its communications with the banks other computers. Naval Fire-Control systems keep a record of every target that they track.

Example: Bank Automatic Teller Machine (ATM). PC system with added security and security software (Difficulty 10, Time 6).

Typical office computers: Word processors and spreadsheets account for over 50% of all computer use. Databases account for another 25%.

Typical home computers: Games account for about 80% of home computer software and word processing accounts for 15%.

Programming: This classic computer operation requires a number of successes determined by the Storyteller (generally 10-25) rolled against a difficulty set by the Storyteller (generally 7). Each roll requires two hours.

Computers at Work

Valis Zilber, an Anarch, has decided to hack his way into The Metropolitan Bank and wreak havoc with the Prince's accounts. Val sits down at his system and begins plotting out his assault. He knows he cannot use his home telephone to call the bank as the likelihood of the calls eventually being traced is very high. Therefore, Val will use a portable computer from a payphone. The Storyteller sets the difficulty of hacking into the Bank computer has follows: Mainframe Computer — 4 hours per roll, difficulty 8. Security =+4 hours per roll, difficulty +4 (total 8 hours per roll, 12 difficulty). Cracking software = -4 hours per roll, -2 difficulty (total 4 hours per roll, 10 difficulty).

Val can roll as often as he likes to break into the computer and rearrange the Prince's accounts. In order to succeed he must accumulate 8 successes. Each roll will take 4 hours of game time. The Storyteller rules that even if Val is successful, the damage to the prince will be temporary (the bank has

back-up records) unless Val accumulated 16 successes, in which case the effects on the prince's accounts would be permanent. Any botched roll Val makes will set off the computer security system and alert the operators that something is wrong.

MEDICAL SUPPLIES

Blood Bags/Bottles: This is a convenient way of storing cold blood. Medical quality blood containers cost $15 per quart bottle and are made of Pyrex, an oven-safe glass.

Drugs & Poisons

Poisons have a vector (how they enter the system), sensory information on how to detect the toxin, and an effect, which is normally loss of health levels along with specific affects. Also listed are the means of protection/antidotes for the substance, and the effect a Kindred will feel consuming the blood of an affected human.

Tear Gas: Vector: Contact/Inhalant

Sensory: Colorless (frequently mixed with smoke), distinct odor.

Effect: Coughing, gagging, severe irritation of the eyes and mucus membranes. Subtract two dice to all dice pools until clear of the gas cloud for 10 minutes.

Protection: Gas mask will protect fully, scuba mask or goggles will protect the eyes, and breathing through a wet cloth will protect the lungs. Vampires do not breathe, so this gas has a very limited effect on them. They subtract one die to dice pools involving use of vision as their eyes fill up with blood.

NOTE: Using tear gas (or mace) as a civilian is considered felonious assault unless you are actively engaged in self defense.

Drinking the blood: No effect

Mustard Gas: Vector: Contact/Inhaled

Sensory: Faintly Yellowish, Distinctive odor

Effect: Caustic, causes blisters to exposed flesh, if inhaled, may be fatal due to blistering inside the lungs. Subtract one health level per turn the skin is exposed to the gas. Subtract two health levels for turn of breathing the gas.

Protection: Full-skin coverage and gas mask are necessary for any protection. Ordinary clothing will protect for one turn only.

Drinking the blood: No effect, Mustard Gas is a contact Poison and does not enter the bloodstream.

Vomit Gas (Nausea Gas): Vector: Inhaled

Sensory: Colorless, Odorless

Effect: Causes nearly instant projectile vomiting and extreme disorientation. Vomiting will continue for 10 minutes - Stamina. Extreme nausea and disorientation will persist for 10 - Stamina hours. Subtract three to all Dice Pools for the duration of effect. You may roll Stamina + Fortitude, Difficulty 7, every turn to stop retching. Five successes are required to cease. These successes may be accumulated over any length of time, but you may do **nothing** until retching ceases.

Protection: sealed NBC suit. Gas masks are completely ineffective.

Drinking the blood: Dry heaves and disorientation lasting for 5 hours minus Stamina.

Nerve Gas (Sarin): Vector: Inhaled, Contact

Sensory: Colorless, Odorless

Effect: High concentration: One health level per turn

Low concentration: One health level per minute

Trace concentration: One health level per hour

These cause nausea and disorientation followed by death. It is important to realize that the lethal effects of Sarin occur at a concentration of 10 - 100 parts-per-million, and that the effects are **always** lethal. (Chances of non-lethal but still symptom causing exposure are less than 1 in 10,000)

Protection: Sealed NBC Gear

Drinking the blood: Dizziness, bleeding from the rectum (the body will attempt to eliminate the contaminated blood), and loss of one health level per hour.

Antidote: Atropine (must be administered before symptoms begin. Atropine taken without exposure to Sarin becomes a toxin.)

NOTE: It may be possible to protect oneself from Sarin by sealing a room in a high place. Israel used this approach to protect its population during the 1991 Gulf War, but the effectiveness was not tested (there were no gas attacks).

Atropine: Vector: Injected

Sensory: Odorless, Colorless liquid

Effect: Over a period of 3 plus Stamina hours, Nausea, Cramps and Vomiting, Disorientation, Difficulty Breathing and Death.

Antidote: Blood Transfusion, Hospital Care

Drinking the blood: Disorientation and intestinal pains lasting 6 - Stamina hours, as well as the loss of 3 health levels. Obviously the Vampire cannot use contaminated blood to heal these wounds.

Salmonella (food poisoning): Vector: Oral

Sensory: Roll Perception against a difficulty of 8 to detect a sour smell or taste in food. Cooking and spices will make this roll much more difficult.

Effect: Extreme nausea, vomiting and diarrhea. General Malaise and weakness lasting 7 - Stamina days.

Antidote: Stomach pumping, bed rest, lots of water.

Drinking the blood: Intestinal pain, nausea causing inability to drink more blood (roll Stamina + Fortitude to overcome), loss of two health levels over a one-day period.

Amphetamines & Cocaine (Speed, Uppers, Crack): Vector: Oral, nasal, injected

Sensory: Speed is usually in pill or tablet form, coke is normally powder, and crack is small "rocks" of crystallized cocaine.

Effect: These drugs confer the same effect as one level of Celerity. The effect will last 12 - Stamina hours, after which all Attributes will be lowered by one and the character will feel tired and listless, although able to function normally.

Amphetamines (particularly cocaine) also confer a feeling of superiority and invincibility, but this must be roleplayed.

Overdose: Uncontrollable shaking and shivering, difficulty breathing, loss of bladder and bowel control, high heart rate and blood pressure can lead to heart attack and/or stroke. Paranoia, loss of judgement, inability to make realistic risk assessments and willingness to try suicidal maneuvers.

Antidote: Thorazine, Depressants

Drinking the blood: An added level of Celerity for 10 - Stamina minutes after drinking. The feelings of superiority and invincibility last 8 - Stamina hours as well as increasing the difficulty levels on frenzy rolls.

Depressants: Vector: Oral

Sensory: Almost always pills, although cough syrup contains codeine, and heroin and morphine can be smoked or injected

Effect: Subtract two from Dexterity. Also give feelings of detachment, the sense the world is not real, and poor judgement. Subtract two from any Ability. Effects last 12 - Stamina +Fortitude hours. After the effects wear off, the character will have to concentrate and spend extra time or suffer a negative one penalty to all rolls involving Dexterity for the next full day.

Overdose: Unconsciousness leading to coma and/or death. Unwillingness and inability to move voluntary muscles, cannot stand or even sit.

Antidote: Amphetamines, keeping awake

Drinking the blood: Subtract two from Dexterity and all Abilities for 10 - Stamina minutes. Dreamlike quality will last for 12 - Stamina hours. The difficulty for frenzy rolls are **decreased** by one.

Hallucinogens (Psilocybin Mushrooms, LSD, Peyote, etc.): Vector: Oral (dried Mushrooms can be smoked and liquid LSD can be dropped in eyes or added to skin-contact ointments like DMSO)

Sensory: LSD is typically sold soaked into sheets of Blotter Paper or in liquid form; mushrooms are dried; and peyote is small "buttons" of dried cactus.

Effect: Hallucinogens alter the perceptions and thought processes in poorly understood ways. For game purposes, consider the abilities and attributes to remain unchanged, but apply one or more of the following effects as the Storyteller sees fit.

• Lower all dice pools by 1 - 3 due to an inability to concentrate. Persons under the effect of Hallucinogens are easily distracted and are very suggestible.

• Raise an ability score by 1 - 3 while the character is actively working on a project. Persons under the effect of hallucinogens can fixate on one task and apply all their energy to it.

• Allow sudden insights and/or leaps of logic due to the altered state in which the character is thinking.

These effects last 15 - Stamina hours, but will begin to fade starting with the fifth hour. It is possible for someone on hallucinogens to fixate on troubling or panicked thoughts and to panic themselves, losing track of where they are, who their friends are, and even forgetting that they have taken

drugs. The exact effects must be played out, but are up to the Storyteller.

Antidote: Thorazine

Drinking the blood: Effects as above lasting 8 - Stamina hours

Marijuana: Vector: Inhaled (Usually smoked, but it can be used as a spice and eaten)

Sensory: Dried buds and leaves

Effect: Mild euphoria, inability to concentrate, poor short term memory. Altered perception of time, as minutes seem to last forever but hours fly by. Low dosage has no game effect. High dosage will decrease all Knowledges by one, and will make the character listless and unenergetic. A low dose will last 5 - Stamina hours, a high dose will last 2 or even 3 times as long.

Drinking the blood: Effects as above, lasting 1/2 as long.

Alcohol: Vector: Oral

Effect: Euphoria, relaxation, lack of judgement. Subtract 1 from Dexterity, and Intelligence for every ounce of alcohol after the first. These effects go away at the rate of one point per hour. Assume one beer, a glass of wine, and a shot of liquor all contain one ounce of alcohol.

Overdose: Incoherence, fixation, inability to reason or remember, unconsciousness. Death can result from alcohol

toxicity, but is very rare. A character who drinks to the point where her Intelligence has reached one will be noticeably tipsy, at negative two she will be drunk, at negative five she will be unconscious. She will remain unconscious for 15 - stamina hours, when she will awaken with a hangover.

Drinking the blood: Effects as above, except 1/2 as severe.

HAVENS

My house! It's out of the ordinary!
That's right! I'm gonna' hurt somebody!
— *Talking Heads*, Burning Down The House

Storage for the Gangrel

Lailen melds with the earth in the park by the lake, every day just at dawn. It is odd for Kindred to ever witness the glowing of the sky, but Lailen misses the sun on her face. She waits until the last moment before she allows the earth to swallow her again. She keeps a collection of her things, spare clothing, books, and a gun that she stole from a cop she seduced, carefully hidden under an old slab of concrete in the woods at one end of the park. The concrete there is part of an old sidewalk, long since forgotten. She keeps these possessions wrapped in several plastic tarpaulins (of the sort used by road crews), to protect them from wetness.

The Rich and Powerful

Mr. and Mrs. Ionesco of clan Ventrue, live in a large, well-appointed estate in the fashionable west end of town. "Wealth," Clark Ionesco will tell you, "does not solve one's problems — it changes them into problems that can be solved."

They sleep in a comfortable room in the basement, on a large antique bed with silk sheets.

The estate is protected by an eight-foot high stone wall topped with sharp, ornamental spikes. Set along the top of the wall is a wire-based motion detector [on/off sensor, difficulty 8 to spot while climbing wall, will trigger if any pressure is applied to spikes (like using them for a handhold), cannot be spotted from the ground]. The wall-top detector triggers a silent alarm inside the house, where a monitor shows the ghoul on duty where along the wall the alarm was triggered. Standard procedure is to call the police and then send another ghoul out with two attack-trained dogs. The house itself has an intercom and video camera at the front door, along with an iron security gate. The walls are two foot thick stone and the windows have iron burglar bars as well as breakage alarms. The house has a tastefully concealed fire extinguisher in each room in addition to a sprinkler system. In the event of a fire during the day, a 90 decibel siren will sound in the basement.

Brujah's Highway

This large RV was converted from an old diesel touring bus. It comfortably sleeps Nathan, his two Progeny, and their four ghouls for a total of seven adults, plus three large ghoul dogs. The RV has blacked-out sections inside where the Kindred sleep during the day, while the ghouls and dogs keep the privacy or drive. Strapped onto the back of the bus are two BMW R-75 motorcycles to make getting around town a little easier.

Nathan and each of his crew carry large handguns and the RV has been modified to provide firing ports for the five AK-74s Nathan owns. All glass is bulletproof.

Nathan keeps a dozen fully charged fire extinguishers inside and house rules state that one person must be awake at all times. Just in case, the RV is also equipped with 5

battery-operated smoke detectors, each separately wired to a large air-raid siren (140 decibels) on the roof. Take 1 die damage to hearing for one week if you are exposed to this.

Sewer Manse

Gabrial, of clan Nosferatu, lives in the sewers of a large city on the eastern seaboard. He has built his home in an odd corner of the sewer system shut off from the rest of the sewers by more recent construction. Gabrial's haven is a deadend tunnel with only a crawlway for a door, as the tunnel is nearly blocked by a large pile of fallen masonry. He lives here without electricity or need of it, as his daytime security system consists of a section of masonry wall that he thrusts into the crawlway, making it appear as if the pile of debris is at the tunnels end.

Over the years Gabrial has gathered many books and curios in his hole, and they sit along the curving walls on cinder block and board shelves. He has also made a large rack for candles, and this is normally unlit in the center of the room.

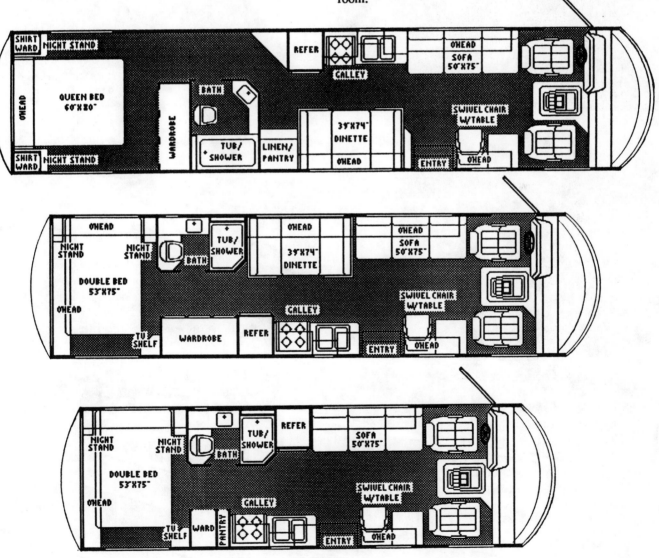

Chapter Seven:
Survival of the Fittest

What a piece of work is man! how noble in reason! how infinite in faculties! in form and moving how express and admirable! in action how like an angel! in apprehension how like a god! the beauty of the world, the paragon of animals! And yet to me what is the quintessence of dust? Man delights not me...

Shakespeare, *Hamlet*

 n uninvited guest in my chambers? How curious. No, please do not go, stay a spell. It has been some time since I have been visited.

Well, do not simply stand before me. You may sit, I no longer insist upon such petty vanities. Those days are long distant. And after all, are we not both Kindred?

Your visage is unfamiliar to myself. I trust you have not long been among the dead? One can always tell by looking at the eyes. The neonates always look so defiant, so undaunted. That shall not last long, it never does. You shall learn the truth of this sordid existence soon enough.

I know what you think, I can see your dreams. You are no longer mortal. No longer a fragile and powerless human. You are now a creature of power and neither bullets nor blades can end your existence. Death no longer hangs over you like a Damocles Sword, ready to fall at any moment and wink out your existence.

Guess again.

Just because you died once doesn't mean it can't happen again. It can, only the next time is forever. The final death it is called, and though it is almost never accidental, it can and, unfortunately, usually does happen. Immortality lasts only as long as you avoid the few dangers that can bring you harm and end your lease on unlife: fire, the Sun, beheadings and witch Hunters with sharp stakes. Only these few things are of danger to you, but they are enough.

Most of use want to eke out as much of our immortal existence as possible. In fact, after an initial ecstatic phase of vampiric life, we are usually more fearful about the cessation of existence than ever before. An old Vampire is a paranoid Vampire, or else one who has achieved Golconda and is willing to meet such termination meekly.

If you want to grow old, you will need to become just as paranoid. There are many who seek to end your existence, and the moment you drop your guard they will rush to extinguish you. Though they may not watch you all the time, and though they may not always be ready to attack you, your existence is so protracted that sometime you will forget your fear and they will be waiting. It will be the end of you.

You may find my advice callous and brutal, but listen closely and do as I bid. I will not teach you the ways of Golconda. That is the path of cowards. I will merely relate to you the techniques of survival, and to survive you must be strong and pitiless. Among our kind, survival is the only measure of success — survival and the number of toys you collect.

MANAGING YOUR DEATH:

 ost Kindred, after the Embrace, disappear from mortal society. If they were loner types, not many questions will arise, but if they were well-known, their deaths must be faked. In this instance, funeral services should be endured for relatives to lay memories

to rest. Then the Kindred can walk the night without fear of being found by police as a "missing person."

Often the Sire will arrange things, but sometimes the Kindred will maintain mortal contacts for a time and hold on to mortal power and wealth long enough to transfer some amount of it to the new existence. It's guaranteed that there's a funeral home in town with a vampiric retainer ready to arrange these matters. It may require owing a Kindred a favor, but it is a most useful service.

Without it, relatives and friends may continually be on the search for missing loved ones. If you're seen prowling town at night and recognized, word may get around, and that attracts the attention of witch-hunters: "Strange disappearance of relative, seen walking streets at night, pale. Ran away when named called. Strange assaults found in same area, victims weak as if from loss of blood. Hmmm..."

Some Kindred pretend they are still alive, finding that they would lose too much if they were to "die." Generally, only loners who were recluses in life can get away with this and have no fear of friends dropping over unannounced. However, some who were particularly wealthy or powerful can continue to arrange things to their satisfaction. Among the wealthy, radical changes in life style are not all that uncommon, and are considered their divine prerogative. Others who worked a night job, such as a cop or security guard, can handle the transition with difficulty. Otherwise, this is not a wise option, but it can be continued for a time.

Your mortal "death" is one of the most important factors in your new life. Make sure all your loose ends are tied up. Of course, it's rarely as simple as it sounds. Most Vampires have a hard time escaping the spectre of their previous life, but those who adapt to the Embrace quickly are usually the survivors.

THE TIES THAT BIND:

here are not too many people who could literally spend eternity together. This may sound strange, but it is better to watch them grow old and die from a distance than to know it did not work out. Dreams are always kinder than reality.

It is especially hard at first if you have family that loves you. It is a simple thing to stand before a mirror and talk yourself up to be a cold, ruthless creature of the night, but one look at your mother, growing old and dying, is enough to make you break down and cry bloody tears.

You go about your new life, sucking blood where you can on the streets, praying that your sister never sees what you have become. You are no longer a part of their lives. They

grow old, get married, have children, and die. All without you.

It has happened to some of my progeny. I tried to do what I could for them, but the best thing for you is to get away. Do not see them anymore, forget they existed.

If this affects you also: let it. Soak it up, while you still can. Many new Kindred exalt in the fact that they are now inhuman. Believe me, there is enough time for that later. Eventually, you will get to a point when you won't be able to act human if you wanted to. Then you will come miss those fleeting moments of sorrow and joy that you get from watching your family or friends go about their lives.

Do not be in a hurry to become the creature which most mortals dread. You will be that soon enough, regardless. An when you are, your existence will become all the more complicated — if you survive at all. For that, you must be security conscious, and security starts in the home.

HAVENS:

he choice of where you spend your days in seclusion from the abominable rays of the sun is of utmost concern. You're most vulnerable during the day when you are deep in sleep and have extremely constrained movement. Day is when the Hunters will always come after you, and thus you should be most protected then.

If you can Earth Meld, just be careful what mud you sink into. Make sure no one is going to come digging by day. This is what can make graveyards dangerous. If you are careful, however, you have one of the most valuable keys to survival that our kind possesses. At five minutes to dawn, if someone is in your Haven who doesn't belong, you have little concern. There's usually a park within running distance of wherever you are. Even in the city, you can usually find a bare patch of earth (unless you are in the Hive). Therefore, it can be quite dangerous to be in the Hive close to morning, unless your Haven is located there, and that in itself may need to be reconsidered.

Not all Kindred are lucky enough to have a relationship with the earth. For them, house hunting is an important skill. Of course, we have a different set of priorities than most fickle mortals. Everyone, of course, has their own requirements. If it were not so, we would be constantly fighting over the same few caves.

Some Kindred think a haven close to their feeding site is the best. This allows them to stay out as late as they want and rush home at the last minute. This makes some sense. But, if you ever do anything to attract attention, you might have police combing your neighborhood while you sleep. Unless they are in your pocket, this is not prudent.

Now, assume you obtain a more regular abode such as an apartment. People come knocking on apartment doors all day. What you have to do is let everyone know you work at night. That way, they do not think it odd that you sleep by day. Also, change the locks, so the landlord will not barge in with his key anytime he feels. Never be late with rent. Always be on good terms with your haven-lord.

Some Vampires make havens of the same place they lived in mortal life. The old, family house with its single occupant, never seen by day, can be a marvelous Haven. The lights may burn all night and figures are seen through the windows pacing the rooms, but only the children of the neighborhood will suspect the resident is something other than human. Fortunately, this is just a game to them, and who's going to believe a bunch of kids anyway? Such a strategy may seem to rely too much on luck, but do not yourself overlook the fact that mortals seem to most often miss what is right in front of their faces. The strength of the Masquerade is that at times we can make daring use of it and still be safe.

If you do choose to retain your old residence, then be most careful. If you remain too active in the mortal world, you risk mortals discovering your true nature. Again, only loners can usually live in the same old apartment. But watch out for "Miss Crabblipp" in Apt. 1. She's awfully nosy about you staying out so late and if she hears strange noises she just might call the police...

You make your haven in a place fitting of your vampiric needs: close to a feeding source and well-secured against entry by anyone during the day. An ideal Haven should be three things: secret, secure and guarded.

No one should know the location your Haven except for yourself and your retainers. Not even other Kindred. Especially other Kindred! Each time you leave and enter you Haven, you should make sure you are not being watched or seen, and this can be difficult if you do not have much time before before the suns rises. This is why you should always return to your Haven well before dawn. Don't let anyone follow you for too long even if you find it an amusing game. They may simply be trying to find where you hide. If you live near where you feed, you must be especially careful not to be seen and followed back to your Haven. The police won't conveniently wait until night to capture what they believe to be a psycho killer.

Many Kindred today laugh at coffins, but there are few things as sturdy and light-tight as a casket. The problem is that it will clue any mortal to your true nature if they see it. There are few excuses one can give for having a coffin in one's house than that one is a Vampire. So, I recommend large, walk-in closets with heavy doors and room to lie down. I realize it is a bit cramped, but it is normal. Normality is important if you will live where mortals will come and go often.

If the room is really light-tight, you can sleep on a bed like you used to. This way you have ample room to move if anyone breaks in on you with malicious intent.

Your Haven should be reinforced so it is difficult for others to break in. This is especially true for the room or coffin in which you sleep. The doors should be solid and the hinges reinforced. The lock should be strong, perhaps with multiple dead bolts. If someone is trying to break down a door, the lock is always the first to go. Make sure the windows are all blackened against sunlight. Spray paint covering the windows helps, but this can peel and you might miss some spots.]

"Black wrap," a heavy metal foil used in the film industry with lighting equipment to block outside light, is great for plastering the windows. It comes in rolls, like aluminum foil, so it's a good thing to carry around to create makeshift Haven protection on the run. Most walls to the outside have small cracks and holes, so it is essential to cover them up.

Lastly, your Haven should be protected either by retainers or traps. Do not make it easy for those who come to extinguish you — get at them first. Even you, a simple neonate, can create traps and possess mortals guards, though it will not equal the complexity and devilishness of the devices and guards of the Elders. You can make a ghoul of some animal, preferably a large dog, and set it to guard you. It is quite simple to set a gun trap with a wire, but such devices often do not work. You may even be able to hire private detectives who will watch your residence during the day. I once knew a Kindred from somewhere in the Latin nations who managed to get himself placed under house arrest soon after his change. A wonderful protection during those first dangerous weeks.

You need some sort of means to rouse you if anyone enters your Haven. In these modern times, all types of advanced electronic alarms are common, but many Hunters know how to disarm them, and many Kindred have the means to disable them. I find that the most simple of alarms, such as row of cans on a string attached to the door, work the best. The intruder does not expect them, and they are exceedingly simple to install. Best of all, you can do it yourself — there is no need to bring others into your Haven. Each mortal you employ is another potential traitor.

YOUR DRINKING PROBLEM:

There is no "Bloodsuckers Anonymous" to help you cope with that thirst of yours, so you are on your own. This is the trickiest part of survival: who to drink from and when.

Finding sources of Vitæ can be a major problem early on in your new life. It is dangerous to feed, and difficult to ever find enough. The best thing to do is to gather a Herd as soon as you can, mortals from whom you can drink without worry of being caught. Neighborhood derelicts are good. Render them unconscious, drink, and when they revive they will believe it to have been an alcohol-soaked delusion. The only trouble is the alcohol content of their blood, which can be severely disabling. You can get around this, however, by feeding early in the night, before they have feasted on their own golden nectar.

Some Kindred, unwilling yet to give up any of their precious morality, drink only from animals. In the city, however, animals can be very difficult to procure, and they do not provide enough sustenance for any Kindred interested in long-term survival. You can travel to the countryside, but the Lupines live there, and it is a most dangerous practice. These vegetarians also have the contempt of most Vampires, so if your survival will depend on some modicum of social success in the Kindred world, I recommend you give in to your desire and take a bite from mortal flesh. More than anything else, it is a pleasure not to be missed.

Some timid Kindred go for the easy route: they suck from the sleeping. These Sandmen have to be good at sneaking into houses and not waking their victims. A good knowledge of how to foil burglar alarms is necessary, as is an ability to move quickly and silently. The few of these Sandmen who keep a Herd sometimes cause their vessels to take sleeping pills at night to ensure they don't awaken. However, the effects of these pills will effect the Kindred to some degree, so all but the most feckless avoid this method. This is an excellent survival tactic, if you can tolerate the boredom. Most Kindred tire of this very quickly. We exist for the excitement of life, not the dullness of death.

Real, live, wake victims are much more difficult to handle — it is an art above anything else. For this, you need the city. In a rural area, everybody knows immediately when old Jeb goes missing. In a city, there's an ample supply of drifters who will never be missed. This is one of the primary reasons why we live where we do.

The homeless are the prime targets. While they can be unhealthy due to disease or perhaps alcohol, they are a guaranteed drink. No one will believe them if they remember it anyway. You just need to be careful where you take the blood and how much of it you take.

Never take enough blood to kill a Vessel, though sometimes it can be difficult to hold back your thirst. Though few of us care about one more death among the mortals, each death raises suspicion and usually is the cause of some sort of investigation.

Many Princes frown upon killings, especially those done without good reason. They are especially angry with those who do not even lick the wounds on their victims, those who in effect refuse to conceal the means of the loss of blood. You need to follow custom when you hunt, and do nothing which will attract attention to you or the others. Those who betray the Masquerade are hunted down, as we do not tolerate those who are sloppy in their methods or are ravenous in their appetites. Don't be among those few who have had a blood hunt called against them. If you are that stupid, then feel certain that I will be among those who pursue you. The taste of Kindred blood, as you will doubtlessly learn, is unparalleled.

If you have the power to "cloud men's minds" (such quaint expressions those writers come up with), you will have none of these problems. This a most useful device when you must drink from someone who knows what you are doing but who you cannot risk killing. This can backfire if you are not careful. Cases of vessels fainting due to inexplicable blood loss have been known to attract attention at times. You must be careful. Drink as little as you can stand to, lick the wound and wipe the memory clean.

There are always blood banks, but unless you're starving, stay away from them. Few things will create more media attention than mysteriously stolen blood. If you can arrange for a retainer who works in the bank, though, then this option is a safe bet, but only if you take a little bit of blood at a time. It's not fine dining, and you'll probably get sick of it after a while, but it's an excellent fallback option. If you can get someone on the inside to work for you, you can even set up business selling to other Kindred who are hard on their luck. You could make them pay thousands of dollars, or you could simply collect a much more valuable commodity, like favors. No Elder would take such a risk, but if you are ambitious it is a fast way to gain power.

Sex is an exceptional pretense for sneaking a nip without someone noticing. It is natural for a couple to go off in the darkness together to be alone, and no one suspects anything unusual from it. The object of your desire will likely not notice anything either, and you must merely make sure that the vessel is well prepared. Alcohol is a useful device to make them amenable to your seductions, and if you have powers of Domination you should certainly be able to control them. However, you must be careful of such control, for often when it ends, your hold on them will be broken suddenly and they may remember what occurred. I find the natural methods more reliable, and use my force of Presence to bring them to me and into my bed.

When you do feed from a lover you must make sure you do not drink too much. Many will know you were with the mortal, and they may point the finger at you if a mutual acquaintance is missing. You must also engage them deeply into the act of sexual conquest. They must feel great arousal before you begin to drink, and they must think it is the sex which makes them feel as wonderful as the Kiss does. They will become addicted to the pleasure of it, and will return to you often, hoping for more, but you must not take too much nor can you take from them too often. Change your partners often, for like any pleasure, the vitality of what they feel will eventually diminish and they may come to realize what is actually happening.

If this does occur, of course, there is but one solution. It should never have to come to that, however.

You can often use the institutions the mortals themselves have created in order to control them. You can become a charismatic religious leader, such as a New Age guru or one of those evangelists. A mortal in any sort of transcendental state is a prime target. You can tell them that that strange feeling of loss and weakness they experienced while meditating was actually the loss of ego or self, and that the pleasure came from the realization of the divine. They'll keep coming back for more. It is quite pathetic, but incredibly amusing.

There are many different methods, and all must be tailored to the individual or group. Creativity is necessary here, but tempered with a conservative awareness of escape in the chance of mishaps. Always leave a back door.

PSYCHOLOGY 101:

 ll too many of us have assumed too much of people, to our own misfortune. They have free will. There is no escaping it. No matter how conditioned you have made them, they will find a way to break out. Then you might wake up to what some call "stake and eggs." A stake in your heart and egg on your face.

Before I go any further, I had best set the stage with a bit of psychology. I recommend that everyone study some of this. You need to understand the enemy better.

Perhaps I sound as if I am talking of an alien race. But you must understand that we really are different from them now, physically as well as psychologically. We have that need for blood above all else, and that has nothing to do with whether I want to screw my mother or not. Darwin probably explains us better than Freud.

It is mortal behavior that you should be concerned about: cause and effect. Again, like I said before, free will gets in your way here. But it is this chaos and unpredictability that makes the centuries pass by without as much boredom. However, to some extent they are predictable, and you can use this to your advantage.

Let us say you are hungry and must drink. If you do not have the ability to make mortals forget they made your acquaintance, you could be in trouble. But, if you choose right, you can find some who will never report seeing you, or at least will not be believed. Mortals such as winos, drunks. Who is going to listen to their sob story about a Vampire attack?

The rich society types are also prime targets. If they go around talking about the night they were attacked by a Vampire, the best they can hope for is a chuckle around the punch bowl, and the worst is being tagged as a loony eccentric. They have a reputation to protect, so you can be sure they will not report any inexplicable incidents.

The ones to avoid are the middle-of-the-road, normal-looking types. If they have been good little boys and girls all their lives and all of a sudden start screaming about Vampires, someone may listen.

Especially avoid the ones who live in trailer parks. A lot of witch-hunters grew up in trailer parks, weaned on tabloids and T.V. The gossip will never end if you drink from one of these fringe dwellers.

So keep to the predictable ones, the ones everyone else has stereotyped.

Now, who can you use among the human population to help you with your daily existence? The fact is, you cannot get along alone, at least not for the first few centuries unless you're going live in a cave, and I have done that. It becomes dull very quick.

Sometimes, if you can trust your friends, you can take them into the fold with you. You can make them Ghouls, or if they are particularly well-balanced, just tell them what has happened to you and they may want to help. But you must be very careful who you tell. If they talk to others, regardless of whether anybody else believes them, a witch-hunter just might. Then this "friend" is leading hunters right up to your haven.

If you can find a friend who you trust, one who will not go into neurotic fits knowing you're an "undead" creature, then use them all you can. I did, and it worked out fine for me. Sometimes, just having a friend "on the outside" is the only thing that keeps you sane.

Police are very important to have control of, being the major paramilitary force among mortals. They are most often already in the hands of Kindred, and can be used against you by these Kindred.

You will probably only be able to gain low-level officers as retainers. The big ones are already taken. Still, any officer is of invaluable use to you. Who you try to get should depend on your particular needs. If you feed off derelicts, then gain the retainership of a policeman who walks that beat. He can look the other way for you. The guard at the city lockup is good too, especially if you can make him a Ghoul. He can then let you in to drink from those incarcerated therein. They will have no place to run.

Just be careful when gaining their aid, however you go about it. You might accidently try to get one who is already taken, and his "patron" might not like your interference. If the patron is an Elder, you could be in a merry bit of trouble.

HOW TO BREAK THE LAW AND GET AWAY WITH IT

 If you get in trouble, you need to do something fast. Kindred justice is not like mortal justice. There are no appeals courts or juries. If you attract the wrath of an Elder you have to deal with it on your own, and you need to know what to do. Fortunately you have a number of choices.

Probably the easiest method is to blame it on someone else. It is an ancient practice, tried and true, used by many on frequent occasion. You can gain enemies in this way, but that is inevitable, especially for an ambitious neonate like you. When you are new in town, do not know anyone and no one knows you, it is abominably easy for some Cainite to arrange for you to be in the wrong place at the right time. The right time for him at least, with you catching the blame for any trespasses she cares to pull.

All I can tell you is to be wary of this, never allowing yourself to be put in a situation where you could be blamed. However, if you can, pull off the same kind of scam on someone else as soon as you get the chance. It is a bloody world we exist in, and there is not enough blood to go around. Sometimes you just have to break the rules, and if there is someone around to conveniently take the blame, let them.

The best idea, though, is to not let anyone know what you're doing. If no one discovers you have broken the rules, can you then really be considered to have broken them? I am sure you are aware of the old adage "if a tree falls in the woods, and there's no one there to hear it, does it make a sound?" Well, if there's no one to witness a blunder with the Masquerade, then there was no blunder.

Yet another method, the one which is best for neonates, is to run. A lot of Kindred are not comfortable with travel, certainly not as much as I am. I tend to come and go often. This does not endear me to Princes. You see, they are thus unaware of my actions. But I have managed to make enough friends to ensure my safety in such a lifestyle. To sum up, if you must breaking the rules, simply break them and then leave. Don't wait around to see what happens. That could be fatal, so simply leave town as quickly as you possibly can, and don't look back.

Don't come back either, at least not until a reasonable period of time has passed (and there is a new Prince on the throne!). Remember, a reasonable amount of time for one of us is a lot longer than it is for mortals.

I have discovered a real secret, one not many of us Anarchs have learned. Before you go around breaking the rules, get to know your Prince. Usually he is more than happy to befriend an Anarch, thinking he may discover something of the plots against him by speaking with you. The Prince is certainly the one who will take retribution against you if you are caught—and one is always more lenient with his friends.

Don't get cocky and think you have him around your finger, however. Princes are Princes because they are good at it. It is certain they know things you do not. They are juggling many problems at once, and you do not know how many balls they have in the air or what might happen if they drop one. Perhaps it will land on you.

The best thing to do is play the game cautiously and find out as much as you can from the Prince before you try anything at all. This is the information age, and the more informed you are, the more freedom you have. To use an old cliche, an adage even older than myself, knowledge is power.

Where to get your information is a matter of no small import. There is so much going on behind the scenes of a city that it is sometimes hard to tell which is the doing of Kindred or kine. When you find someone in the know, then make friends with them immediately. They will make for excellent contacts later on.

Seek out the Nosferatu of the city (just make sure you never mention their smell). They almost always have the best networks running. Sometimes they know even more than the Prince does, not that they will tell you everything. Of course, few partake of their wealth of information due to their ugly countenances, so often they are eager to talk to a good listener. If you can put aside ascetics and deal with them, you are ahead of the game. They may warn you if you are about to be blamed for some crime, or even worse, that you have been found out.

If you are able to befriend them, they will become stout and loyal allies. This may take a while though. They will be paranoid at first, and may not believe your sincerity for many years. But this is a task worthy of your time. There are few among us who will hold out a friendly hand to them, thinking they to be monstrous (as if all of us were not). You should be one of the few.

In general, you should get to know as many of the city's Kindred as you can. The more you now, the better chance you have of controlling the conspiracies you are involved in, whether they be yours or someone else's.

Now, another way to break the rules is have powerful friends behind you. By powerful friends, we mean Elders (or, even better, Primogen). This is difficult to arrange, and can cause you to owe favors to dangerous and mysterious Cainites. However, if you can get the consent and aid of an Elder, then do not hesitate to do so. Princes and other Elders will think twice before moving against you.

One danger of this, however, if that they may begin to think of you as their retainers and treat you as a pawn. You may also become embroiled in plots in which you do not below, and be in over your head, as the quaint aphorism goes.

You see, when you are as involved in politics as a Prince is, you are doing so much behind other's backs that you just assume everyone else is also. The fact is, everyone is doing something behind someone's back. But if you can paralyze a Prince with worrying what your "real" motive is behind an action, you can get away with quite a lot. The trick is to act mysterious, so be a walking secret society.

How do you pull this off? By actually doing it. You have to make a lot of contacts. But this is Kindred politics, and if you are like me, and do not possess the stomach for it, do not even play the game at all. If you seek such political advice, then find a Tremere or Ventrue. They are overly experienced in such things.

There is only a little advice I can give you in this arena. As I said before, you must make many contacts, friends among Kindred who you can turn or come to for favors. For this you must be able to return the favors yourself. You see, you must use others to achieve your own ends, but they must use you.

There are many conspiracies among Kindred that you cannot avoid them all. Your only choice is to master them. To do this, you must become very informed: who's who, who's where and what are they up to. A calculating mind helps, for there will be many different permutations of action possible by those involved in your plans.

Many conspiracies will involve long periods of time and careful planning. Few will be as simple as the one we have described. My purpose was anarchy. But if you have a longer lasting goal, then you must immerse yourself heavily in Kindred politics. This involves getting to know your Prince very well, and knowing exactly how to manipulate him.

PROGENY:

Progeny are one of the most valued rewards that can be bestowed by a Prince. The delight in having a child is almost as great a boon as having an ally tied to you by blood. Carefully weigh the benefits of having progeny against the danger. Remember that you are responsible for them until they are presented to the Prince, and some rulers might hold you responsible even after.

Choosing your progeny should be difficult, for they can be dangerous to you if you choose unwisely. There have been neonates in the past who have turned on their Sires and destroyed them in revenge for the Curse they bestowed. You must be sure the person you choose will not see it as a curse, but a gift. Make them aware that you are the provider of this wondrous benefaction.

Until the Childe has adjusted to the new urges, he is hazardous to your existence and a threat to the Masquerade. Being confused, naive and unused to the world of Kindred, Childer can blow the Masquerade wide open. They do not yet know the rules, and are a danger to us all. They can get you in much trouble with the Prince and probably extinguished as well. You must hold your Childe on a very short leash, watching him carefully until you are satisfied that he will not be a danger to others.

Train him well and do not let him out of your sight until he is of drinking age. A new Vampire, flush with fresh blood and unsure how to handle it, makes a lot of mistakes, like walking off and leaving blood drained bodies lying around. Mortal police pay much attention to these "drunk drivers."

Once you have reached a certain age, you will need Progeny to aid in your survival. They are essential if you wish to have power and influence in the city, and hope to hold on to it. If you choose wisely, they will be your most loyal companions. They can protect you as no other can.

You may decide to tie your Childe to yourself through the Blood Bond, but I advise against this. First of all, other Kindred are very wary about those who other Kindred bind so tightly to them. They are highly fearful of the power such an army provides, and will focus their attention on you. Indeed, the Prince may dislike what you have done, for the same reasons, and use any excuse to call a Blood Hunt against you. Furthermore, in time your neonate will resent what you have done, and no longer will you have a companion in whom you can place your full confidence. They will do as you say, but will not do it as well as they possibly could. You could just as well have a ghoul, for all such a Childe is worth.

If you plan to survive a very long time, you will need to add greatly to the Vampire population to ensure that you will have enough blood to drink from when mortal Vitæ no longer satisfies. Remember, the key to survival is to think ahead.

I do not recommend doing it at all until you have at least a few decades behind you. It is more of a hassle than you can imagine. In many ways, it is much like having a child. You have to clean up behind them before they learn to do it themselves. They tend to leave bodies behind.

If you do decide to Embrace someone, just be careful who you pick. I do not know why you would do it. Perhaps you're lonely, maybe you want revenge, maybe you want a pawn. I do not care. Whatever your motive, you have to deal with them. Besides all the red tape you have to wade through, such as securing the Prince's permission, you must to make sure you can get along with them when they become Kindred, and that they can get along with you.

Neither do I recommend Embracing someone you love — it always turns sour. Love is not an emotion capable of surviving death, or lust for that matter. The love stories stories…? They all lie.

FRIENDS & ALLIES

hose you associate with are more a matter of survival and less a matter of taste. Many Kindred would eliminate you from eternity if given the opportunity and an advantage to be gained by it. Beware of those of your kind you call your friends.

However, you also need such friends to guard your back, especially when you are but a neonate. It is in them you must trust and can turn to in times of need, and it is with them you have strength. You must value your coterie, and do everything you can to keep their faith in you. Some coteries are very tightly bound and survive for centuries, while others are affairs of convenience and last for only weeks or even days.

Choose your friends wisely, and interact only with those you can trust. Know where and how much you can trust them, and when you must be wary. Know too that a coterie cannot be strong when its members constantly quarrel. Do not long remain with such a group. A coterie is what you make of it and what the others make of you. Do not betray them without good reason.

When you are betrayed, do everything in your power to punish the offenders and make them regret what they did. Forge a reputation for being a creature of vengeance, thus making others more reluctant to break faith. Do not let a Judas go unpunished, do not let others know that you have

turned the other cheek, and do not let them know your weaknesses.

It is vital to be on good terms with your local Prince. Do not let the Elders think you are there enemy, for thereby will the dangers of your existence be vastly increased. Even if you are not one of them, they must not think of you as a danger. If you cannot be their friend and ally, be autonomous.

Many modern Kindred are Anarchs, and constantly skirt the anger of the Prince. They may get away with it most of the time, but causing trouble isn't a noted survival trait. They live for the vibrant present, throwing caution to the winds. But, in the world of vampires, an ill wind is always soon to blow.

The surest way to live long years is to withdraw from Vampire society. This is usually only done when one is strong enough in both years and power to enforce one's isolation. The most survival-minded Cainites are the Inconnu — they hide and take no part in the affairs of Kindred or kine. Their air of mystery aids their survival, though someday their silence is likely to be revealed a ruse for hiding weakness.

Likewise, projecting an image of danger and mystery is one way to have Kindred avoid embroiling you in their plots. If you are a wild card, few Kindred will risk betting on you, and they will leave you alone.

RETAINERS

ventually you'll need the help of mortals, and for this you will need influence among them. It's hard to find good help these days, and to control them you'll need the assistance of traitors among them. It requires a critical screening process to choose your pawns. Here, more than most areas, you've really got to watch where you step. Letting a mortal into the secret world of the Kindred is dangerous, but if you want power over them, it is at some point essential.

When mortals discovers the existence of Vampires, they usually react in one of two ways. The first is horror and revulsion. You may have to kill them, but sometimes you can use this to enforce a fear-driven domination upon them. The second reaction may seem better, but it can be more complicated in the end: they want in on it — they want to be Embraced. You must know what to do with either reaction, and you must never rely upon them so much that you cannot kill them. If you have the slightest distrust of your servants, then spare no pity.

If you don't provide your servants with what they want, they may attempt to leave you, or even (if they know enough) go behind your back to another Cainite. If you've got Kindred enemies, intelligent servants are the weakest link in your chain of survival. Proceed carefully. Only tell the most loyal of your servants your secrets. The judicious among your servants may in fact request to know as little as possible.

If you can manage it, it's best not to let your retainers know you're a Vampire. Simply assume a guise which they will accept. If they figure you to be a wealthy and decadent patron, all the easier it will be to use them without danger to yourself. They can work for you, pulling strings by day you can't by night. If they do discover what you are, then watch out. If they don't like it, they're likely to find a hunter somewhere and perhaps beg to drive the stake in themselves.

Ghouls are your most loyal tools in the mortal world. They are able to walk the sunlit streets on your dark errands with some fraction of your powers. You must choose these servants wisely as well. You need ghouls who do not have close families so that their strange behavior will not be noticed. You also need ghouls who will resist domination and will not resist being blood bound to you.

But I must confess: Ghouls make me nervous. They are only partially dead, and you can never fully trust them. But, I'll not argue that they are one of the best tools available for your survival.

They have the best of both worlds: the power, but without the curse. They can partake of the daily activities of mortals that are closed to us.

They can eat food which is forever lost to me. They can kiss a woman without fear that they may loose control and kill her. They can still watch a sunset.

Perhaps I am just envious.

There are disadvantages, though. They are junkies. You have Ghouls on a leash: the blood. They have to have it, you have to make them think you are the only one whose going give it to them, at least until they have had enough to be Bound. Once they are Bound to you, they are putty in your hands. Pets. But until then, watch them very carefully.

If you have not been giving them enough blood, they may go behind your back to one of your enemies and make a deal for a sip. They can trade the only thing they possess — information about you.

But, if you keep them well-fed, they are quite tame. They can even be taught not to bite.

Stay away from hunters. Many young Cainites have gotten themselves literally burned by cocky dealings with them. Hunters are dangerous because they know we exist. Not only that, but the eradication of Vampires is of prime importance in their lives. In fact, it is their obsession. If the harsh light of faith shines from them, then the best method of survival is to run and hide.

If a Hunter has tagged you as a Vampire, there's nothing much you can do to shake his convictions. In this case it's you or them. Bite to kill.

If you do manage to get them first, then you have to cover it up well. It's a crazy kind of fate, but if foul play is discovered, they usually have an heir to take over and get revenge. It's like a fun-house mirror — they're everywhere you turn.

If you can, get your mortal retainers to guide them off the path. Some Kindred have retainers who are especially trained at leading Hunters away. Sometimes, retainers pretend to be Hunters. The problem is, what if they fooled you too, and really are Hunters?

If you are not most careful with your drinking, you will eventually discover one of them your trail. I might sound somewhat paranoid concerning the witch-hunters, but one can never be to careful with these lunatics. They are certifiably insane by mortal standards. Both of us would have thought so before becoming what we are today. However, they are the ones who know we exist, and are all the more enraged that they are not believed. They are capable of anything, that is for sure.

They certainly do not understand us. They do not understand our needs. We have to drink to survive. If the situations were reversed, I am sure they would do the same. In fact I know it to be true. I was there when Vladmicov tested this hypothesis with a most fanatical and rabid example of their kind. He failed in a most pathetic way, protesting and weeping while he slurped. No living thing could resist the urge; it is senseless to try. But they have it in their heads that we do this for fun, that we seek to do evil. I grow so weary of them, I could wish them all dead if they did not provide amusement in my otherwise tedious existence.

It is because they are mad enough to chase us down that we have to watch out for them. A mad man is capable of anything, he is unpredictable and thus dangerous. Yet we do not dare to kill them, at least openly, for people might begin to believe them if they all suddenly began to die. Thus we must merely avoid them, and hope that we can lead them into a trap.

Be forewarned, your Prince will not be pleased if you openly slay a witch-hunter and thereby bring attention onto the city (though she does not always need to know about it). Some of the more conservative Elders would consider that breaking the Masquerade, and would not tolerate it. Only if you can first discredit the hunter will you not be punished for slaying him. Our kind rewards success.

Most mortals, if given hard evidence of our existence, would simply become paranoid wrecks. But these hunters are of a strong stock, and actually decide to do something about it. Perhaps some of them sense that they have special powers.

Those that possess the peculiar ability to repel Kindred are the very worst sort. It is a bewildering sensation, indeed maddening, and many believe it is the faith of these mortals acting upon our supposed curse that allows them power over us. Perhaps, as I believe, it is a parapsychological ability, never studied by science because of our Masquerade. Who can say for sure? There is certainly evidence for both sides.

All that matters is that these creatures can cause us pain.

You will not often realize you are being followed. It will come as a surprise to you. You will say, "Why me, what did I do wrong?", and you will begin to grow afraid. It is the fear that will destroy you, for it will cause you to make mistakes, and that is what they are waiting for you to do. They want you to lead them to others, so that they can work their way up to the "Kingpin" (they are obsessed with hierarchy). Indeed you may have already led the hunter to other Kindred, for they may have been following you for some time. These hunters usually work alone or in very small groups, and are quite antisocial. They simply do not mix well with their fellow man. They look at you with beady fanatic eyes, full of hatred and obsession. Their obsession is a desire, and I believe it to be a desire to feed upon us — they wish to devour us with their fanaticism.

If they begin murdering people near you, some Kindred might make a case to the Prince that you are responsible. It has happened before. You must never put your trust in the goodwill of other Kindred when you are being pursued. They care only for their own safety, and would throw you to the dogs sooner than save you from them. Whatever assures them the most security they will do.

Remember, you've got to take risks in order to set yourself up with the proper security, but these must be measured risks. Your task is to survive, to protect yourself, and to do so in comfort. Take only those risks which take you towards this end, and insist upon a proper return on your effort.

In the end, survival of the fittest is the rule with Kindred just as in nature. As the years peel past, only those who desire it the strongest do indeed survive. Even then it is a long, hard struggle. Immortality is not easily won. It takes more than a bite. It takes raw, steely determination and paranoia. But then again, you're not paranoid if they really are all out to get you.

And they are.

SHEDDING THE MORTAL COIL:

 las, dawn is but an hour away, and I must depart this city and go to earth before then. But let me say one more thing. Listen closely.

Never forget that you were once mortal, too. Never forget that you were born from the womb of a mortal woman, created from the seed of a mortal man. If you forget who you once were, you will forget who are you, and what someday you might have become. That which is you will be gone, and only the Beast will remain.

After enough centuries, some of us become are so alienated from our roots that it can be difficult to even communicate with them. Those who do fall to such a state do not last long. The beast is not a cautious creature. Eventually it leads those who have surrendered to it into a situation which they cannot escape.

It can be terrifying, all the urges that you cannot ignore tugging constantly at your sleeve. Sometimes it just erupts, and no amount of compassion or milk of human kindness can stop it. Listen to me when I say this: it is not your fault. I know you're not going to believe that, and maybe I don't either. But, it keeps me from completely loosing my grip on reality.

The Beast is out there, and in here as well, waiting for you to join him. It is impossible to elude it, and eventually it will catch up with you. So why bother running?

I do not know. I suppose I have always been a gambler, and I am going to give it a good run for its money. Maybe I can pull in the long haul, and discover at long last, Eldorado. The game?

Jokers Wild...